STOP!

This is the back of the book.
You wouldn't want to spoil a great ending!

This book is printed "manga-style," in the authentic Japanese right-to-left format. Since none of the artwork has been flipped or altered, readers get to experience the story just as the creator intended. You've been asking for it, so TOKYOPOP® delivered: authentic, hot-off-the-press, and far more fun!

DIRECTIONS

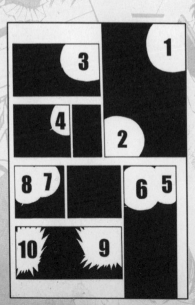

If this is your first time reading manga-style, here's a quick guide to help you understand how it works.

It's easy... just start in the top right panel and follow the numbers. Have fun, and look for more 100% authentic manga from TOKYOPOP®!

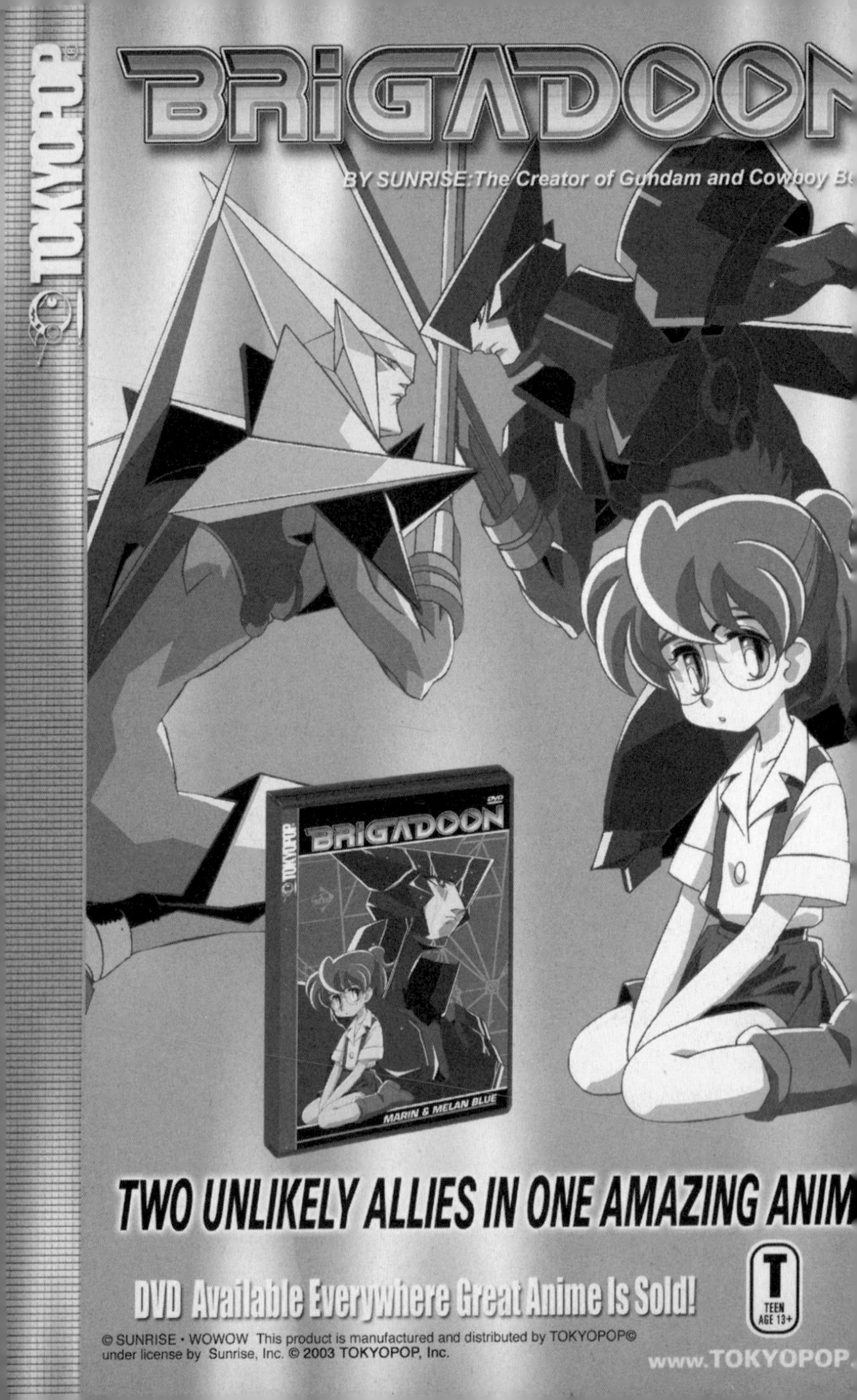
TOKYOPOP
BRIGADOON
BY SUNRISE: The Creator of Gundam and Cowboy
DVD
BRIGADOON
TOKYOPOP
MARIN & MELAN BLUE
TWO UNLIKELY ALLIES IN ONE AMAZING
DVD Available Everywhere Great Anime Is Sold!
T
TEEN
AGE 13+
© SUNRISE • WOWOW This product is manufactured and distributed by TOKYOPOP©
under license by Sunrise, Inc. © 2003 TOKYOPOP, Inc.
www.TOKYOPOP

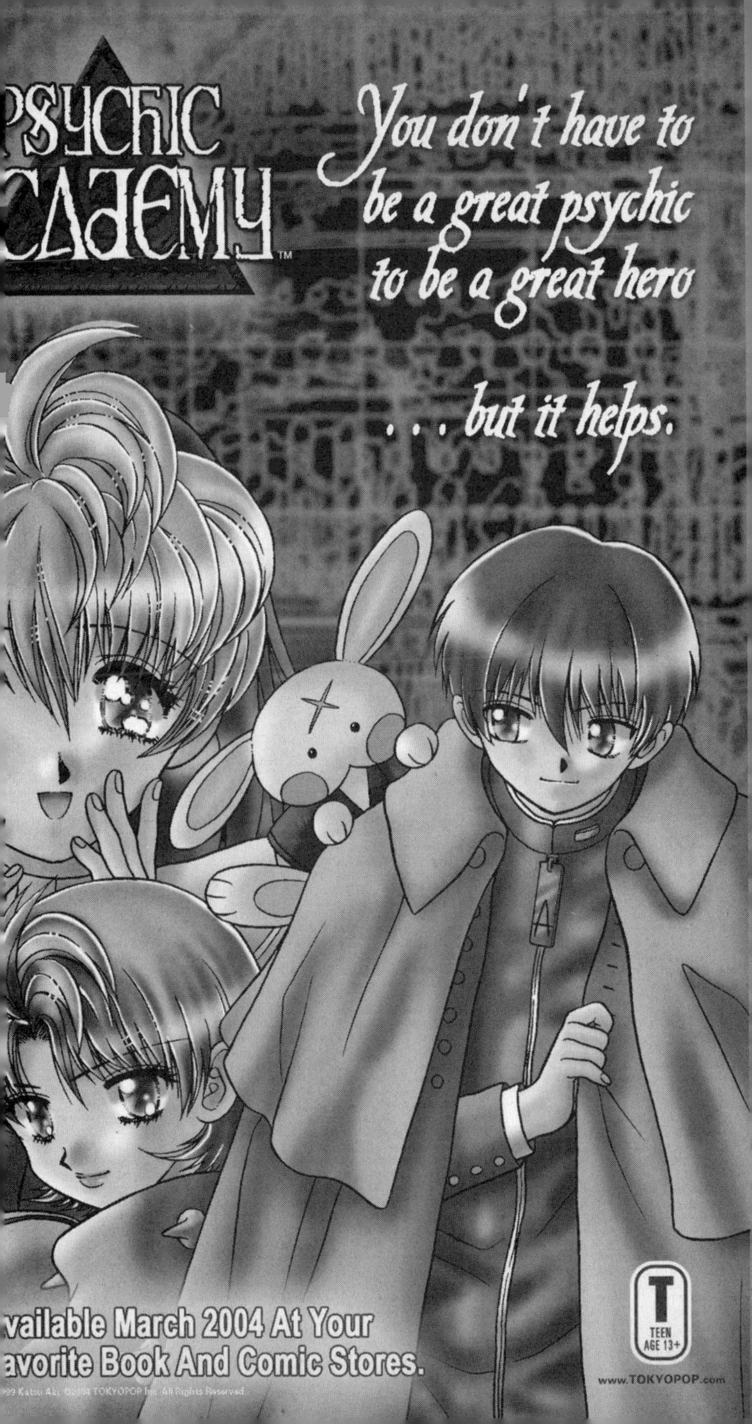

PSYCHIC ACADEMY™
You don't have to be a great psychic to be a great hero
. . . but it helps.
T TEEN AGE 13+
vailable March 2004 At Your
avorite Book And Comic Stores.
www.TOKYOPOP.com

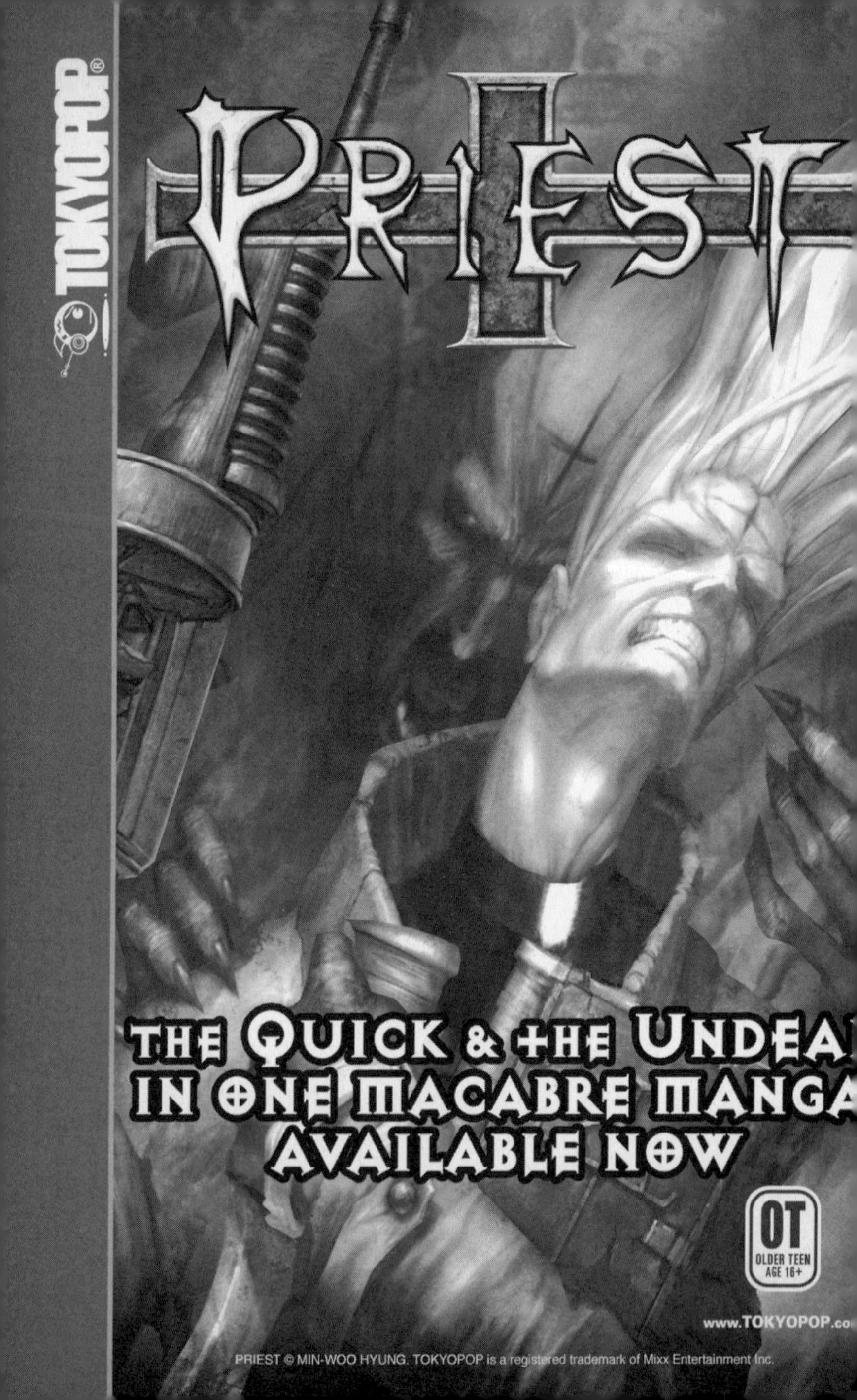
TOKYOPOP®
PRIEST
THE QUICK & THE UNDEA
IN ONE MACABRE MANGA
AVAILABLE NOW
OT
OLDER TEEN
AGE 16+
www.TOKYOPOP.co
PRIEST © MIN-WOO HYUNG. TOKYOPOP is a registered trademark of Mixx Entertainment Inc.

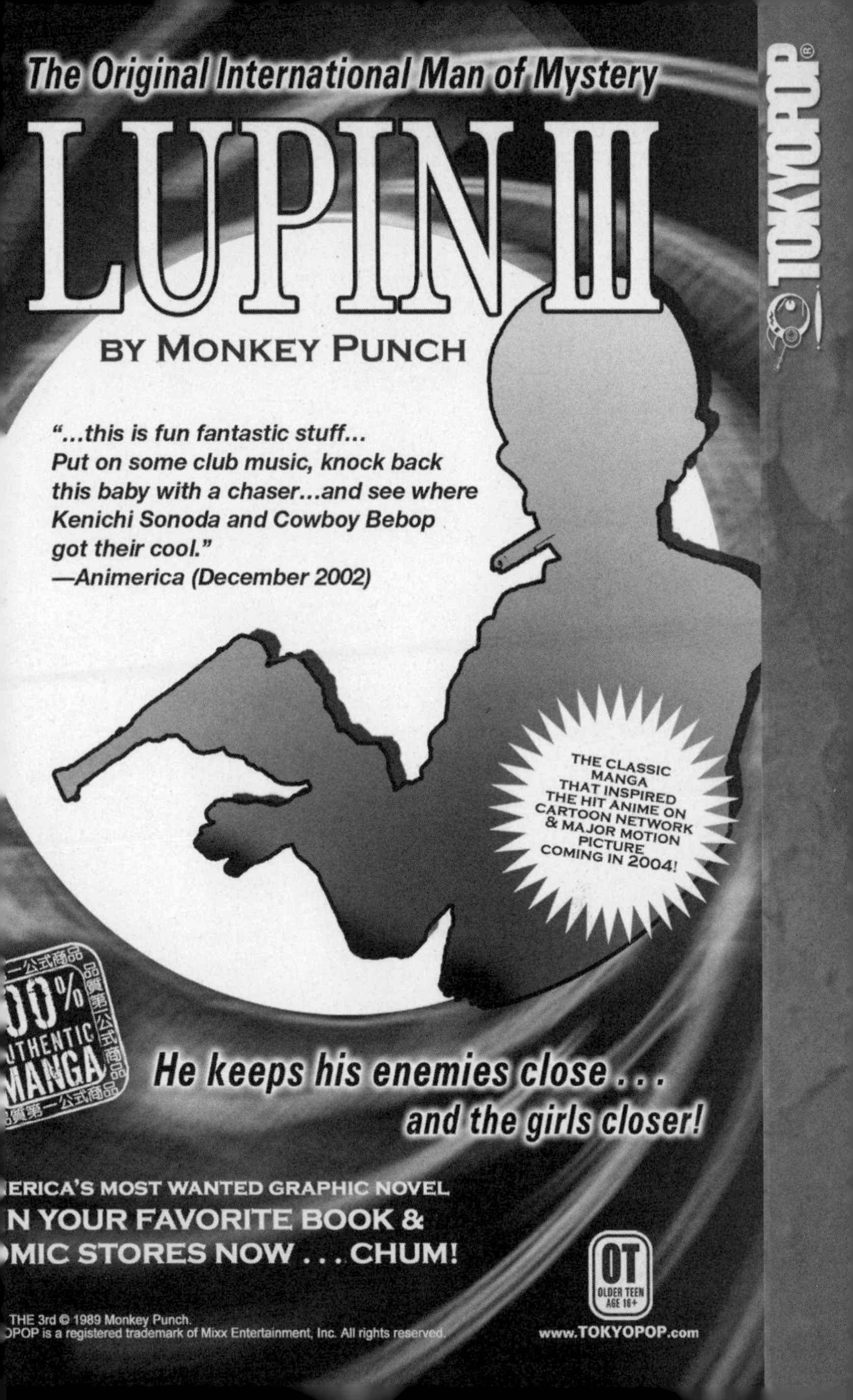
The Original International Man of Mystery
LUPIN III
BY MONKEY PUNCH
"...this is fun fantastic stuff... Put on some club music, knock back this baby with a chaser...and see where Kenichi Sonoda and Cowboy Bebop got their cool."
—Animerica (December 2002)
THE CLASSIC MANGA THAT INSPIRED THE HIT ANIME ON CARTOON NETWORK & MAJOR MOTION PICTURE COMING IN 2004!
00%
UTHENTIC
MANGA
He keeps his enemies close . . .
and the girls closer!
ERICA'S MOST WANTED GRAPHIC NOVEL
N YOUR FAVORITE BOOK &
MIC STORES NOW . . . CHUM!
OT
OLDER TEEN AGE 16+
THE 3rd © 1989 Monkey Punch.
OPOP is a registered trademark of Mixx Entertainment, Inc. All rights reserved.
www.TOKYOPOP.com
TOKYOPOP®

MANGA

.HACK//LEGEND OF THE TWILIGHT
@LARGE
A.I. LOVE YOU February 2004
AI YORI AOSHI January 2004
ANGELIC LAYER
BABY BIRTH
BATTLE ROYALE
BATTLE VIXENS April 2004
BIRTH May 2004
BRAIN POWERED
BRIGADOON
B'TX January 2004
CARDCAPTOR SAKURA
CARDCAPTOR SAKURA: MASTER OF THE CLOW
CARDCAPTOR SAKURA: BOXED SET COLLECTION 1
CARDCAPTOR SAKURA: BOXED SET COLLECTION 2
   March 2004
CHOBITS
CHRONICLES OF THE CURSED SWORD
CLAMP SCHOOL DETECTIVES
CLOVER
COMIC PARTY June 2004
CONFIDENTIAL CONFESSIONS
CORRECTOR YUI
COWBOY BEBOP: BOXED SET THE COMPLETE
   COLLECTION
CRESCENT MOON May 2004
CREST OF THE STARS June 2004
CYBORG 009
DEMON DIARY
DIGIMON
DIGIMON SERIES 3 April 2004
DIGIMON ZERO TWO February 2004
DNANGEL April 2004
DOLL May 2004
DRAGON HUNTER
DRAGON KNIGHTS
DUKLYON: CLAMP SCHOOL DEFENDERS
DV June 2004
ERICA SAKURAZAWA
FAERIES' LANDING January 2004
FAKE
FLCL
FORBIDDEN DANCE
FRUITS BASKET February 2004
G GUNDAM
GATEKEEPERS
GETBACKERS February 2004
GHOST! March 2004
GIRL GOT GAME January 2004
GRAVITATION
GTO

GUNDAM WING
GUNDAM WING: BATTLEFIELD OF PACIFISTS
GUNDAM WING: ENDLESS WALTZ
GUNDAM WING: THE LAST OUTPOST
HAPPY MANIA
HARLEM BEAT
I.N.V.U.
INITIAL D
ISLAND
JING: KING OF BANDITS
JULINE
JUROR 13 March 2004
KARE KANO
KILL ME, KISS ME February 2004
KINDAICHI CASE FILES, THE
KING OF HELL
KODOCHA: SANA'S STAGE
LAMENT OF THE LAMB May 2004
LES BIJOUX February 2004
LIZZIE MCGUIRE
LOVE HINA
LUPIN III
LUPIN III SERIES 2
MAGIC KNIGHT RAYEARTH I
MAGIC KNIGHT RAYEARTH II February 2004
MAHOROMATIC: AUTOMATIC MAIDEN May 2004
MAN OF MANY FACES
MARMALADE BOY
MARS
METEOR METHUSELA June 2004
METROID June 2004
MINK April 2004
MIRACLE GIRLS
MIYUKI-CHAN IN WONDERLAND
MODEL May 2004
NELLY MUSIC MANGA April 2004
ONE April 2004
PARADISE KISS
PARASYTE
PEACH GIRL
PEACH GIRL CHANGE OF HEART
PEACH GIRL RELAUNCH BOX SET
PET SHOP OF HORRORS
PITA-TEN January 2004
PLANET LADDER February 2004
PLANETES
PRIEST
PRINCESS AI April 2004
PSYCHIC ACADEMY March 2004
RAGNAROK
RAGNAROK: BOXED SET COLLECTION 1
RAVE MASTER
RAVE MASTER: BOXED SET March 2004

VOL. 2

BY
MAKOTO YUKIMURA

TOKYOPOP®

LOS ANGELES • TOKYO • LONDON

Translator - Yuki Nakamura
English Adaptation - Anna Wenger
Copy Editors - Aaron Sparrow & Jodi Bryson
Retouch and Lettering - Alex Santaclara
Cover Layout - Gary Shum

Editor - Luis Reyes
Managing Editor - Jill Freshney
Production Coordinator - Antonio DePietro
Production Managers - Jennifer Miller, Mutsumi Miyazaki
Art Director - Matt Alford
Editorial Director - Jeremy Ross
VP of Production - Ron Klamert
President & C.O.O. - John Parker
Publisher & C.E.O. - Stuart Levy

Email: editor@TOKYOPOP.com
Come visit us online at www.TOKYOPOP.com

A TOKYOPOP® Manga

TOKYOPOP Inc.
5900 Wilshire Blvd. Suite 2000
Los Angeles, CA 90036

Planetes Volume 2

First published in Japan in 2001 by Kodansha Ltd., Tokyo
English publication rights arranged through Kodansha Ltd.

ISBN: 1-59182-509-1

First TOKYOPOP printing: January 2004

10 9 8 7 6 5 4 3 2 1

Printed in the USA

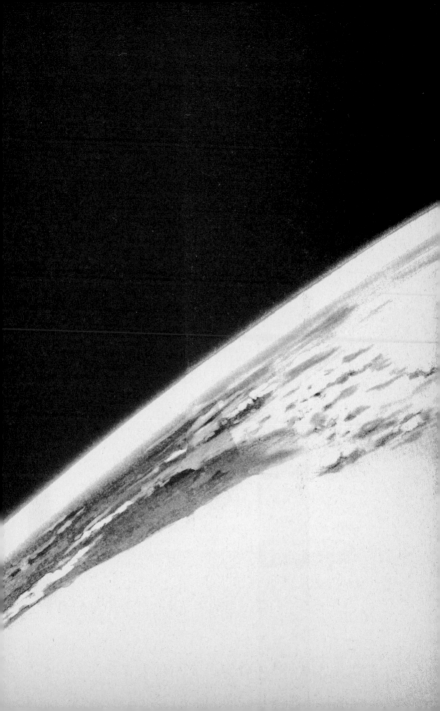

At the Threshold of the Future

In the history of space travel, many great men have forged the way into new frontiers, and many great men have died so that others may continue further into the great reaches of space. On the periphery of man's emergence as a space-faring species, Hachimaki Hoshino works with a small team of debris collectors toiling day and night clearing Earth's orbit of the ever-amounting refuse from space-bound vessels. But the young pilot's ambitions lie beyond Earth's orbit. Now, whether he longs to travel beyond the asteroid belt and into the Jovian region of our Solar System for the betterment of mankind or to satiate his own personal longing for wealth and fame is a question he has yet to answer. The first step, however, is finding a way to be a part of the first manned space expedition to Jupiter.

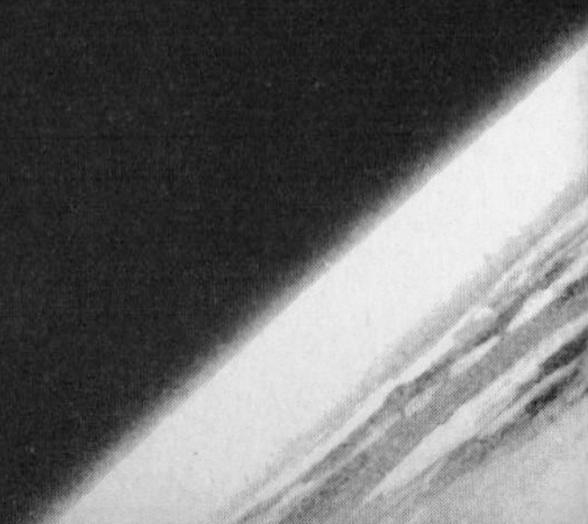

PLANETES 2

CONTENTS

//PHASE 6//
Running man ....PAGE 0001

//PHASE 7//
Tanabe ....PAGE 0046

//PHASE 8//
A BLACK FLOWER NAMED
SAKINOHAKA (PART 1) ....PAGE 0093

//PHASE 9//
A BLACK FLOWER NAMED
SAKINOHAKA (PART 2) ....PAGE 0126

//PHASE 10//
LOST SOULS ....PAGE 0166

//PHASE 11//
СПАСИБО ....PAGE 0206

NOVEMBER, 2075

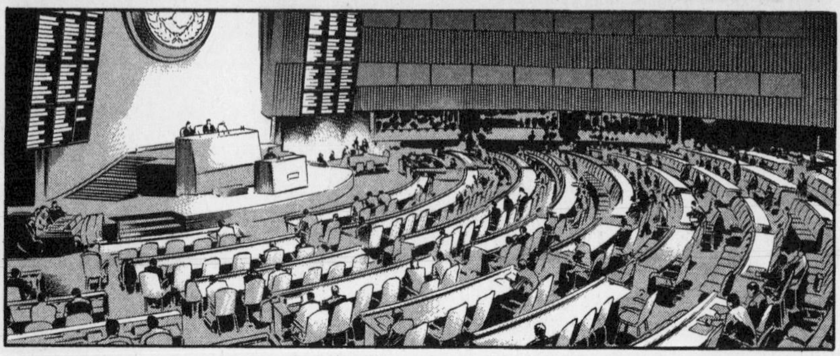

THE EDC (EARTH DEVELOPMENT COMMUNITY) HAS DECLARED IT WILL BEGIN CONSTRUCTION ON A PERMANENT RESOURCE BASE; A MINE; ON JUPITER BEFORE THE END OF THE CENTURY.

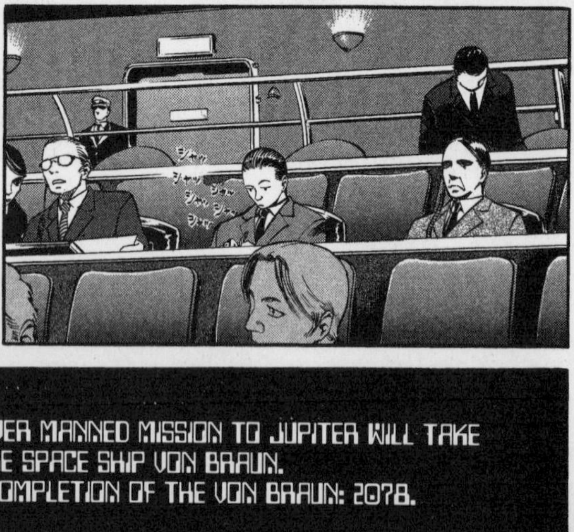

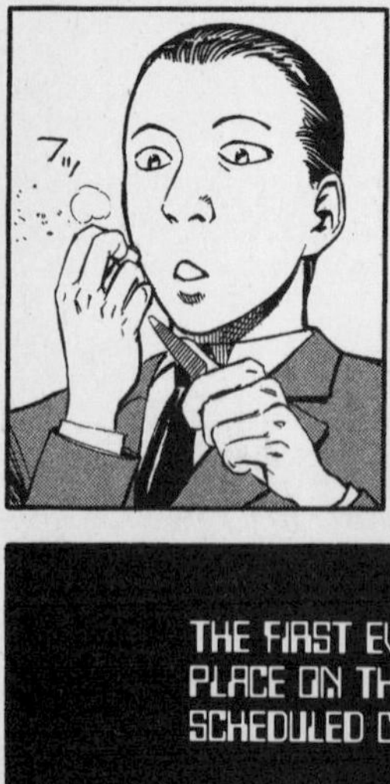
フッ

THE FIRST EVER MANNED MISSION TO JUPITER WILL TAKE PLACE ON THE SPACE SHIP VON BRAUN.
SCHEDULED COMPLETION OF THE VON BRAUN: 2078.

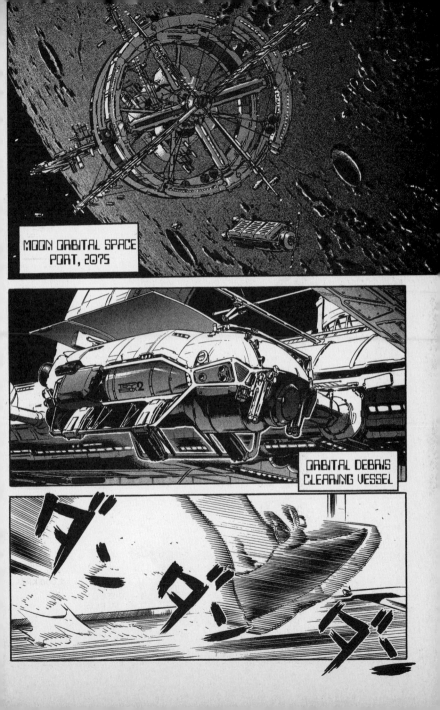

MOON ORBITAL SPACE PORT, 2075

ORBITAL DEBRIS CLEARING VESSEL

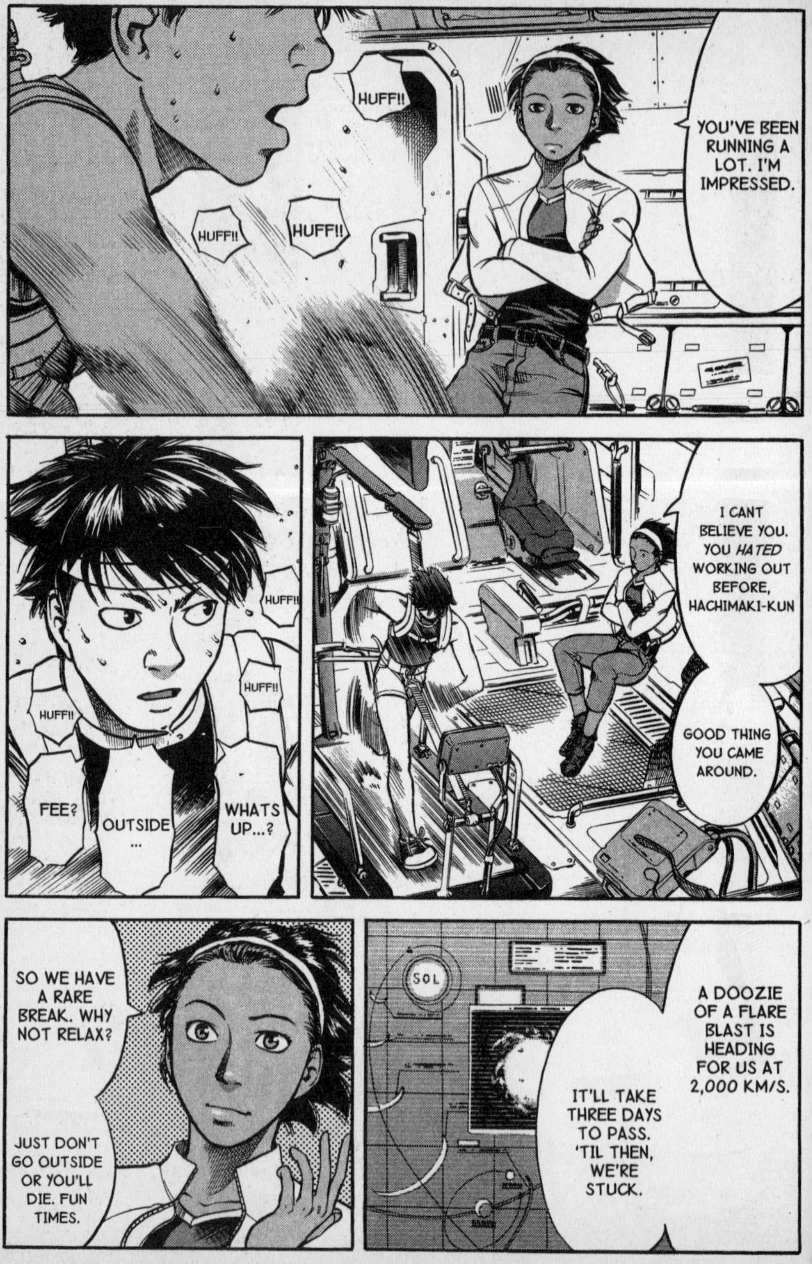
YOU'VE BEEN RUNNING A LOT. I'M IMPRESSED.
HUFF!!
HUFF!!
HUFF!!
I CANT BELIEVE YOU. YOU *HATED* WORKING OUT BEFORE, HACHIMAKI-KUN
GOOD THING YOU CAME AROUND.
HUFF!!
HUFF!!
HUFF!!
WHATS UP...?
OUTSIDE ...
FEE?
A DOOZIE OF A FLARE BLAST IS HEADING FOR US AT 2,000 KM/S.
IT'LL TAKE THREE DAYS TO PASS. 'TIL THEN, WE'RE STUCK.
SOL
SO WE HAVE A RARE BREAK. WHY NOT RELAX?
JUST DON'T GO OUTSIDE OR YOU'LL DIE. FUN TIMES.

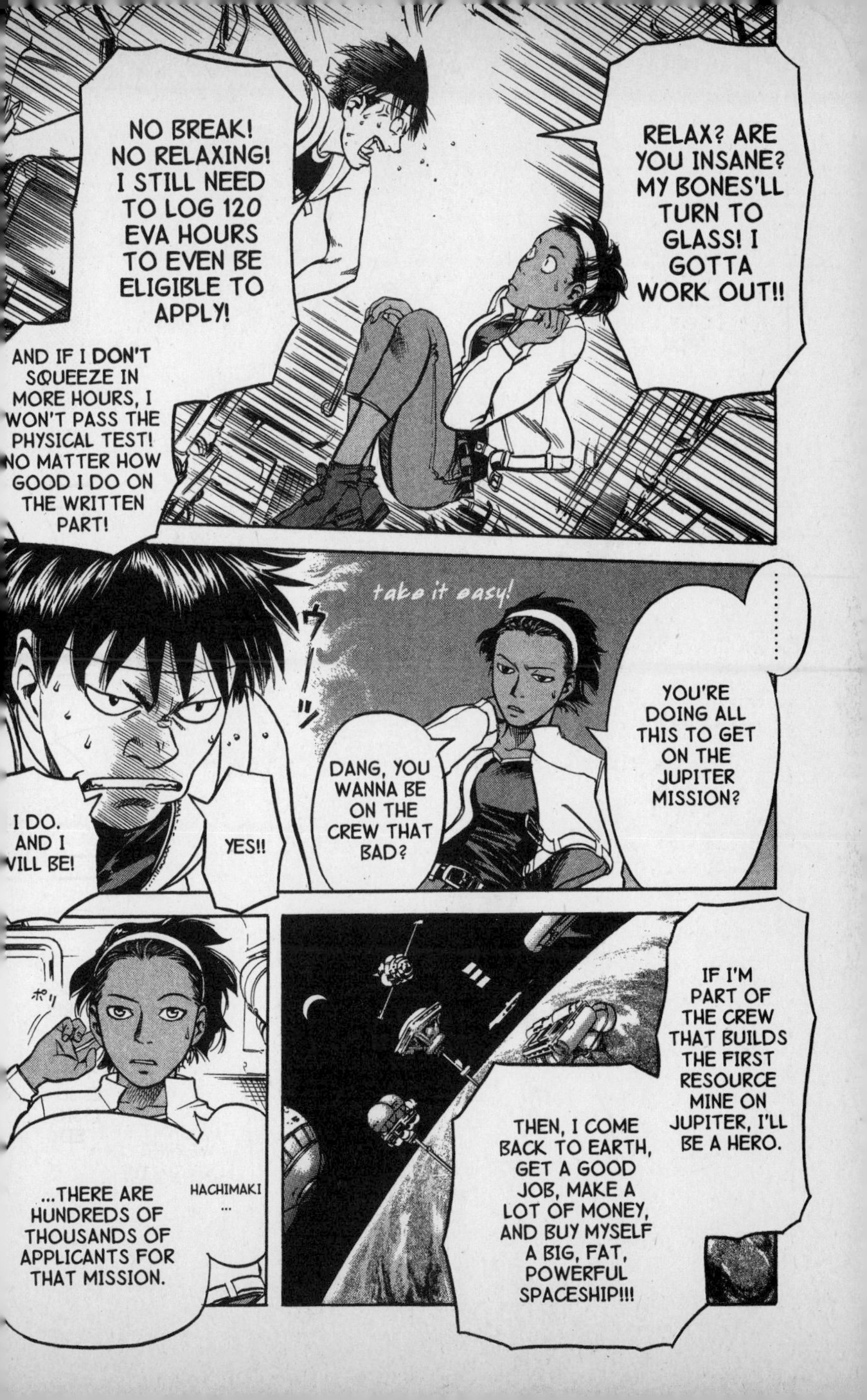
RELAX? ARE YOU INSANE? MY BONES'LL TURN TO GLASS! I GOTTA WORK OUT!!
NO BREAK! NO RELAXING! I STILL NEED TO LOG 120 EVA HOURS TO EVEN BE ELIGIBLE TO APPLY!
AND IF I DON'T SQUEEZE IN MORE HOURS, I WON'T PASS THE PHYSICAL TEST! NO MATTER HOW GOOD I DO ON THE WRITTEN PART!
......
YOU'RE DOING ALL THIS TO GET ON THE JUPITER MISSION?
take it easy!
DANG, YOU WANNA BE ON THE CREW THAT BAD?
YES!!
I DO. AND I VILL BE!
IF I'M PART OF THE CREW THAT BUILDS THE FIRST RESOURCE MINE ON JUPITER, I'LL BE A HERO.
THEN, I COME BACK TO EARTH, GET A GOOD JOB, MAKE A LOT OF MONEY, AND BUY MYSELF A BIG, FAT, POWERFUL SPACESHIP!!!
ポリ
HACHIMAKI ...
...THERE ARE HUNDREDS OF THOUSANDS OF APPLICANTS FOR THAT MISSION.

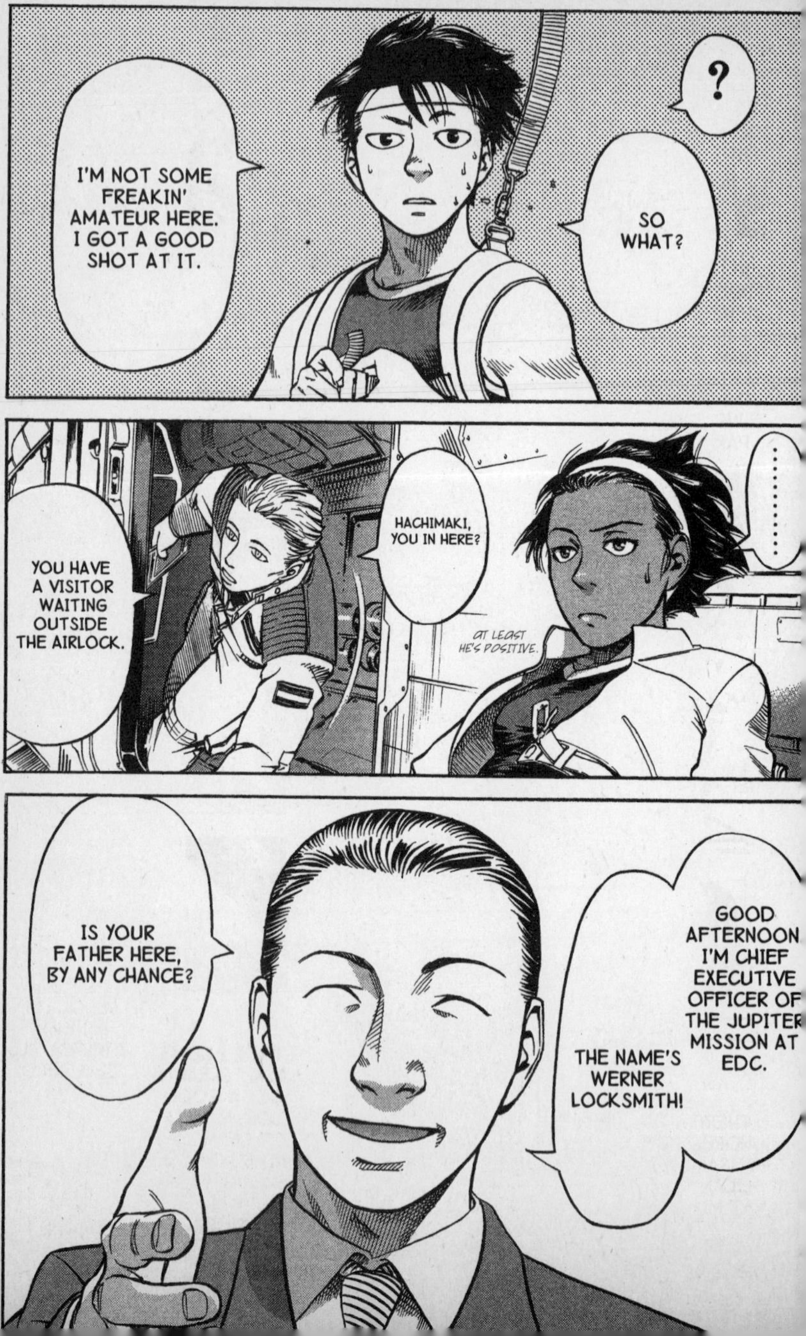
?
SO WHAT?
I'M NOT SOME FREAKIN' AMATEUR HERE. I GOT A GOOD SHOT AT IT.
......
AT LEAST HE'S POSITIVE.
HACHIMAKI, YOU IN HERE?
YOU HAVE A VISITOR WAITING OUTSIDE THE AIRLOCK.
GOOD AFTERNOON I'M CHIEF EXECUTIVE OFFICER OF THE JUPITER MISSION AT EDC.
THE NAME'S WERNER LOCKSMITH!
IS YOUR FATHER HERE, BY ANY CHANCE?

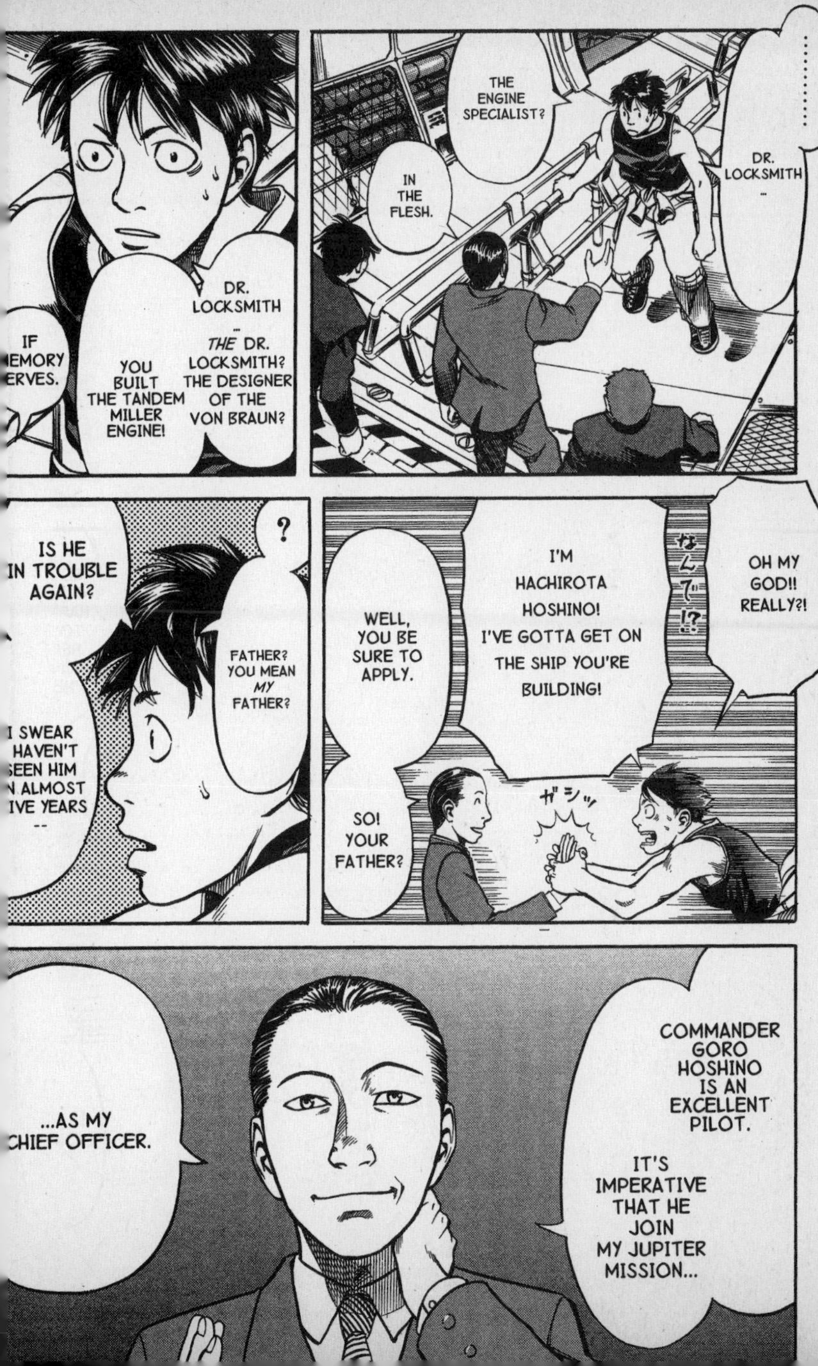

......
DR. LOCKSMITH -
THE ENGINE SPECIALIST?
IN THE FLESH.
DR. LOCKSMITH ... *THE* DR. LOCKSMITH? THE DESIGNER OF THE VON BRAUN?
YOU BUILT THE TANDEM MILLER ENGINE!
IF EMORY ERVES.
OH MY GOD!! REALLY?!
なんで!?
I'M HACHIROTA HOSHINO! I'VE GOTTA GET ON THE SHIP YOU'RE BUILDING!
WELL, YOU BE SURE TO APPLY.
ガシッ
SO! YOUR FATHER?
?
FATHER? YOU MEAN *MY* FATHER?
IS HE IN TROUBLE AGAIN?
I SWEAR HAVEN'T SEEN HIM N ALMOST IVE YEARS --
COMMANDER GORO HOSHINO IS AN EXCELLENT PILOT.
IT'S IMPERATIVE THAT HE JOIN MY JUPITER MISSION...
...AS MY HIEF OFFICER.

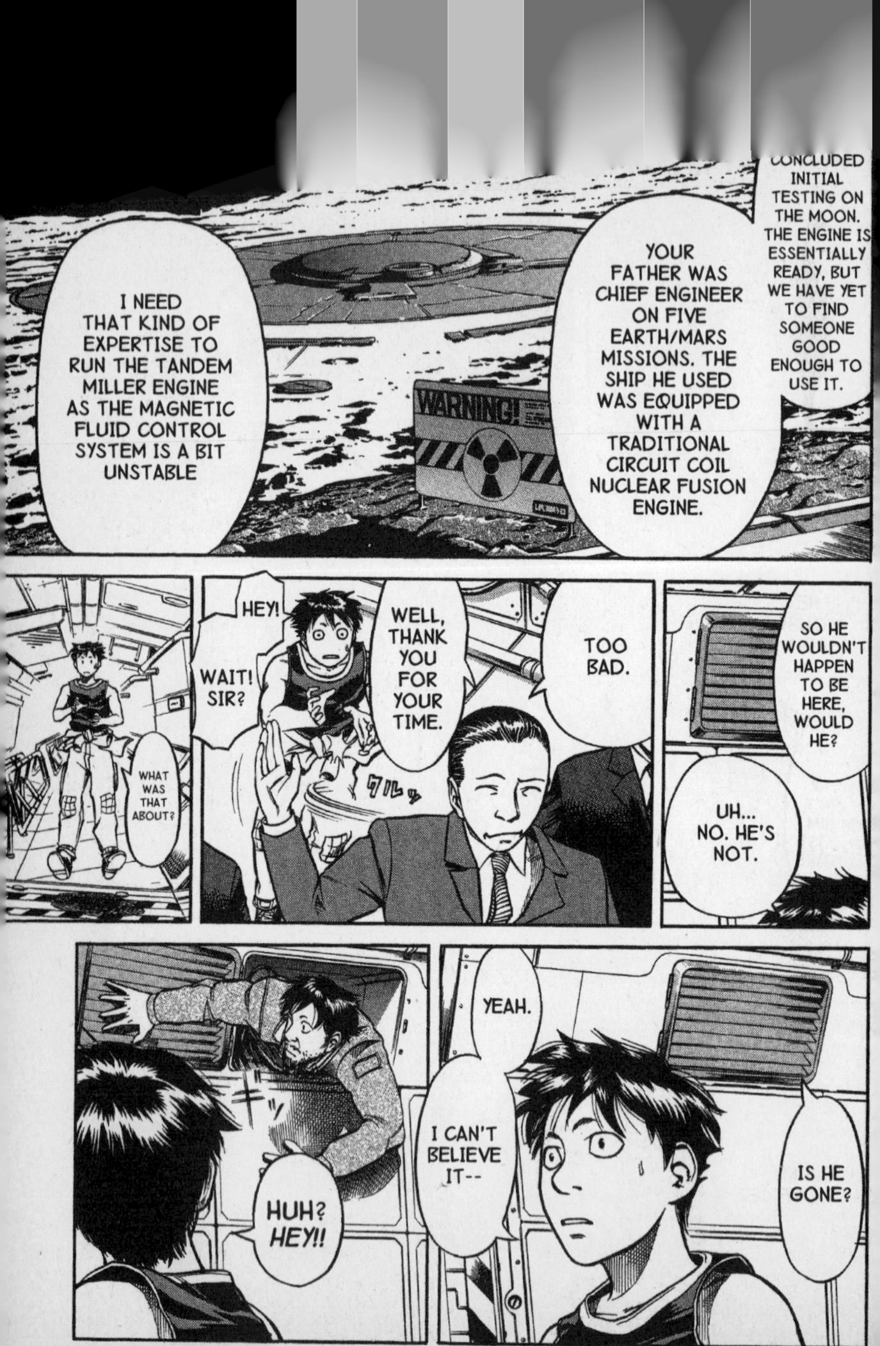
CONCLUDED INITIAL TESTING ON THE MOON. THE ENGINE IS ESSENTIALLY READY, BUT WE HAVE YET TO FIND SOMEONE GOOD ENOUGH TO USE IT.
YOUR FATHER WAS CHIEF ENGINEER ON FIVE EARTH/MARS MISSIONS. THE SHIP HE USED WAS EQUIPPED WITH A TRADITIONAL CIRCUIT COIL NUCLEAR FUSION ENGINE.
WARNING!
I NEED THAT KIND OF EXPERTISE TO RUN THE TANDEM MILLER ENGINE AS THE MAGNETIC FLUID CONTROL SYSTEM IS A BIT UNSTABLE
SO HE WOULDN'T HAPPEN TO BE HERE, WOULD HE?
UH... NO. HE'S NOT.
TOO BAD.
WELL, THANK YOU FOR YOUR TIME.
HEY!
WAIT! SIR?
クルッ
WHAT WAS THAT ABOUT?
IS HE GONE?
YEAH.
I CAN'T BELIEVE IT--
HUH? HEY!!

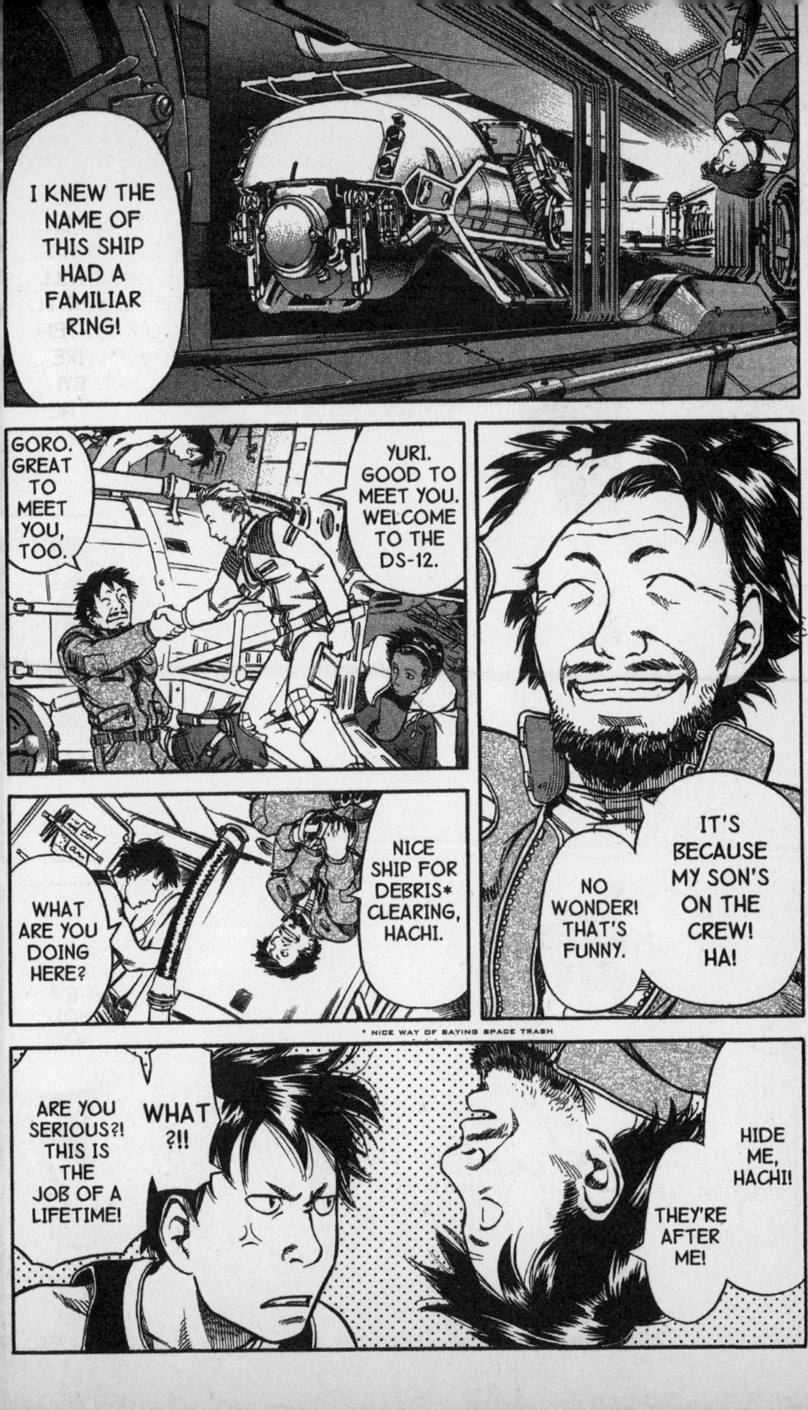
I KNEW THE NAME OF THIS SHIP HAD A FAMILIAR RING!
IT'S BECAUSE MY SON'S ON THE CREW! HA!
NO WONDER! THAT'S FUNNY.
YURI. GOOD TO MEET YOU. WELCOME TO THE DS-12.
GORO. GREAT TO MEET YOU, TOO.
NICE SHIP FOR DEBRIS* CLEARING, HACHI.
WHAT ARE YOU DOING HERE?
HIDE ME, HACHI!
THEY'RE AFTER ME!
WHAT?!!
ARE YOU SERIOUS?! THIS IS THE JOB OF A LIFETIME!

* NICE WAY OF SAYING SPACE TRASH

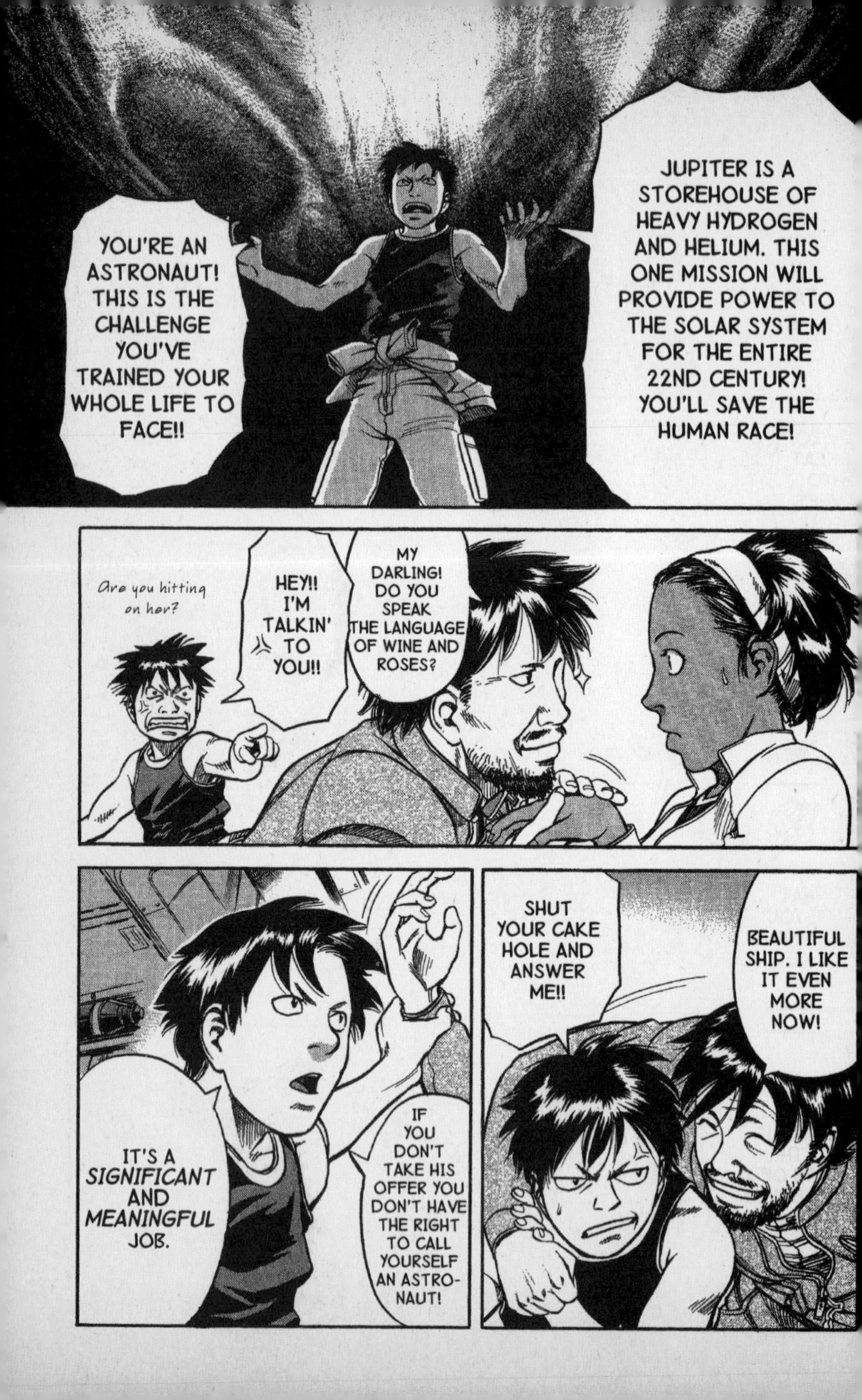
JUPITER IS A STOREHOUSE OF HEAVY HYDROGEN AND HELIUM. THIS ONE MISSION WILL PROVIDE POWER TO THE SOLAR SYSTEM FOR THE ENTIRE 22ND CENTURY! YOU'LL SAVE THE HUMAN RACE!
YOU'RE AN ASTRONAUT! THIS IS THE CHALLENGE YOU'VE TRAINED YOUR WHOLE LIFE TO FACE!!
MY DARLING! DO YOU SPEAK THE LANGUAGE OF WINE AND ROSES?
HEY!! I'M TALKIN' TO YOU!!
Are you hitting on her?
BEAUTIFUL SHIP. I LIKE IT EVEN MORE NOW!
SHUT YOUR CAKE HOLE AND ANSWER ME!!
IF YOU DON'T TAKE HIS OFFER YOU DON'T HAVE THE RIGHT TO CALL YOURSELF AN ASTRO-NAUT!
IT'S A *SIGNIFICANT* AND *MEANINGFUL* JOB.

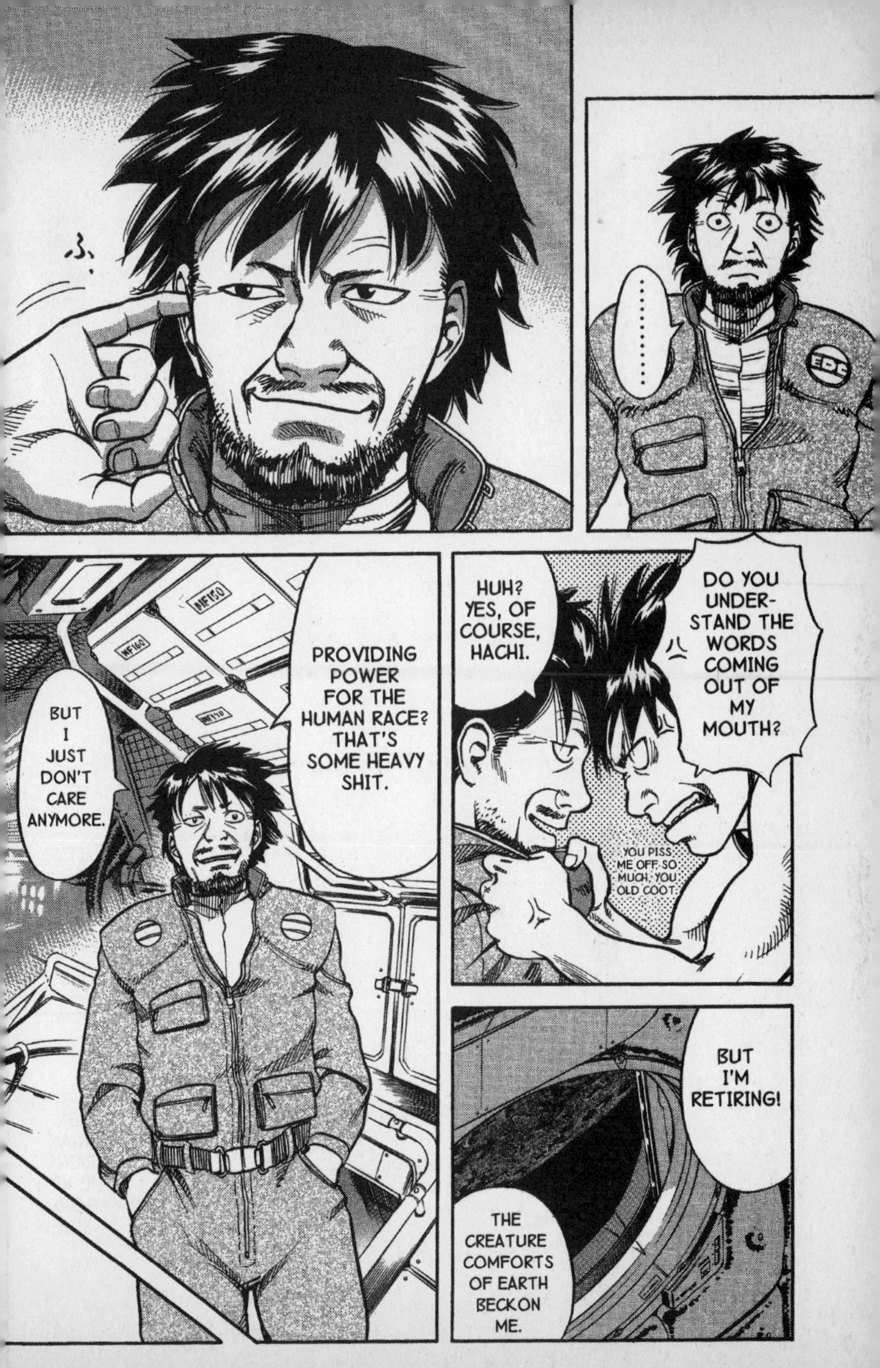
……
ふ
DO YOU UNDER-STAND THE WORDS COMING OUT OF MY MOUTH?
HUH? YES, OF COURSE, HACHI.
YOU PISS ME OFF SO MUCH, YOU OLD COOT.
BUT I'M RETIRING!
THE CREATURE COMFORTS OF EARTH BECKON ME.
PROVIDING POWER FOR THE HUMAN RACE? THAT'S SOME HEAVY SHIT.
BUT I JUST DON'T CARE ANYMORE.

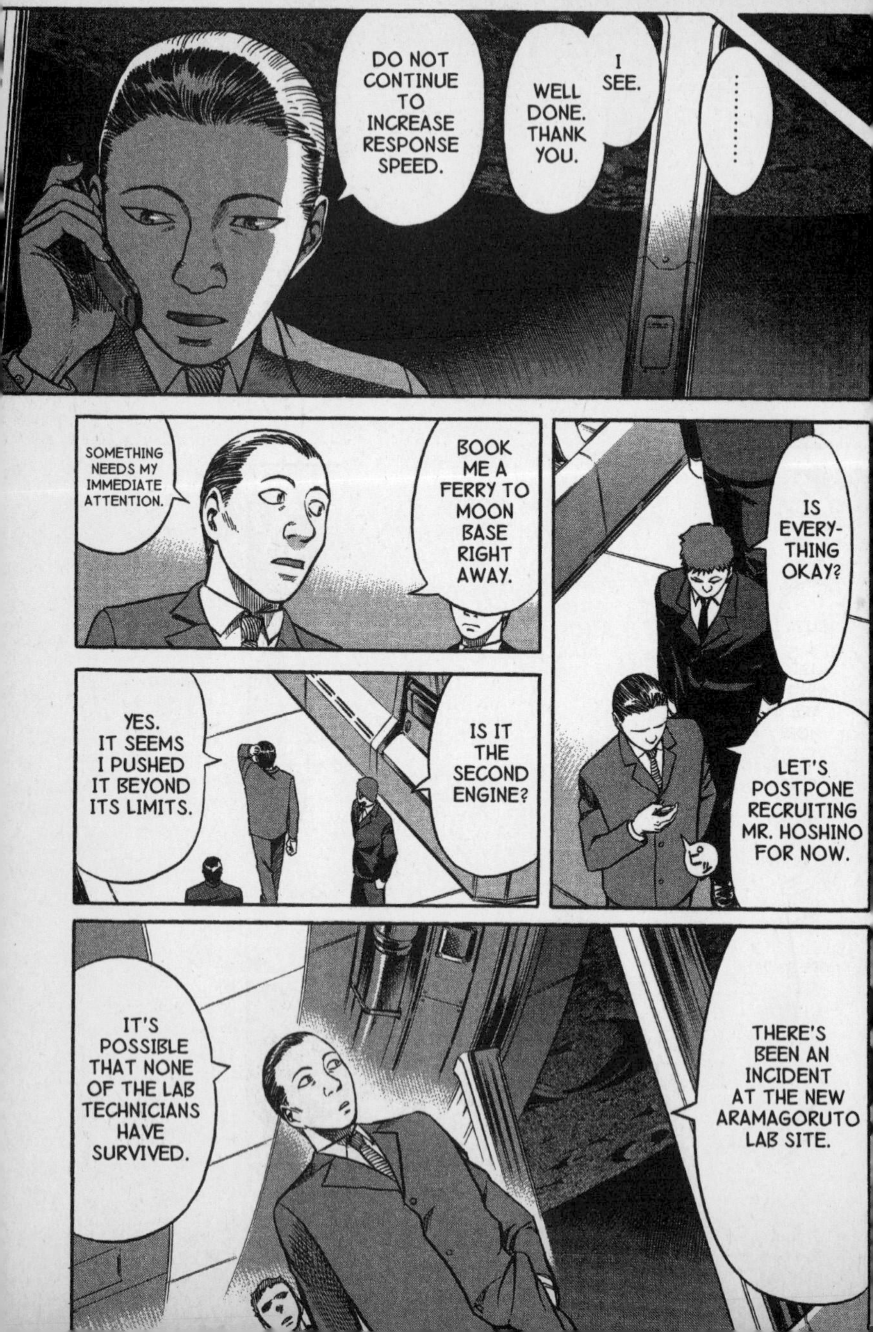
....
I SEE.
WELL DONE. THANK YOU.
DO NOT CONTINUE TO INCREASE RESPONSE SPEED.
IS EVERYTHING OKAY?
LET'S POSTPONE RECRUITING MR. HOSHINO FOR NOW.
BOOK ME A FERRY TO MOON BASE RIGHT AWAY.
SOMETHING NEEDS MY IMMEDIATE ATTENTION.
IS IT THE SECOND ENGINE?
YES. IT SEEMS I PUSHED IT BEYOND ITS LIMITS.
THERE'S BEEN AN INCIDENT AT THE NEW ARAMAGORUTO LAB SITE.
IT'S POSSIBLE THAT NONE OF THE LAB TECHNICIANS HAVE SURVIVED.

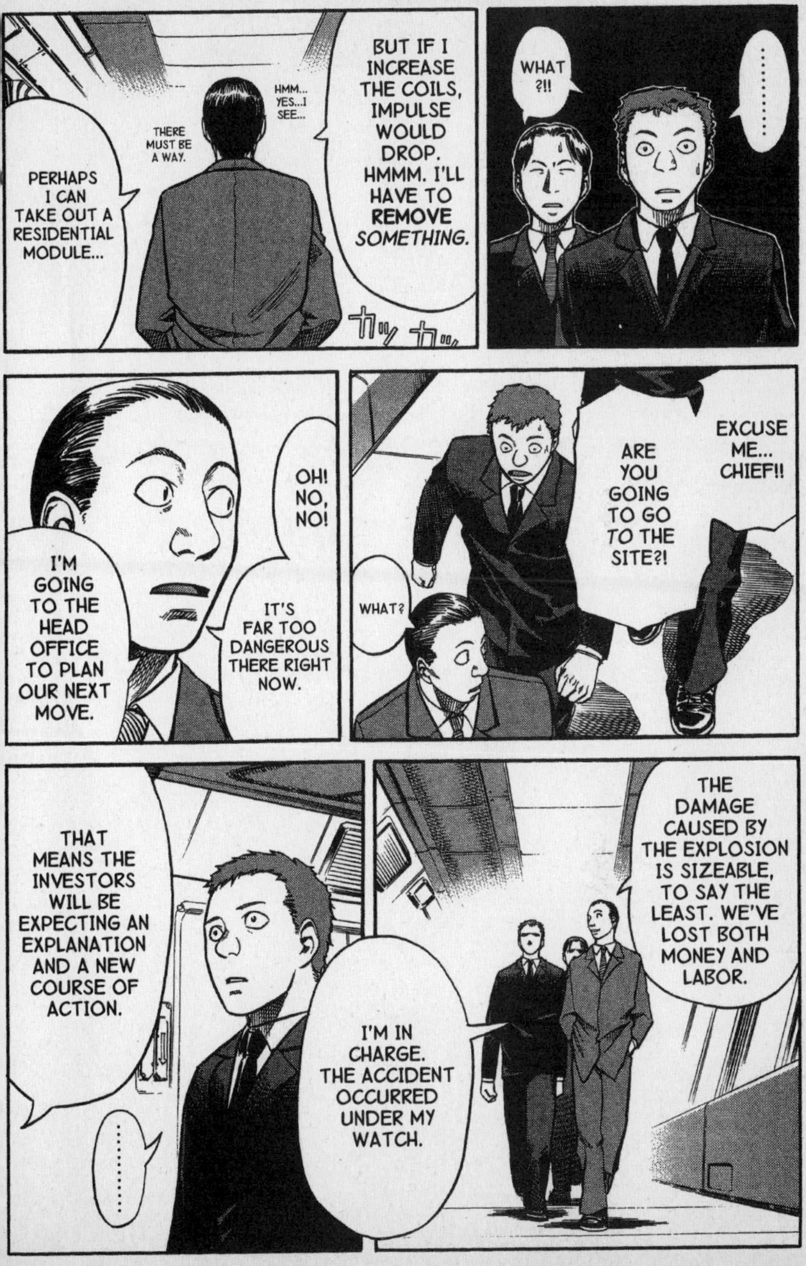

....
WHAT ?!!
BUT IF I INCREASE THE COILS, IMPULSE WOULD DROP. HMMM. I'LL HAVE TO **REMOVE** *SOMETHING.*
HMM... YES...I SEE...
THERE MUST BE A WAY.
PERHAPS I CAN TAKE OUT A RESIDENTIAL MODULE...
カッ カッ
EXCUSE ME... CHIEF!!
ARE YOU GOING TO GO *TO* THE SITE?!
WHAT?
OH! NO, NO!
IT'S FAR TOO DANGEROUS THERE RIGHT NOW.
I'M GOING TO THE HEAD OFFICE TO PLAN OUR NEXT MOVE.
THE DAMAGE CAUSED BY THE EXPLOSION IS SIZEABLE, TO SAY THE LEAST. WE'VE LOST BOTH MONEY AND LABOR.
I'M IN CHARGE. THE ACCIDENT OCCURRED UNDER MY WATCH.
THAT MEANS THE INVESTORS WILL BE EXPECTING AN EXPLANATION AND A NEW COURSE OF ACTION.
....

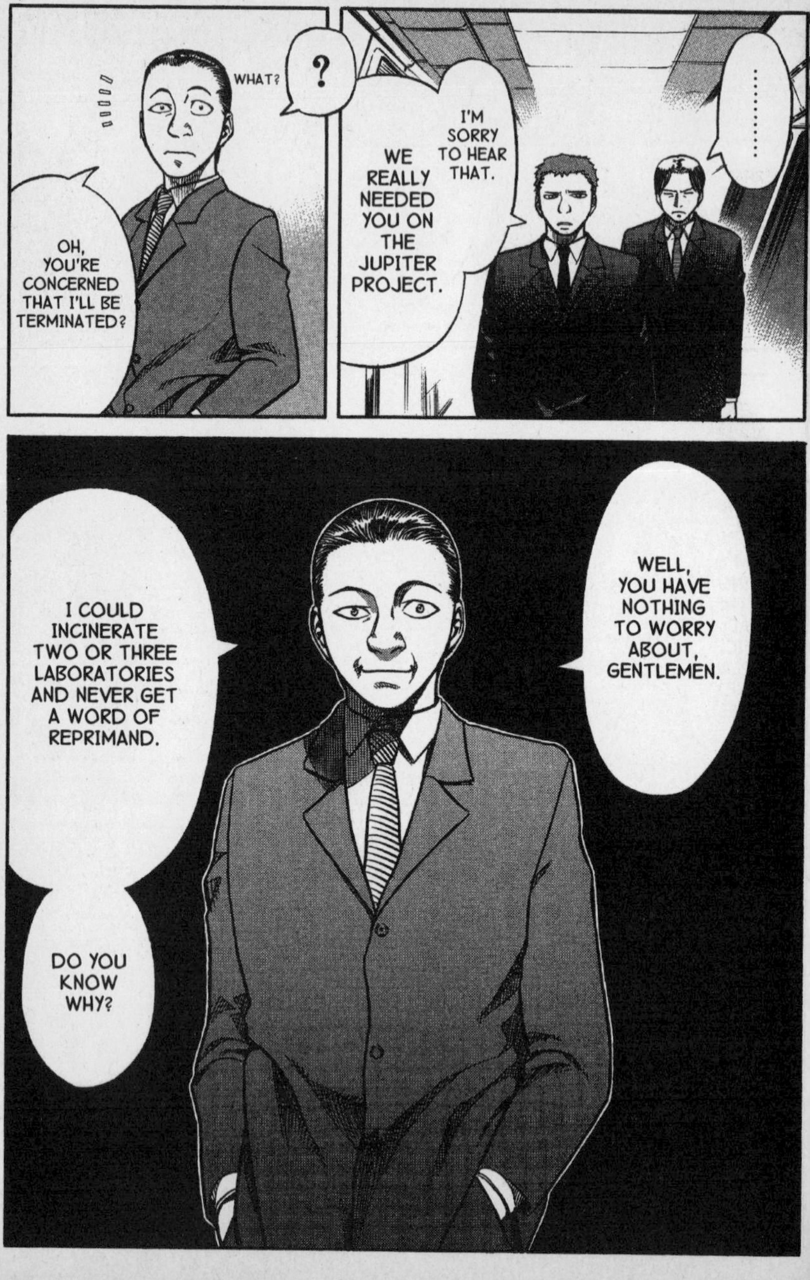
......
I'M SORRY TO HEAR THAT.
WE REALLY NEEDED YOU ON THE JUPITER PROJECT.
?
WHAT?
OH, YOU'RE CONCERNED THAT I'LL BE TERMINATED?
WELL, YOU HAVE NOTHING TO WORRY ABOUT, GENTLEMEN.
I COULD INCINERATE TWO OR THREE LABORATORIES AND NEVER GET A WORD OF REPRIMAND.
DO YOU KNOW WHY?

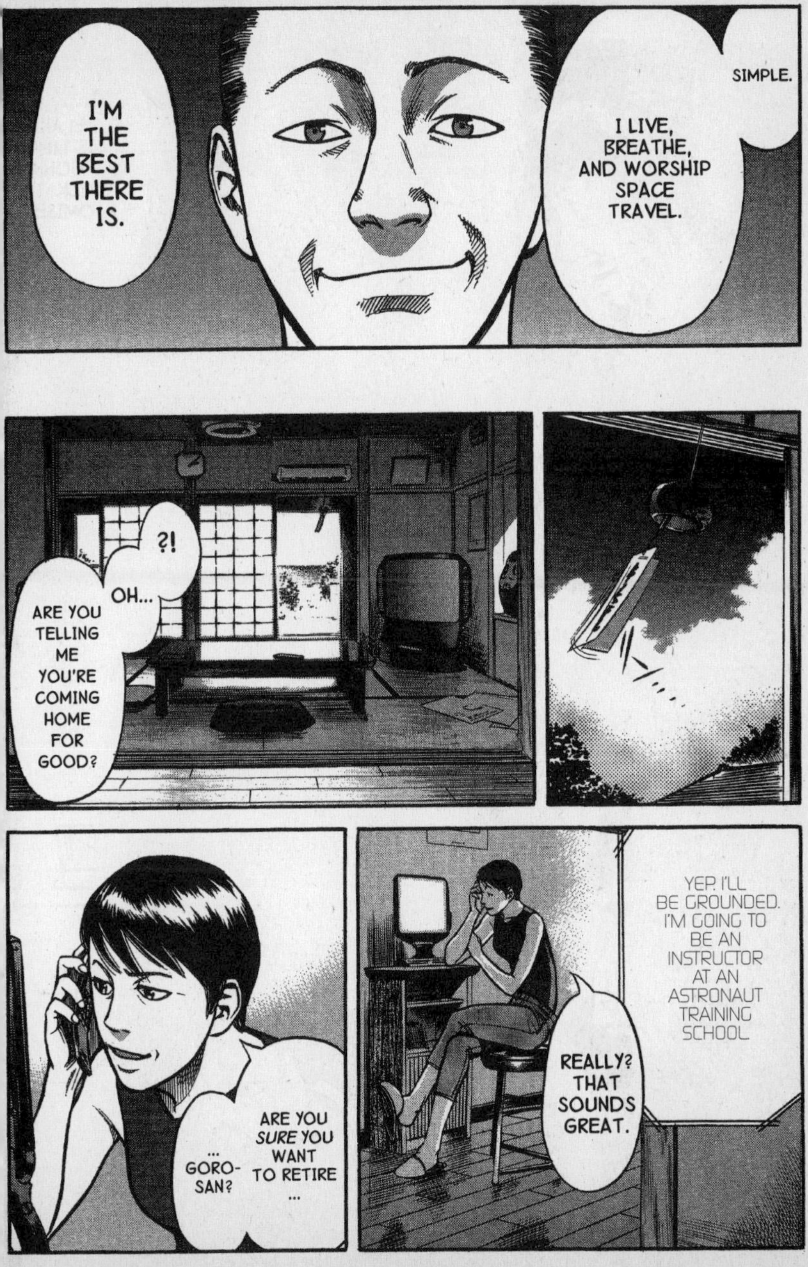
SIMPLE.
I LIVE, BREATHE, AND WORSHIP SPACE TRAVEL.
I'M THE BEST THERE IS.
?!
OH...
ARE YOU TELLING ME YOU'RE COMING HOME FOR GOOD?
YEP. I'LL BE GROUNDED. I'M GOING TO BE AN INSTRUCTOR AT AN ASTRONAUT TRAINING SCHOOL.
REALLY? THAT SOUNDS GREAT.
ARE YOU *SURE* YOU WANT TO RETIRE ...
... GORO-SAN?

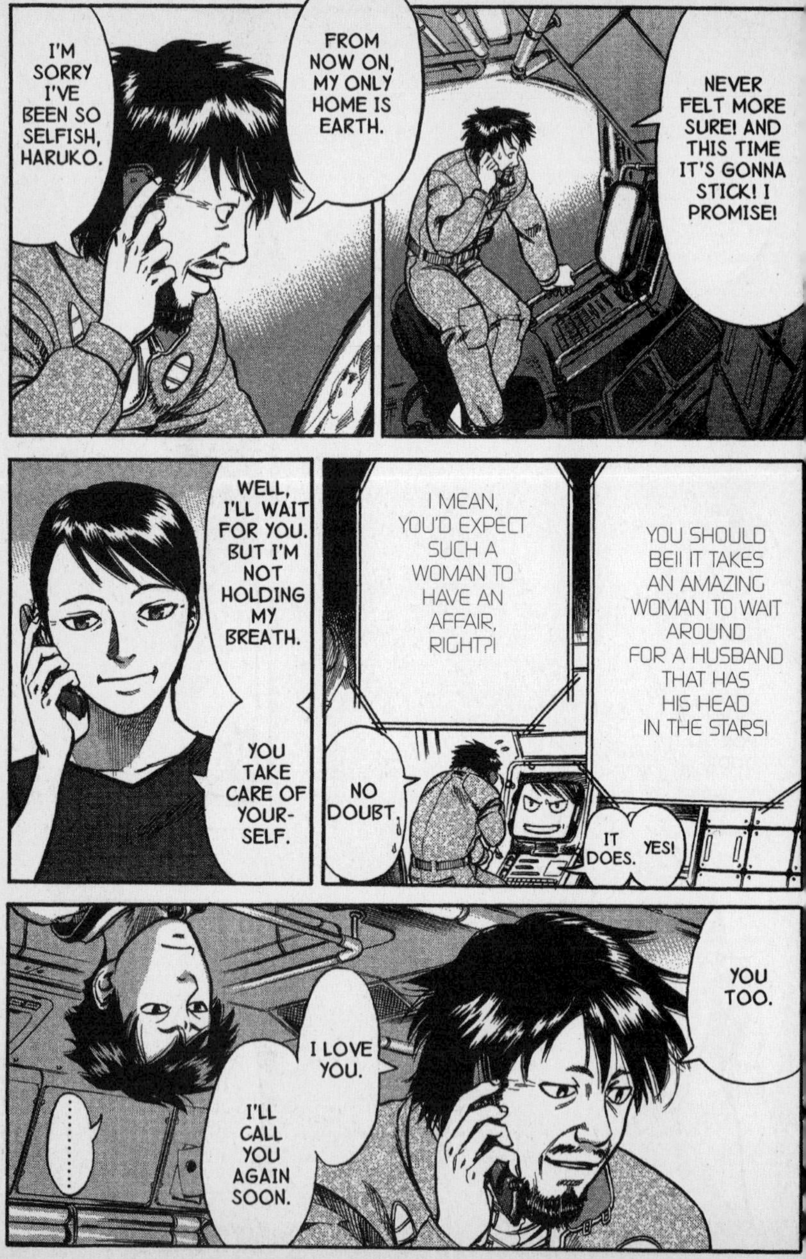
NEVER FELT MORE SURE! AND THIS TIME IT'S GONNA STICK! I PROMISE!
FROM NOW ON, MY ONLY HOME IS EARTH.
I'M SORRY I'VE BEEN SO SELFISH, HARUKO.
YOU SHOULD BE!! IT TAKES AN AMAZING WOMAN TO WAIT AROUND FOR A HUSBAND THAT HAS HIS HEAD IN THE STARS!
I MEAN, YOU'D EXPECT SUCH A WOMAN TO HAVE AN AFFAIR, RIGHT?!
YES!
IT DOES.
NO DOUBT.
WELL, I'LL WAIT FOR YOU. BUT I'M NOT HOLDING MY BREATH.
YOU TAKE CARE OF YOUR-SELF.
YOU TOO.
I LOVE YOU.
I'LL CALL YOU AGAIN SOON.
……

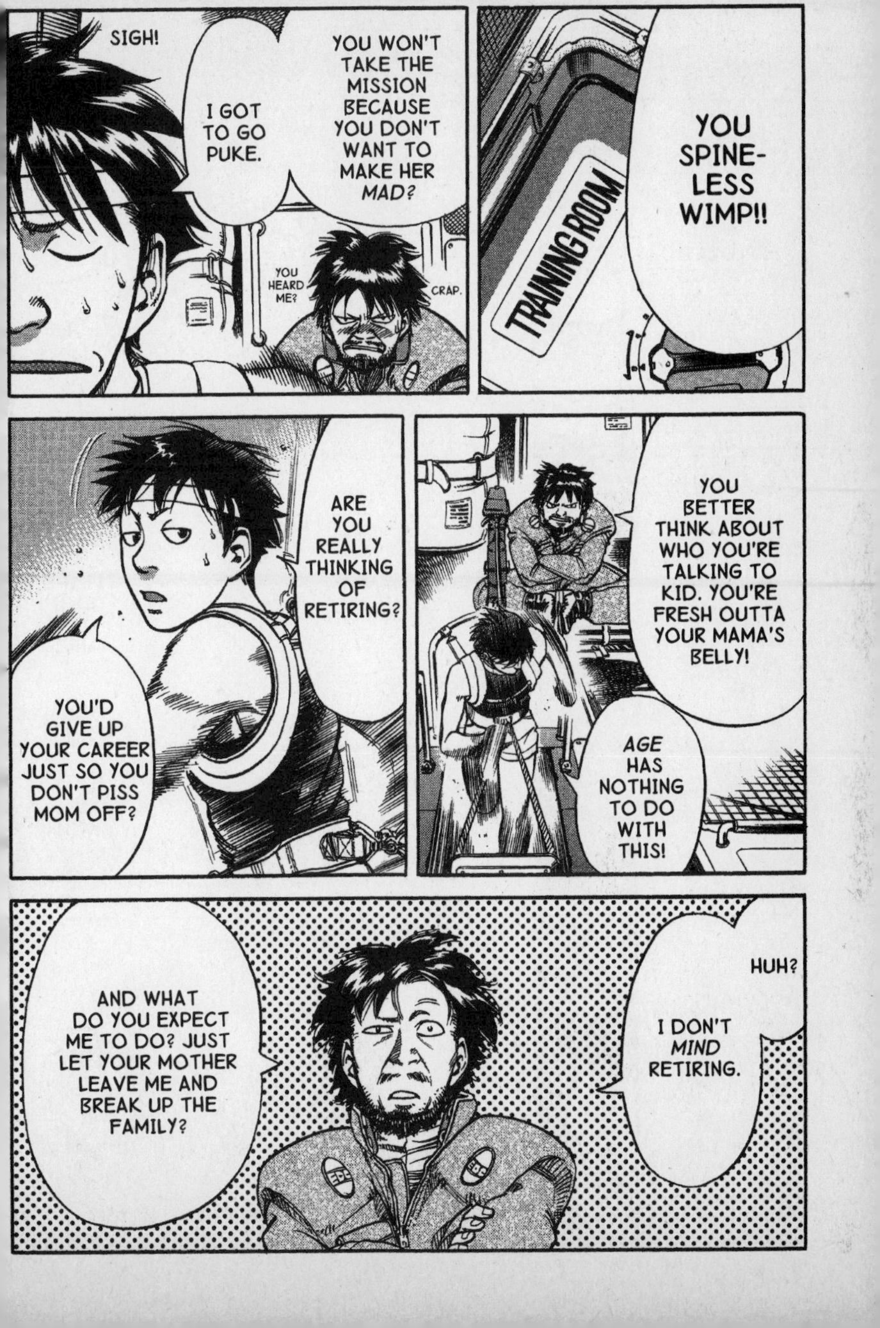
YOU SPINE-LESS WIMP!!
TRAINING ROOM
YOU WON'T TAKE THE MISSION BECAUSE YOU DON'T WANT TO MAKE HER *MAD*?
I GOT TO GO PUKE.
SIGH!
CRAP.
YOU HEARD ME?
YOU BETTER THINK ABOUT WHO YOU'RE TALKING TO KID. YOU'RE FRESH OUTTA YOUR MAMA'S BELLY!
AGE HAS NOTHING TO DO WITH THIS!
ARE YOU REALLY THINKING OF RETIRING?
YOU'D GIVE UP YOUR CAREER JUST SO YOU DON'T PISS MOM OFF?
HUH?
I DON'T *MIND* RETIRING.
AND WHAT DO YOU EXPECT ME TO DO? JUST LET YOUR MOTHER LEAVE ME AND BREAK UP THE FAMILY?

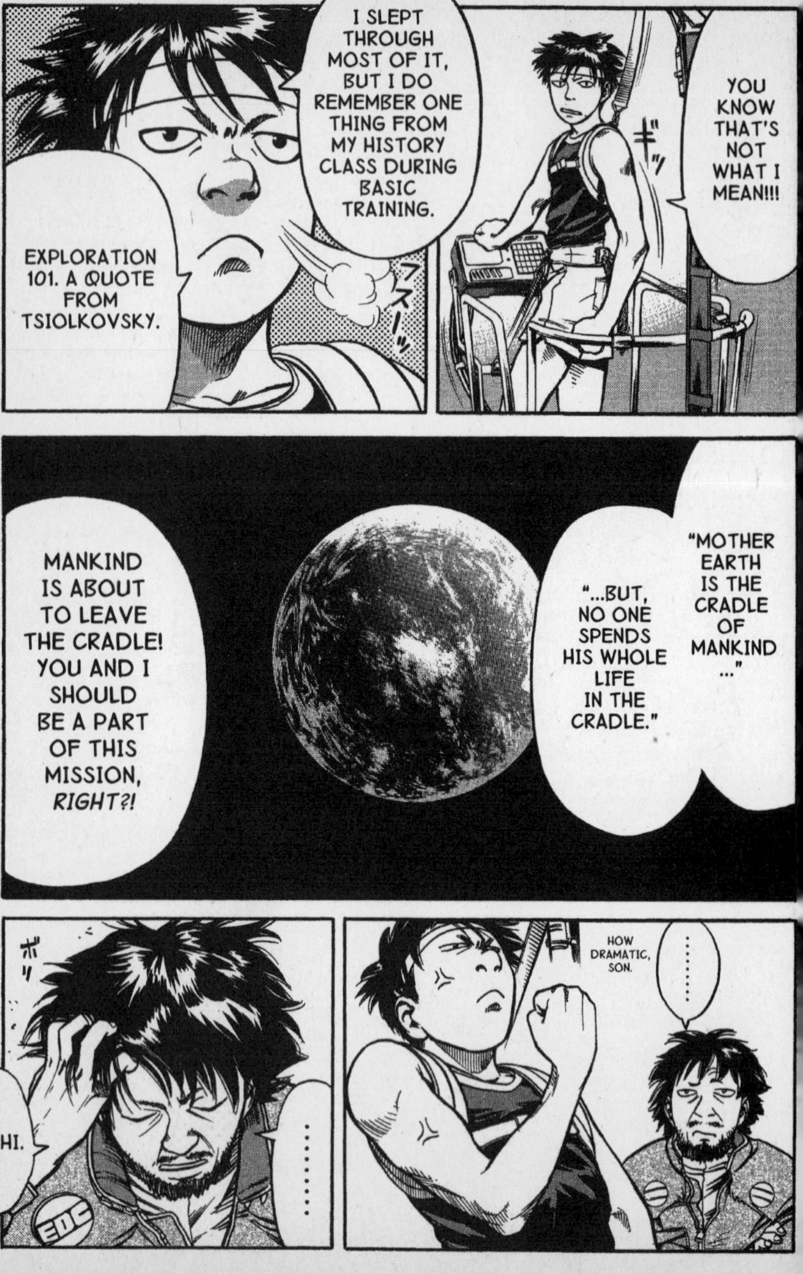
YOU KNOW THAT'S NOT WHAT I MEAN!!!
ギッ
I SLEPT THROUGH MOST OF IT, BUT I DO REMEMBER ONE THING FROM MY HISTORY CLASS DURING BASIC TRAINING.
フスーッ
EXPLORATION 101. A QUOTE FROM TSIOLKOVSKY.
"MOTHER EARTH IS THE CRADLE OF MANKIND ..."
"...BUT, NO ONE SPENDS HIS WHOLE LIFE IN THE CRADLE."
MANKIND IS ABOUT TO LEAVE THE CRADLE! YOU AND I SHOULD BE A PART OF THIS MISSION, *RIGHT?!*
......
HOW DRAMATIC, SON.
ボリ
......
HACHI.

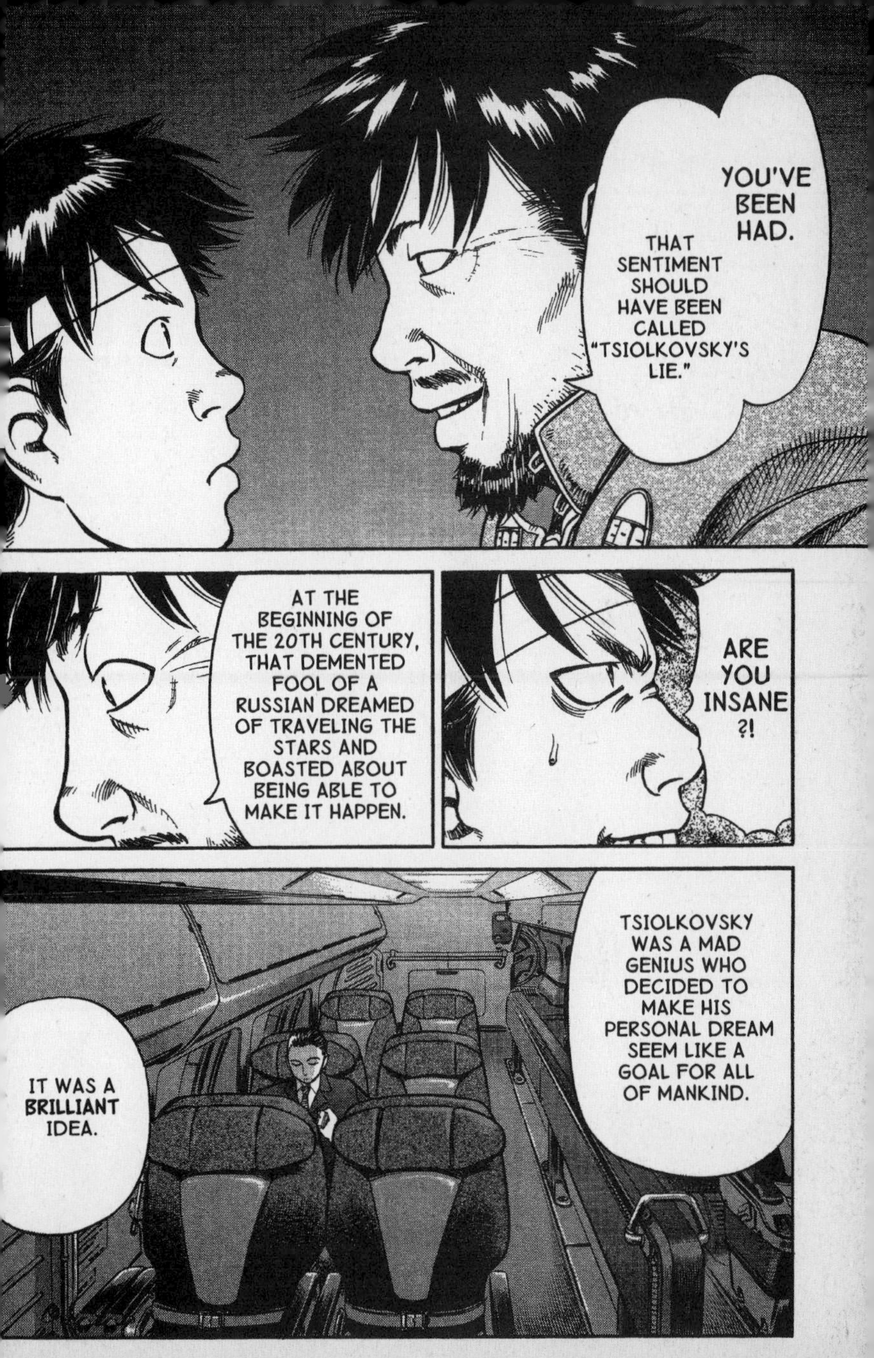
YOU'VE BEEN HAD.
THAT SENTIMENT SHOULD HAVE BEEN CALLED "TSIOLKOVSKY'S LIE."
ARE YOU INSANE?!
AT THE BEGINNING OF THE 20TH CENTURY, THAT DEMENTED FOOL OF A RUSSIAN DREAMED OF TRAVELING THE STARS AND BOASTED ABOUT BEING ABLE TO MAKE IT HAPPEN.
TSIOLKOVSKY WAS A MAD GENIUS WHO DECIDED TO MAKE HIS PERSONAL DREAM SEEM LIKE A GOAL FOR ALL OF MANKIND.
IT WAS A BRILLIANT IDEA.

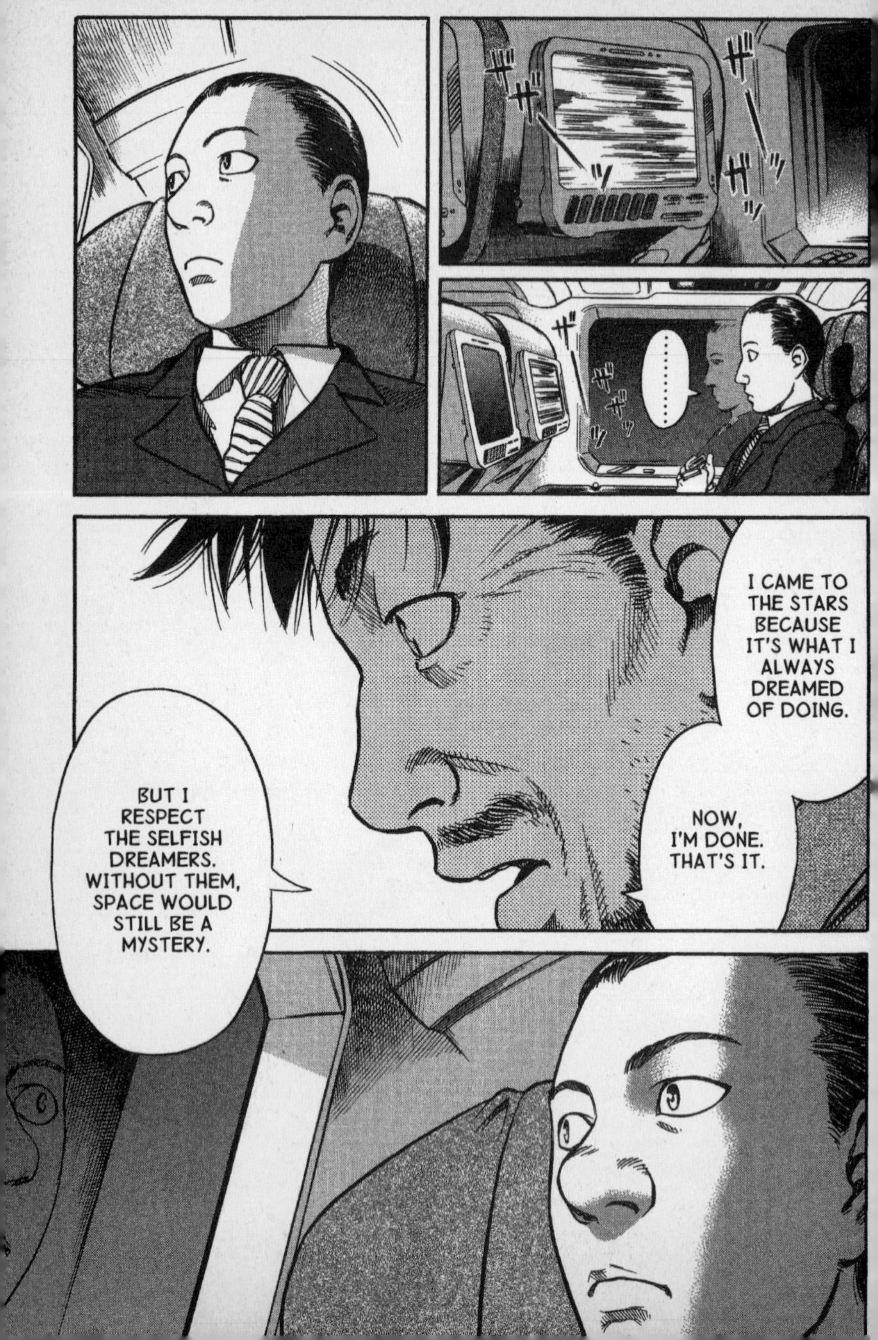
....
I CAME TO THE STARS BECAUSE IT'S WHAT I ALWAYS DREAMED OF DOING.
NOW, I'M DONE. THAT'S IT.
BUT I RESPECT THE SELFISH DREAMERS. WITHOUT THEM, SPACE WOULD STILL BE A MYSTERY.

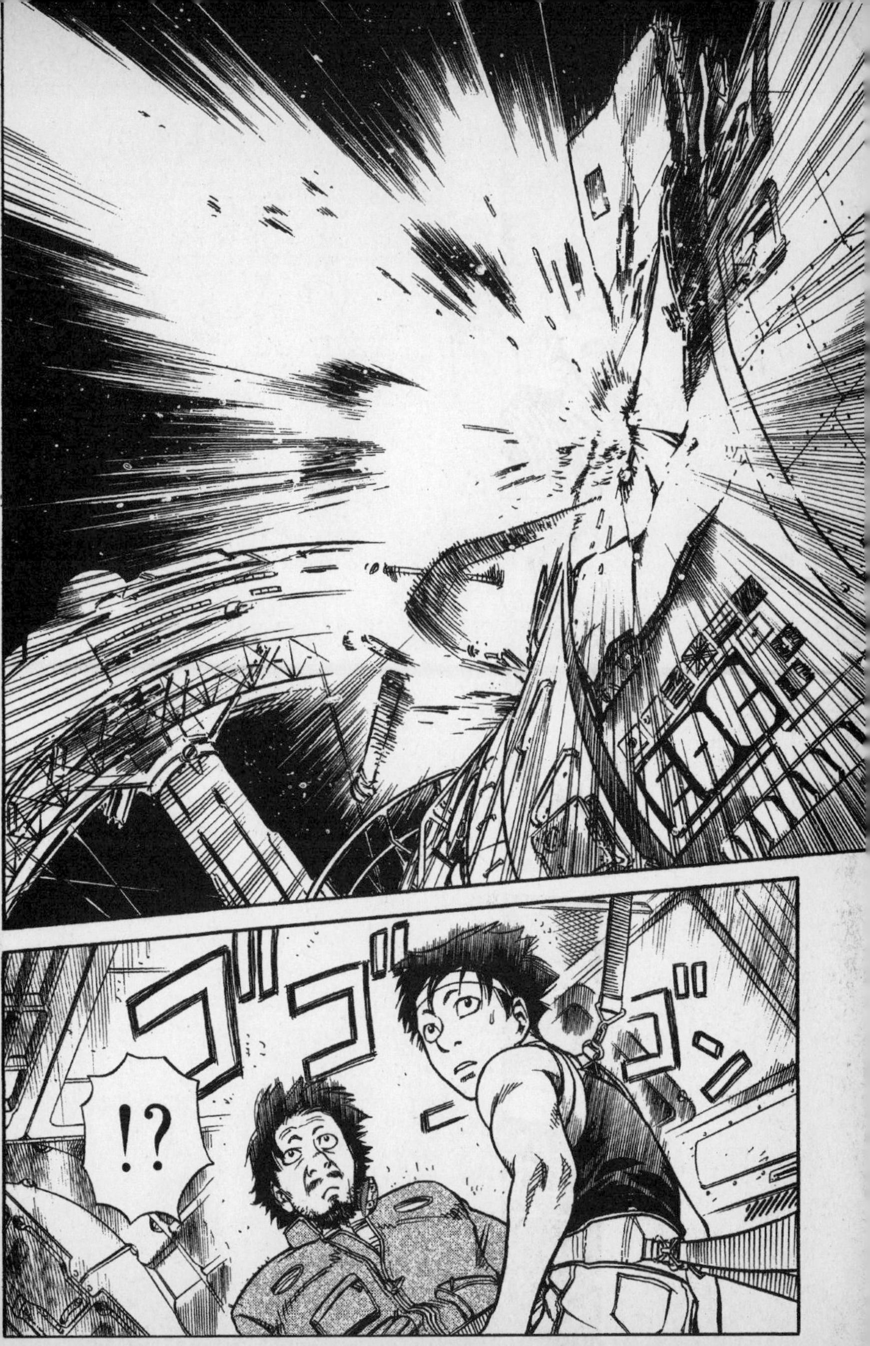
ゴーン
ゴゴ
!?

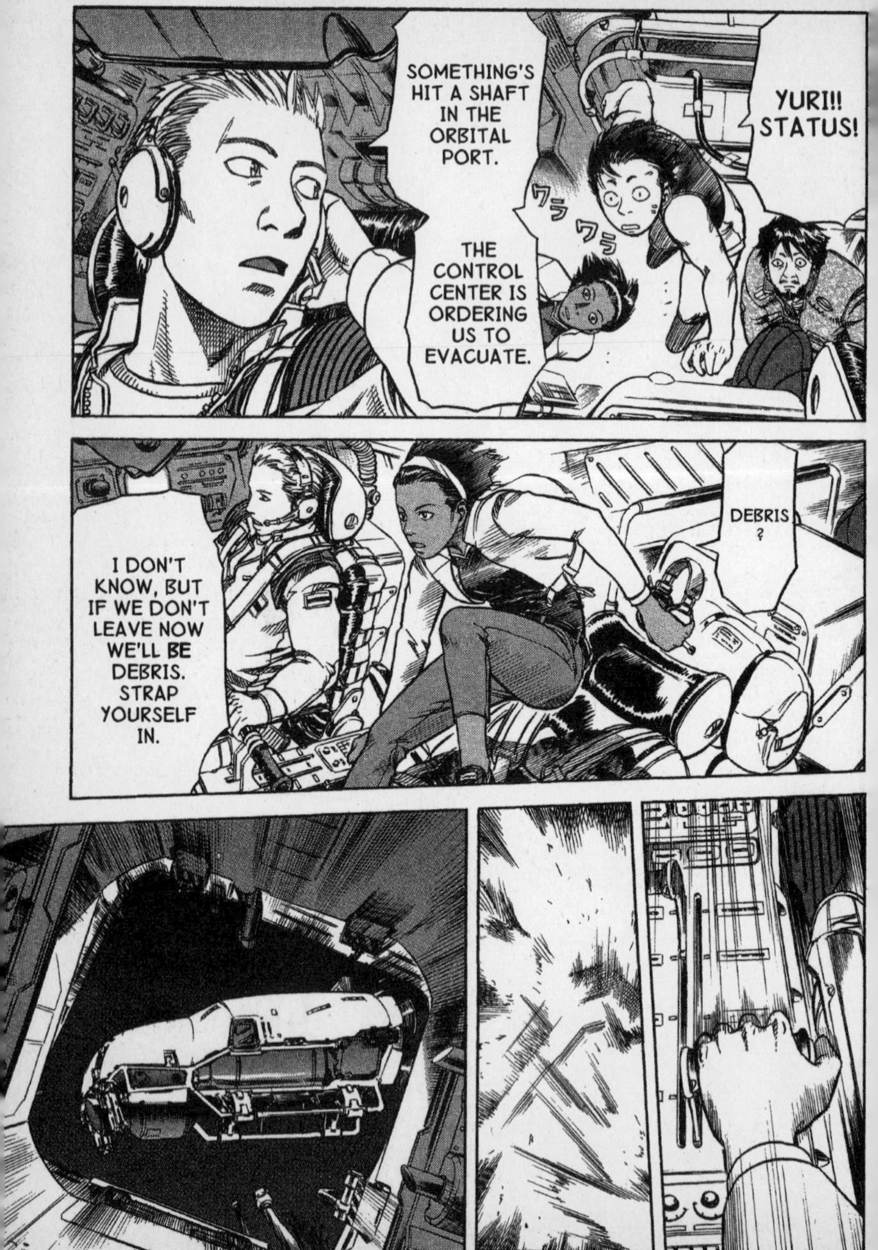
YURI!! STATUS!
SOMETHING'S HIT A SHAFT IN THE ORBITAL PORT.
ワラワラ
THE CONTROL CENTER IS ORDERING US TO EVACUATE.
DEBRIS?
I DON'T KNOW, BUT IF WE DON'T LEAVE NOW WE'LL BE DEBRIS. STRAP YOURSELF IN.

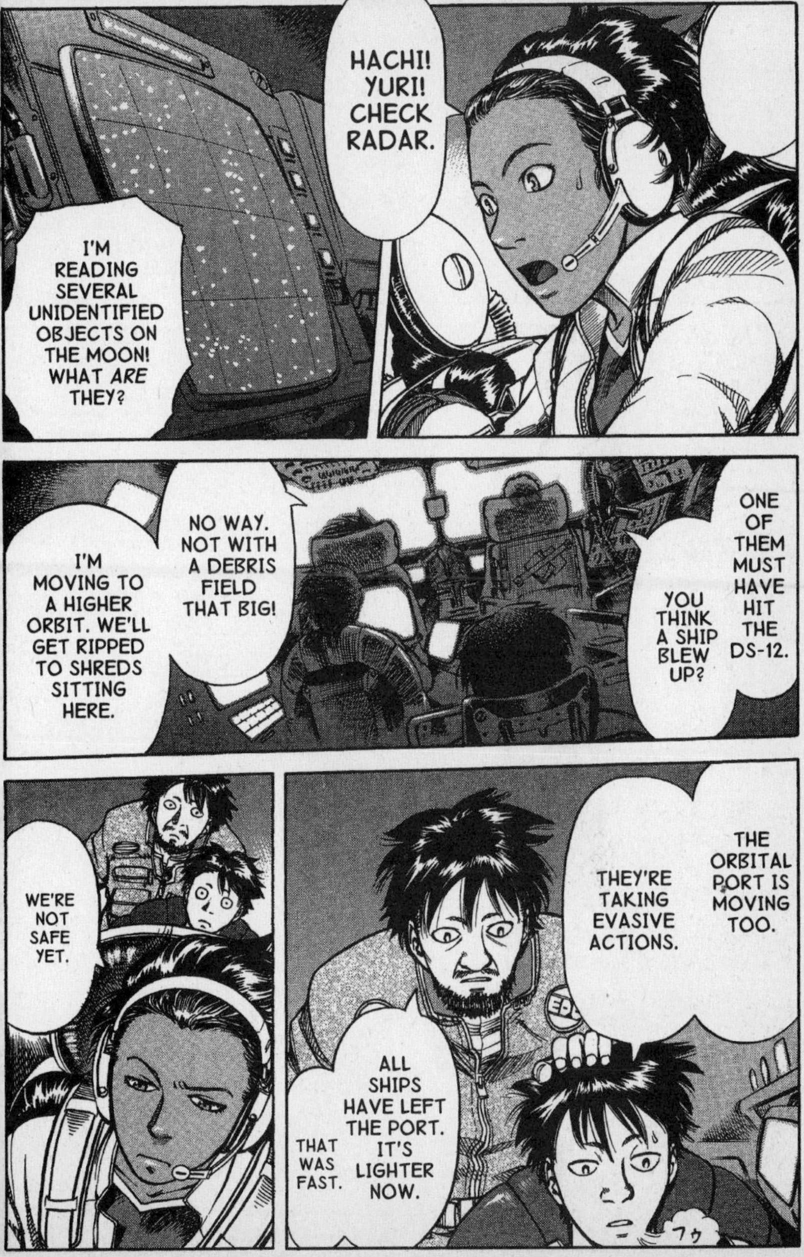
HACHI! YURI! CHECK RADAR.
I'M READING SEVERAL UNIDENTIFIED OBJECTS ON THE MOON! WHAT *ARE* THEY?
ONE OF THEM MUST HAVE HIT THE DS-12.
YOU THINK A SHIP BLEW UP?
NO WAY. NOT WITH A DEBRIS FIELD THAT BIG!
I'M MOVING TO A HIGHER ORBIT. WE'LL GET RIPPED TO SHREDS SITTING HERE.
THE ORBITAL PORT IS MOVING TOO.
THEY'RE TAKING EVASIVE ACTIONS.
ALL SHIPS HAVE LEFT THE PORT. IT'S LIGHTER NOW.
THAT WAS FAST.
フゥ
WE'RE NOT SAFE YET.

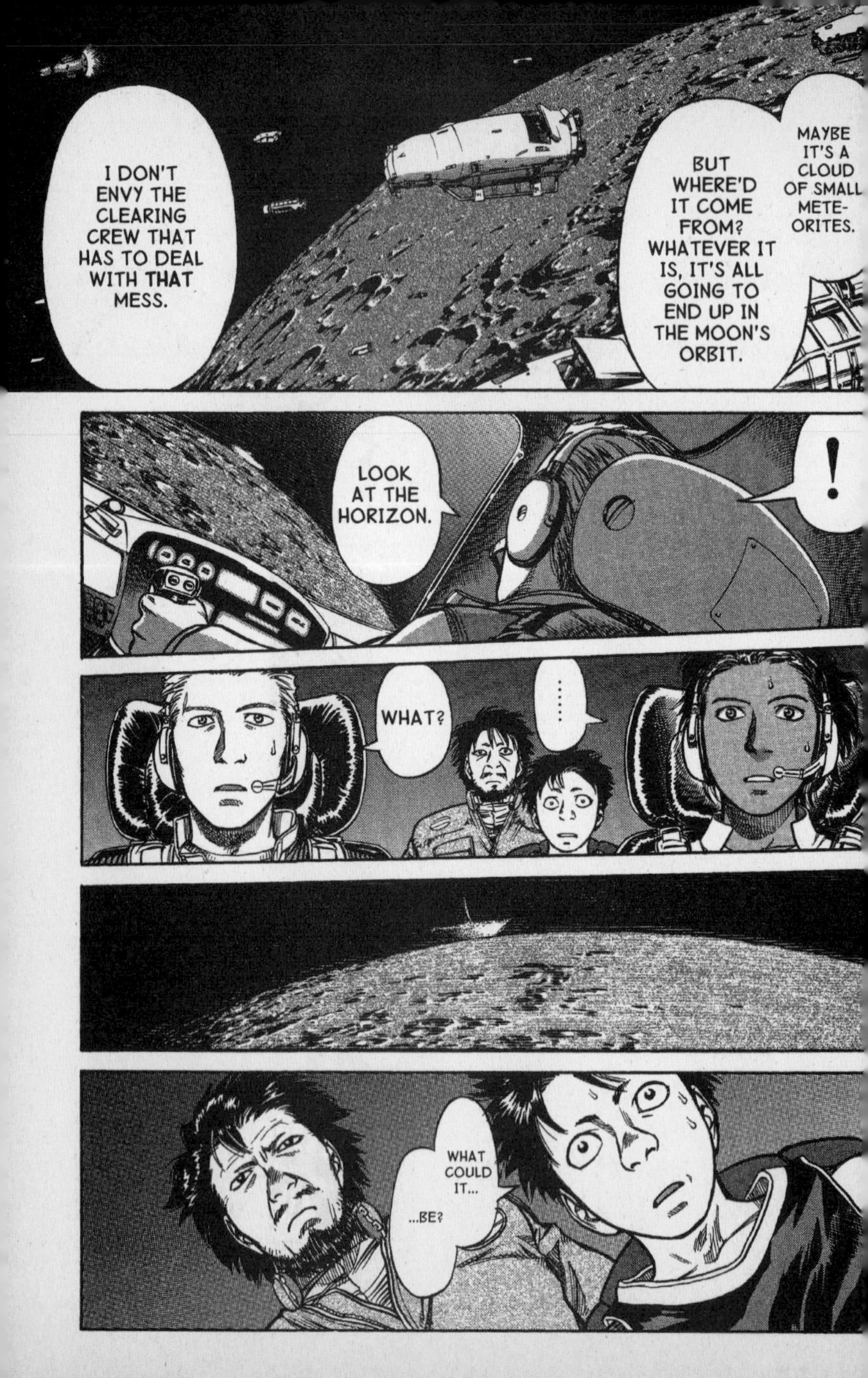
MAYBE IT'S A CLOUD OF SMALL METE-ORITES.
BUT WHERE'D IT COME FROM? WHATEVER IT IS, IT'S ALL GOING TO END UP IN THE MOON'S ORBIT.
I DON'T ENVY THE CLEARING CREW THAT HAS TO DEAL WITH THAT MESS.
!
LOOK AT THE HORIZON.
......
WHAT?
WHAT COULD IT...
...BE?

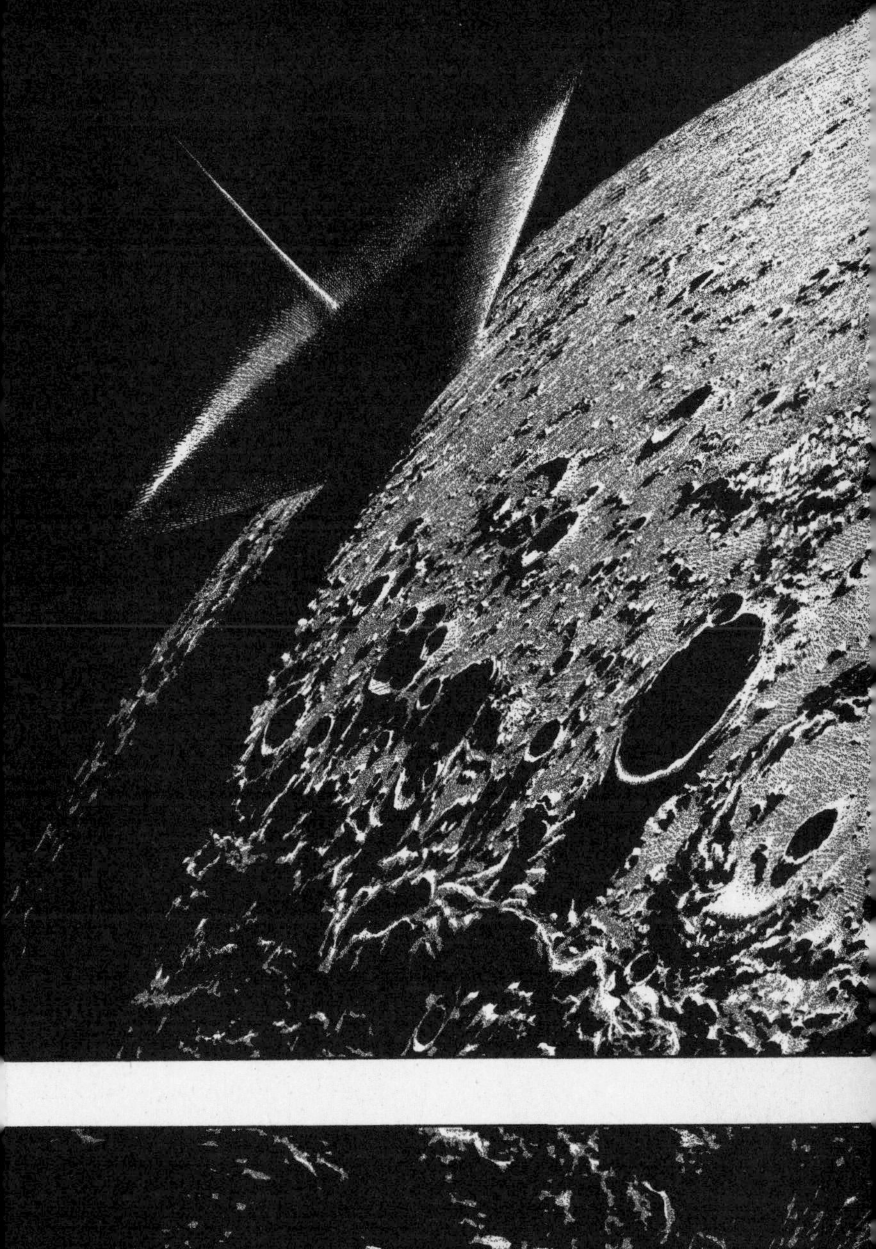

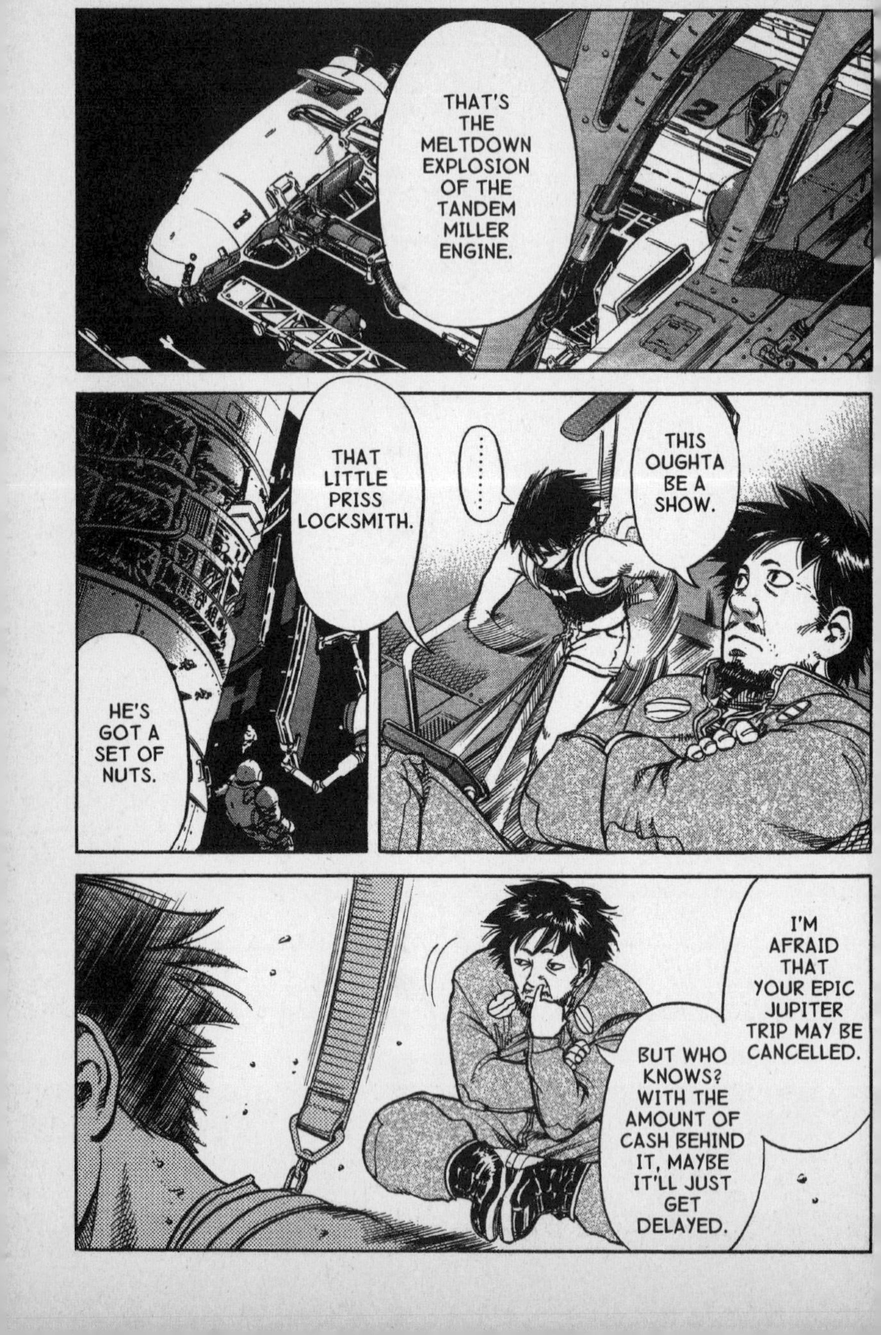
THAT'S THE MELTDOWN EXPLOSION OF THE TANDEM MILLER ENGINE.
THIS OUGHTA BE A SHOW.
......
THAT LITTLE PRISS LOCKSMITH.
HE'S GOT A SET OF NUTS.
I'M AFRAID THAT YOUR EPIC JUPITER TRIP MAY BE CANCELLED.
BUT WHO KNOWS? WITH THE AMOUNT OF CASH BEHIND IT, MAYBE IT'LL JUST GET DELAYED.

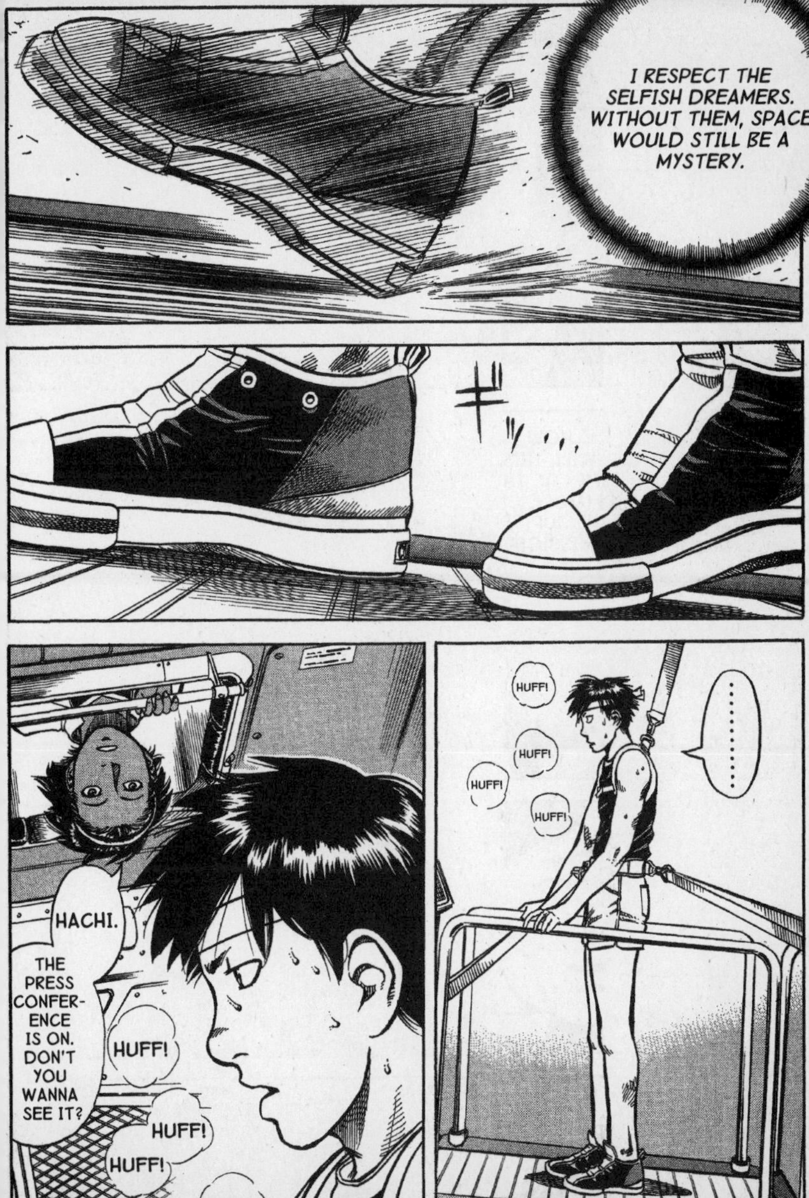
I RESPECT THE SELFISH DREAMERS. WITHOUT THEM, SPACE WOULD STILL BE A MYSTERY.
HUFF!
HUFF!
HUFF!
HUFF!
......
HACHI.
THE PRESS CONFERENCE IS ON. DON'T YOU WANNA SEE IT?
HUFF!
HUFF!
HUFF!
HUFF!

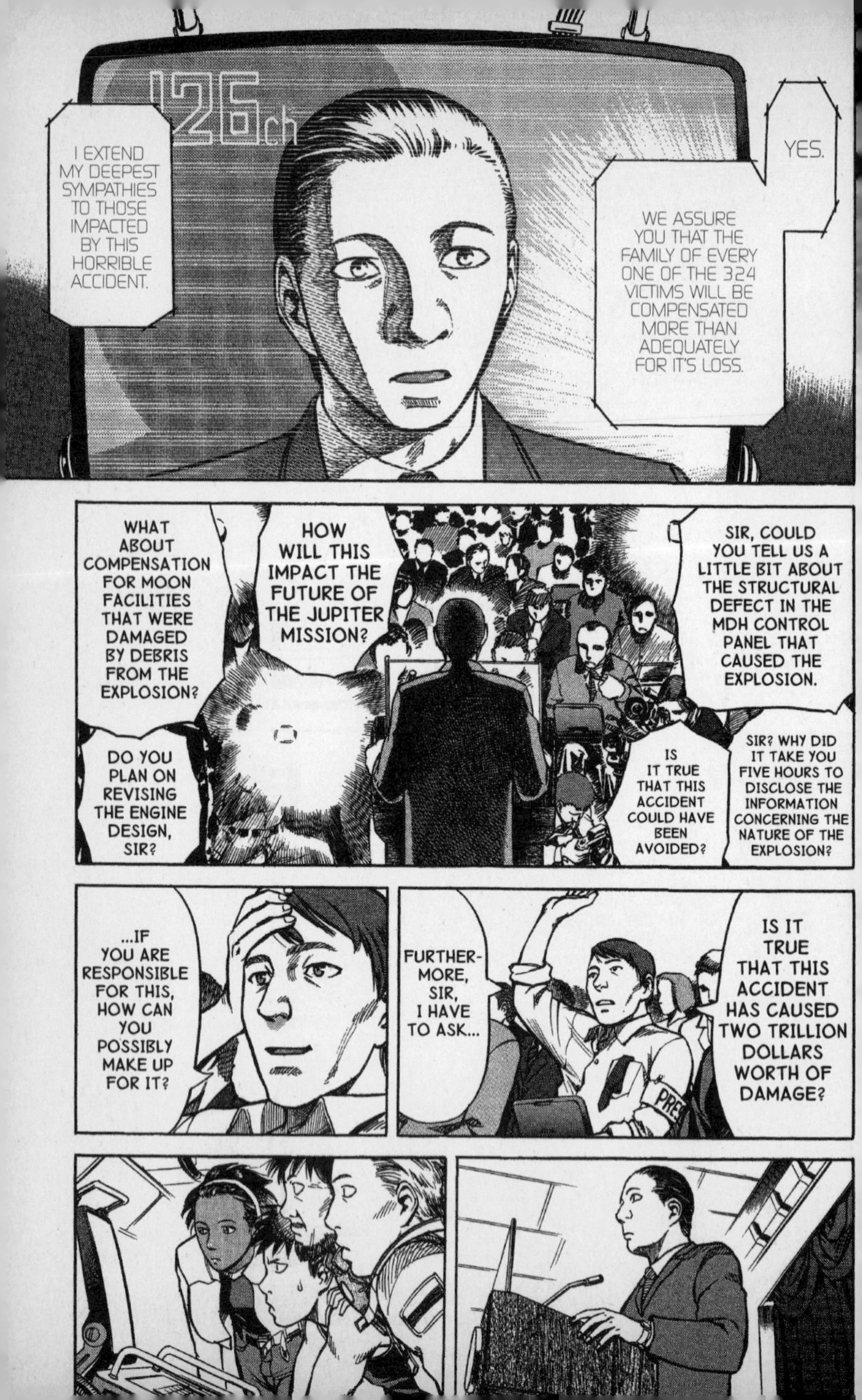
126ch
YES.
WE ASSURE YOU THAT THE FAMILY OF EVERY ONE OF THE 324 VICTIMS WILL BE COMPENSATED MORE THAN ADEQUATELY FOR IT'S LOSS.
I EXTEND MY DEEPEST SYMPATHIES TO THOSE IMPACTED BY THIS HORRIBLE ACCIDENT.
SIR, COULD YOU TELL US A LITTLE BIT ABOUT THE STRUCTURAL DEFECT IN THE MDH CONTROL PANEL THAT CAUSED THE EXPLOSION.
HOW WILL THIS IMPACT THE FUTURE OF THE JUPITER MISSION?
WHAT ABOUT COMPENSATION FOR MOON FACILITIES THAT WERE DAMAGED BY DEBRIS FROM THE EXPLOSION?
SIR? WHY DID IT TAKE YOU FIVE HOURS TO DISCLOSE THE INFORMATION CONCERNING THE NATURE OF THE EXPLOSION?
IS IT TRUE THAT THIS ACCIDENT COULD HAVE BEEN AVOIDED?
DO YOU PLAN ON REVISING THE ENGINE DESIGN, SIR?
IS IT TRUE THAT THIS ACCIDENT HAS CAUSED TWO TRILLION DOLLARS WORTH OF DAMAGE?
FURTHER-MORE, SIR, I HAVE TO ASK...
...IF YOU ARE RESPONSIBLE FOR THIS, HOW CAN YOU POSSIBLY MAKE UP FOR IT?

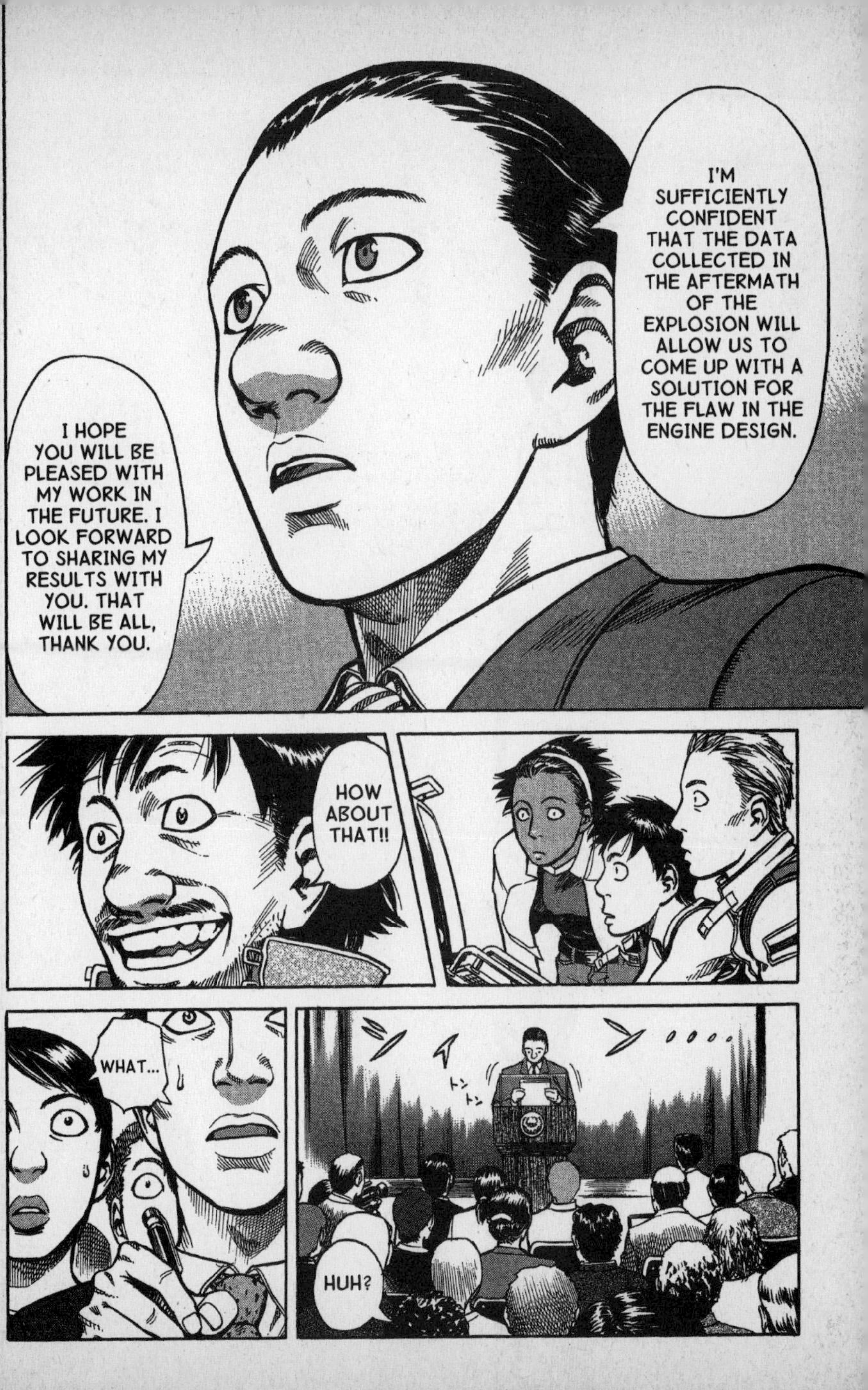
I'M SUFFICIENTLY CONFIDENT THAT THE DATA COLLECTED IN THE AFTERMATH OF THE EXPLOSION WILL ALLOW US TO COME UP WITH A SOLUTION FOR THE FLAW IN THE ENGINE DESIGN.
I HOPE YOU WILL BE PLEASED WITH MY WORK IN THE FUTURE. I LOOK FORWARD TO SHARING MY RESULTS WITH YOU. THAT WILL BE ALL, THANK YOU.
HOW ABOUT THAT!!
トン トン
HUH?
WHAT...

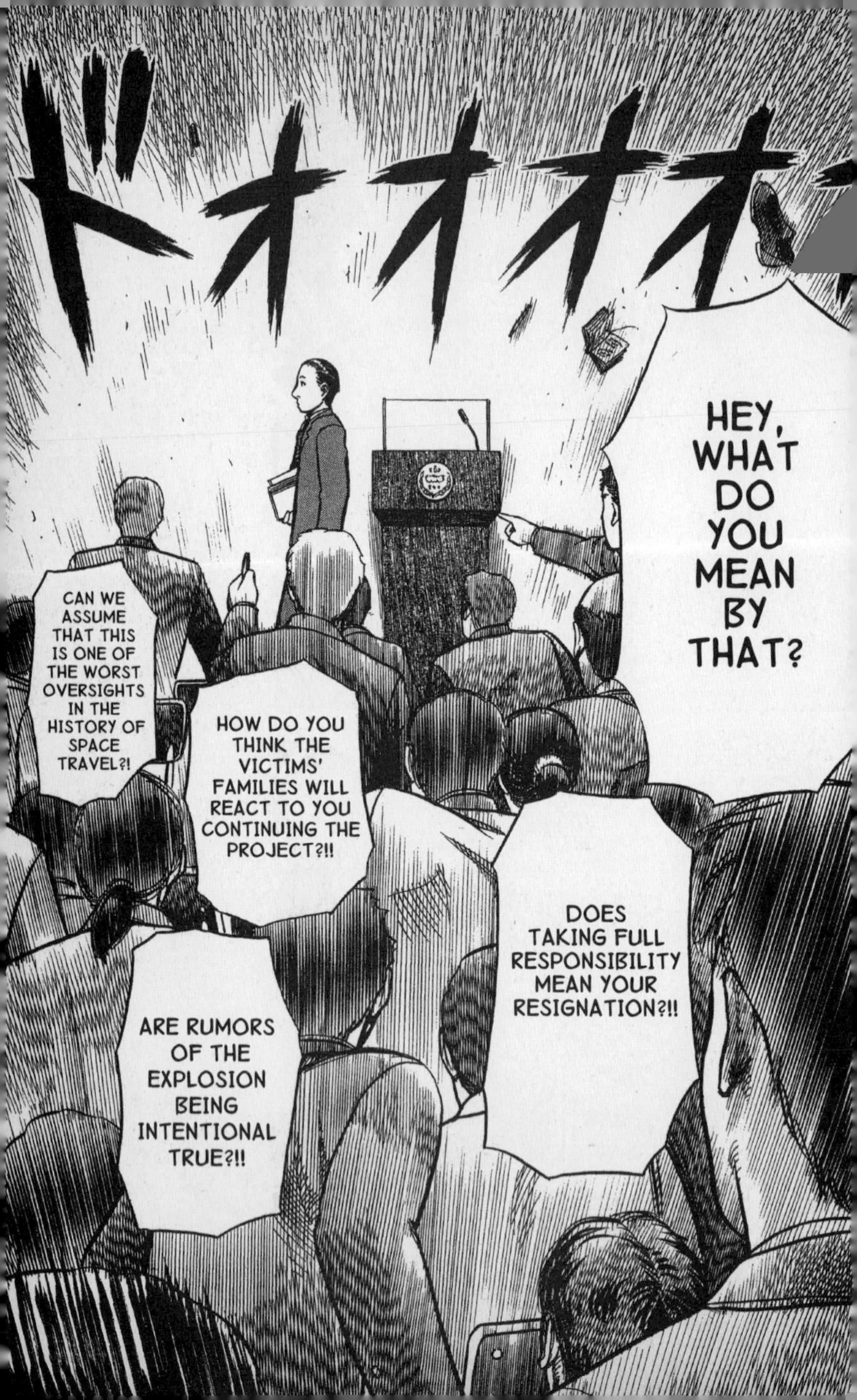
ドオオオオ
HEY, WHAT DO YOU MEAN BY THAT?
CAN WE ASSUME THAT THIS IS ONE OF THE WORST OVERSIGHTS IN THE HISTORY OF SPACE TRAVEL?!
HOW DO YOU THINK THE VICTIMS' FAMILIES WILL REACT TO YOU CONTINUING THE PROJECT?!!
DOES TAKING FULL RESPONSIBILITY MEAN YOUR RESIGNATION?!!
ARE RUMORS OF THE EXPLOSION BEING INTENTIONAL TRUE?!!

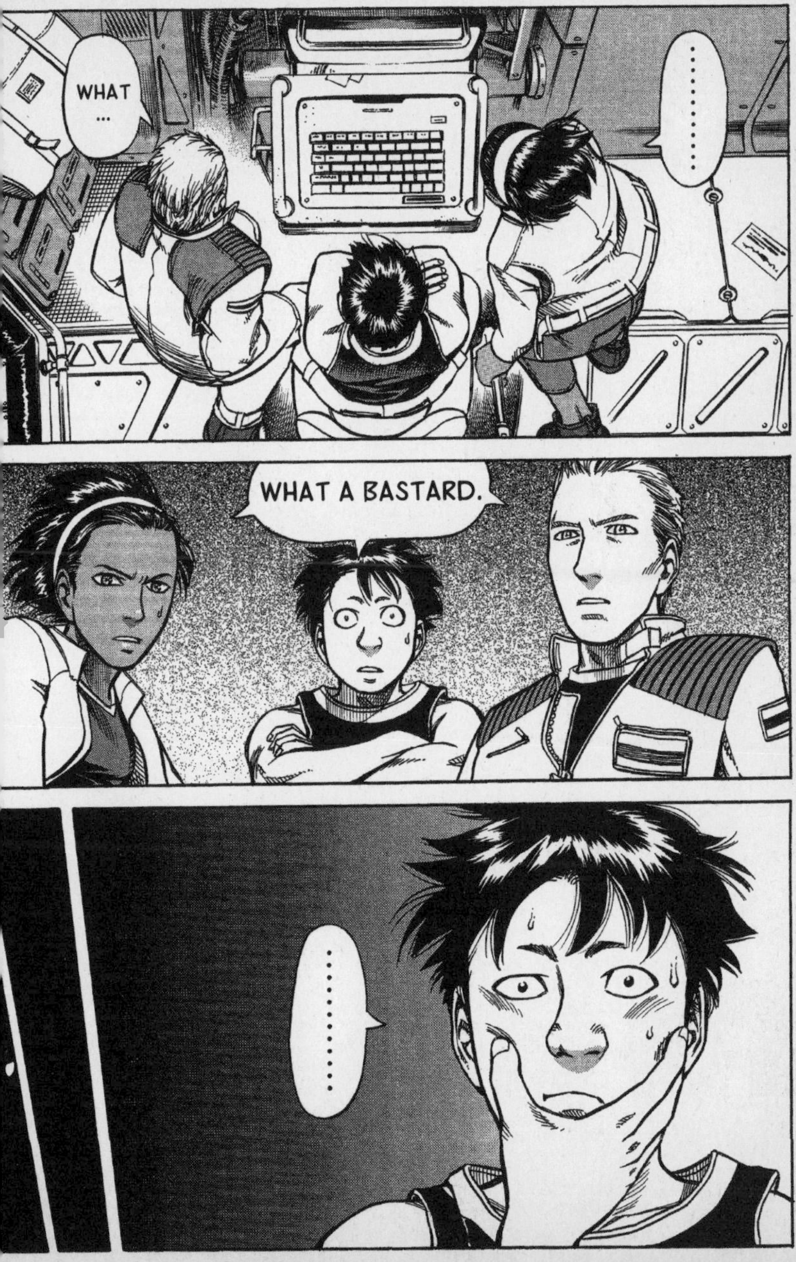
......
WHAT ...
WHAT A BASTARD.
......

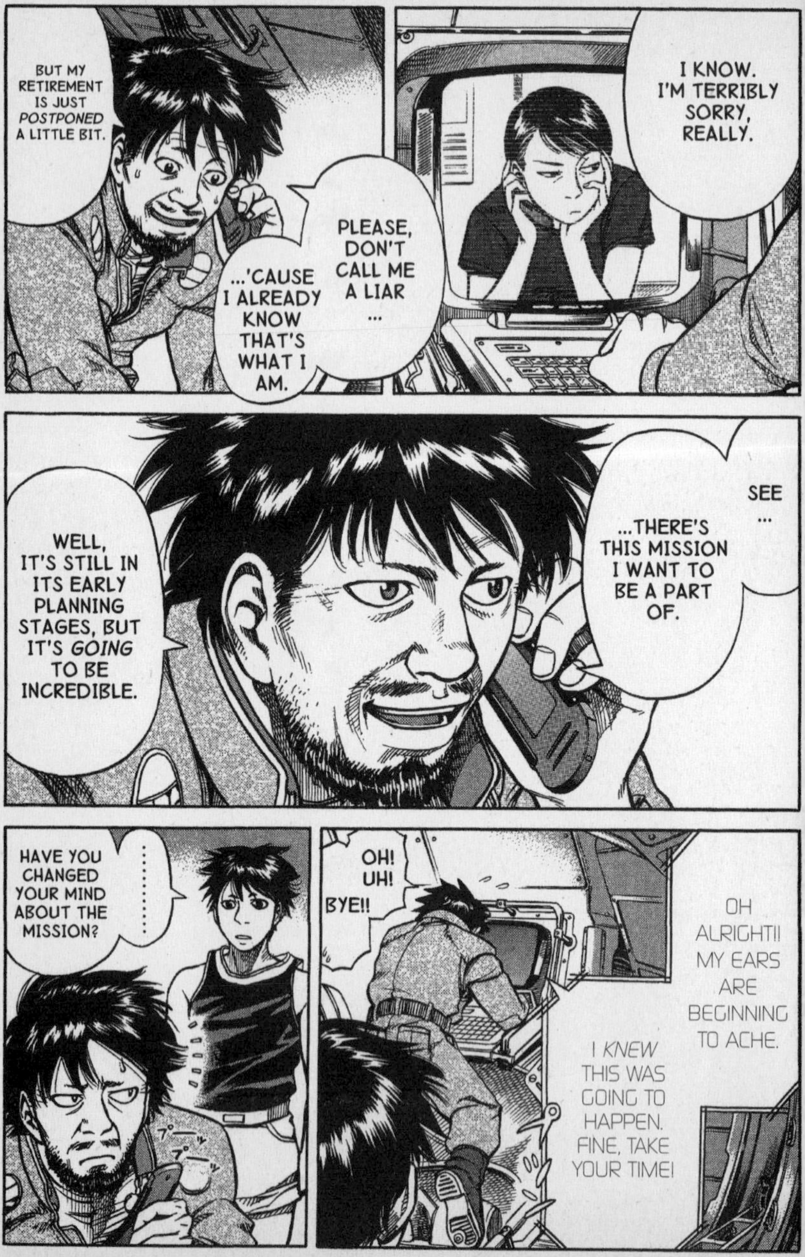
I KNOW. I'M TERRIBLY SORRY, REALLY.
PLEASE, DON'T CALL ME A LIAR ...
...'CAUSE I ALREADY KNOW THAT'S WHAT I AM.
BUT MY RETIREMENT IS JUST *POSTPONED* A LITTLE BIT.
SEE ...
...THERE'S THIS MISSION I WANT TO BE A PART OF.
WELL, IT'S STILL IN ITS EARLY PLANNING STAGES, BUT IT'S *GOING* TO BE INCREDIBLE.
OH ALRIGHT!! MY EARS ARE BEGINNING TO ACHE.
I *KNEW* THIS WAS GOING TO HAPPEN. FINE, TAKE YOUR TIME!
OH! UH! BYE!!
....
HAVE YOU CHANGED YOUR MIND ABOUT THE MISSION?
プーッ
プーッ

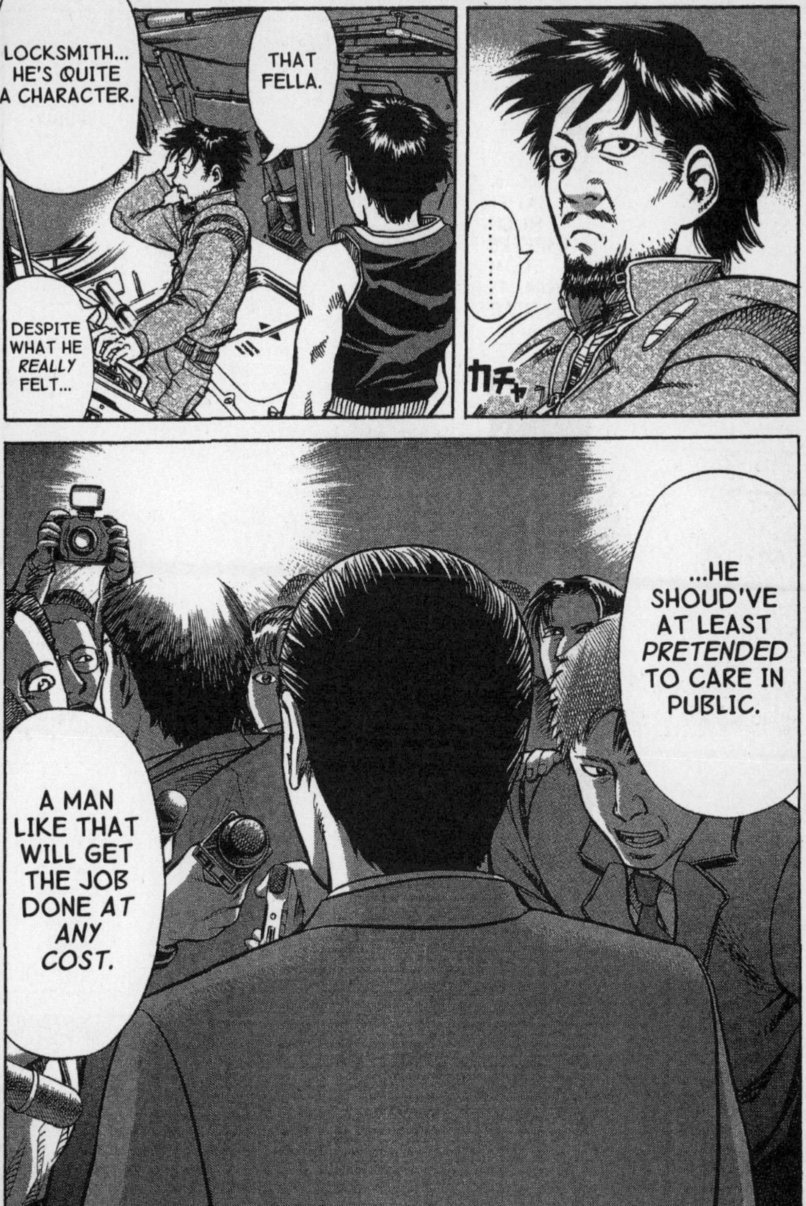
......
カチャ
LOCKSMITH... HE'S QUITE A CHARACTER.
THAT FELLA.
DESPITE WHAT HE *REALLY* FELT...
...HE SHOUD'VE AT LEAST *PRETENDED* TO CARE IN PUBLIC.
A MAN LIKE THAT WILL GET THE JOB DONE AT *ANY* COST.

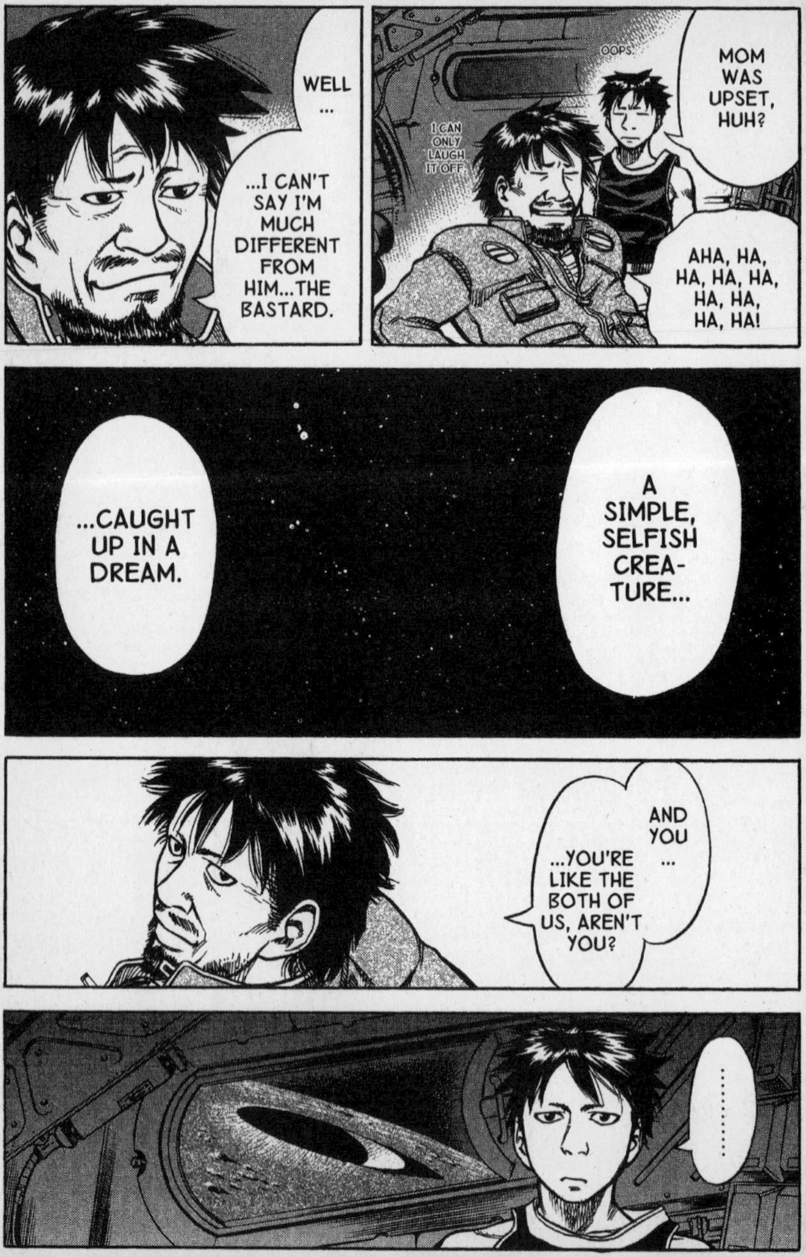
MOM WAS UPSET, HUH?
OOPS.
I CAN ONLY LAUGH IT OFF.
AHA, HA, HA, HA, HA, HA, HA, HA, HA!
WELL ...
...I CAN'T SAY I'M MUCH DIFFERENT FROM HIM...THE BASTARD.
A SIMPLE, SELFISH CREA-TURE...
...CAUGHT UP IN A DREAM.
AND YOU ...
...YOU'RE LIKE THE BOTH OF US, AREN'T YOU?
....

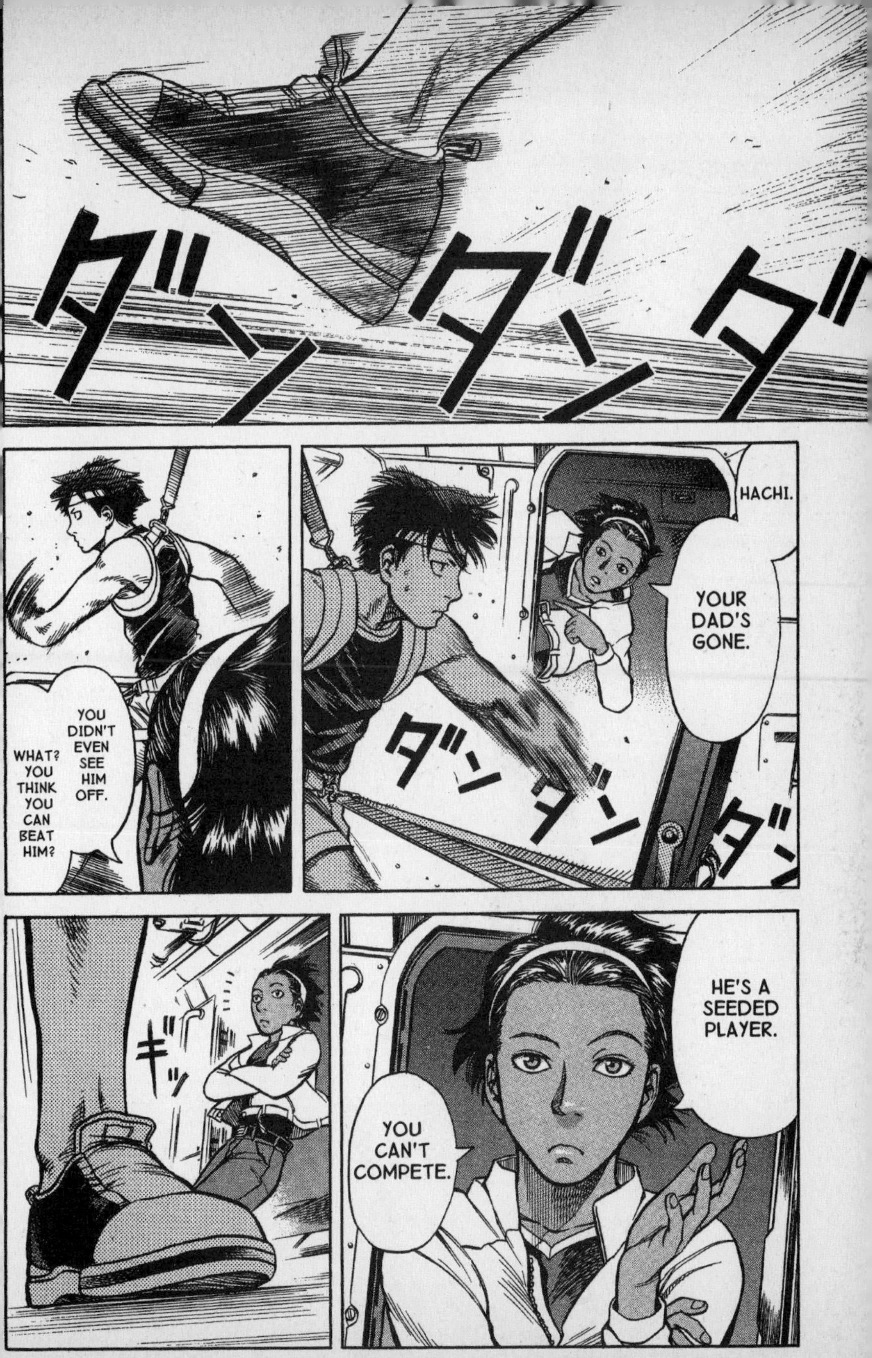
ダン
ダン
ダン
HACHI.
YOUR DAD'S GONE.
ダン
ダン
ダン
YOU DIDN'T EVEN SEE HIM OFF.
WHAT? YOU THINK YOU CAN BEAT HIM?
HE'S A SEEDED PLAYER.
YOU CAN'T COMPETE.
ギッ

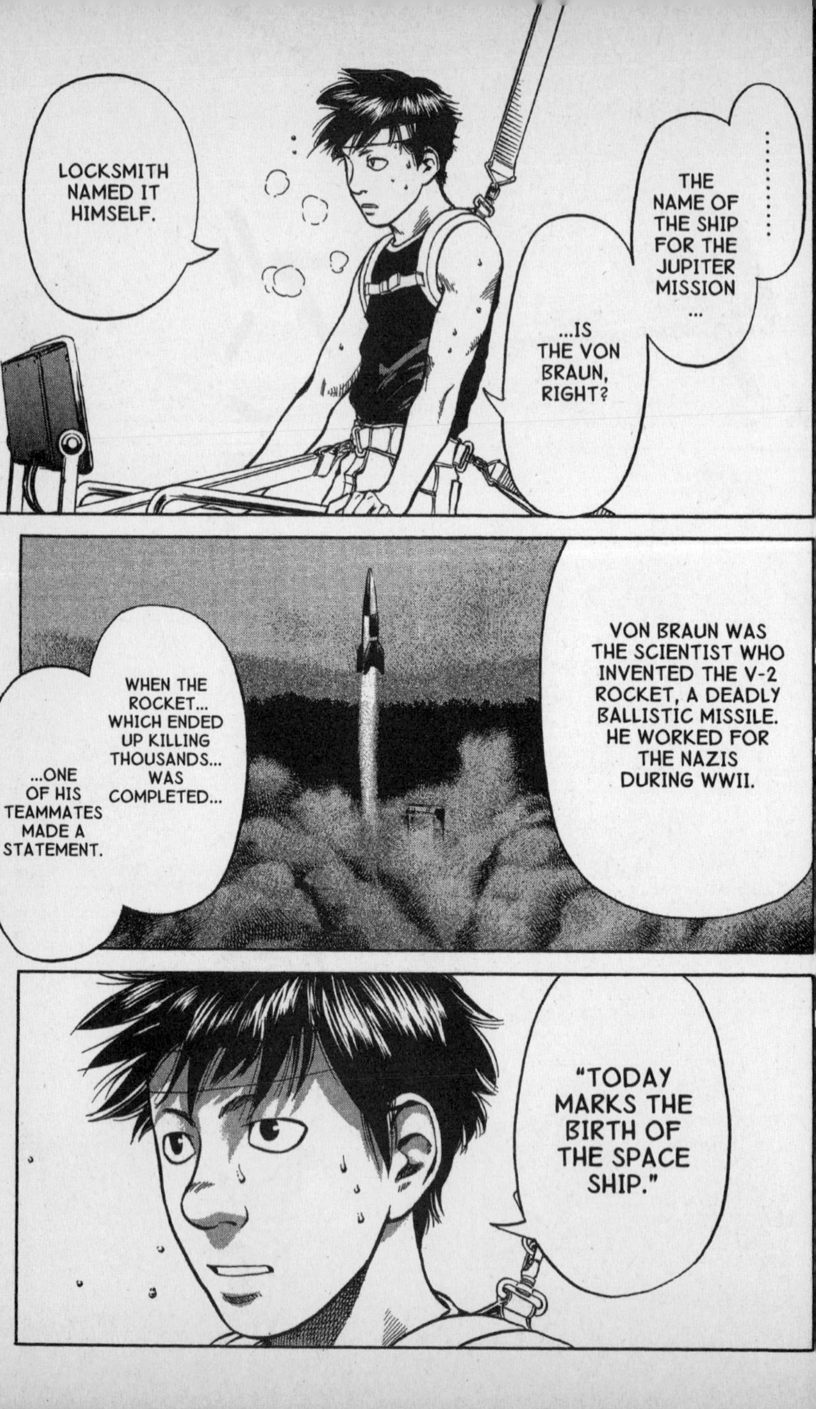

....
THE NAME OF THE SHIP FOR THE JUPITER MISSION ...
...IS THE VON BRAUN, RIGHT?
LOCKSMITH NAMED IT HIMSELF.
VON BRAUN WAS THE SCIENTIST WHO INVENTED THE V-2 ROCKET, A DEADLY BALLISTIC MISSILE. HE WORKED FOR THE NAZIS DURING WWII.
WHEN THE ROCKET... WHICH ENDED UP KILLING THOUSANDS... WAS COMPLETED...
...ONE OF HIS TEAMMATES MADE A STATEMENT.
"TODAY MARKS THE BIRTH OF THE SPACE SHIP."

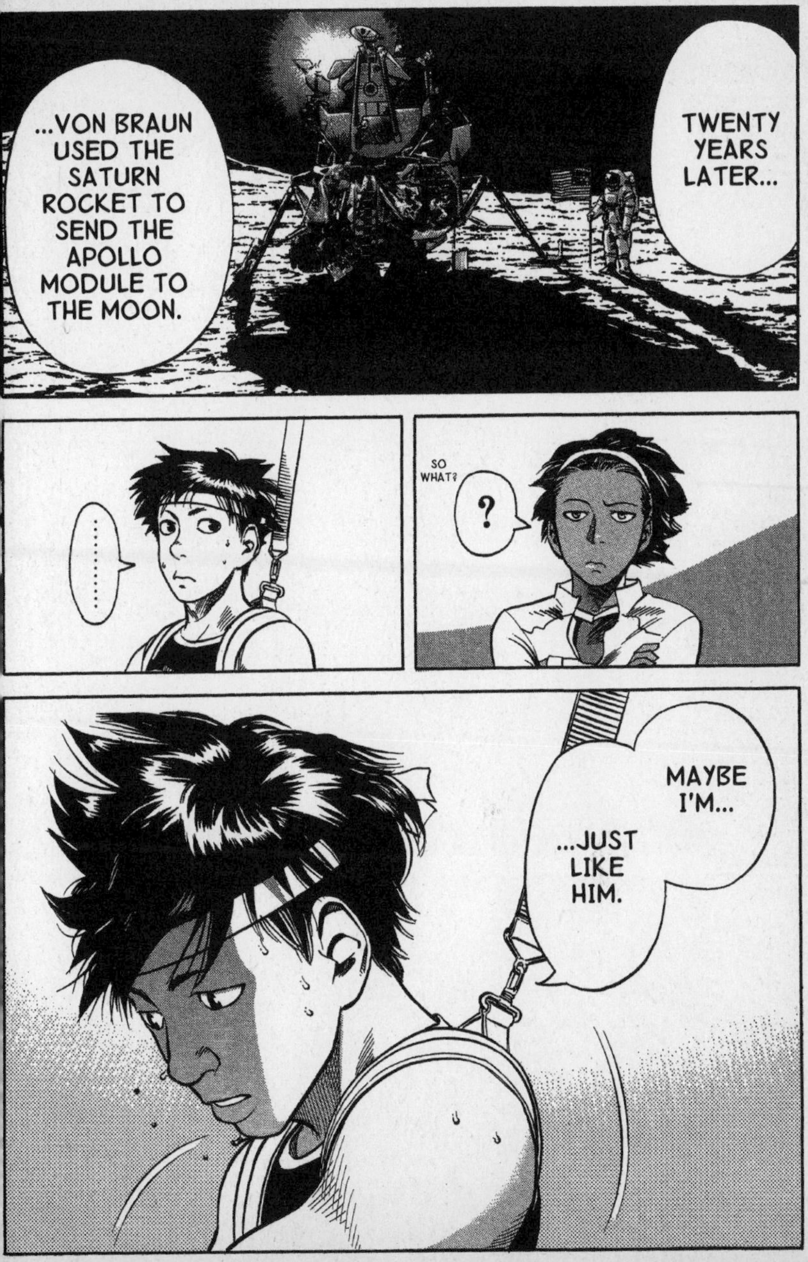
TWENTY YEARS LATER...
...VON BRAUN USED THE SATURN ROCKET TO SEND THE APOLLO MODULE TO THE MOON.
SO WHAT?
?
......
MAYBE I'M...
...JUST LIKE HIM.

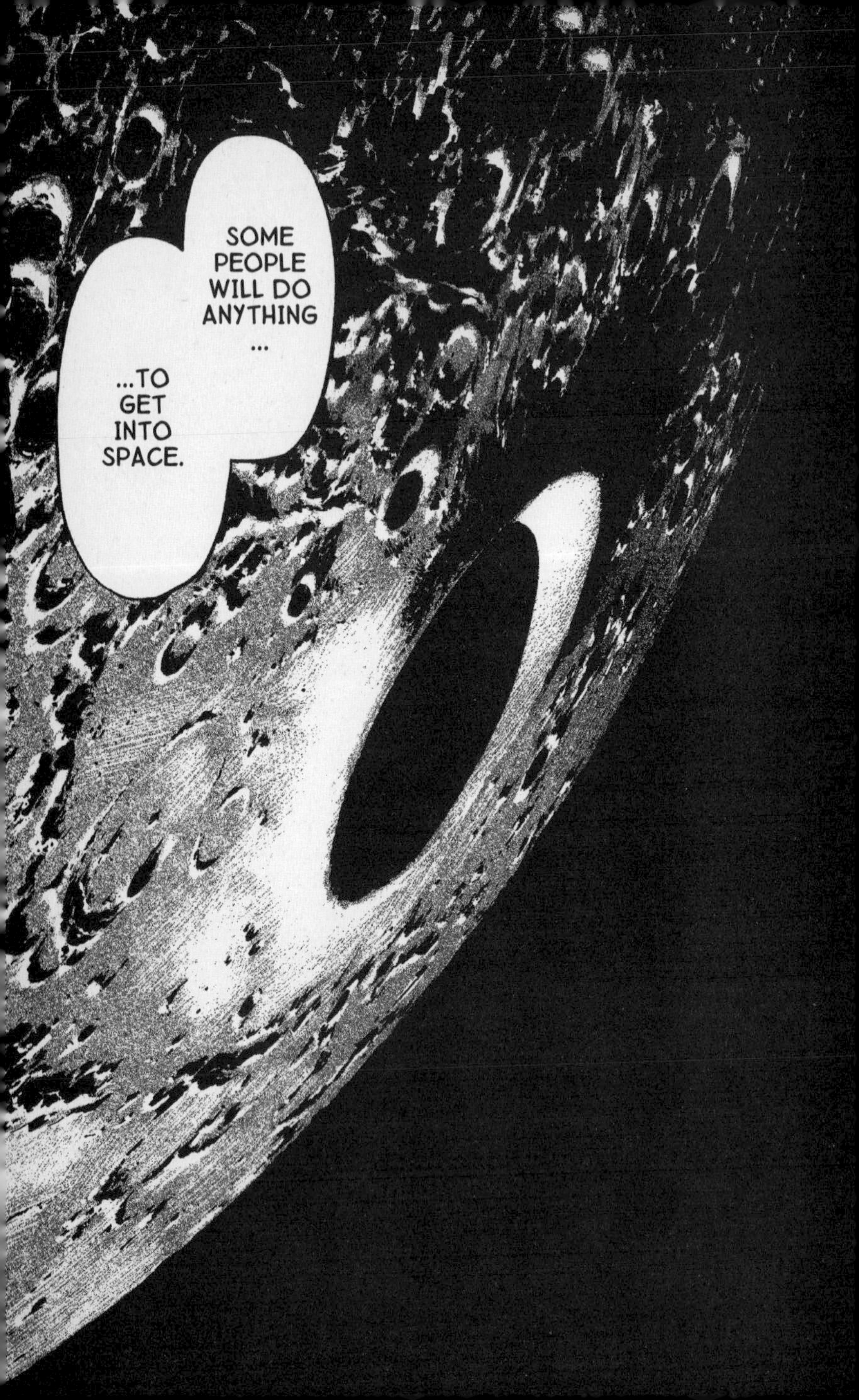
SOME PEOPLE WILL DO ANYTHING ...
...TO GET INTO SPACE.

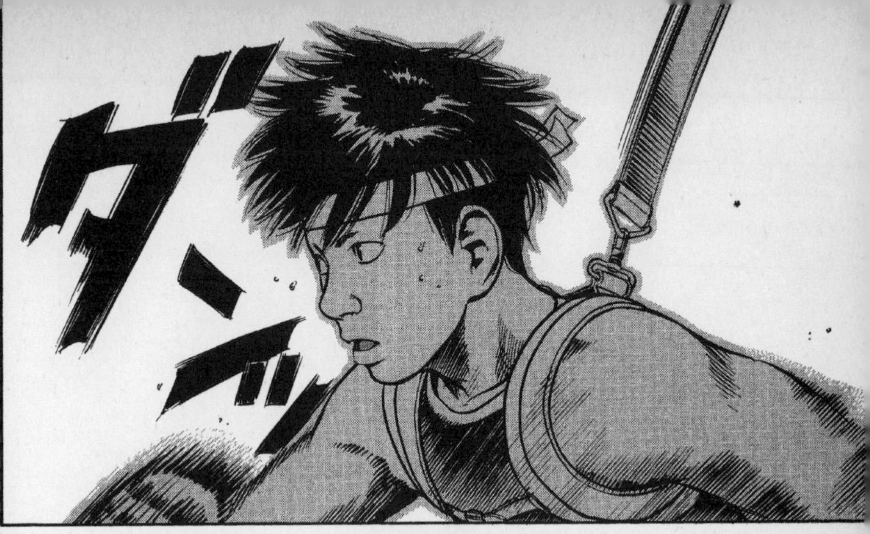
ダンッ

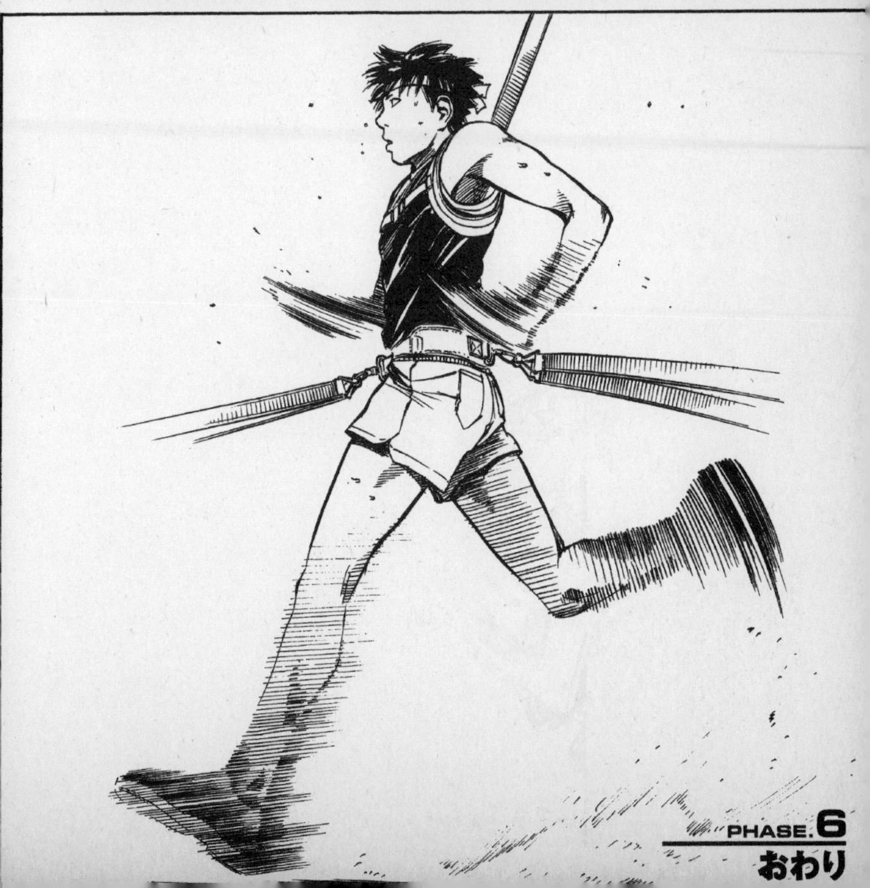
PHASE.6
おわり

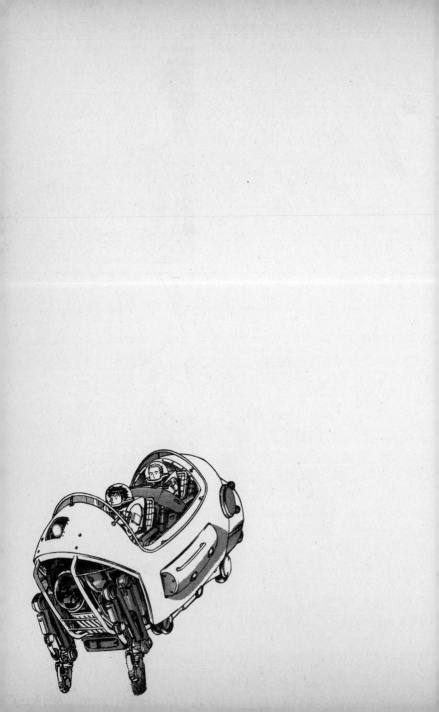

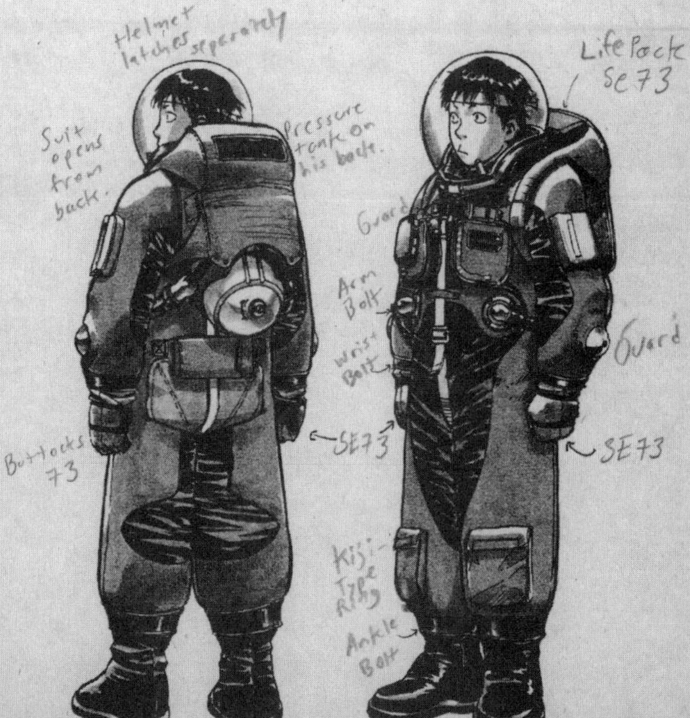
Helmet latches seperately
Suit opens from back.
Pressure tank on his back.
Life Pack SE73
Guard
Arm Bolt
Guard
Wrist Bolt
SE73
SE73
Buttocks 73
Kiji-Type Ring
Ankle Bolt

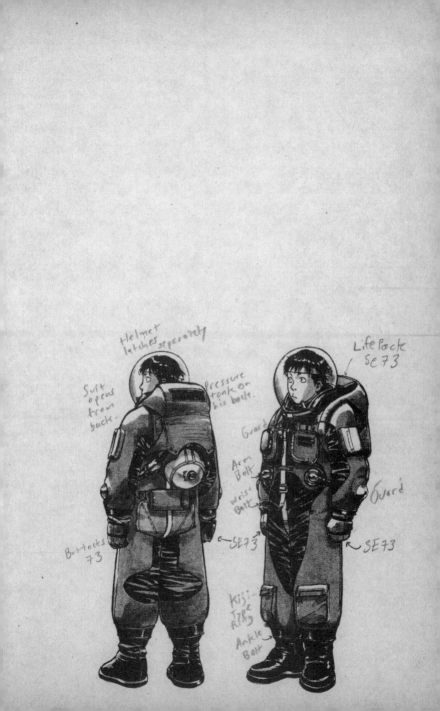

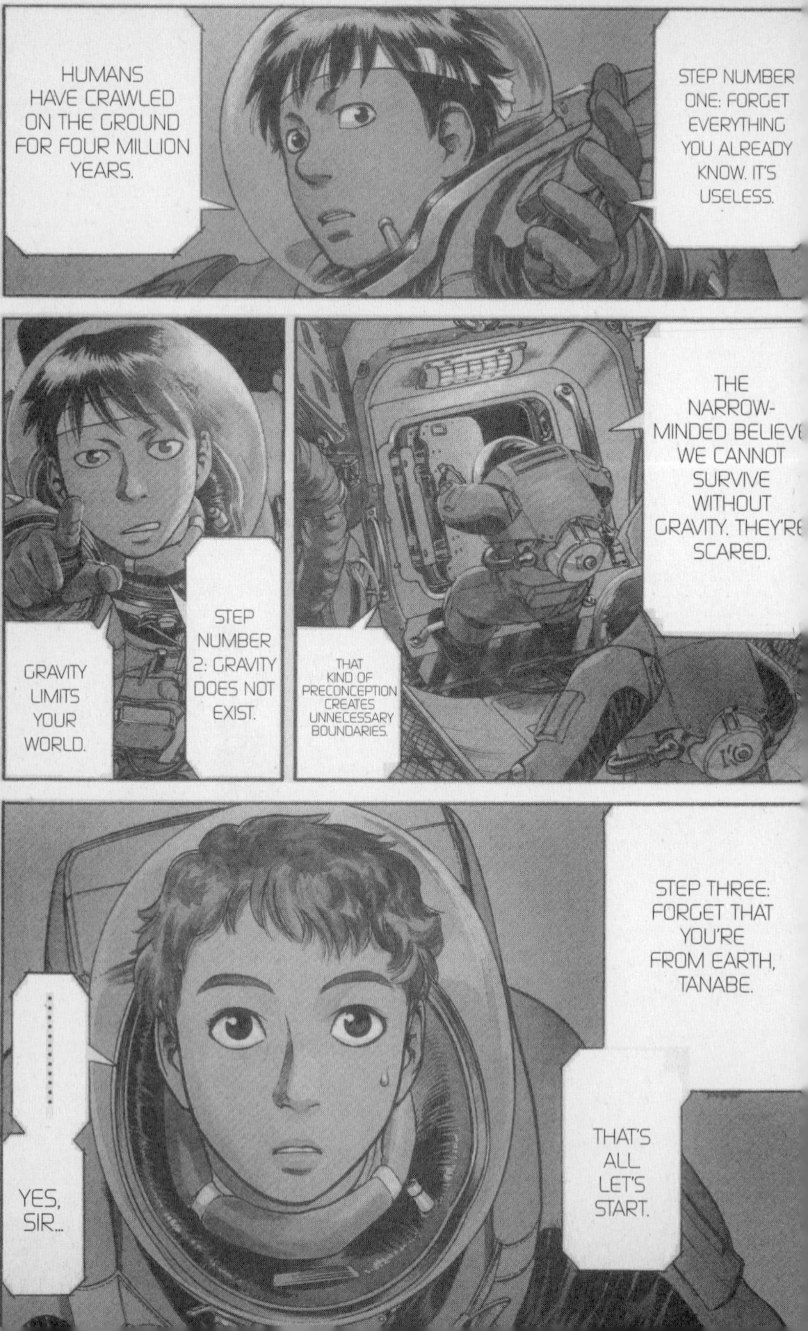
STEP NUMBER ONE: FORGET EVERYTHING YOU ALREADY KNOW. IT'S USELESS.
HUMANS HAVE CRAWLED ON THE GROUND FOR FOUR MILLION YEARS.
THE NARROW-MINDED BELIEV WE CANNOT SURVIVE WITHOUT GRAVITY. THEY'R SCARED.
THAT KIND OF PRECONCEPTION CREATES UNNECESSARY BOUNDARIES.
STEP NUMBER 2: GRAVITY DOES NOT EXIST.
GRAVITY LIMITS YOUR WORLD.
STEP THREE: FORGET THAT YOU'RE FROM EARTH, TANABE.
THAT'S ALL LET'S START.
……
YES, SIR...

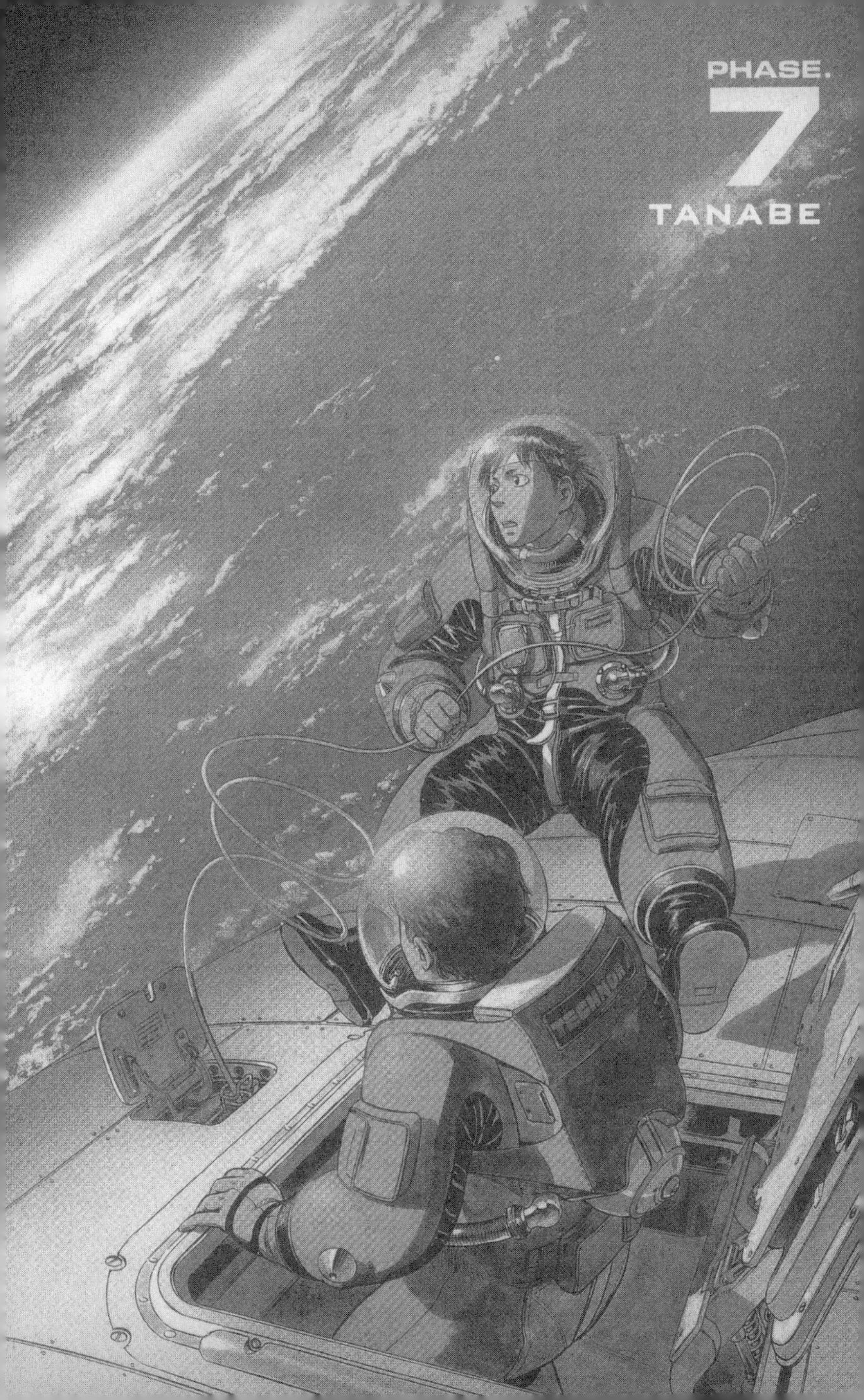
PHASE.
7
TANABE

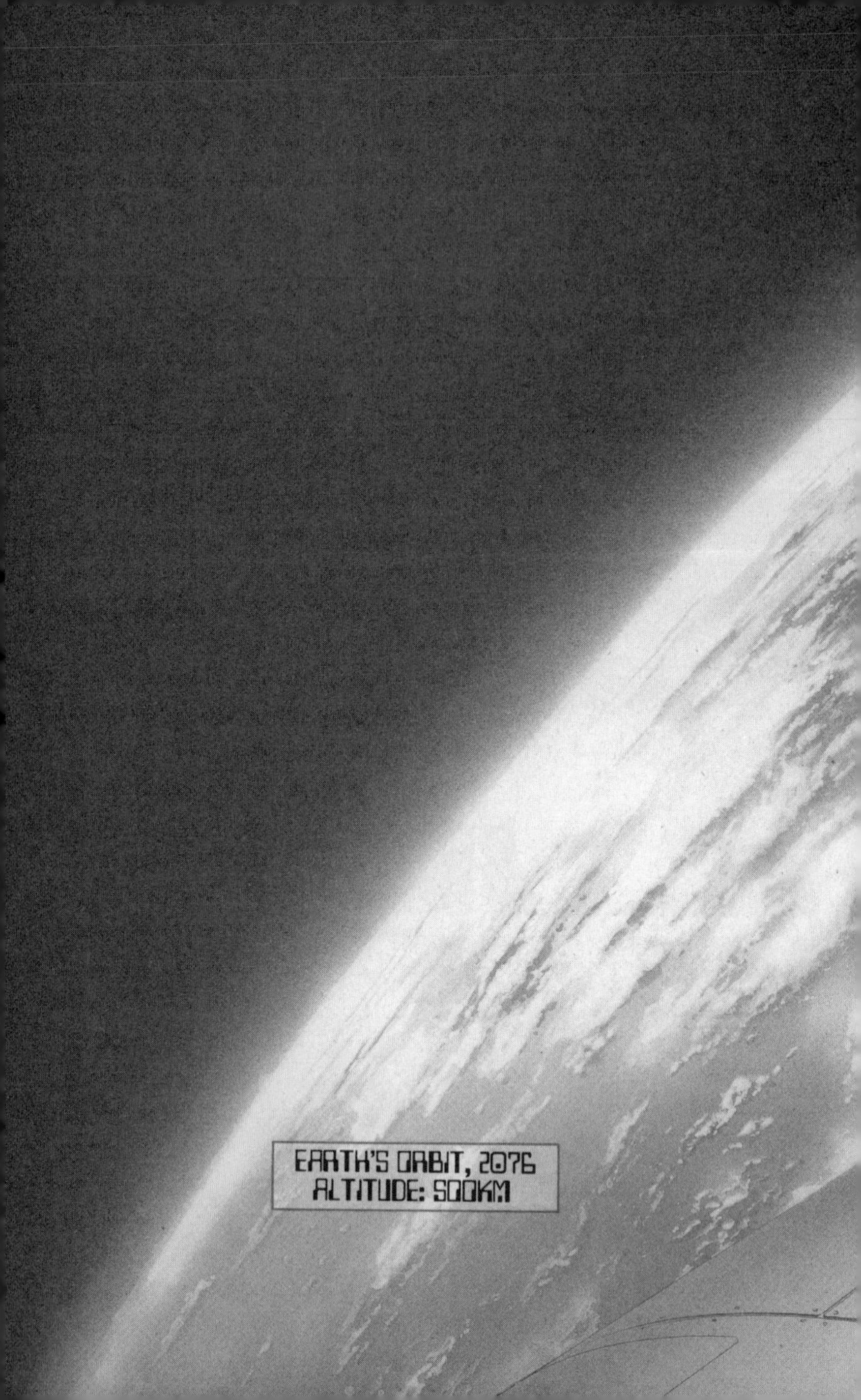
EARTH'S ORBIT, 2076
ALTITUDE: 500KM

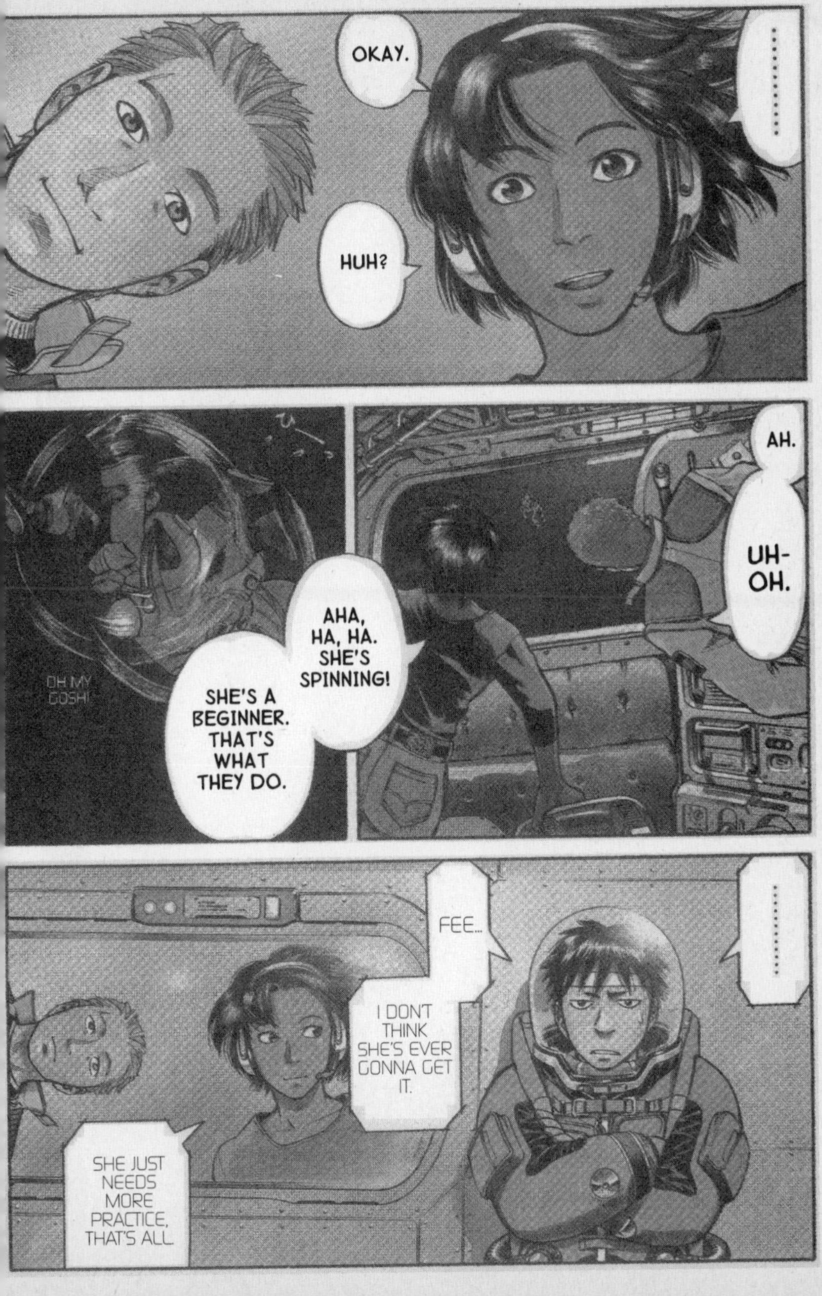
……
OKAY.
HUH?
AH.
UH-OH.
AHA, HA, HA. SHE'S SPINNING!
SHE'S A BEGINNER. THAT'S WHAT THEY DO.
OH MY GOSH!
……
FEE…
I DON'T THINK SHE'S EVER GONNA GET IT.
SHE JUST NEEDS MORE PRACTICE, THAT'S ALL.

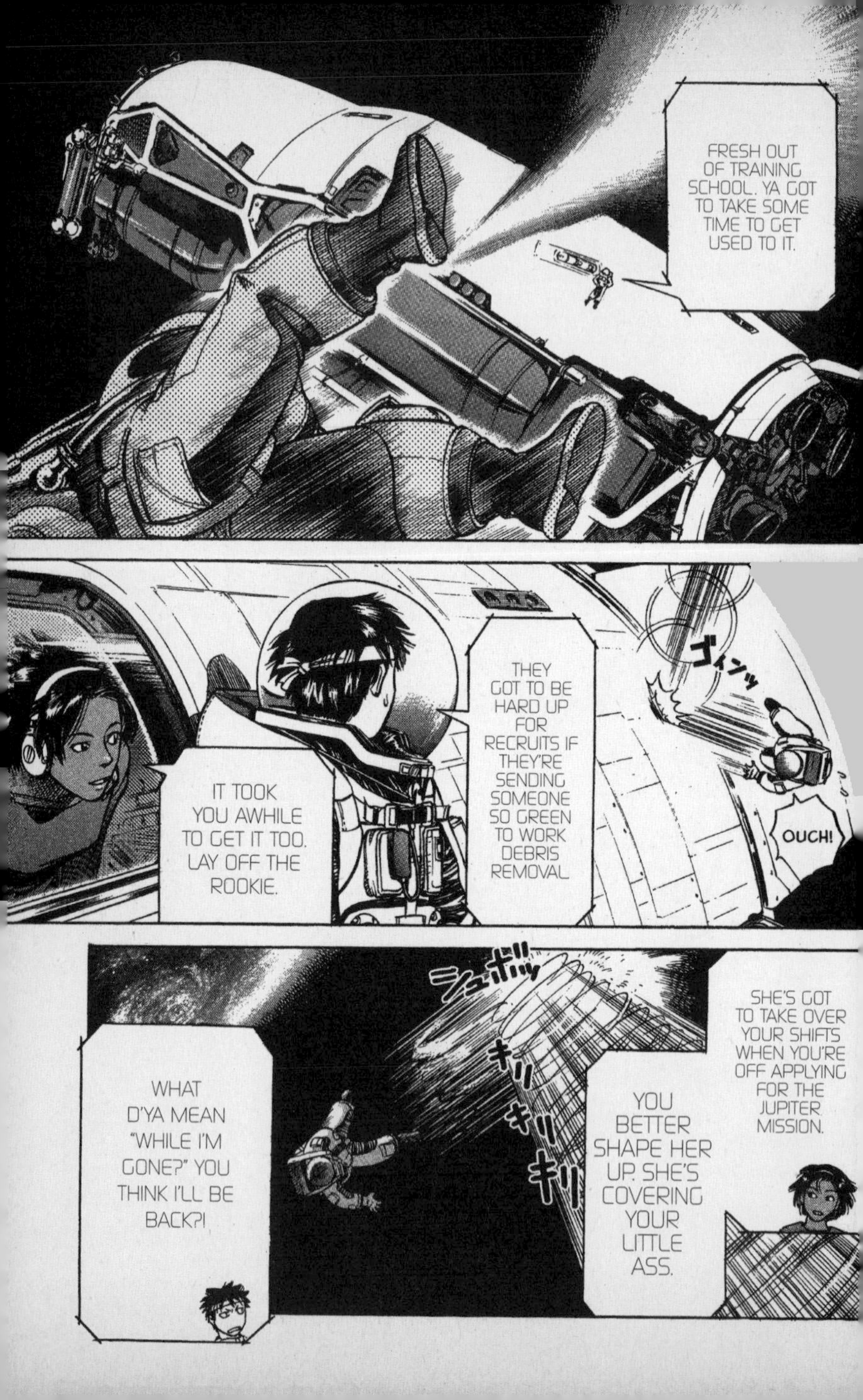
FRESH OUT OF TRAINING SCHOOL. YA GOT TO TAKE SOME TIME TO GET USED TO IT.
ゴィンッ
OUCH!
THEY GOT TO BE HARD UP FOR RECRUITS IF THEY'RE SENDING SOMEONE SO GREEN TO WORK DEBRIS REMOVAL.
IT TOOK YOU AWHILE TO GET IT TOO. LAY OFF THE ROOKIE.
SHE'S GOT TO TAKE OVER YOUR SHIFTS WHEN YOU'RE OFF APPLYING FOR THE JUPITER MISSION.
シュボッ
キリキリキリ
YOU BETTER SHAPE HER UP. SHE'S COVERING YOUR LITTLE ASS.
WHAT D'YA MEAN "WHILE I'M GONE?" YOU THINK I'LL BE BACK?!

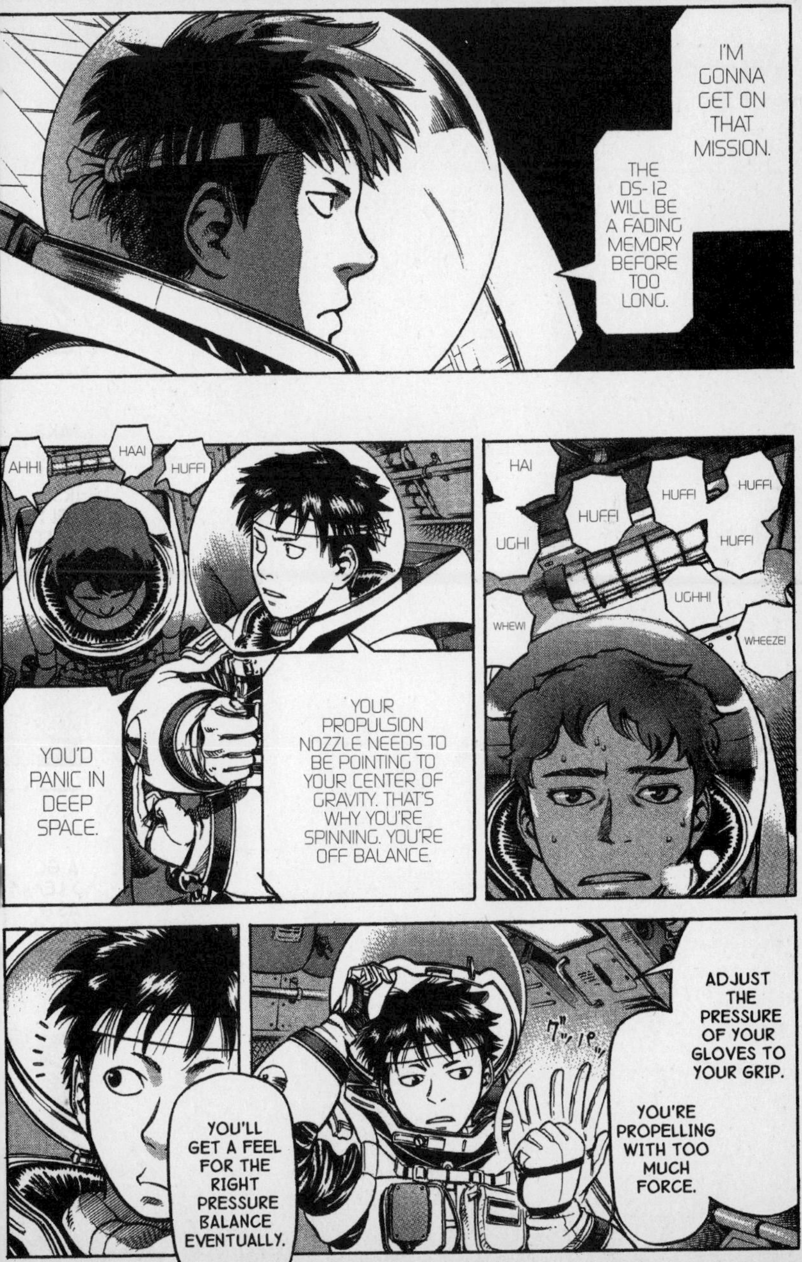
I'M GONNA GET ON THAT MISSION.
THE DS-12 WILL BE A FADING MEMORY BEFORE TOO LONG.
HUFF!
HUFF!
HAI
HUFF!
HUFF!
UGH!
UGHH!
WHEEZE!
WHEW!
HUFF!
HAAI
AHH!
YOUR PROPULSION NOZZLE NEEDS TO BE POINTING TO YOUR CENTER OF GRAVITY. THAT'S WHY YOU'RE SPINNING. YOU'RE OFF BALANCE.
YOU'D PANIC IN DEEP SPACE.
ADJUST THE PRESSURE OF YOUR GLOVES TO YOUR GRIP.
YOU'RE PROPELLING WITH TOO MUCH FORCE.
YOU'LL GET A FEEL FOR THE RIGHT PRESSURE BALANCE EVENTUALLY.

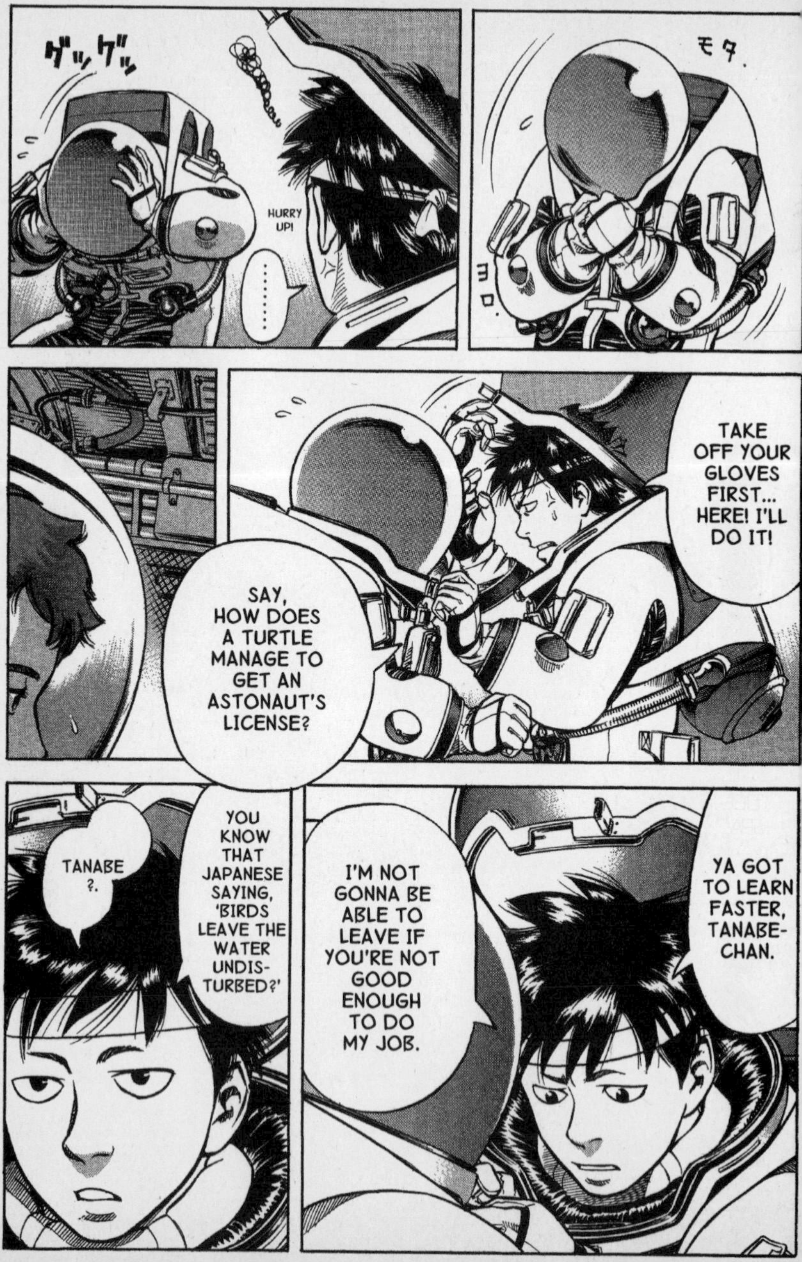
モタ.
ヨロ.
グッグッ
HURRY UP!
....
TAKE OFF YOUR GLOVES FIRST... HERE! I'LL DO IT!
SAY, HOW DOES A TURTLE MANAGE TO GET AN ASTONAUT'S LICENSE?
YA GOT TO LEARN FASTER, TANABE-CHAN.
I'M NOT GONNA BE ABLE TO LEAVE IF YOU'RE NOT GOOD ENOUGH TO DO MY JOB.
YOU KNOW THAT JAPANESE SAYING, 'BIRDS LEAVE THE WATER UNDIS-TURBED?'
TANABE ?.

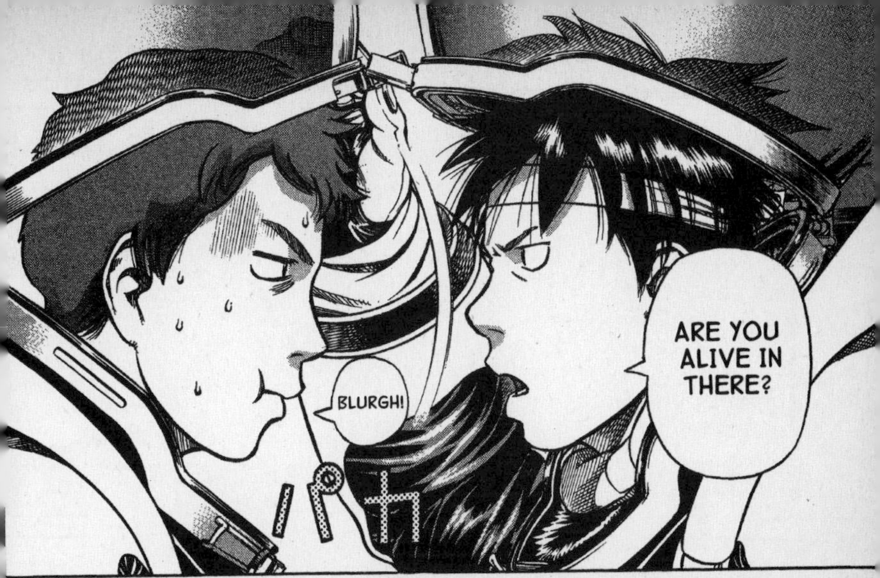
ARE YOU ALIVE IN THERE?
BLURGH!

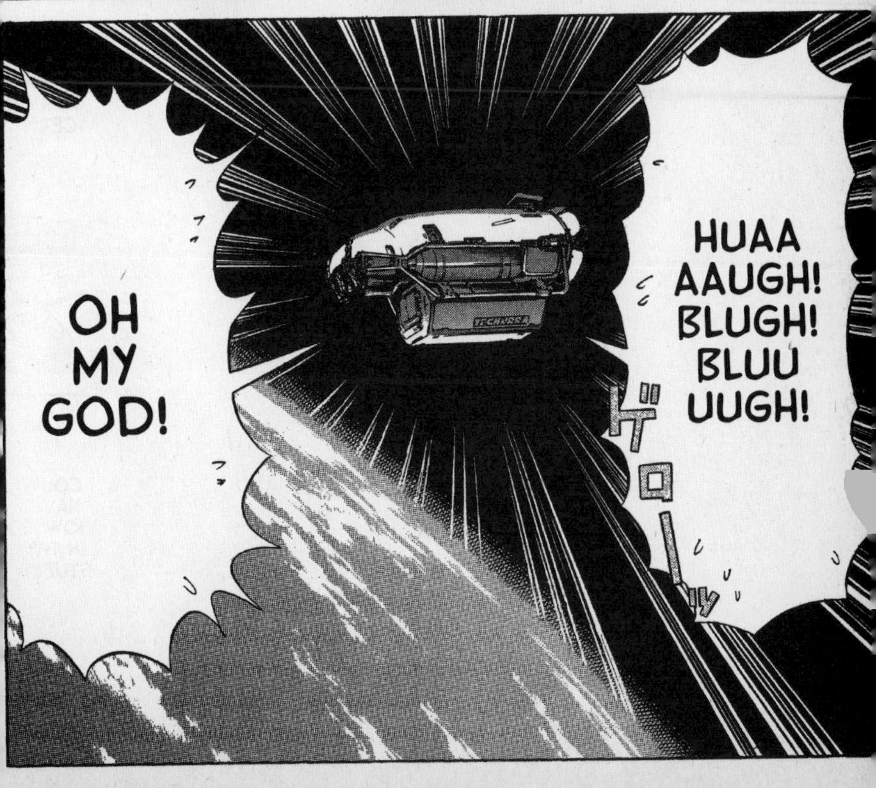
HUAA AAUGH! BLUGH! BLUU UUGH!
OH MY GOD!

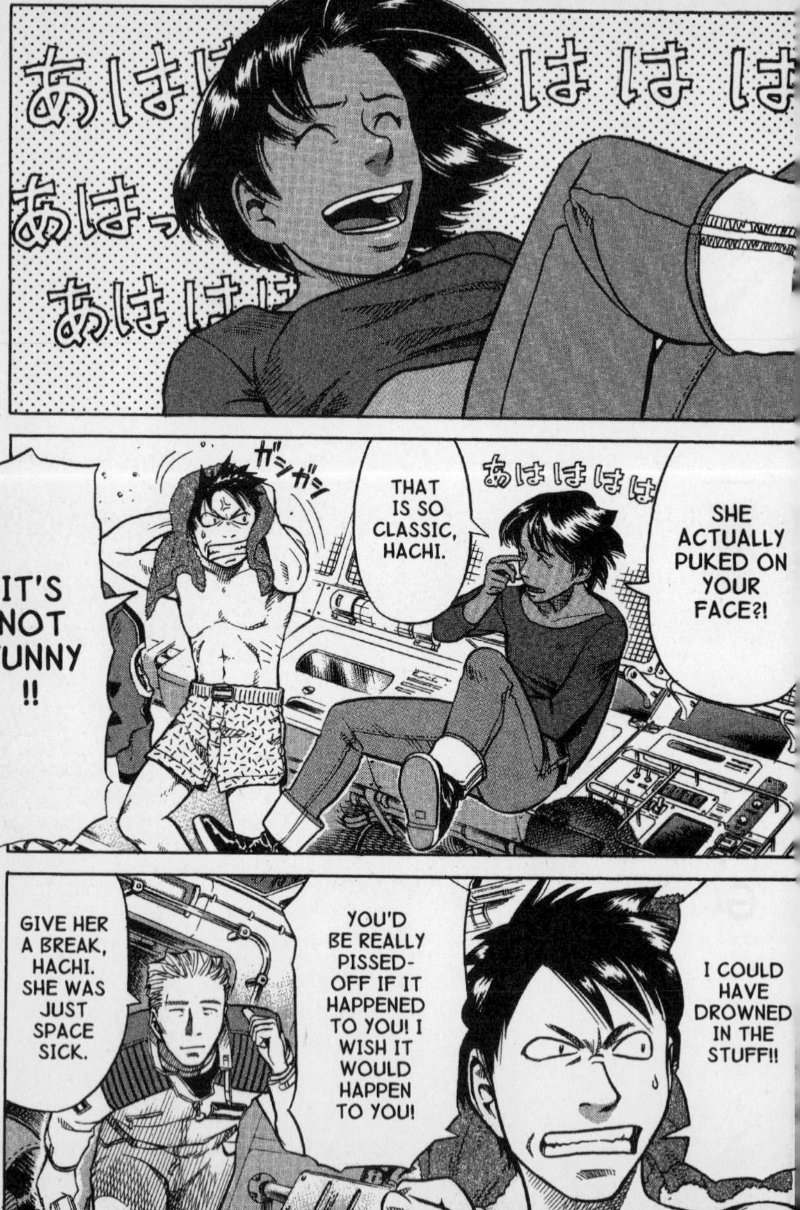
あはは ははは は
あはっ
あははは
SHE ACTUALLY PUKED ON YOUR FACE?!
あははははは
THAT IS SO CLASSIC, HACHI.
ガシガシ
IT'S NOT FUNNY!!
I COULD HAVE DROWNED IN THE STUFF!!
YOU'D BE REALLY PISSED-OFF IF IT HAPPENED TO YOU! I WISH IT WOULD HAPPEN TO YOU!
GIVE HER A BREAK, HACHI. SHE WAS JUST SPACE SICK.

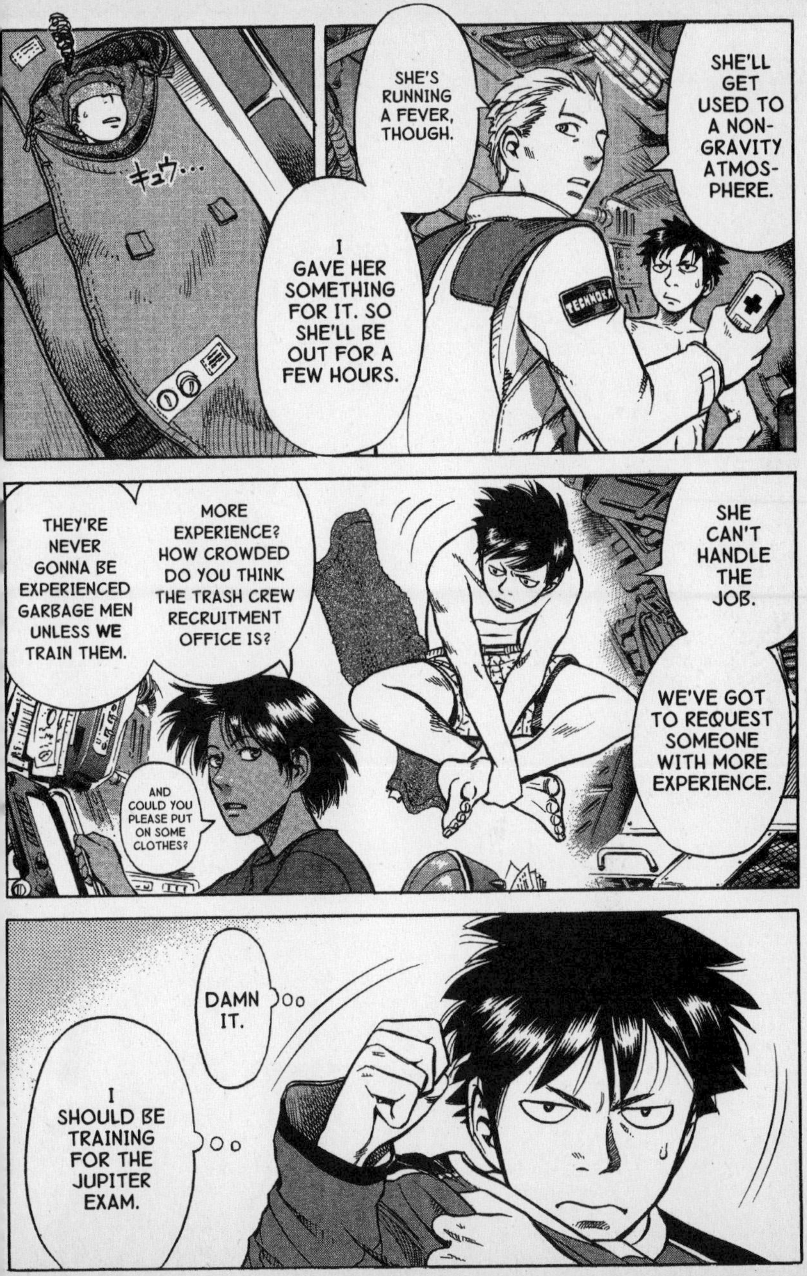
SHE'LL GET USED TO A NON-GRAVITY ATMOSPHERE.
SHE'S RUNNING A FEVER, THOUGH.
TECHNORA
I GAVE HER SOMETHING FOR IT. SO SHE'LL BE OUT FOR A FEW HOURS.
キュウ…
SHE CAN'T HANDLE THE JOB.
WE'VE GOT TO REQUEST SOMEONE WITH MORE EXPERIENCE.
MORE EXPERIENCE? HOW CROWDED DO YOU THINK THE TRASH CREW RECRUITMENT OFFICE IS?
THEY'RE NEVER GONNA BE EXPERIENCED GARBAGE MEN UNLESS WE TRAIN THEM.
AND COULD YOU PLEASE PUT ON SOME CLOTHES?
DAMN IT.
I SHOULD BE TRAINING FOR THE JUPITER EXAM.

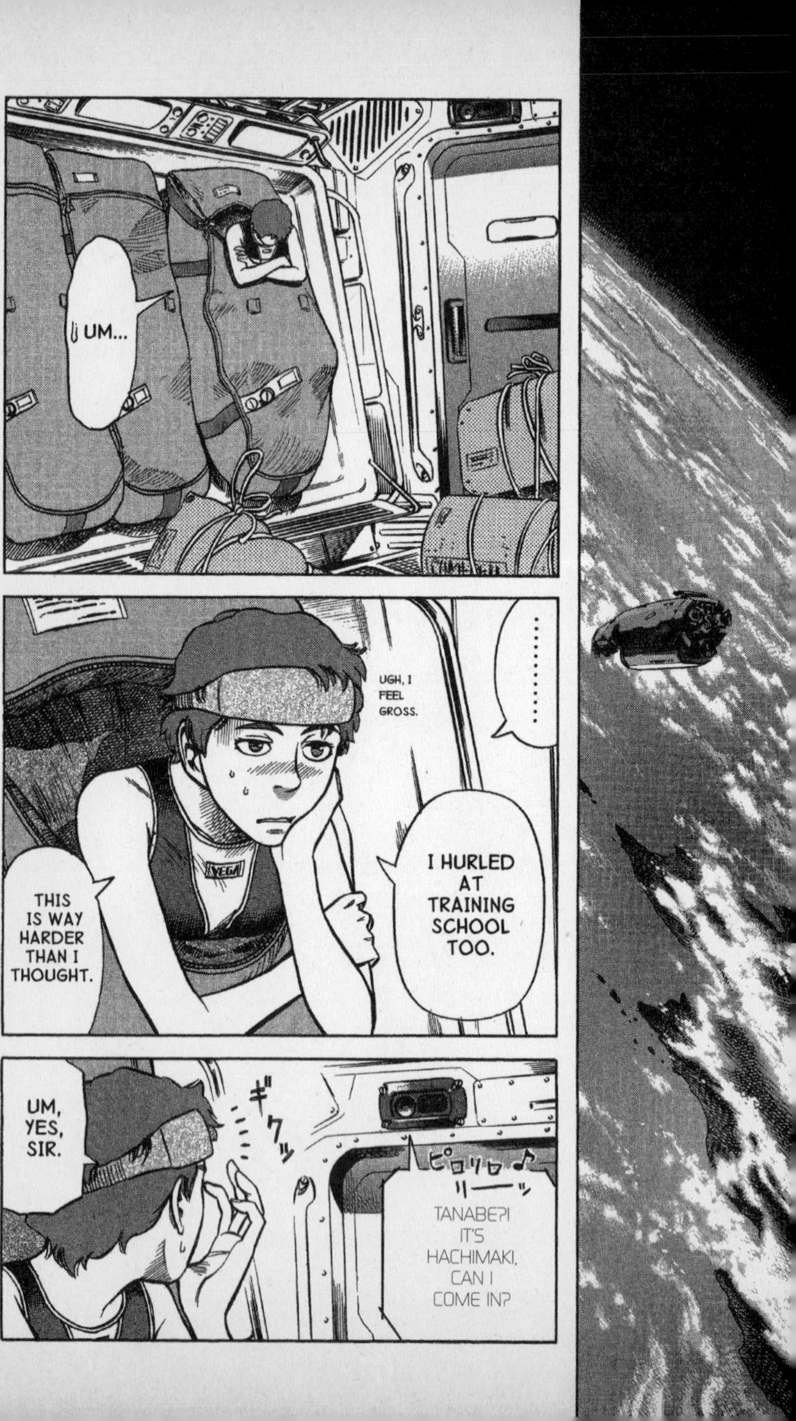
UM...
......
UGH, I FEEL GROSS.
I HURLED AT TRAINING SCHOOL TOO.
THIS IS WAY HARDER THAN I THOUGHT.
ピロリロ♪ リーッ
TANABE?! IT'S HACHIMAKI, CAN I COME IN?
ギクッ
UM, YES, SIR.

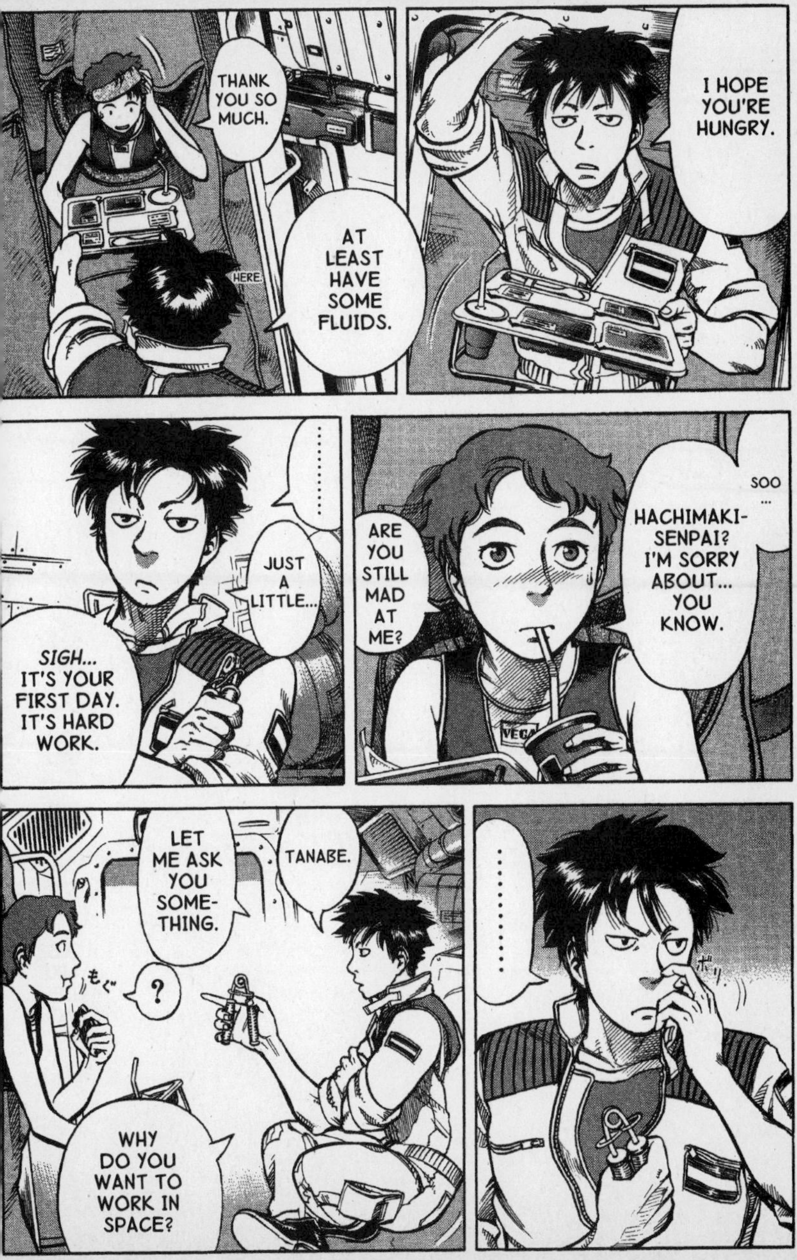
I HOPE YOU'RE HUNGRY.
HERE.
THANK YOU SO MUCH.
AT LEAST HAVE SOME FLUIDS.
SOO ...
HACHIMAKI-SENPAI? I'M SORRY ABOUT... YOU KNOW.
ARE YOU STILL MAD AT ME?
......
JUST A LITTLE...
SIGH... IT'S YOUR FIRST DAY. IT'S HARD WORK.
....
ボリ
TANABE.
LET ME ASK YOU SOME-THING.
もぐ
?
WHY DO YOU WANT TO WORK IN SPACE?

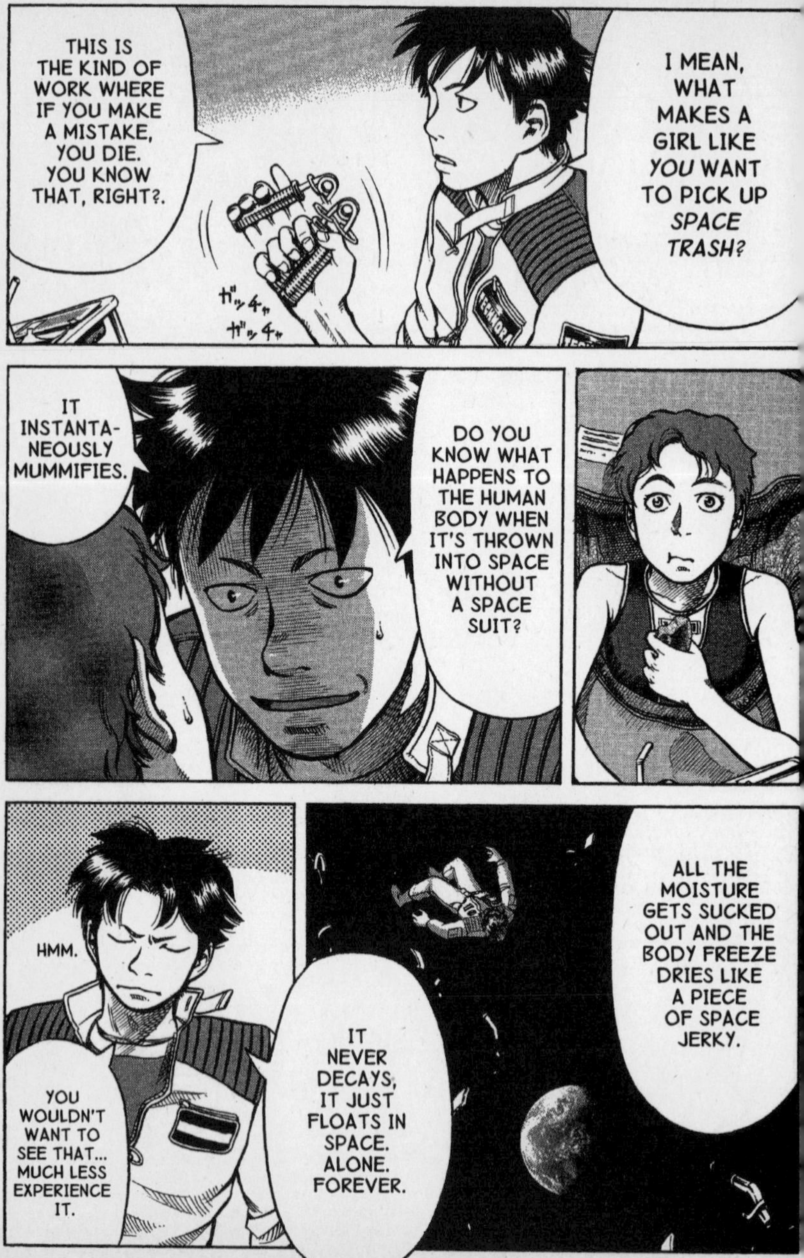
I MEAN, WHAT MAKES A GIRL LIKE *YOU* WANT TO PICK UP *SPACE TRASH?*
THIS IS THE KIND OF WORK WHERE IF YOU MAKE A MISTAKE, YOU DIE. YOU KNOW THAT, RIGHT?.
ガッチャ
ガッチャ
DO YOU KNOW WHAT HAPPENS TO THE HUMAN BODY WHEN IT'S THROWN INTO SPACE WITHOUT A SPACE SUIT?
IT INSTANTA-NEOUSLY MUMMIFIES.
ALL THE MOISTURE GETS SUCKED OUT AND THE BODY FREEZE DRIES LIKE A PIECE OF SPACE JERKY.
IT NEVER DECAYS, IT JUST FLOATS IN SPACE. ALONE. FOREVER.
HMM.
YOU WOULDN'T WANT TO SEE THAT... MUCH LESS EXPERIENCE IT.

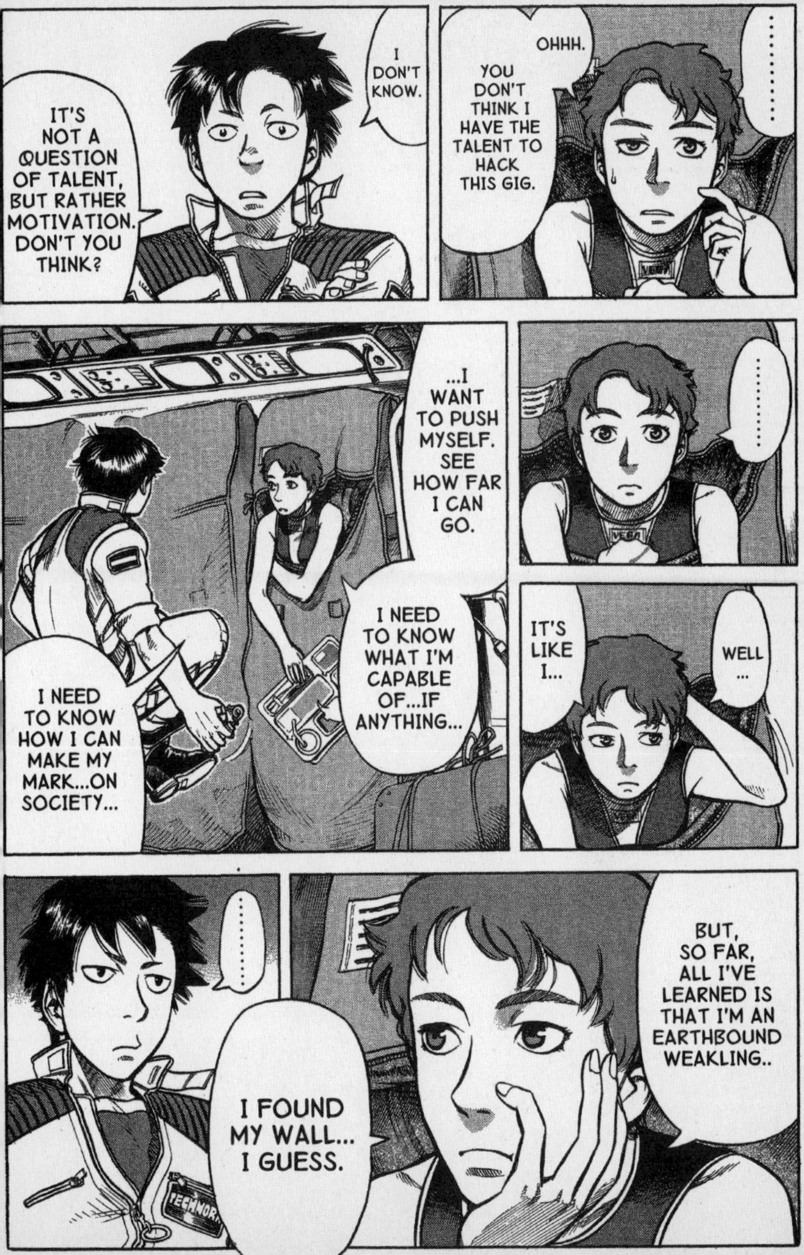
....
OHHH.
YOU DON'T THINK I HAVE THE TALENT TO HACK THIS GIG.
I DON'T KNOW.
IT'S NOT A QUESTION OF TALENT, BUT RATHER MOTIVATION. DON'T YOU THINK?
....
WELL ...
IT'S LIKE I...
...I WANT TO PUSH MYSELF. SEE HOW FAR I CAN GO.
I NEED TO KNOW WHAT I'M CAPABLE OF...IF ANYTHING...
I NEED TO KNOW HOW I CAN MAKE MY MARK...ON SOCIETY...
BUT, SO FAR, ALL I'VE LEARNED IS THAT I'M AN EARTHBOUND WEAKLING..
I FOUND MY WALL... I GUESS.
....

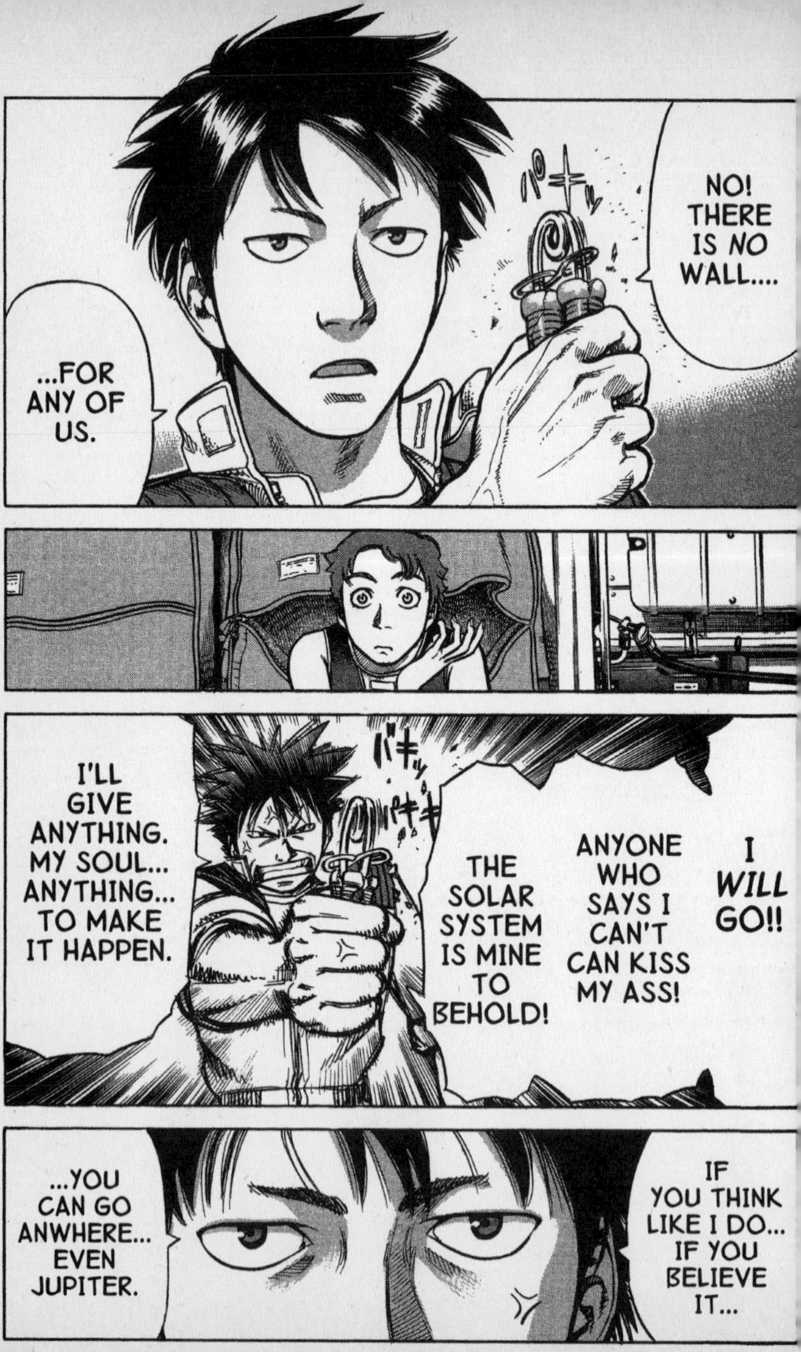
NO! THERE IS *NO* WALL....
...FOR ANY OF US.
I *WILL* GO!!
ANYONE WHO SAYS I CAN'T CAN KISS MY ASS!
THE SOLAR SYSTEM IS MINE TO BEHOLD!
I'LL GIVE ANYTHING. MY SOUL... ANYTHING... TO MAKE IT HAPPEN.
IF YOU THINK LIKE I DO... IF YOU BELIEVE IT...
...YOU CAN GO ANWHERE... EVEN JUPITER.

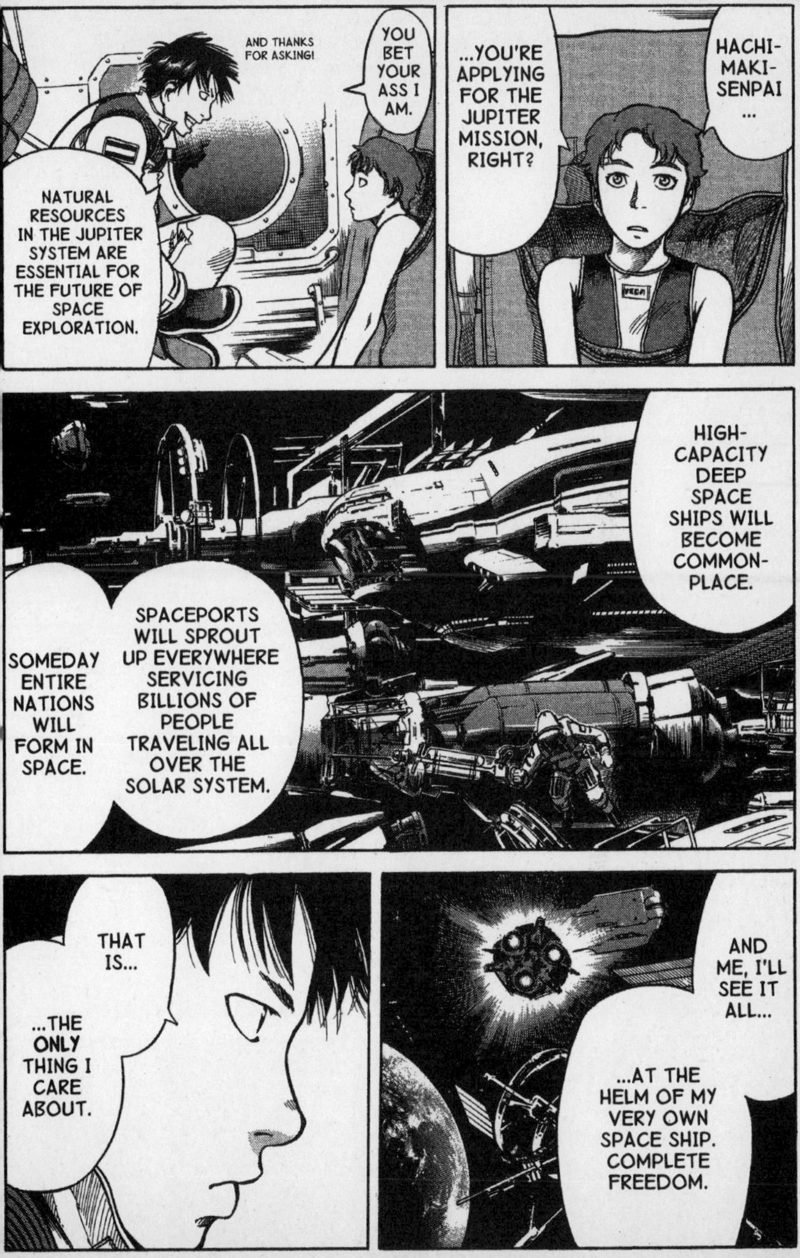
HACHI-MAKI-SENPAI...
...YOU'RE APPLYING FOR THE JUPITER MISSION, RIGHT?
YOU BET YOUR ASS I AM.
AND THANKS FOR ASKING!
NATURAL RESOURCES IN THE JUPITER SYSTEM ARE ESSENTIAL FOR THE FUTURE OF SPACE EXPLORATION.
HIGH-CAPACITY DEEP SPACE SHIPS WILL BECOME COMMON-PLACE.
SPACEPORTS WILL SPROUT UP EVERYWHERE SERVICING BILLIONS OF PEOPLE TRAVELING ALL OVER THE SOLAR SYSTEM.
SOMEDAY ENTIRE NATIONS WILL FORM IN SPACE.
AND ME, I'LL SEE IT ALL...
...AT THE HELM OF MY VERY OWN SPACE SHIP. COMPLETE FREEDOM.
THAT IS...
...THE ONLY THING I CARE ABOUT.

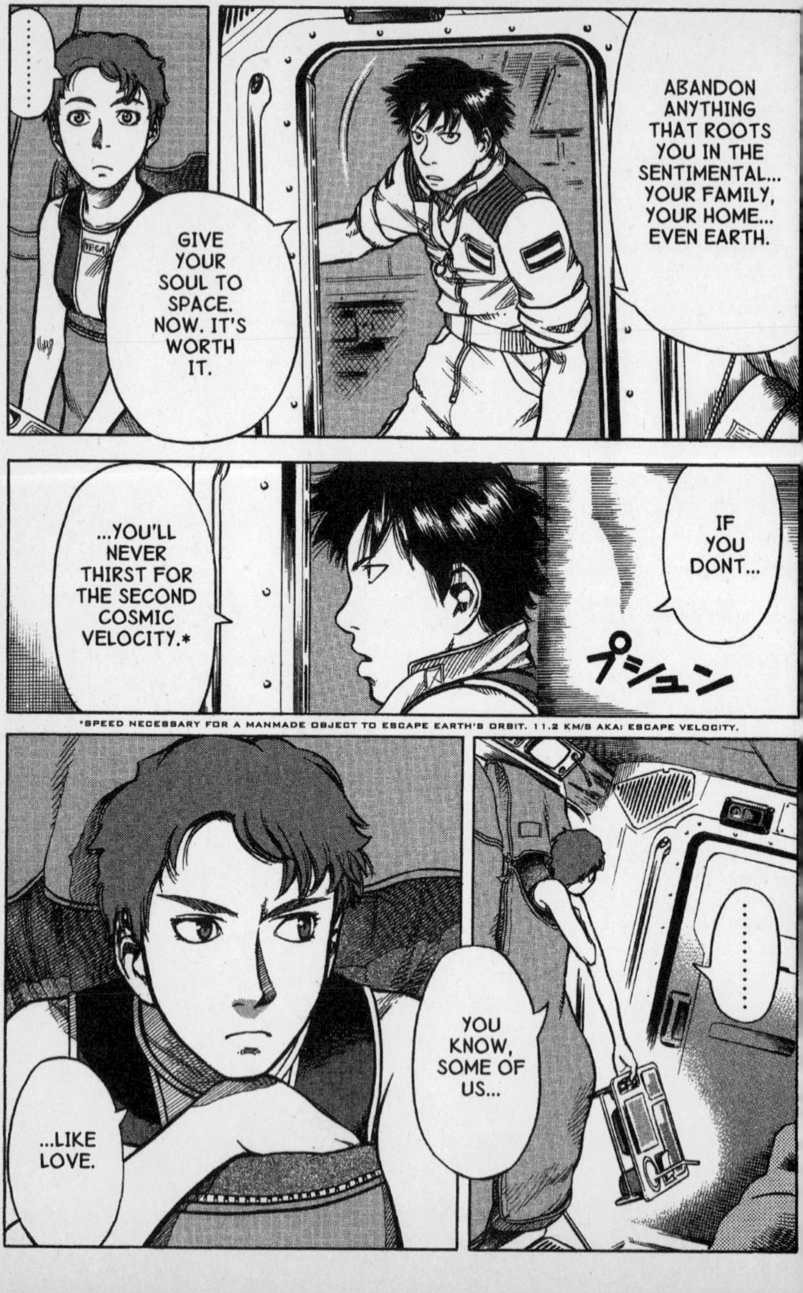
ABANDON ANYTHING THAT ROOTS YOU IN THE SENTIMENTAL... YOUR FAMILY, YOUR HOME... EVEN EARTH.
GIVE YOUR SOUL TO SPACE. NOW. IT'S WORTH IT.
......
IF YOU DONT...
プシュン
...YOU'LL NEVER THIRST FOR THE SECOND COSMIC VELOCITY.*
....
YOU KNOW, SOME OF US...
...LIKE LOVE.

*SPEED NECESSARY FOR A MANMADE OBJECT TO ESCAPE EARTH'S ORBIT. 11.2 KM/S AKA: ESCAPE VELOCITY.

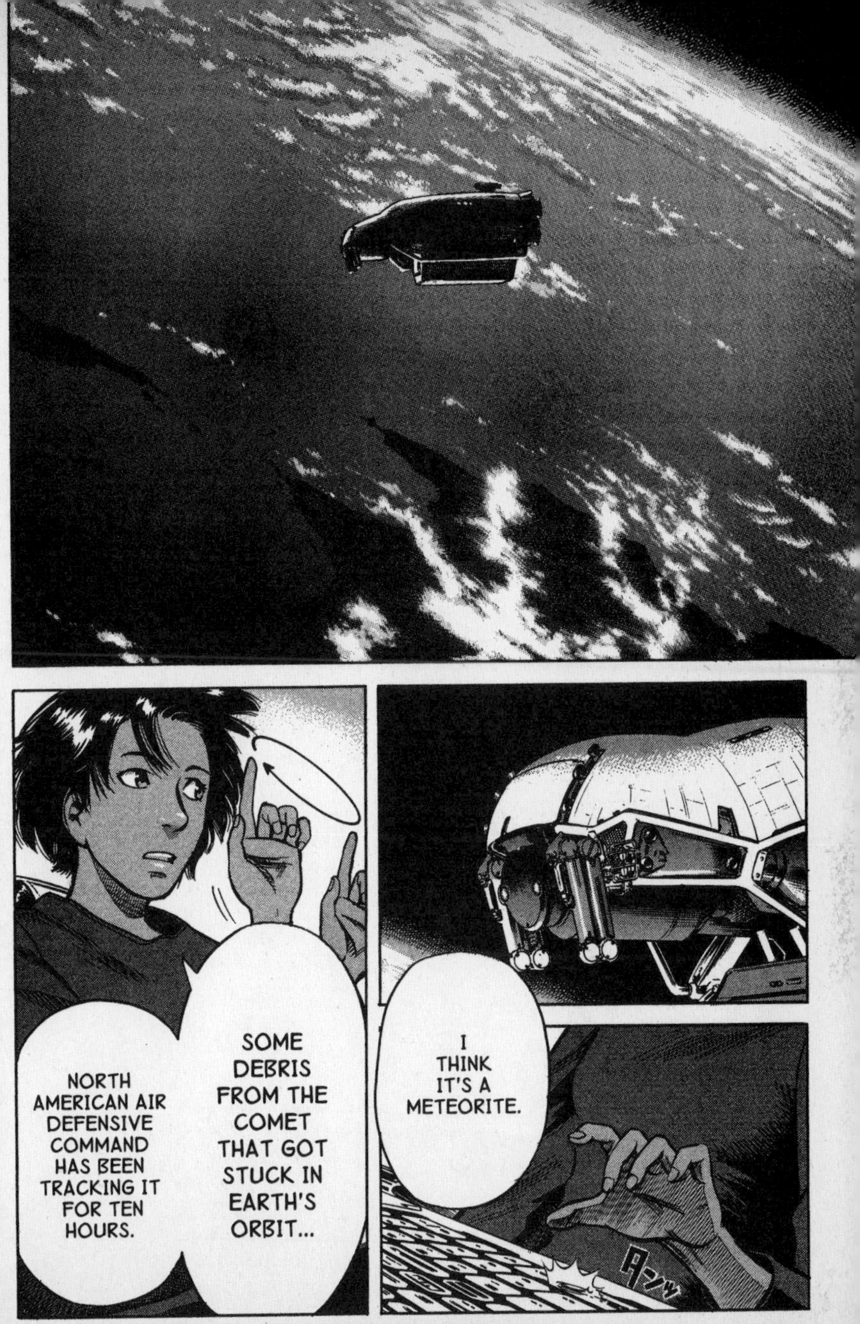
I THINK IT'S A METEORITE.
タンッ
SOME DEBRIS FROM THE COMET THAT GOT STUCK IN EARTH'S ORBIT...
NORTH AMERICAN AIR DEFENSIVE COMMAND HAS BEEN TRACKING IT FOR TEN HOURS.

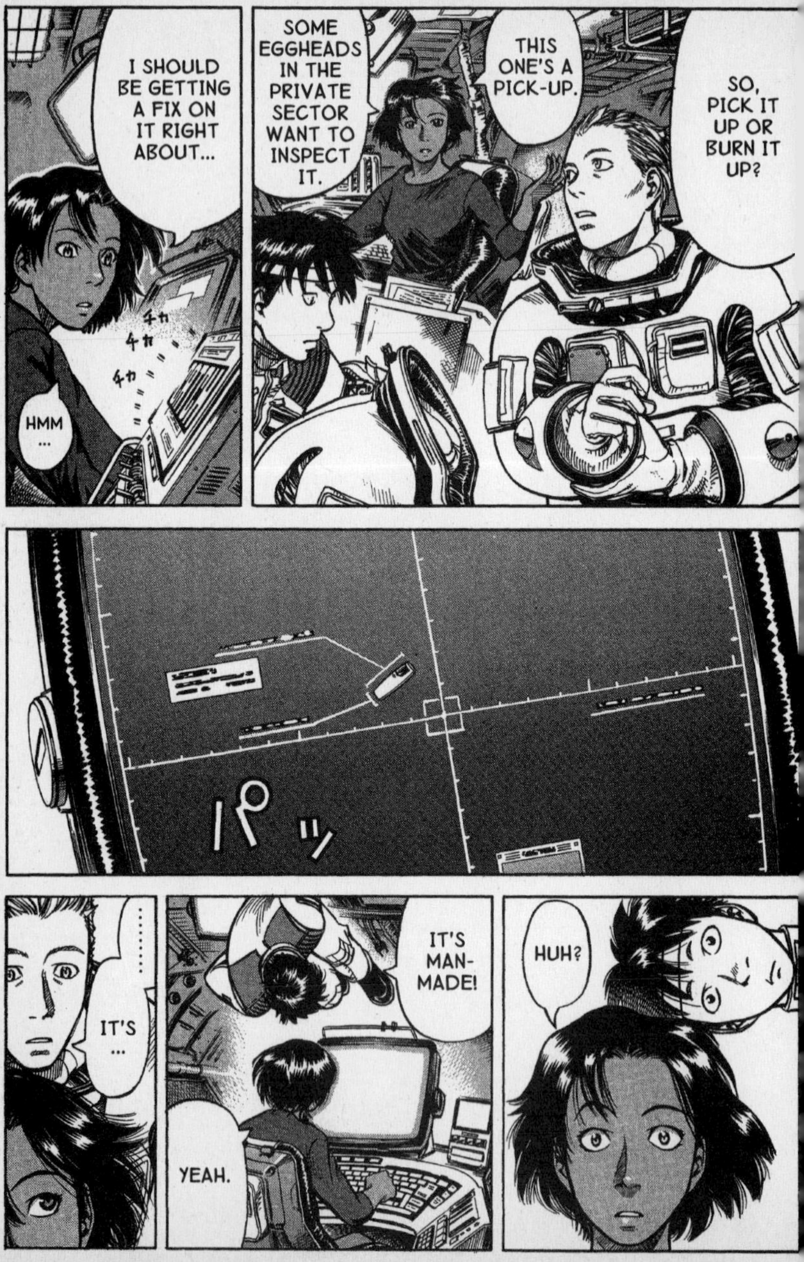
SO, PICK IT UP OR BURN IT UP?
THIS ONE'S A PICK-UP.
SOME EGGHEADS IN THE PRIVATE SECTOR WANT TO INSPECT IT.
I SHOULD BE GETTING A FIX ON IT RIGHT ABOUT...
HMM...
パッ
HUH?
IT'S MAN-MADE!
YEAH.
......
IT'S...

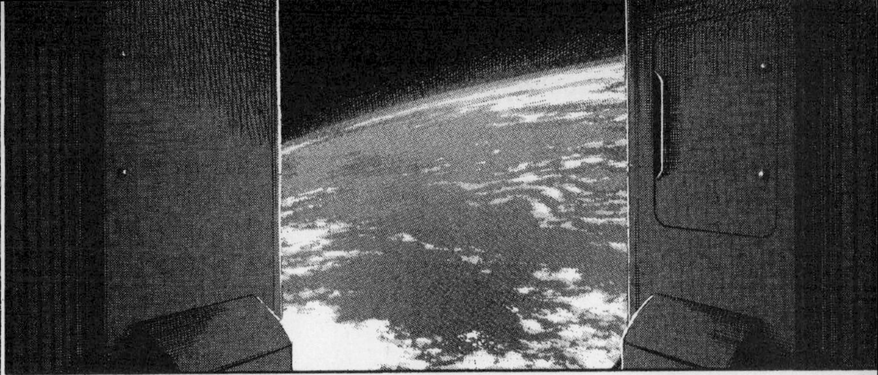

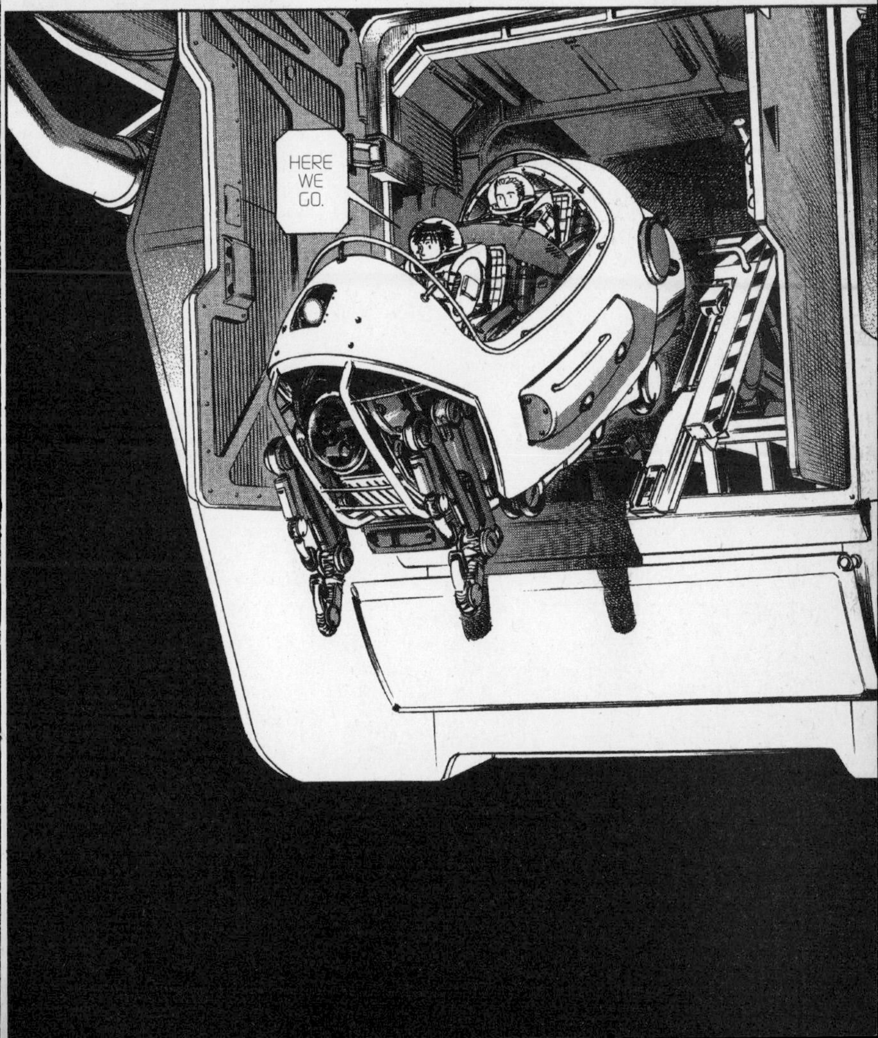
HERE WE GO.

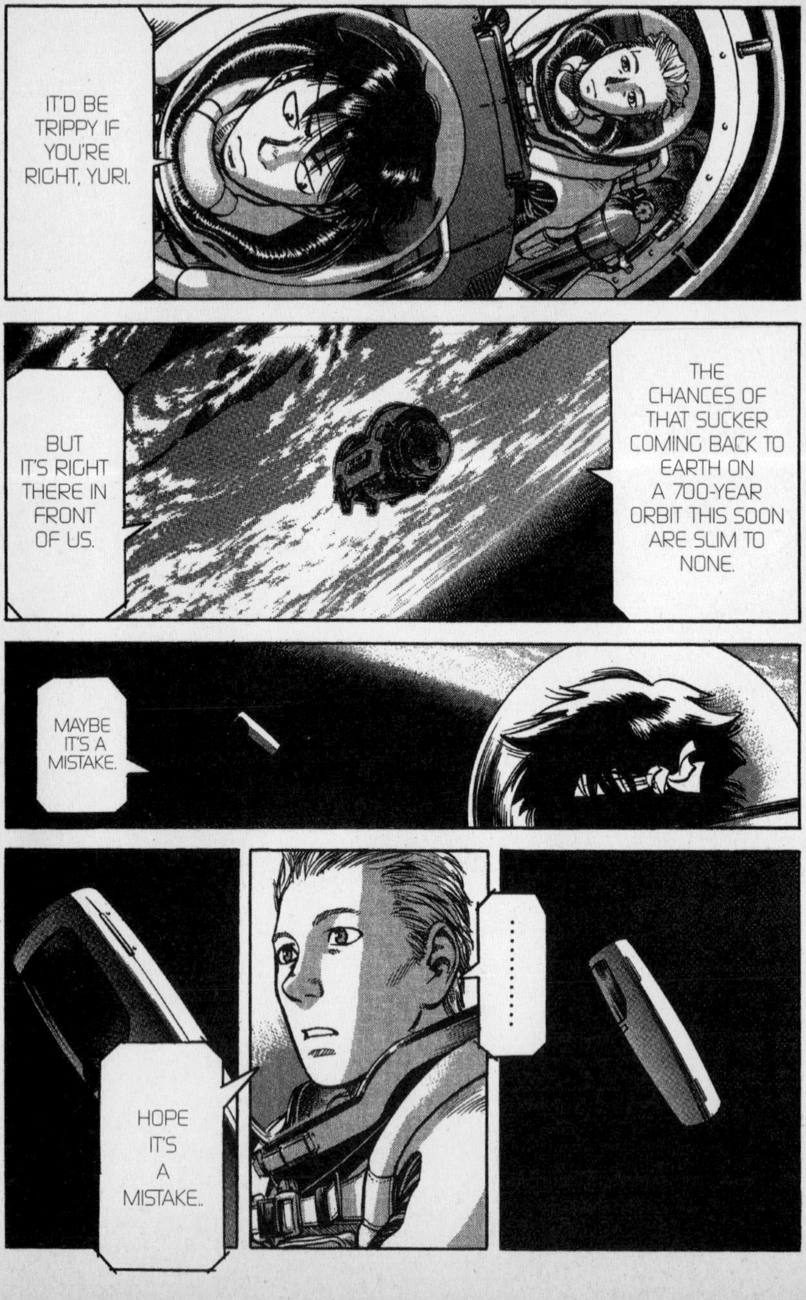
IT'D BE TRIPPY IF YOU'RE RIGHT, YURI.
THE CHANCES OF THAT SUCKER COMING BACK TO EARTH ON A 700-YEAR ORBIT THIS SOON ARE SLIM TO NONE.
BUT IT'S RIGHT THERE IN FRONT OF US.
MAYBE IT'S A MISTAKE.
......
HOPE IT'S A MISTAKE..

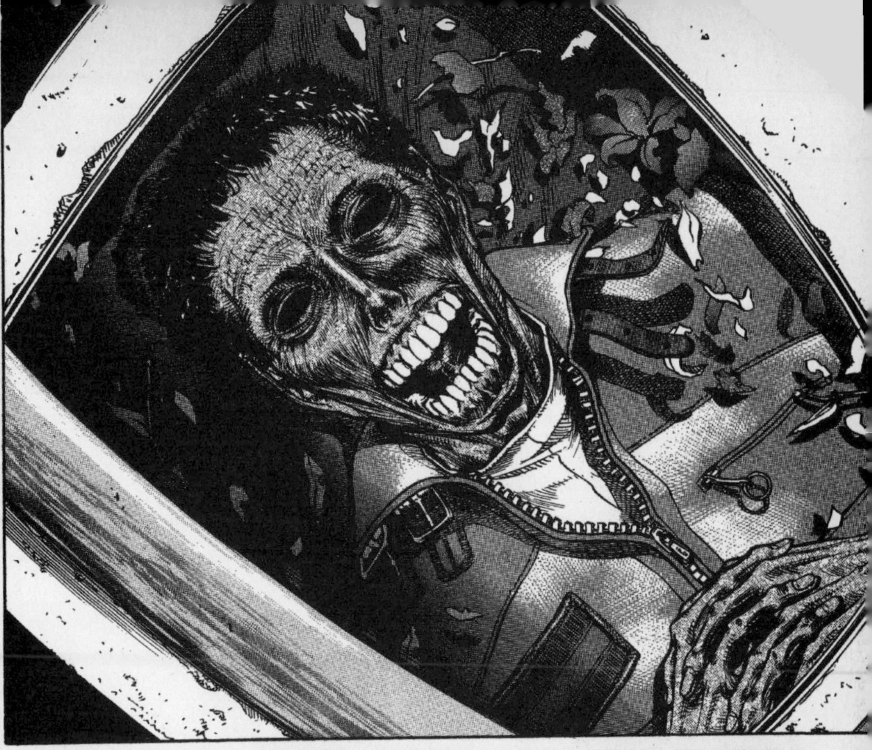

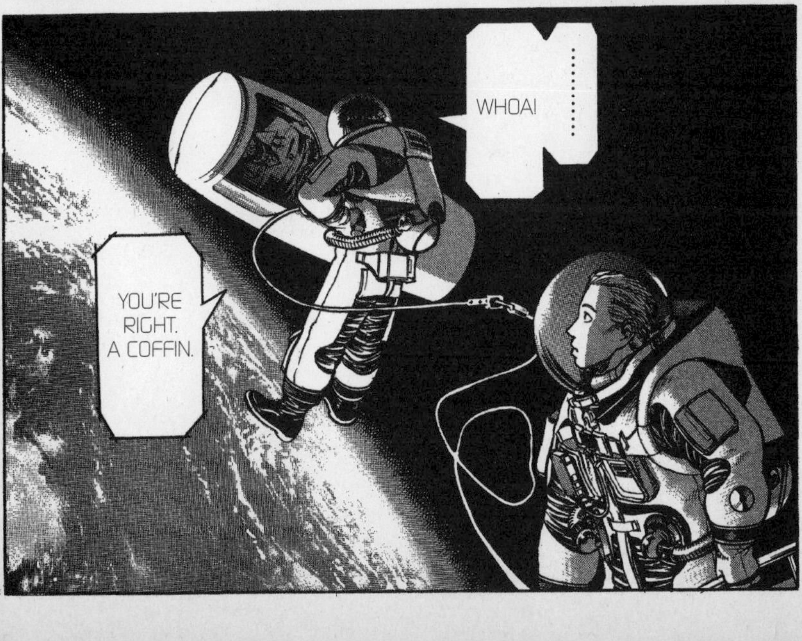
……
WHOA!
YOU'RE RIGHT. A COFFIN.

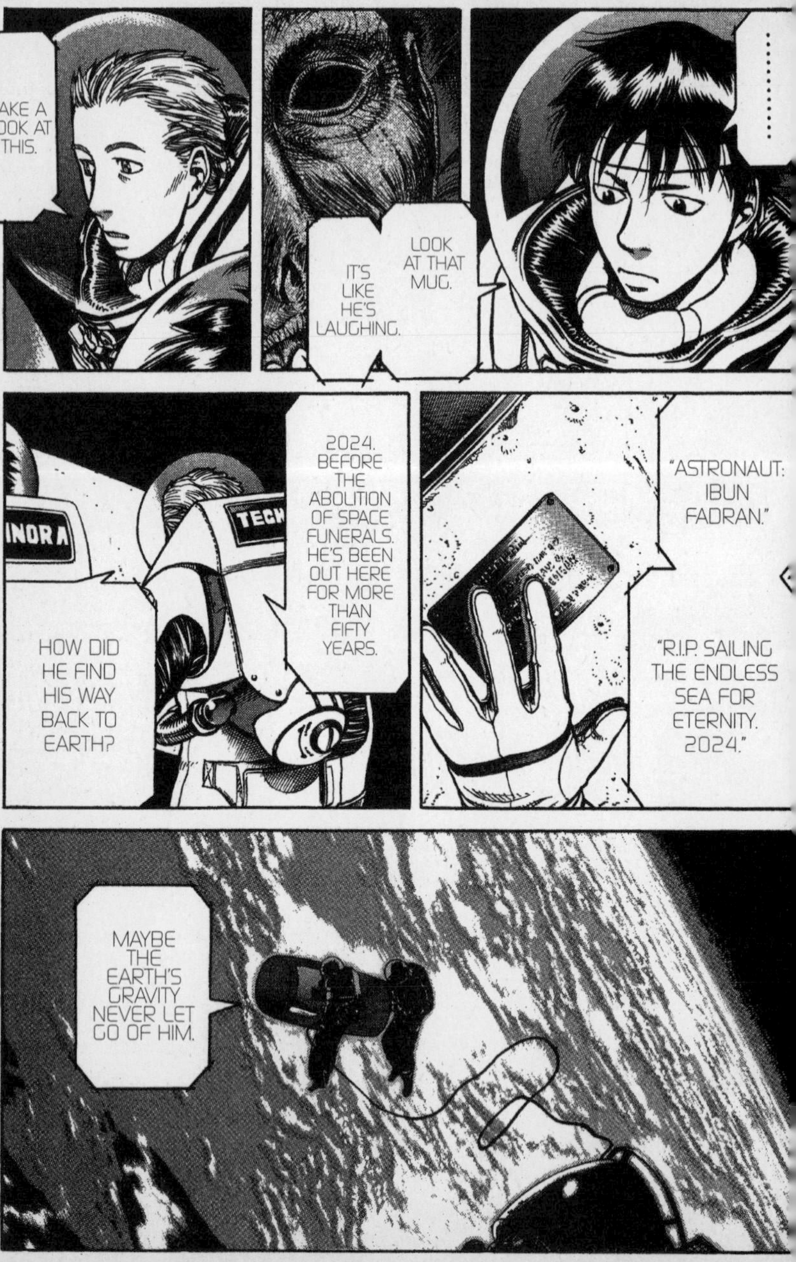
......
LOOK AT THAT MUG.
IT'S LIKE HE'S LAUGHING.
TAKE A LOOK AT THIS.
"ASTRONAUT: IBUN FADRAN."
"R.I.P. SAILING THE ENDLESS SEA FOR ETERNITY. 2024."
2024. BEFORE THE ABOLITION OF SPACE FUNERALS. HE'S BEEN OUT HERE FOR MORE THAN FIFTY YEARS.
TECH
INORA
HOW DID HE FIND HIS WAY BACK TO EARTH?
MAYBE THE EARTH'S GRAVITY NEVER LET GO OF HIM.

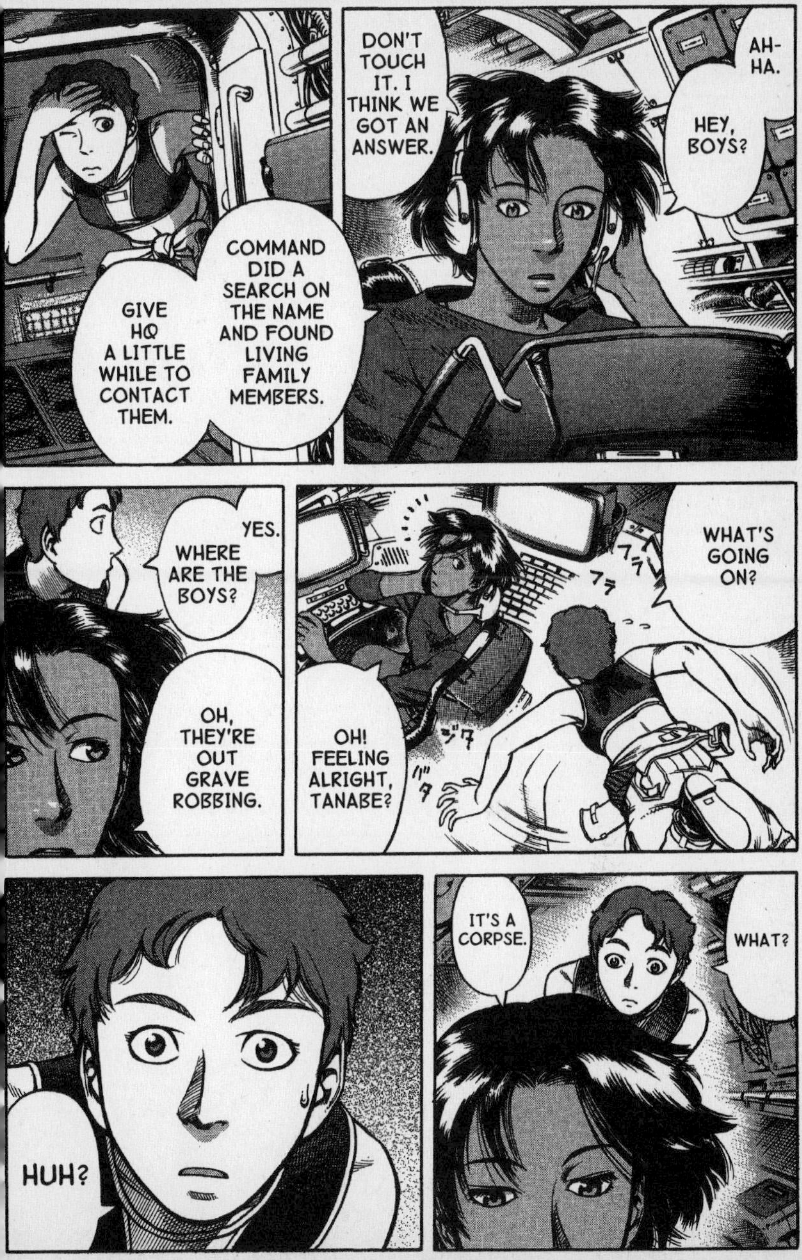
AH-HA.
HEY, BOYS?
DON'T TOUCH IT. I THINK WE GOT AN ANSWER.
COMMAND DID A SEARCH ON THE NAME AND FOUND LIVING FAMILY MEMBERS.
GIVE HQ A LITTLE WHILE TO CONTACT THEM.
WHAT'S GOING ON?
OH! FEELING ALRIGHT, TANABE?
YES. WHERE ARE THE BOYS?
OH, THEY'RE OUT GRAVE ROBBING.
WHAT?
IT'S A CORPSE.
HUH?

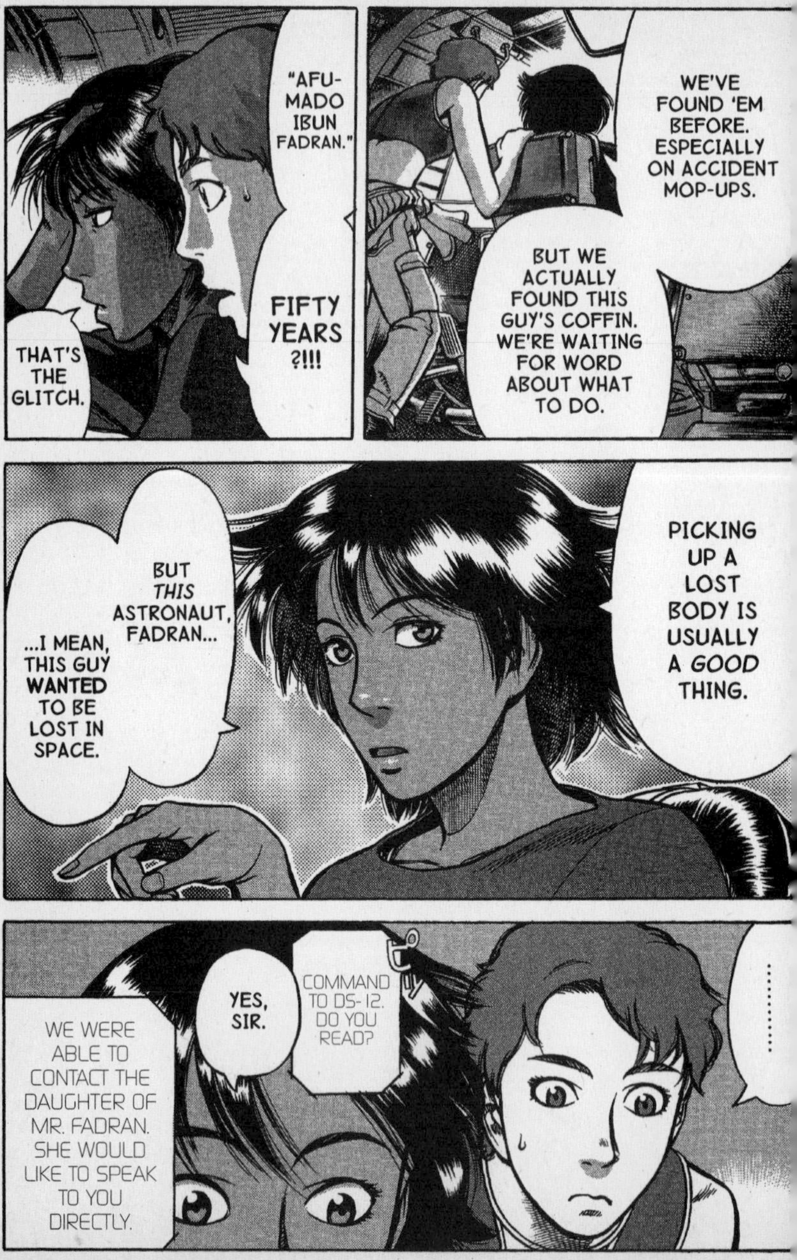
WE'VE FOUND 'EM BEFORE. ESPECIALLY ON ACCIDENT MOP-UPS.
BUT WE ACTUALLY FOUND THIS GUY'S COFFIN. WE'RE WAITING FOR WORD ABOUT WHAT TO DO.
"AFU-MADO IBUN FADRAN."
FIFTY YEARS?!!!
THAT'S THE GLITCH.
PICKING UP A LOST BODY IS USUALLY A *GOOD* THING.
BUT *THIS* ASTRONAUT, FADRAN...
...I MEAN, THIS GUY **WANTED** TO BE LOST IN SPACE.
....
COMMAND TO DS-12. DO YOU READ?
YES, SIR.
WE WERE ABLE TO CONTACT THE DAUGHTER OF MR. FADRAN. SHE WOULD LIKE TO SPEAK TO YOU DIRECTLY.

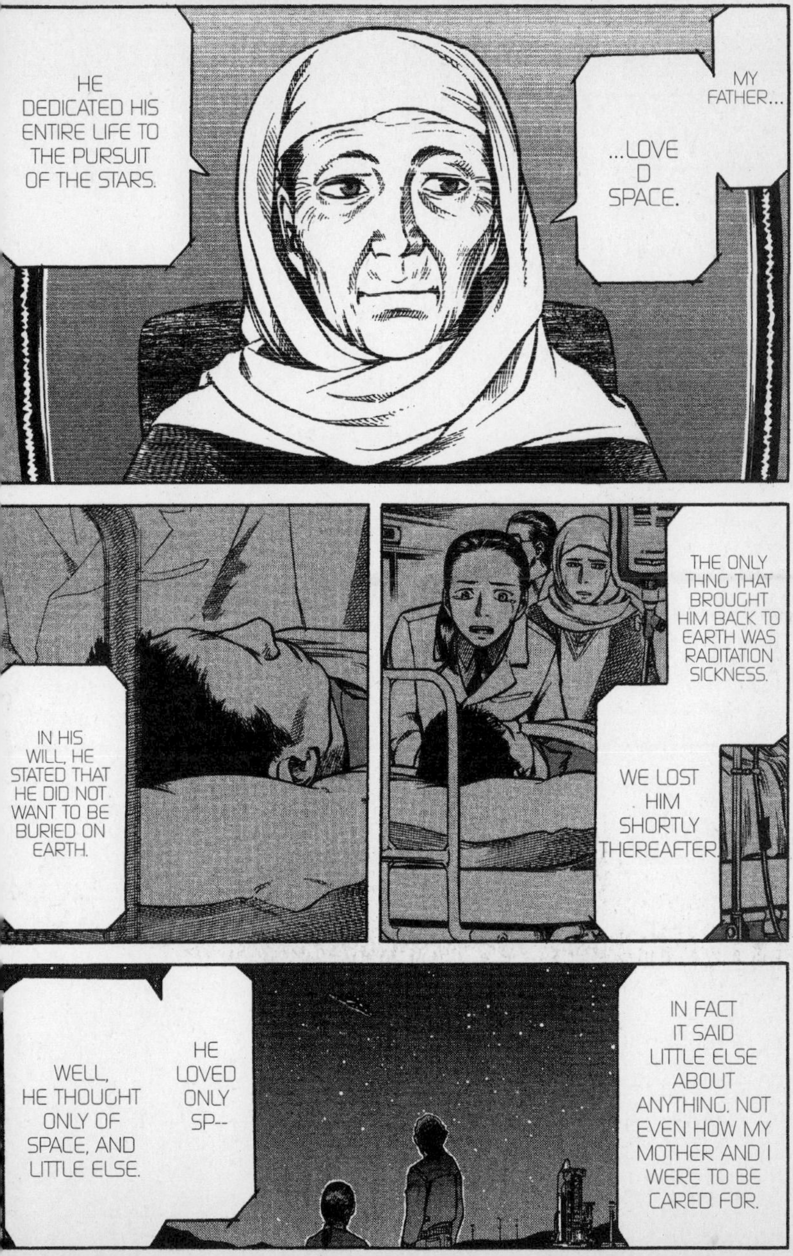
MY FATHER...
...LOVE D SPACE.
HE DEDICATED HIS ENTIRE LIFE TO THE PURSUIT OF THE STARS.
THE ONLY THNG THAT BROUGHT HIM BACK TO EARTH WAS RADITATION SICKNESS.
WE LOST HIM SHORTLY THEREAFTER.
IN HIS WILL, HE STATED THAT HE DID NOT WANT TO BE BURIED ON EARTH.
IN FACT IT SAID LITTLE ELSE ABOUT ANYTHING. NOT EVEN HOW MY MOTHER AND I WERE TO BE CARED FOR.
HE LOVED ONLY SP--
WELL, HE THOUGHT ONLY OF SPACE, AND LITTLE ELSE.

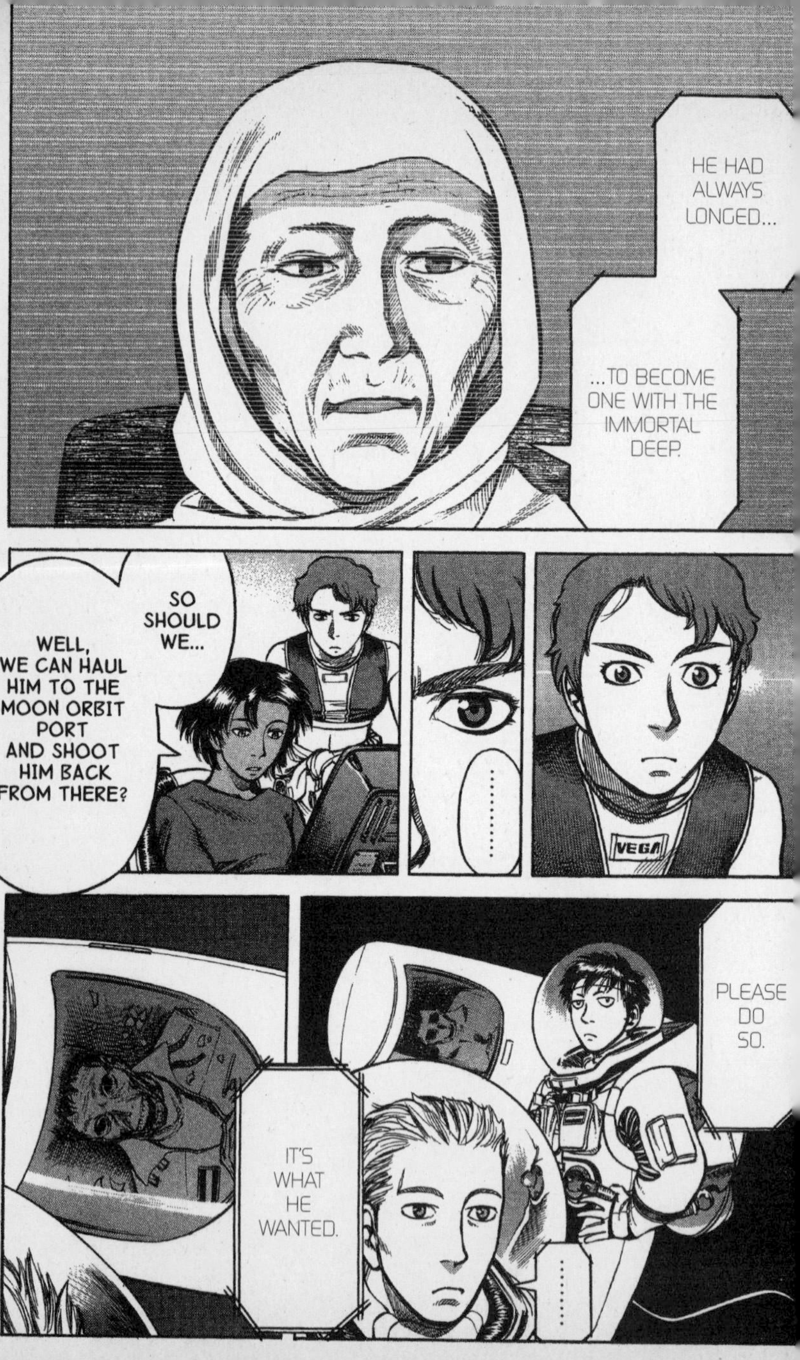
HE HAD ALWAYS LONGED...
...TO BECOME ONE WITH THE IMMORTAL DEEP.
VEGA
......
SO SHOULD WE...
WELL, WE CAN HAUL HIM TO THE MOON ORBIT PORT AND SHOOT HIM BACK FROM THERE?
PLEASE DO SO.
IT'S WHAT HE WANTED.
......

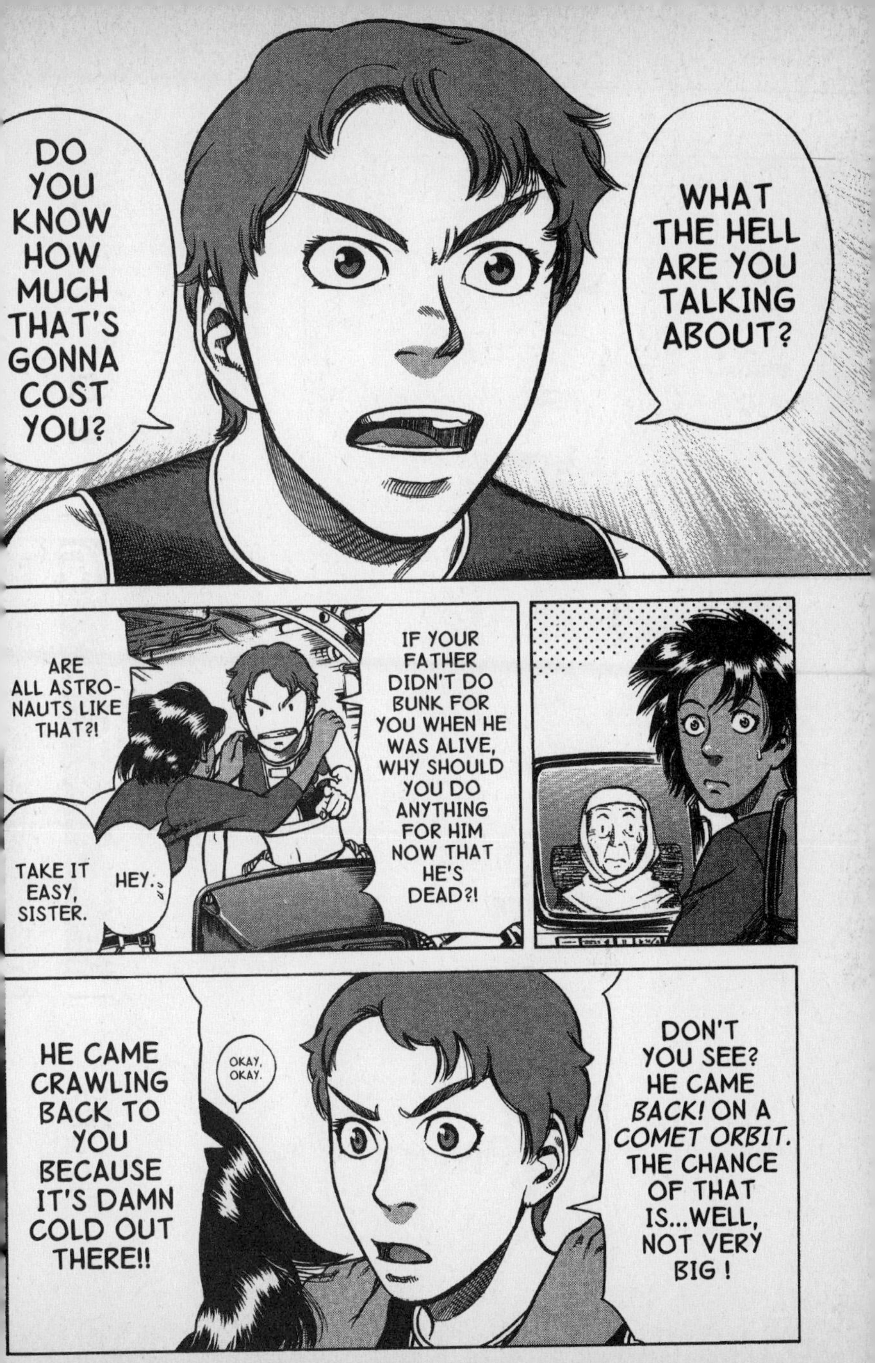
WHAT THE HELL ARE YOU TALKING ABOUT?
DO YOU KNOW HOW MUCH THAT'S GONNA COST YOU?
IF YOUR FATHER DIDN'T DO BUNK FOR YOU WHEN HE WAS ALIVE, WHY SHOULD YOU DO ANYTHING FOR HIM NOW THAT HE'S DEAD?!
ARE ALL ASTRONAUTS LIKE THAT?!
HEY.
TAKE IT EASY, SISTER.
DON'T YOU SEE? HE CAME *BACK!* ON A *COMET ORBIT.* THE CHANCE OF THAT IS...WELL, NOT VERY BIG !
OKAY, OKAY.
HE CAME CRAWLING BACK TO YOU BECAUSE IT'S DAMN COLD OUT THERE!!

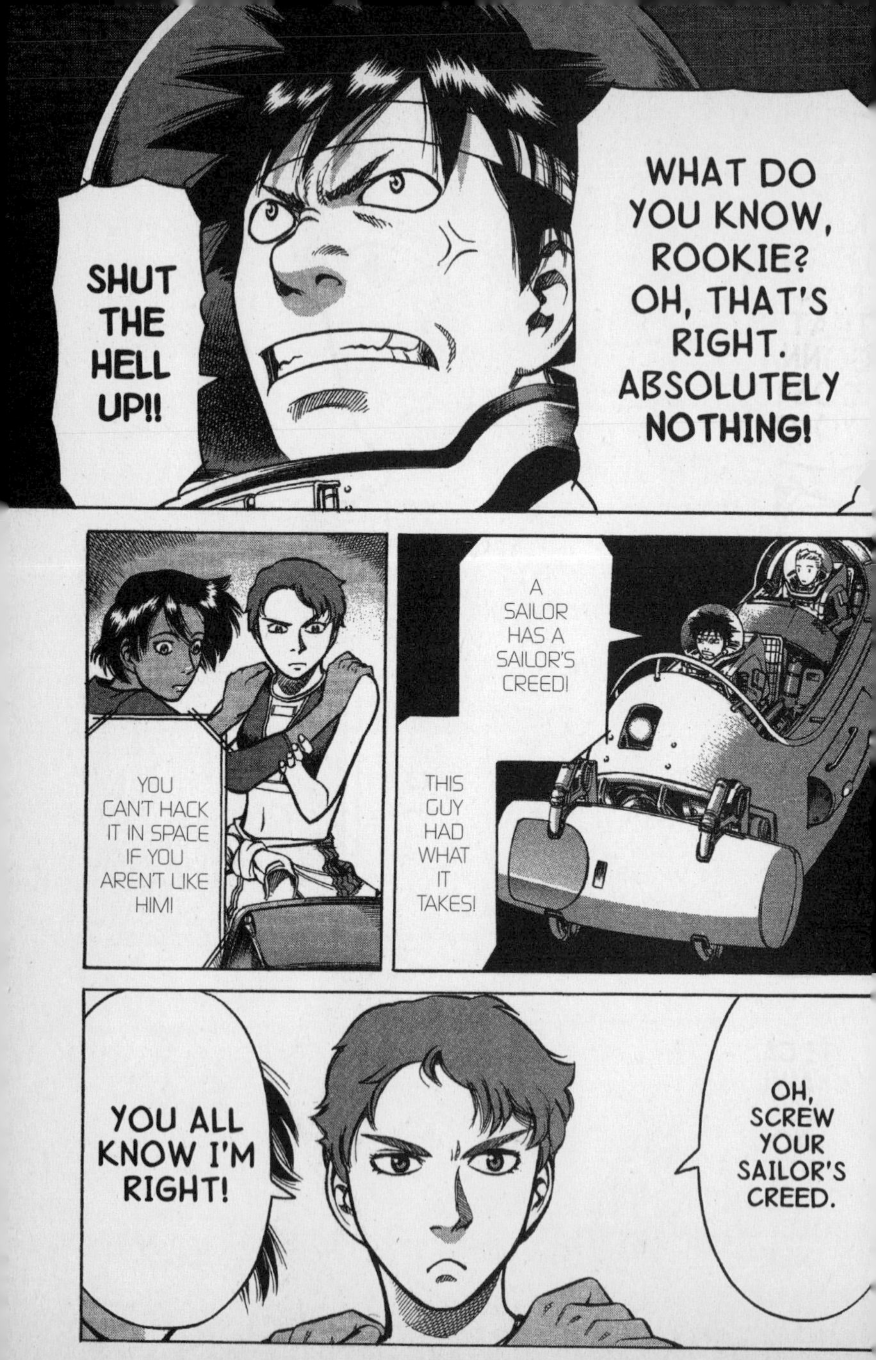
WHAT DO YOU KNOW, ROOKIE? OH, THAT'S RIGHT. ABSOLUTELY NOTHING!
SHUT THE HELL UP!!
A SAILOR HAS A SAILOR'S CREED!
THIS GUY HAD WHAT IT TAKES!
YOU CAN'T HACK IT IN SPACE IF YOU AREN'T LIKE HIM!
OH, SCREW YOUR SAILOR'S CREED.
YOU ALL KNOW I'M RIGHT!

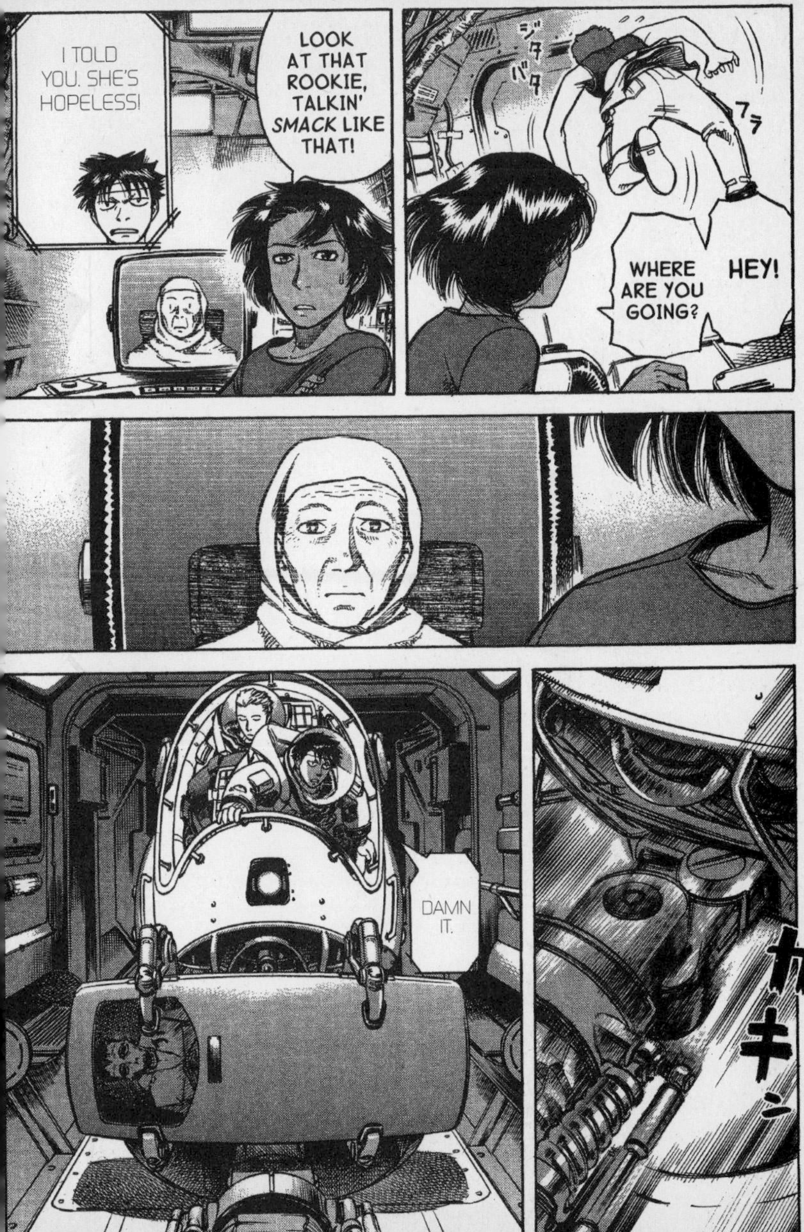
ジタバタ
フラ
HEY!
WHERE ARE YOU GOING?
LOOK AT THAT ROOKIE, TALKIN' *SMACK* LIKE THAT!
I TOLD YOU. SHE'S HOPELESS!
ガキン
DAMN IT.

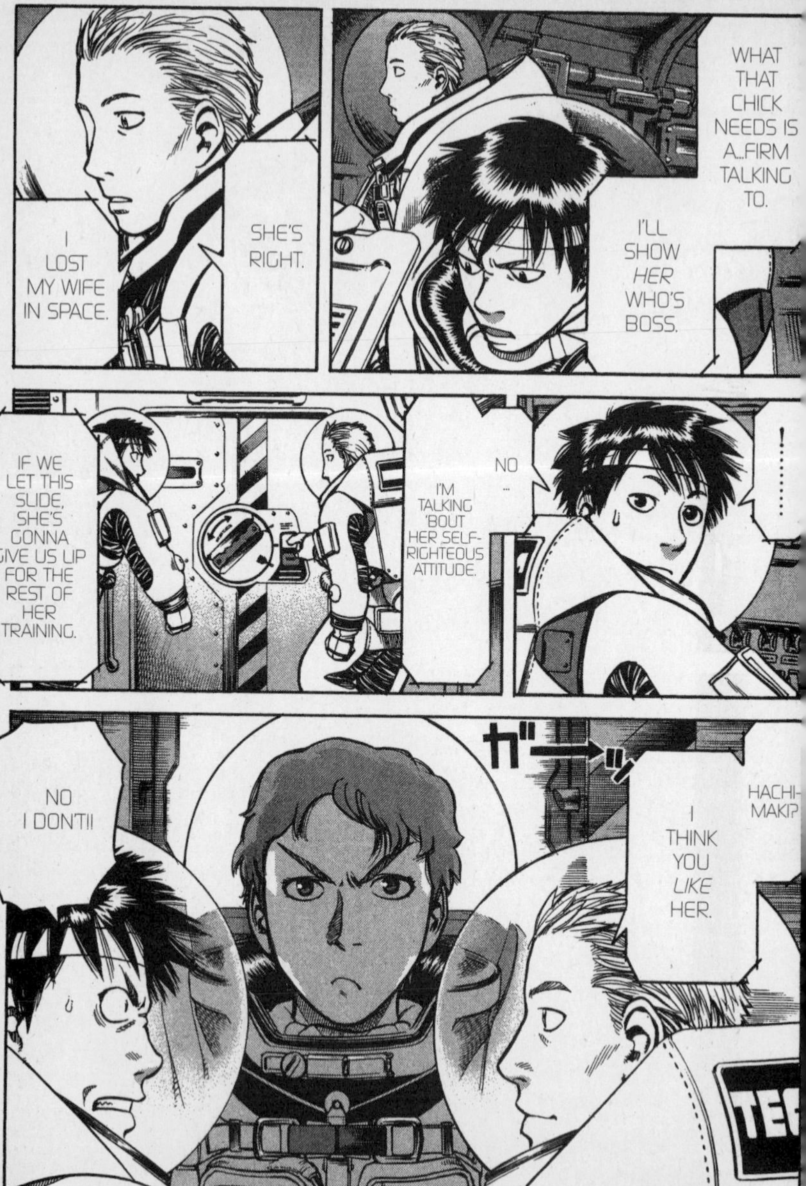
WHAT THAT CHICK NEEDS IS A...FIRM TALKING TO.
I'LL SHOW *HER* WHO'S BOSS.
SHE'S RIGHT.
I LOST MY WIFE IN SPACE.
!......
NO ...
I'M TALKING 'BOUT HER SELF-RIGHTEOUS ATTITUDE.
IF WE LET THIS SLIDE, SHE'S GONNA GIVE US UP FOR THE REST OF HER TRAINING.
HACHI-MAKI?
I THINK YOU *LIKE* HER.
ガーッ
NO I DON'T!!

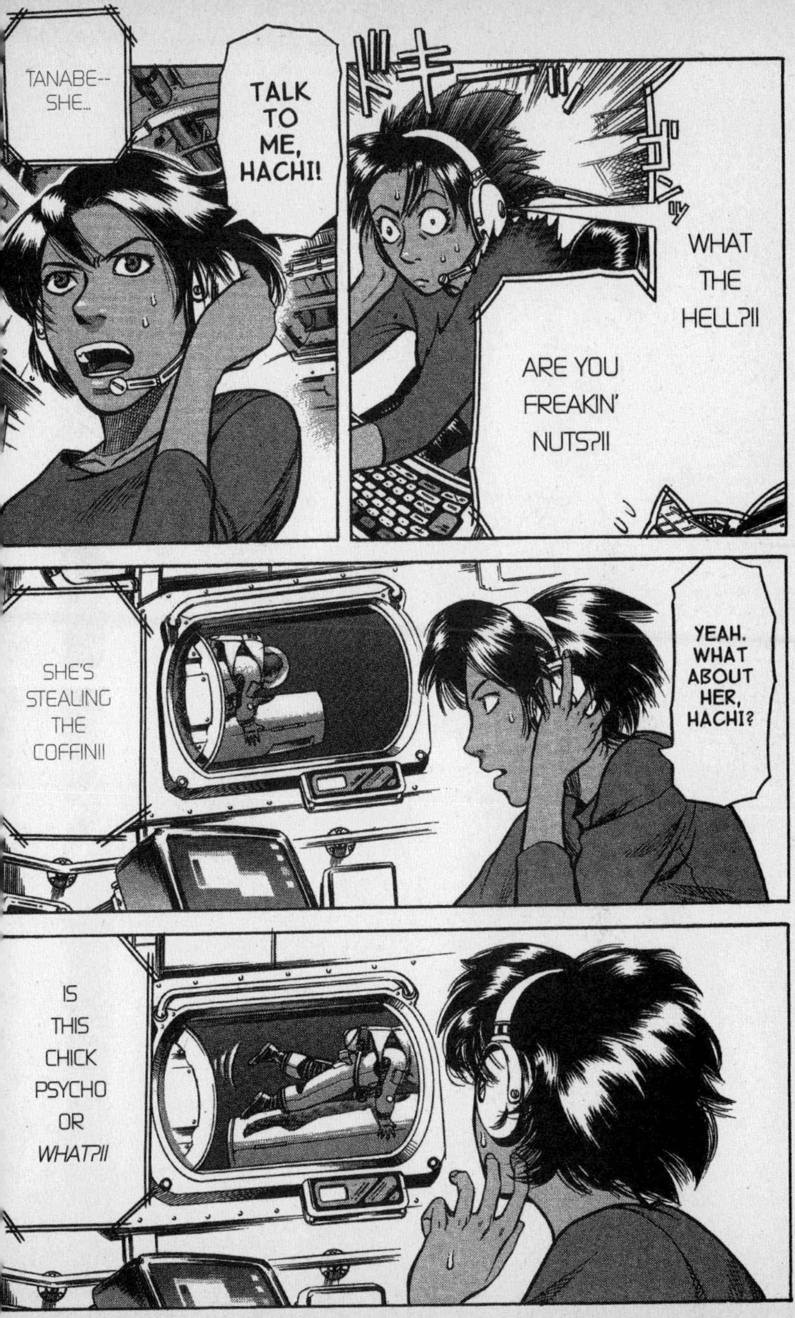
WHAT THE HELL?!!
ARE YOU FREAKIN' NUTS?!!
TALK TO ME, HACHI!!
TANABE-- SHE...
YEAH. WHAT ABOUT HER, HACHI?
SHE'S STEALING THE COFFIN!!
IS THIS CHICK PSYCHO OR *WHAT?!!*

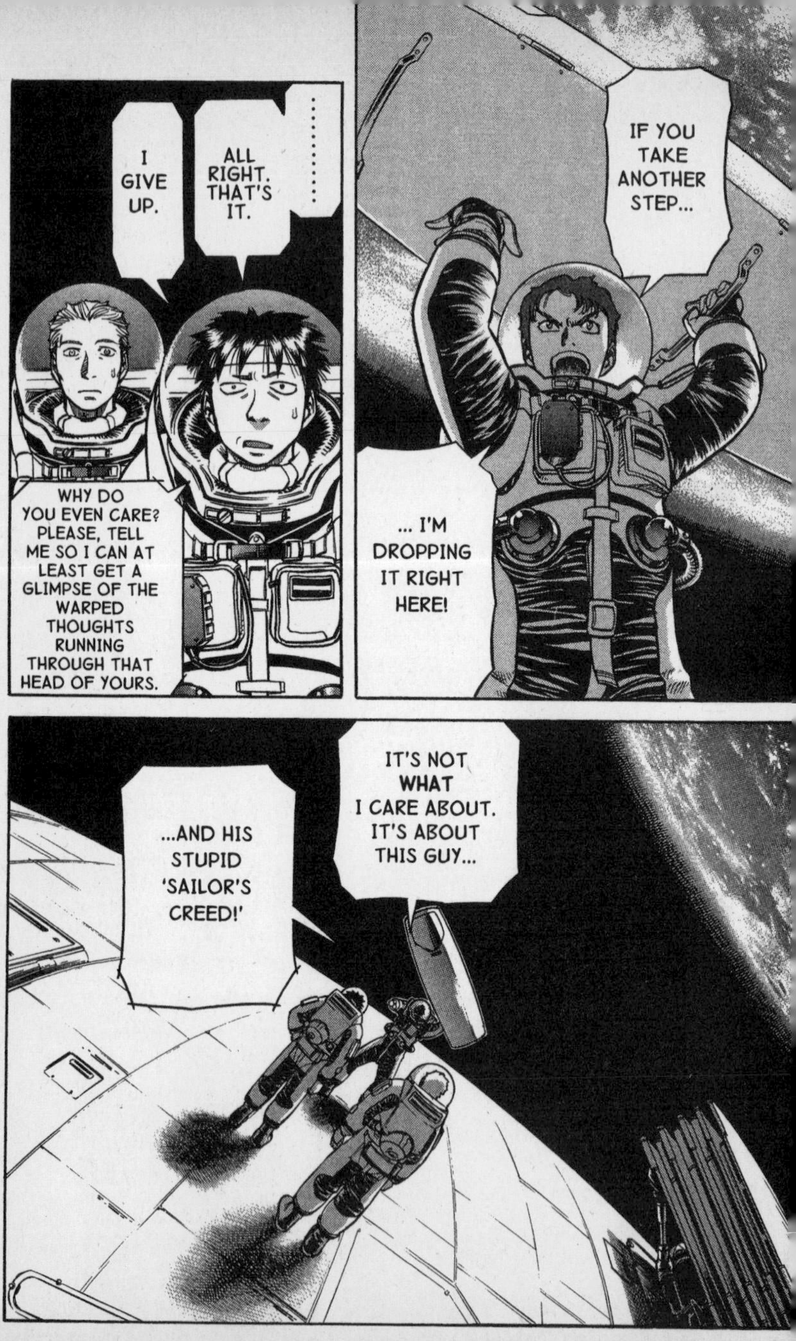
IF YOU TAKE ANOTHER STEP...
... I'M DROPPING IT RIGHT HERE!
....
ALL RIGHT. THAT'S IT.
I GIVE UP.
WHY DO YOU EVEN CARE? PLEASE, TELL ME SO I CAN AT LEAST GET A GLIMPSE OF THE WARPED THOUGHTS RUNNING THROUGH THAT HEAD OF YOURS.
IT'S NOT WHAT I CARE ABOUT. IT'S ABOUT THIS GUY...
...AND HIS STUPID 'SAILOR'S CREED!'

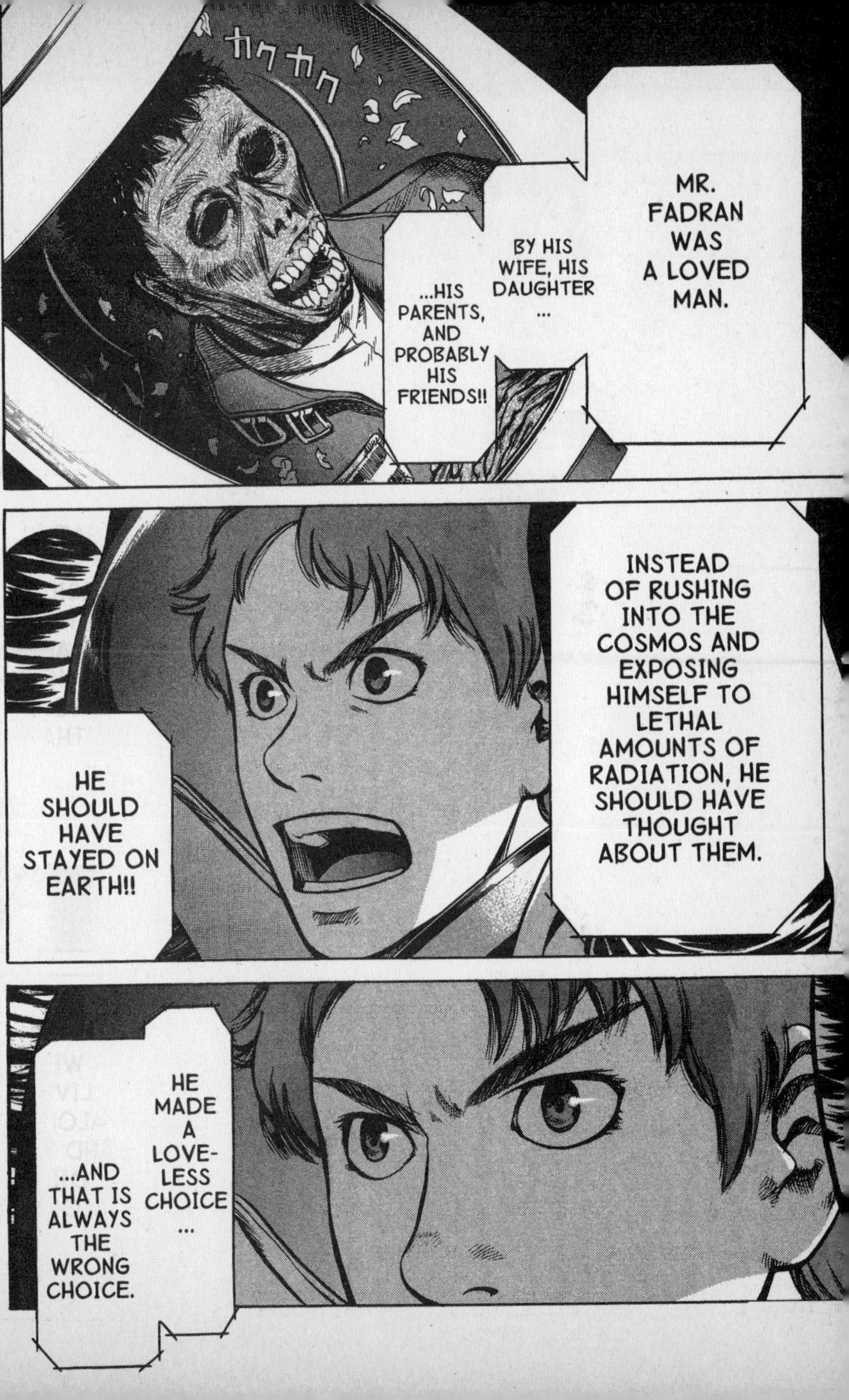
カクカク
MR. FADRAN WAS A LOVED MAN.
BY HIS WIFE, HIS DAUGHTER ...
...HIS PARENTS, AND PROBABLY HIS FRIENDS!!
INSTEAD OF RUSHING INTO THE COSMOS AND EXPOSING HIMSELF TO LETHAL AMOUNTS OF RADIATION, HE SHOULD HAVE THOUGHT ABOUT THEM.
HE SHOULD HAVE STAYED ON EARTH!!
HE MADE A LOVE-LESS CHOICE ...
...AND THAT IS ALWAYS THE WRONG CHOICE.

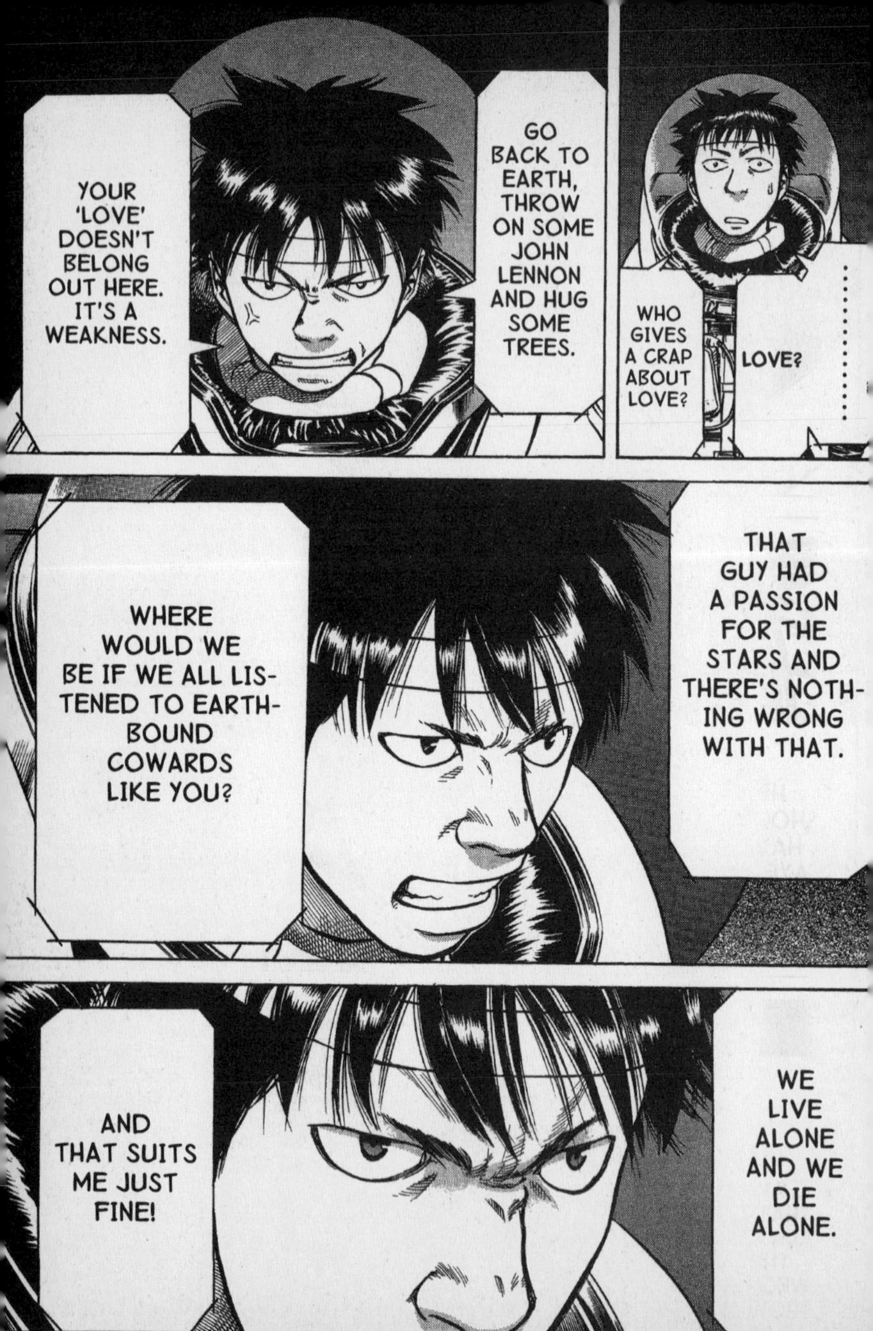
......
LOVE?
WHO GIVES A CRAP ABOUT LOVE?
GO BACK TO EARTH, THROW ON SOME JOHN LENNON AND HUG SOME TREES.
YOUR 'LOVE' DOESN'T BELONG OUT HERE. IT'S A WEAKNESS.
THAT GUY HAD A PASSION FOR THE STARS AND THERE'S NOTHING WRONG WITH THAT.
WHERE WOULD WE BE IF WE ALL LISTENED TO EARTHBOUND COWARDS LIKE YOU?
WE LIVE ALONE AND WE DIE ALONE.
AND THAT SUITS ME JUST FINE!

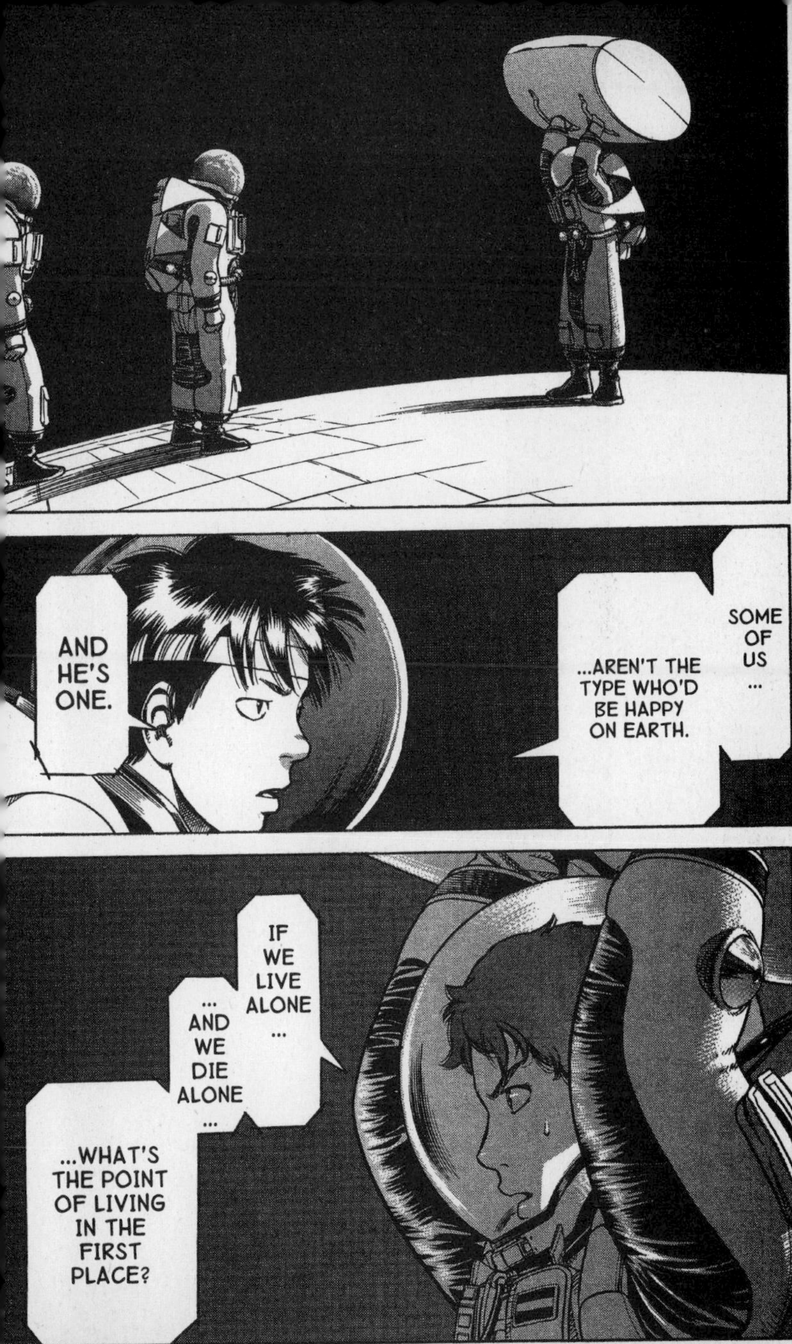
SOME OF US ...
...AREN'T THE TYPE WHO'D BE HAPPY ON EARTH.
AND HE'S ONE.
IF WE LIVE ALONE ...
... AND WE DIE ALONE ...
...WHAT'S THE POINT OF LIVING IN THE FIRST PLACE?

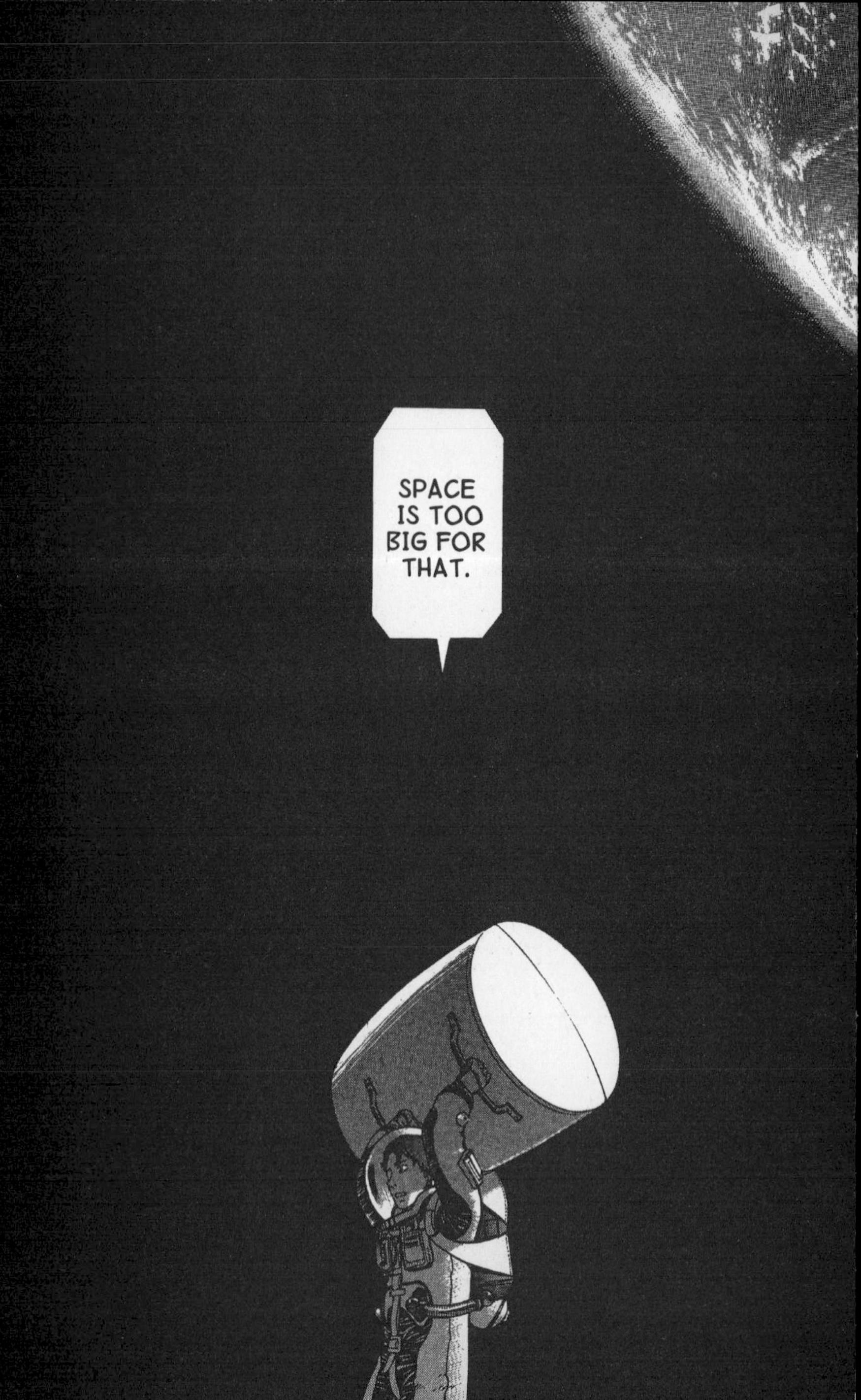
SPACE IS TOO BIG FOR THAT.

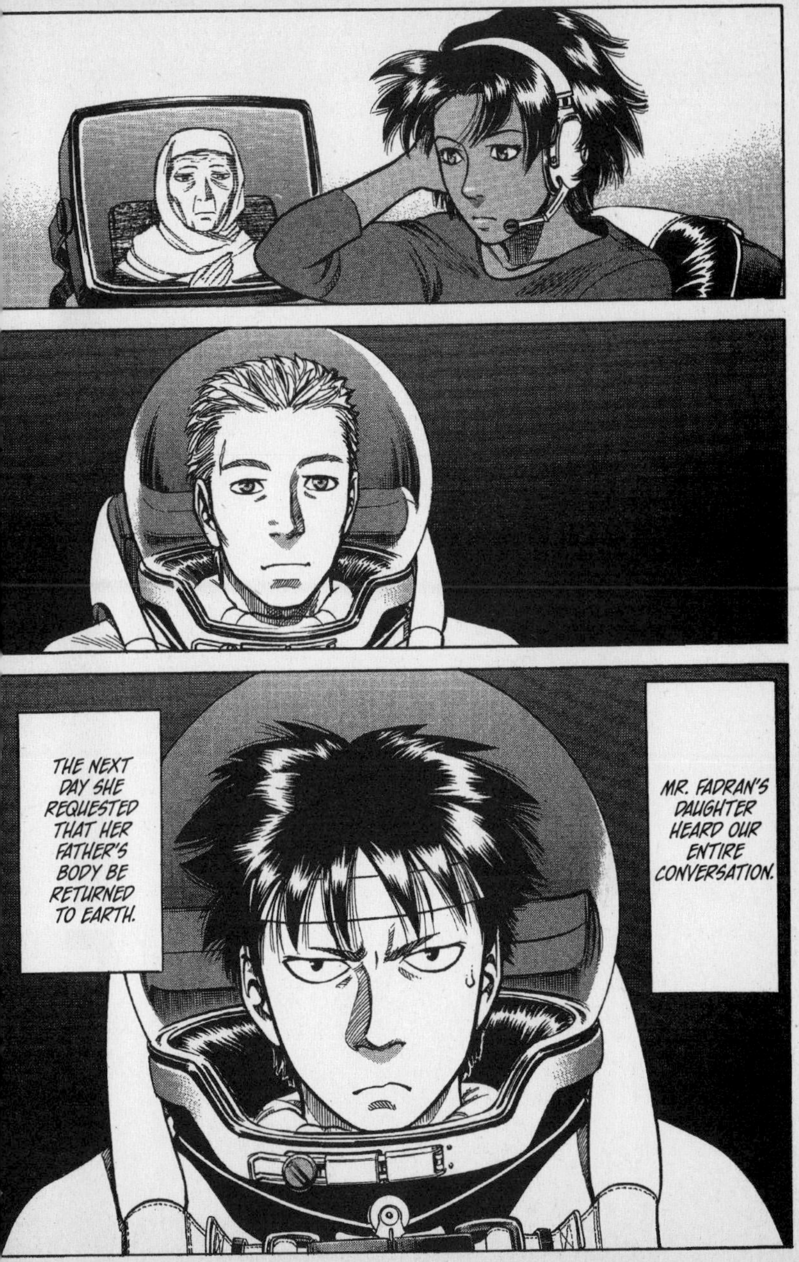
MR. FADRAN'S DAUGHTER HEARD OUR ENTIRE CONVERSATION.
THE NEXT DAY SHE REQUESTED THAT HER FATHER'S BODY BE RETURNED TO EARTH.

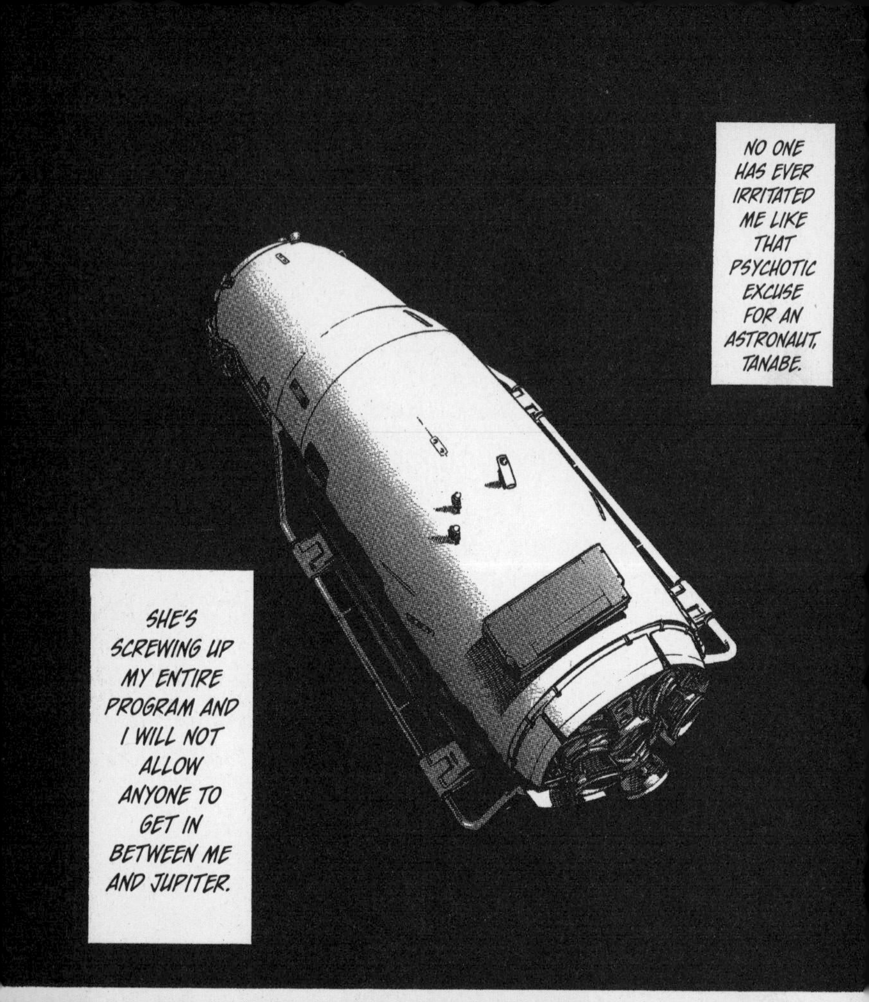
NO ONE HAS EVER IRRITATED ME LIKE THAT PSYCHOTIC EXCUSE FOR AN ASTRONAUT, TANABE.
SHE'S SCREWING UP MY ENTIRE PROGRAM AND I WILL NOT ALLOW ANYONE TO GET IN BETWEEN ME AND JUPITER.
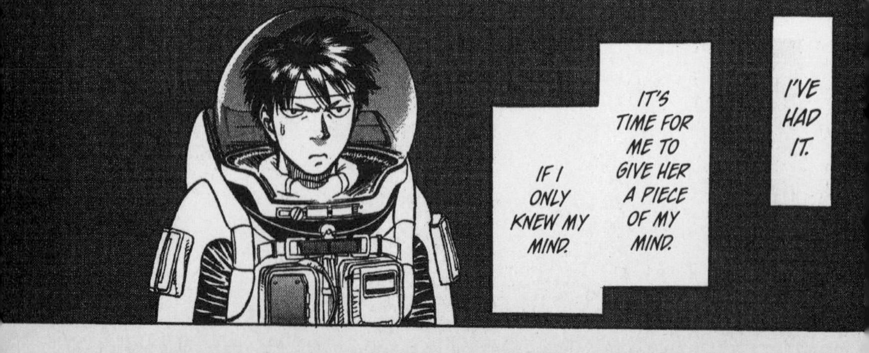
I'VE HAD IT.
IT'S TIME FOR ME TO GIVE HER A PIECE OF MY MIND.
IF I ONLY KNEW MY MIND.

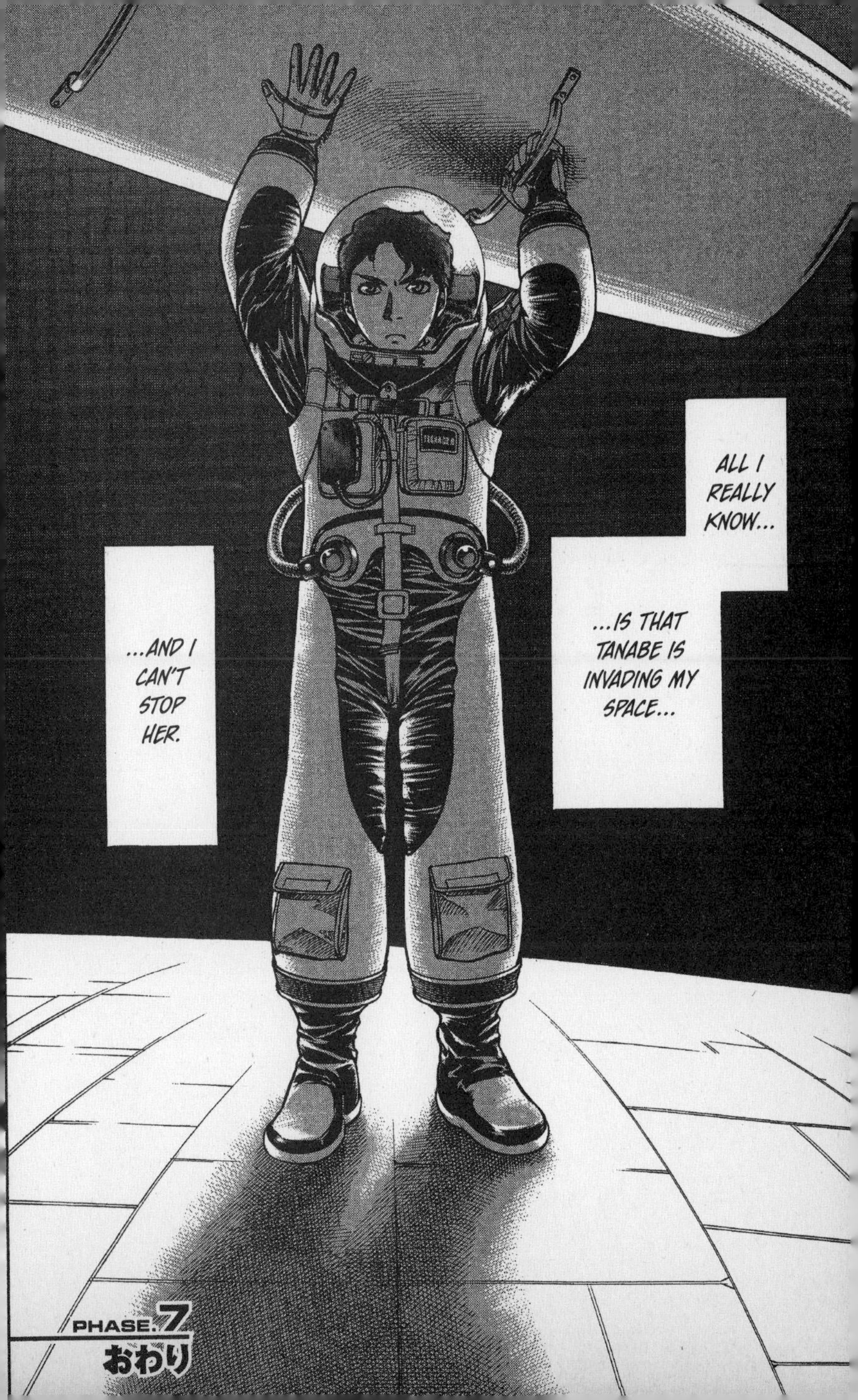
ALL I REALLY KNOW...
...IS THAT TANABE IS INVADING MY SPACE...
...AND I CAN'T STOP HER.
PHASE. 7
おわり

PLANETES
SUPPLEMENT

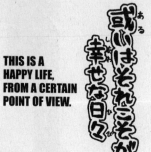

プラネテス超外伝

或いはそれこそが幸せな日々

THIS IS A HAPPY LIFE, FROM A CERTAIN POINT OF VIEW.

BY
MAKOTO
YUKIMURA

作・幸村誠

A FOUR PANEL COMIC

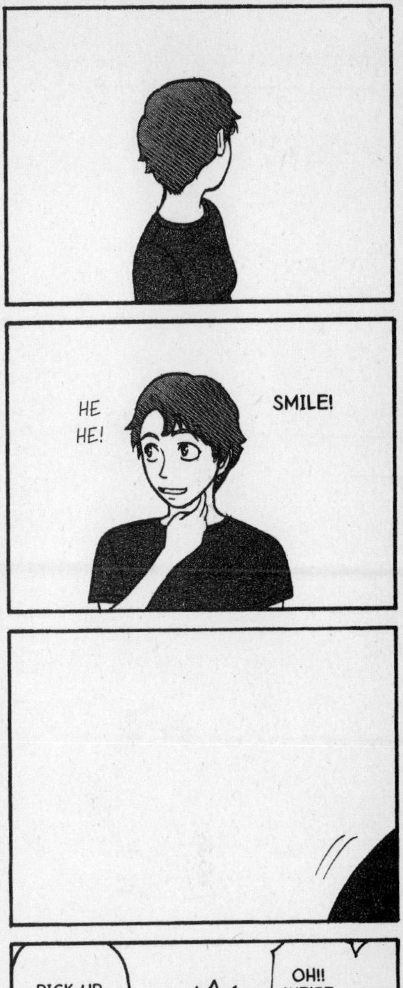
SMILE!
HE HE!
LET ME INTRODUCE MY PET...
OH!! WE'RE ON THE FOURTH PANEL ALREADY?!
PICK UP THE PACE.
BUT I HAVEN'T FINISHED!!

NAMAO-SAN (PRESUMABLY MALE).

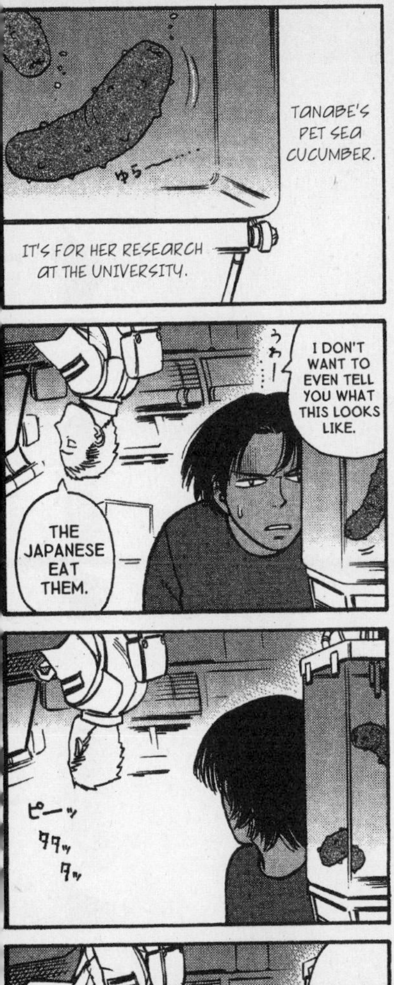
TANABE'S PET SEA CUCUMBER.
ゆら
IT'S FOR HER RESEARCH AT THE UNIVERSITY.
I DON'T WANT TO EVEN TELL YOU WHAT THIS LOOKS LIKE.
うわー…
THE JAPANESE EAT THEM.
ピーッ
タタッ
タッ
AS A PUNISHMENT?
NO, AS AN APPETIZER.
WITH PONZU SAUCE. DELICIOUS.

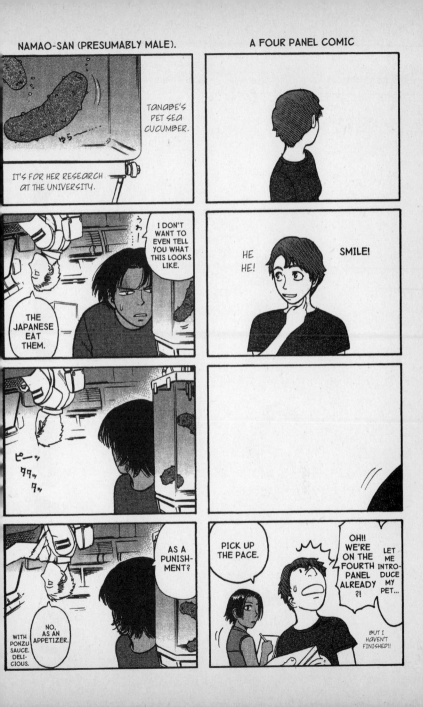

EAT? THAT THING?!

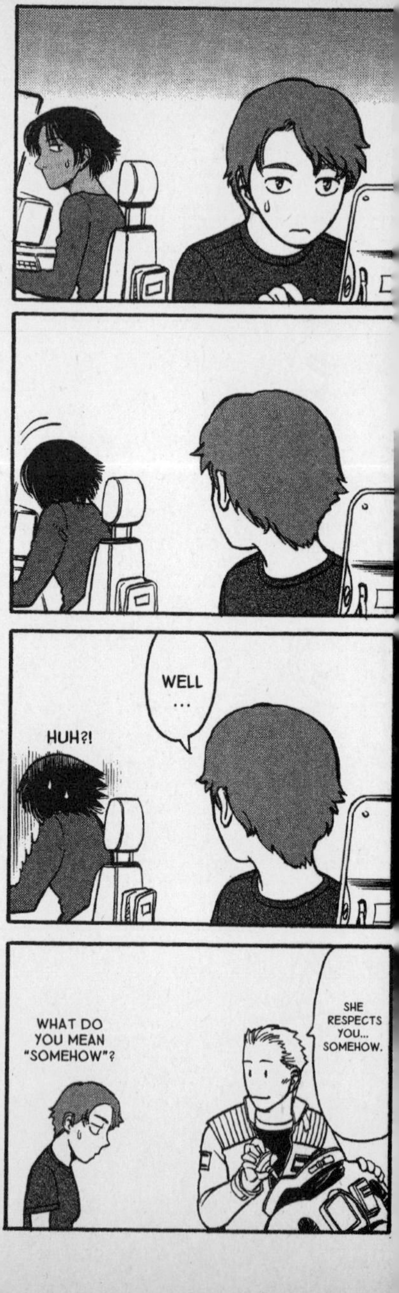
WELL
...
HUH?!
SHE RESPECTS YOU... SOMEHOW.
WHAT DO YOU MEAN "SOMEHOW"?

DRINKING HOT COFFEE THROUGH A STRAW

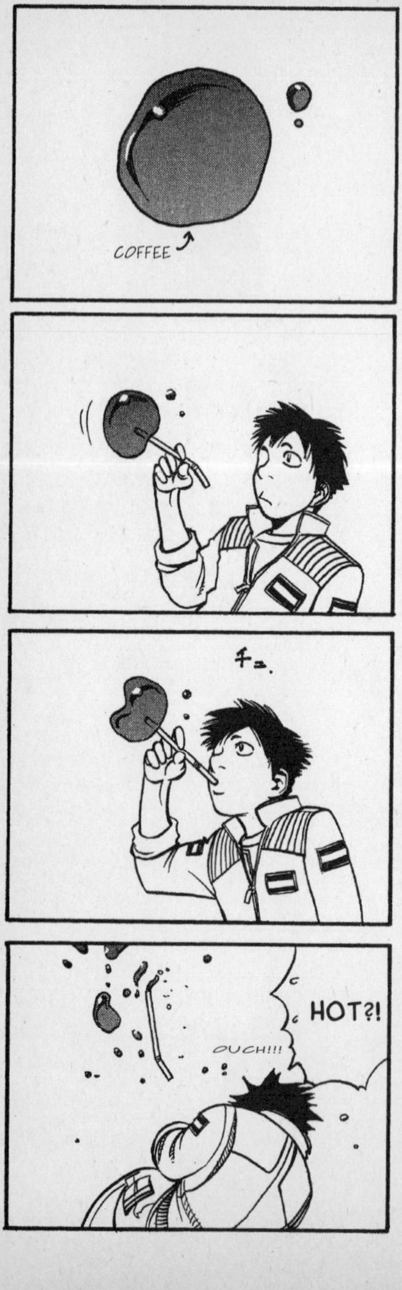
COFFEE
チュ.
HOT?!
OUCH!!!

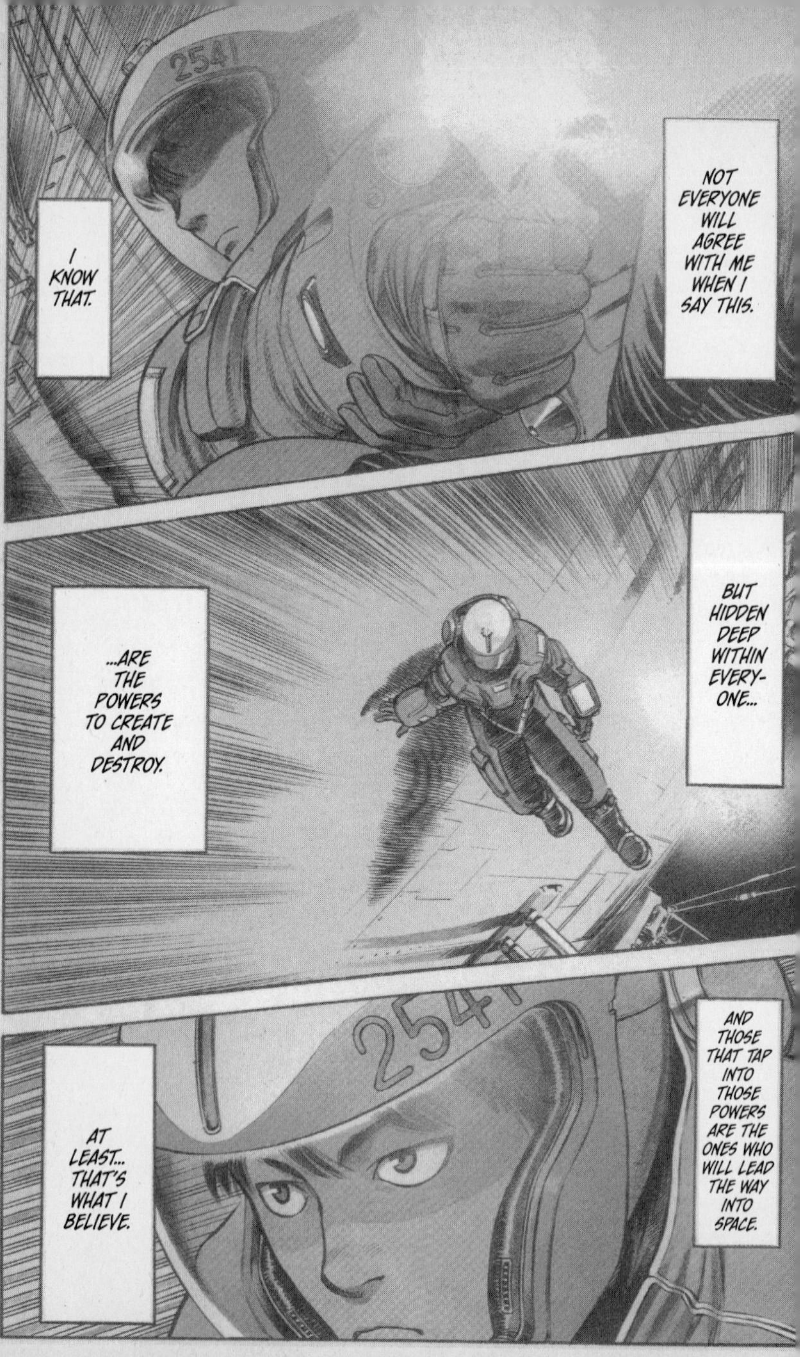
NOT EVERYONE WILL AGREE WITH ME WHEN I SAY THIS.
I KNOW THAT.
BUT HIDDEN DEEP WITHIN EVERY-ONE...
...ARE THE POWERS TO CREATE AND DESTROY.
AND THOSE THAT TAP INTO THOSE POWERS ARE THE ONES WHO WILL LEAD THE WAY INTO SPACE.
AT LEAST... THAT'S WHAT I BELIEVE.

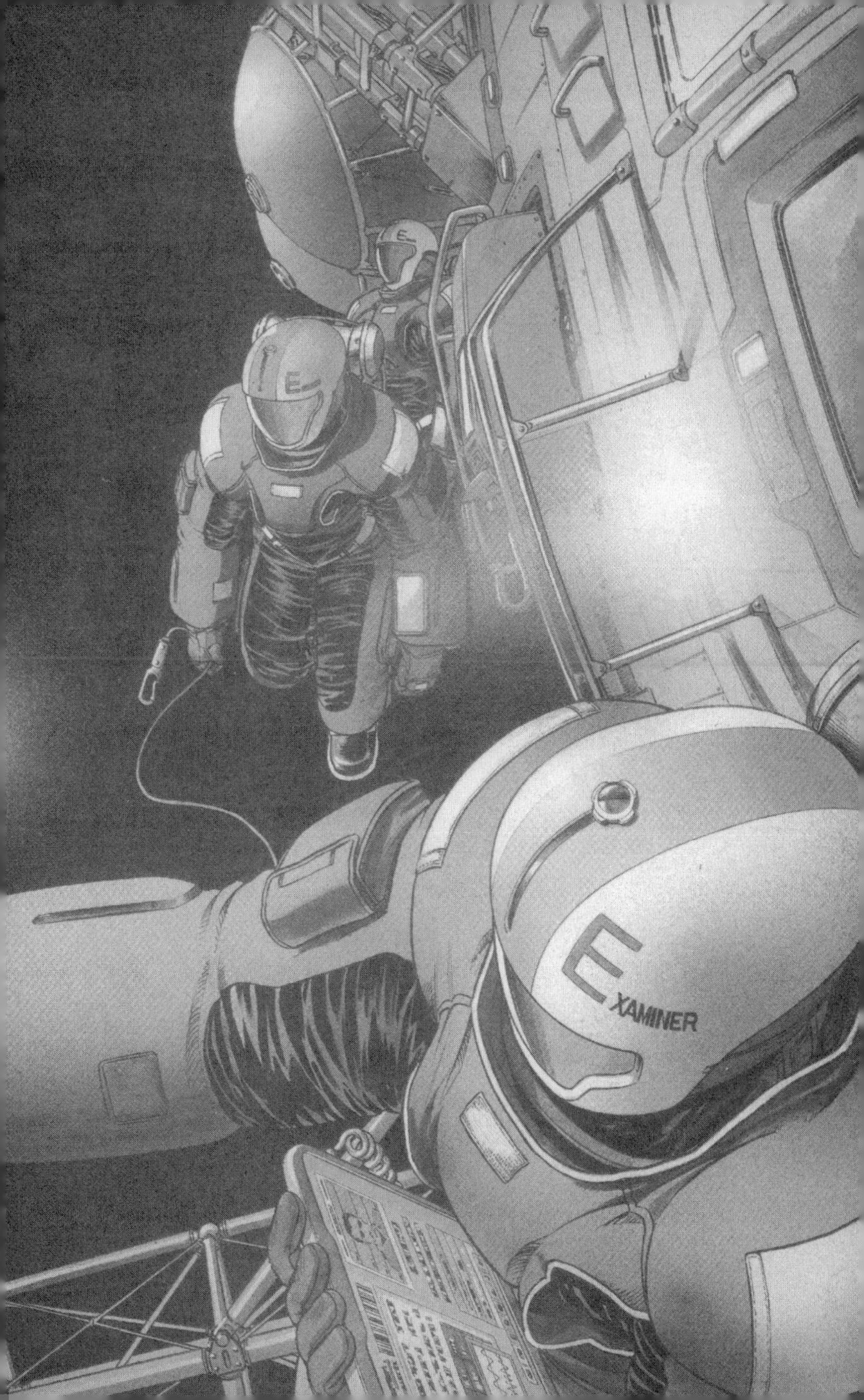
EXAMINER

PHASE. 8
A BLACK FLOWER NAMED SAKINOHAKA (PART 1)

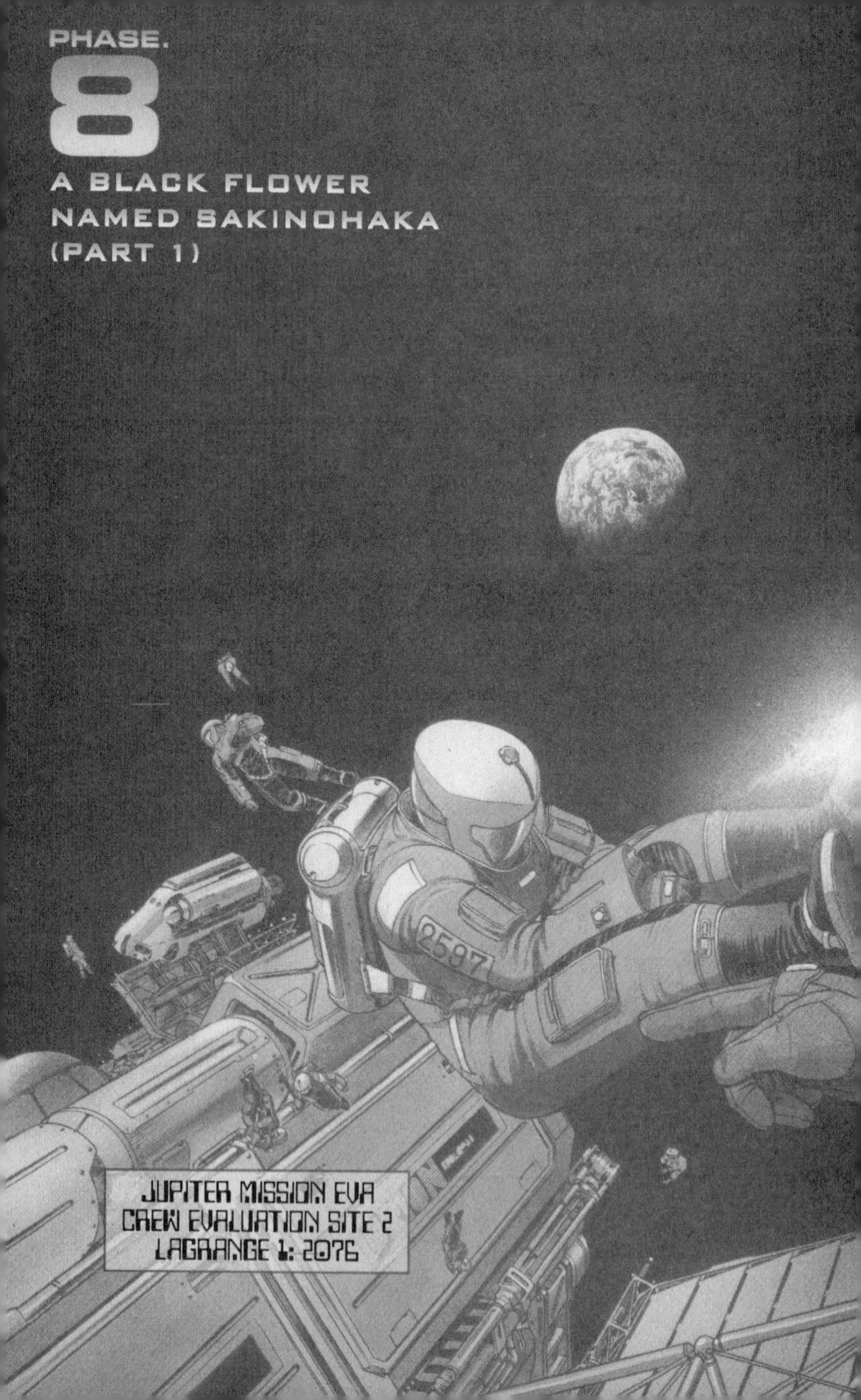
JUPITER MISSION EVA
CREW EVALUATION SITE 2
LAGRANGE 1: 2076
2597

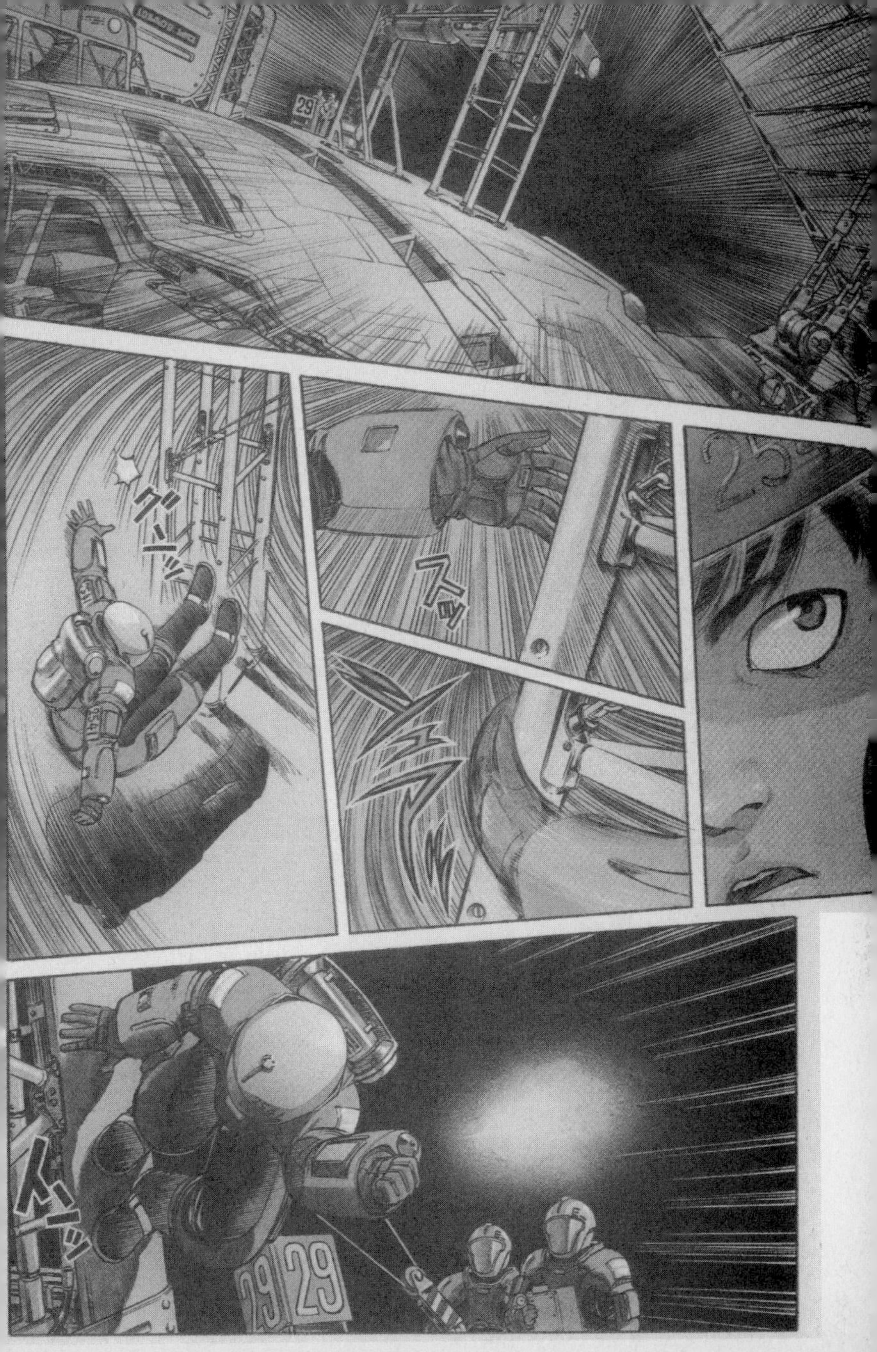
フッ
グイーッ

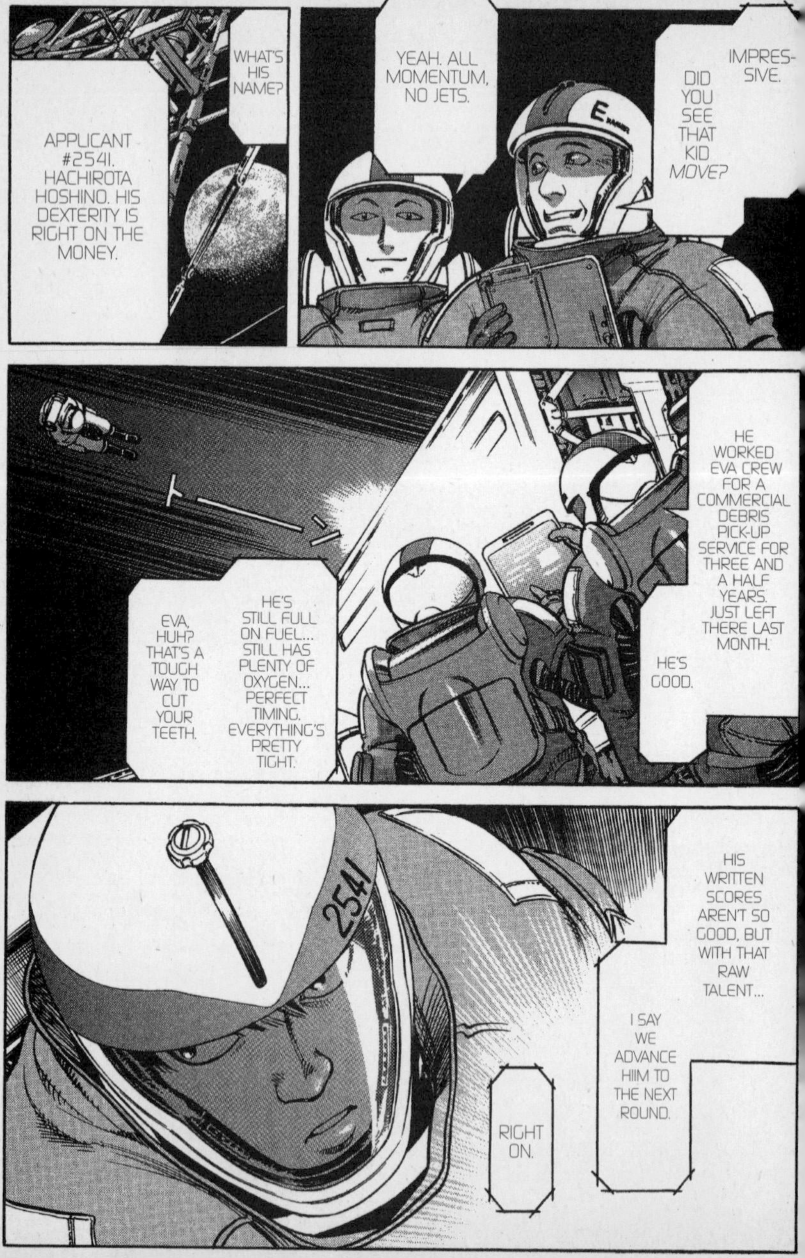

IMPRES-SIVE.
DID YOU SEE THAT KID *MOVE?*
YEAH. ALL MOMENTUM, NO JETS.
WHAT'S HIS NAME?
APPLICANT #2541. HACHIROTA HOSHINO. HIS DEXTERITY IS RIGHT ON THE MONEY.
HE WORKED EVA CREW FOR A COMMERCIAL DEBRIS PICK-UP SERVICE FOR THREE AND A HALF YEARS. JUST LEFT THERE LAST MONTH.
HE'S GOOD.
HE'S STILL FULL ON FUEL... STILL HAS PLENTY OF OXYGEN... PERFECT TIMING. EVERYTHING'S PRETTY TIGHT.
EVA, HUH? THAT'S A TOUGH WAY TO CUT YOUR TEETH.
HIS WRITTEN SCORES AREN'T SO GOOD, BUT WITH THAT RAW TALENT...
I SAY WE ADVANCE HIIM TO THE NEXT ROUND.
RIGHT ON.

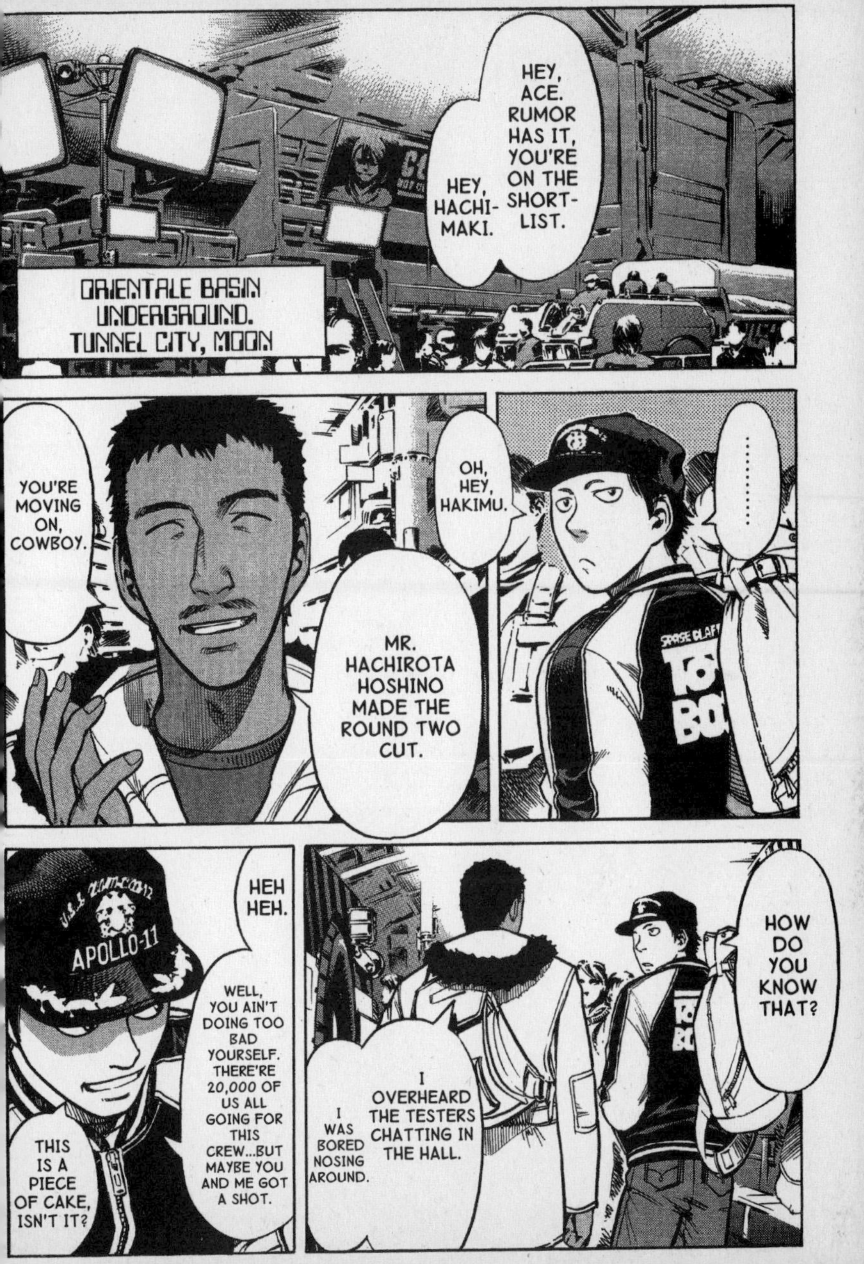
HEY, ACE. RUMOR HAS IT, YOU'RE ON THE SHORT-LIST.
HEY, HACHI-MAKI.
ORIENTALE BASIN UNDERGROUND. TUNNEL CITY, MOON
......
OH, HEY, HAKIMU.
MR. HACHIROTA HOSHINO MADE THE ROUND TWO CUT.
YOU'RE MOVING ON, COWBOY.
HOW DO YOU KNOW THAT?
I OVERHEARD THE TESTERS CHATTING IN THE HALL.
I WAS BORED NOSING AROUND.
HEH HEH.
APOLLO-11
WELL, YOU AIN'T DOING TOO BAD YOURSELF. THERE'RE 20,000 OF US ALL GOING FOR THIS CREW...BUT MAYBE YOU AND ME GOT A SHOT.
THIS IS A PIECE OF CAKE, ISN'T IT?

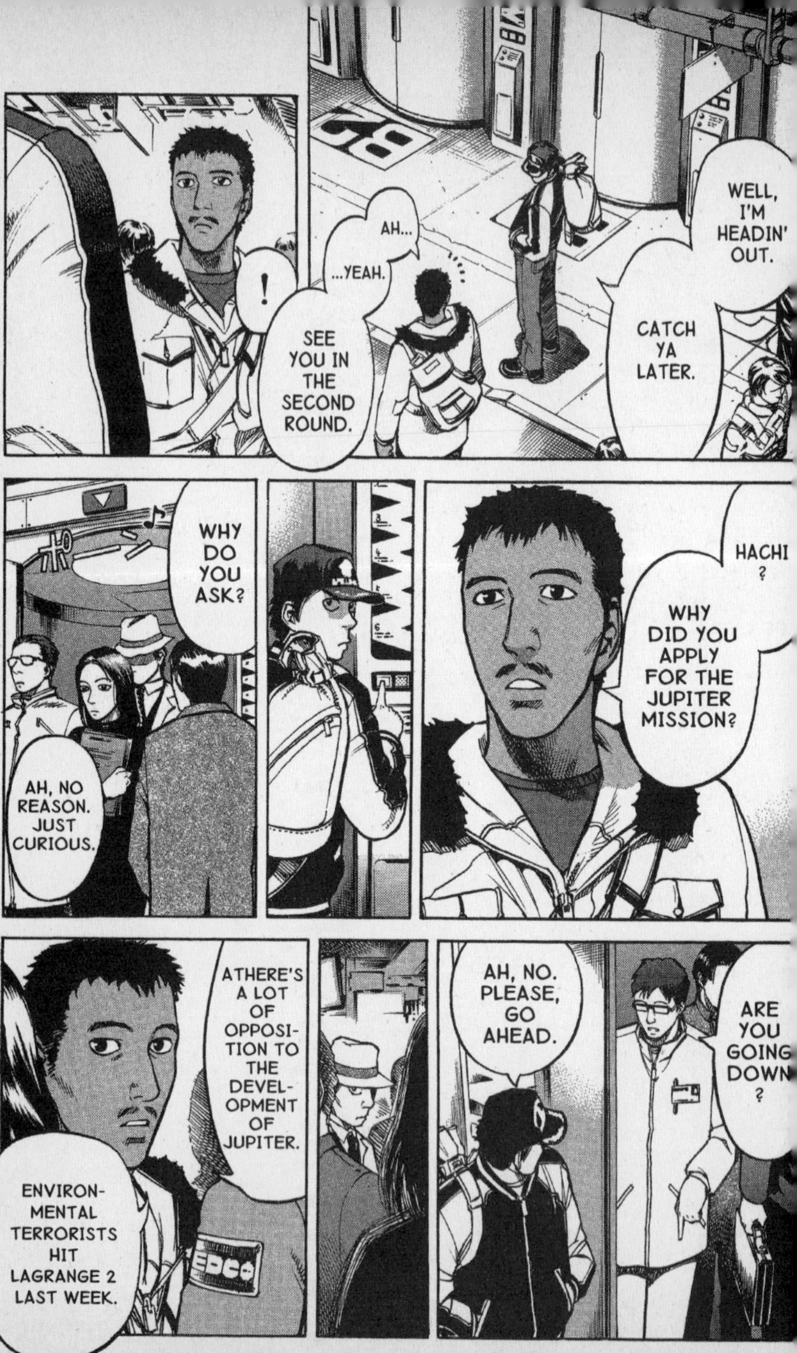
WELL, I'M HEADIN' OUT.
CATCH YA LATER.
AH...
...YEAH.
SEE YOU IN THE SECOND ROUND.
!
HACHI?
WHY DID YOU APPLY FOR THE JUPITER MISSION?
WHY DO YOU ASK?
AH, NO REASON. JUST CURIOUS.
ARE YOU GOING DOWN?
AH, NO. PLEASE, GO AHEAD.
ATHERE'S A LOT OF OPPOSITION TO THE DEVELOPMENT OF JUPITER.
ENVIRONMENTAL TERRORISTS HIT LAGRANGE 2 LAST WEEK.

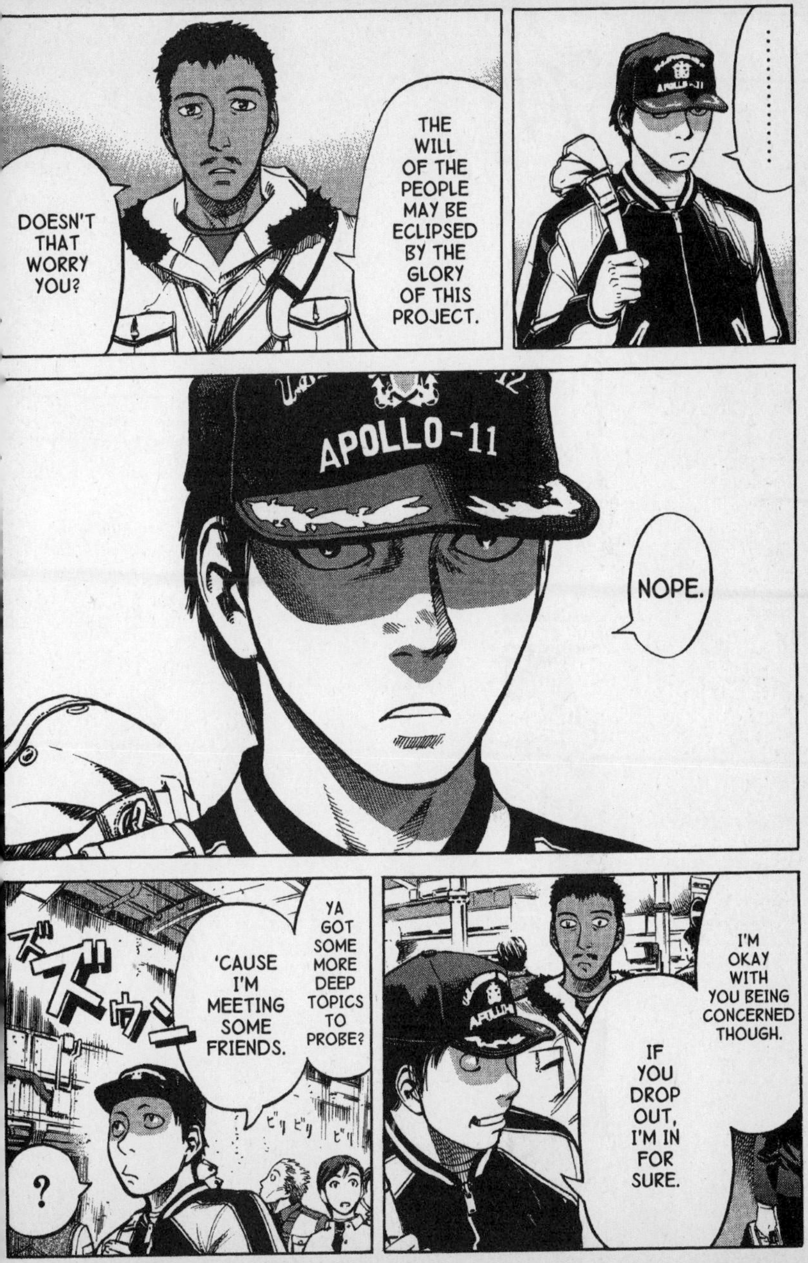
……
THE WILL OF THE PEOPLE MAY BE ECLIPSED BY THE GLORY OF THIS PROJECT.
DOESN'T THAT WORRY YOU?
APOLLO-11
NOPE.
I'M OKAY WITH YOU BEING CONCERNED THOUGH.
IF YOU DROP OUT, I'M IN FOR SURE.
YA GOT SOME MORE DEEP TOPICS TO PROBE?
'CAUSE I'M MEETING SOME FRIENDS.
?

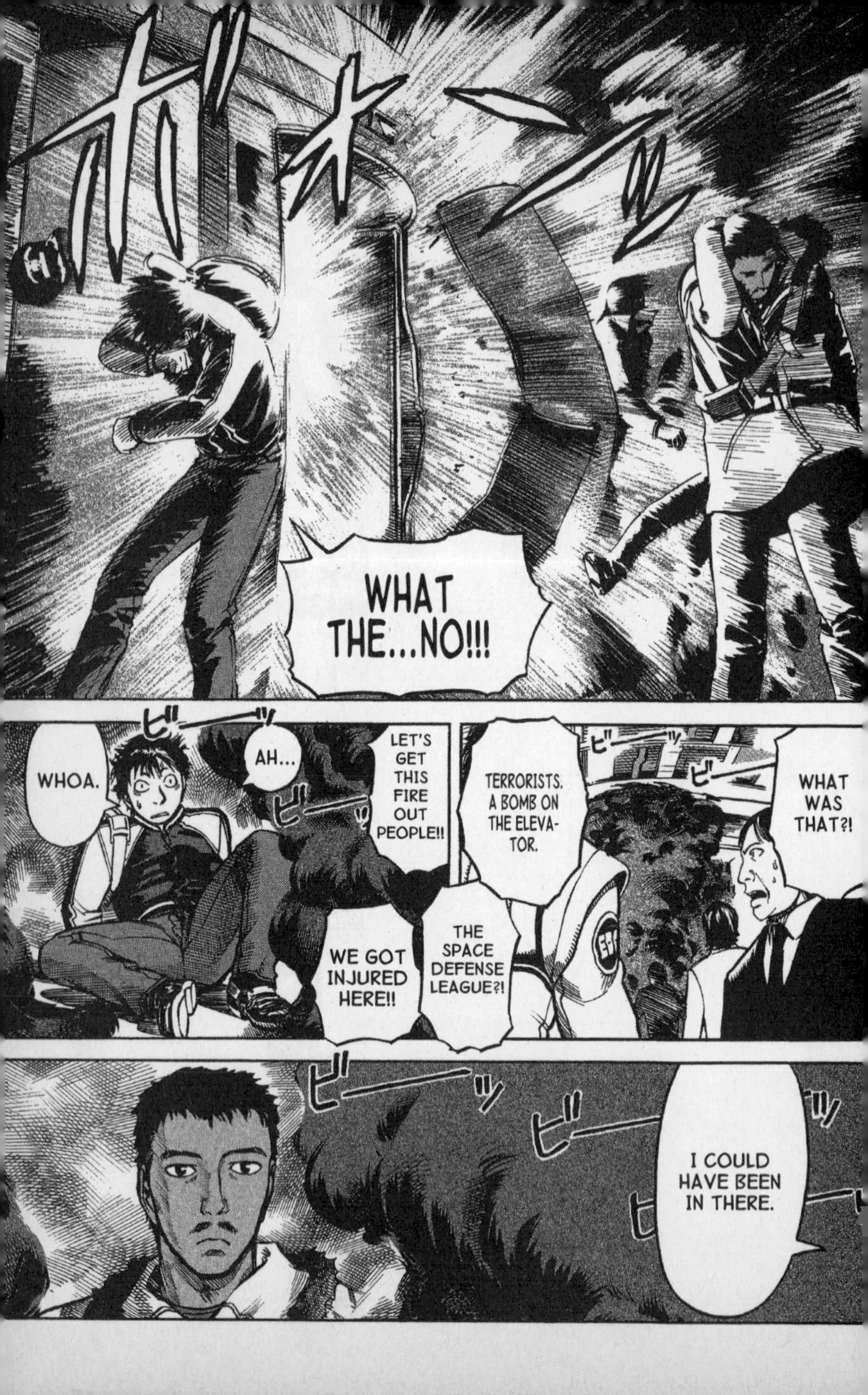
WHAT THE...NO!!!
WHAT WAS THAT?!
TERRORISTS. A BOMB ON THE ELEVATOR.
THE SPACE DEFENSE LEAGUE?!
LET'S GET THIS FIRE OUT PEOPLE!!
WE GOT INJURED HERE!!
AH...
WHOA.
I COULD HAVE BEEN IN THERE.

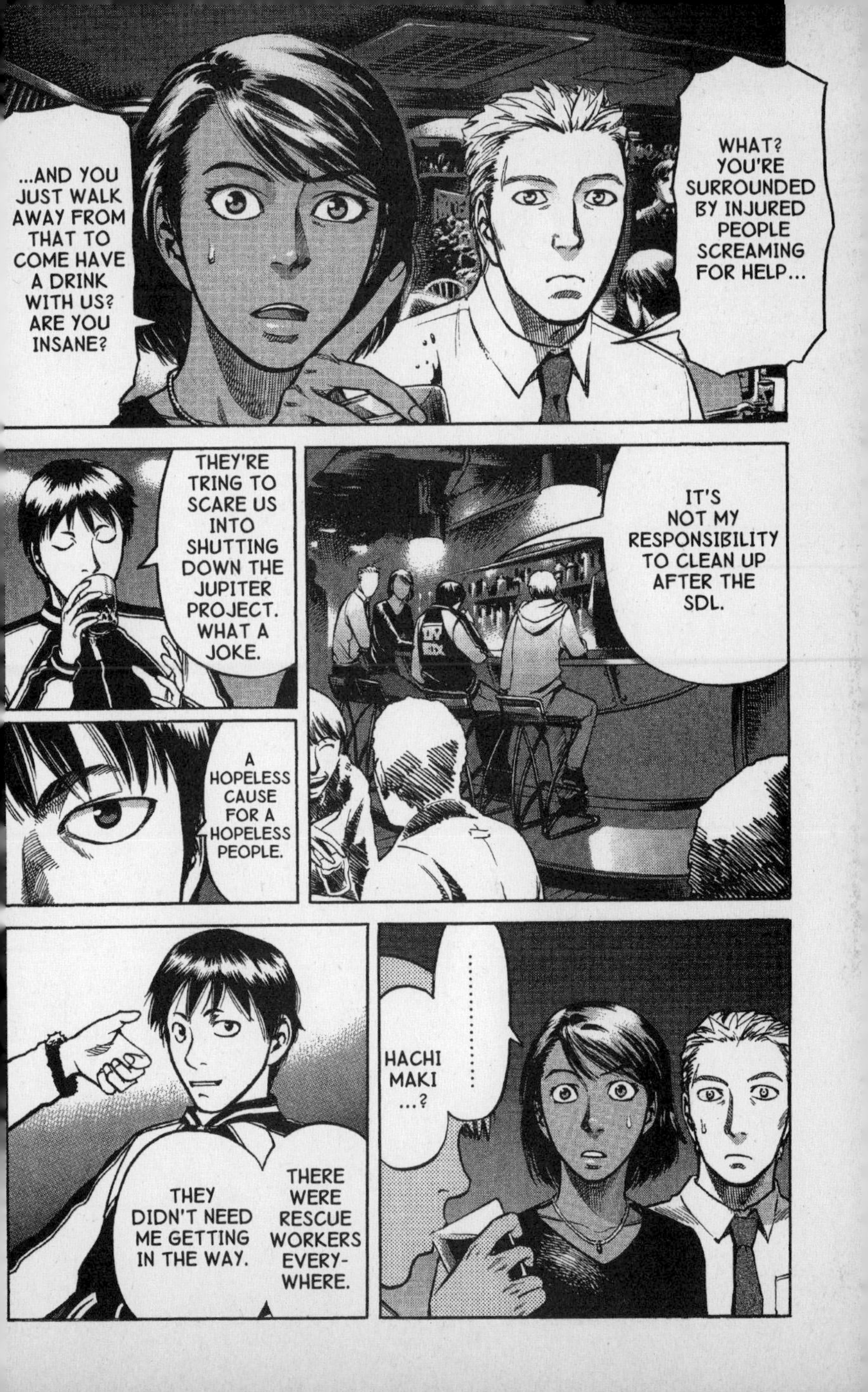
WHAT? YOU'RE SURROUNDED BY INJURED PEOPLE SCREAMING FOR HELP...
...AND YOU JUST WALK AWAY FROM THAT TO COME HAVE A DRINK WITH US? ARE YOU INSANE?
IT'S NOT MY RESPONSIBILITY TO CLEAN UP AFTER THE SDL.
THEY'RE TRING TO SCARE US INTO SHUTTING DOWN THE JUPITER PROJECT. WHAT A JOKE.
A HOPELESS CAUSE FOR A HOPELESS PEOPLE.
....
HACHI MAKI ...?
THERE WERE RESCUE WORKERS EVERY-WHERE.
THEY DIDN'T NEED ME GETTING IN THE WAY.

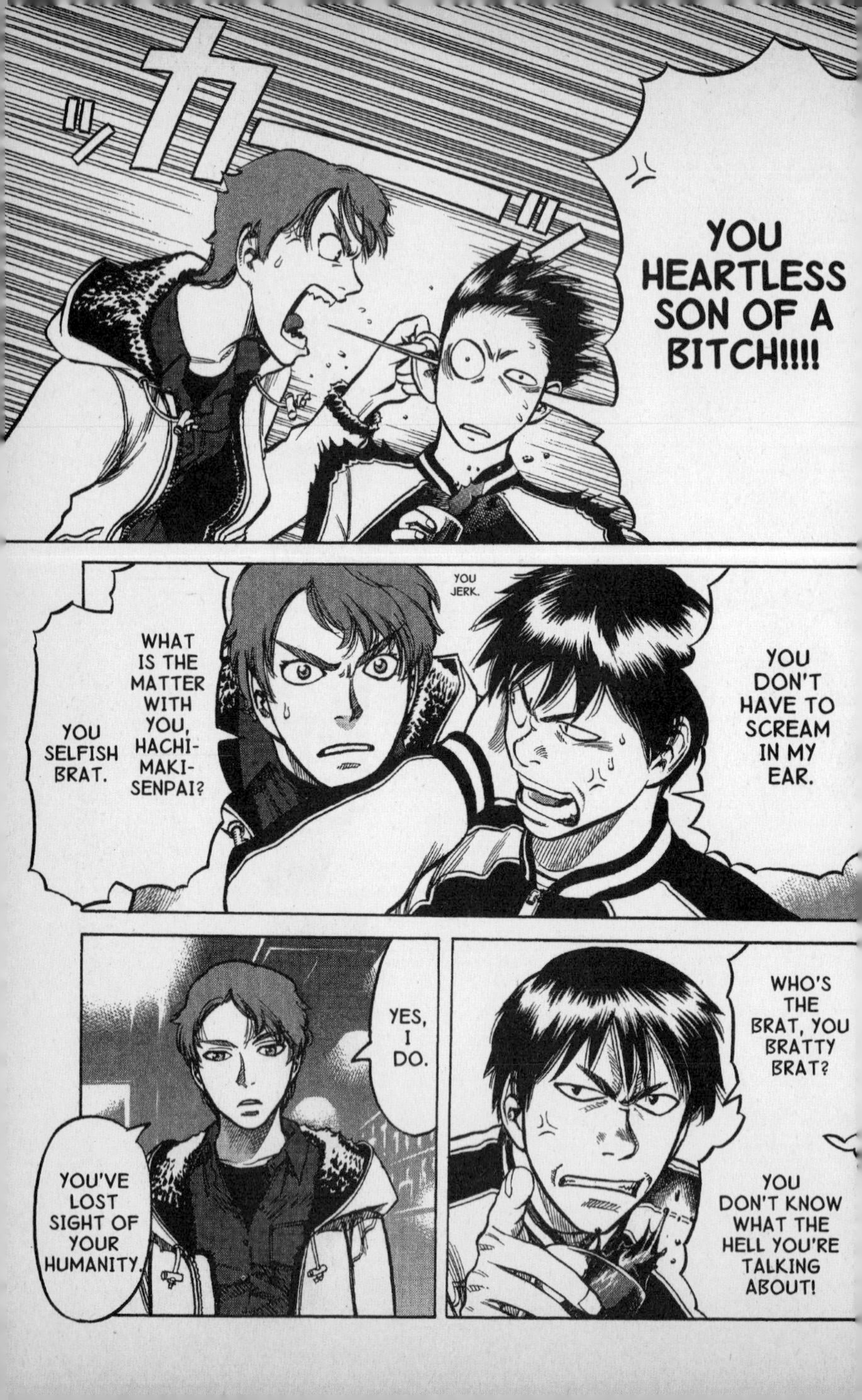
YOU HEARTLESS SON OF A BITCH!!!!
YOU DON'T HAVE TO SCREAM IN MY EAR.
YOU JERK.
WHAT IS THE MATTER WITH YOU, HACHIMAKI-SENPAI?
YOU SELFISH BRAT.
WHO'S THE BRAT, YOU BRATTY BRAT?
YOU DON'T KNOW WHAT THE HELL YOU'RE TALKING ABOUT!
YES, I DO.
YOU'VE LOST SIGHT OF YOUR HUMANITY.

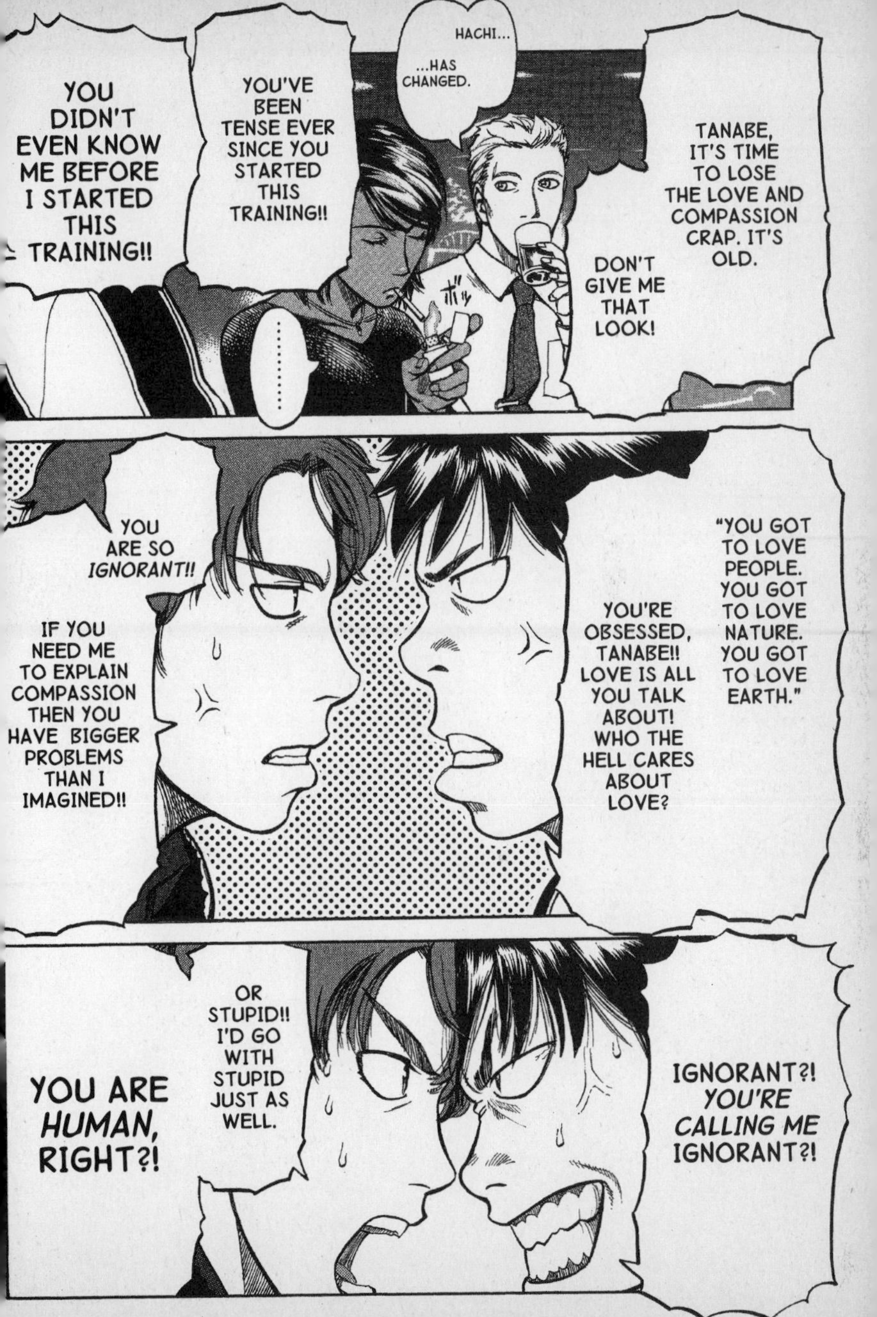
TANABE, IT'S TIME TO LOSE THE LOVE AND COMPASSION CRAP. IT'S OLD.
DON'T GIVE ME THAT LOOK!
HACHI...
...HAS CHANGED.
YOU'VE BEEN TENSE EVER SINCE YOU STARTED THIS TRAINING!!
......
YOU DIDN'T EVEN KNOW ME BEFORE I STARTED THIS TRAINING!!
"YOU GOT TO LOVE PEOPLE. YOU GOT TO LOVE NATURE. YOU GOT TO LOVE EARTH."
YOU'RE OBSESSED, TANABE!! LOVE IS ALL YOU TALK ABOUT! WHO THE HELL CARES ABOUT LOVE?
YOU ARE SO *IGNORANT!!*
IF YOU NEED ME TO EXPLAIN COMPASSION THEN YOU HAVE BIGGER PROBLEMS THAN I IMAGINED!!
IGNORANT?! *YOU'RE CALLING ME* IGNORANT?!
OR STUPID!! I'D GO WITH STUPID JUST AS WELL.
YOU ARE *HUMAN,* RIGHT?!

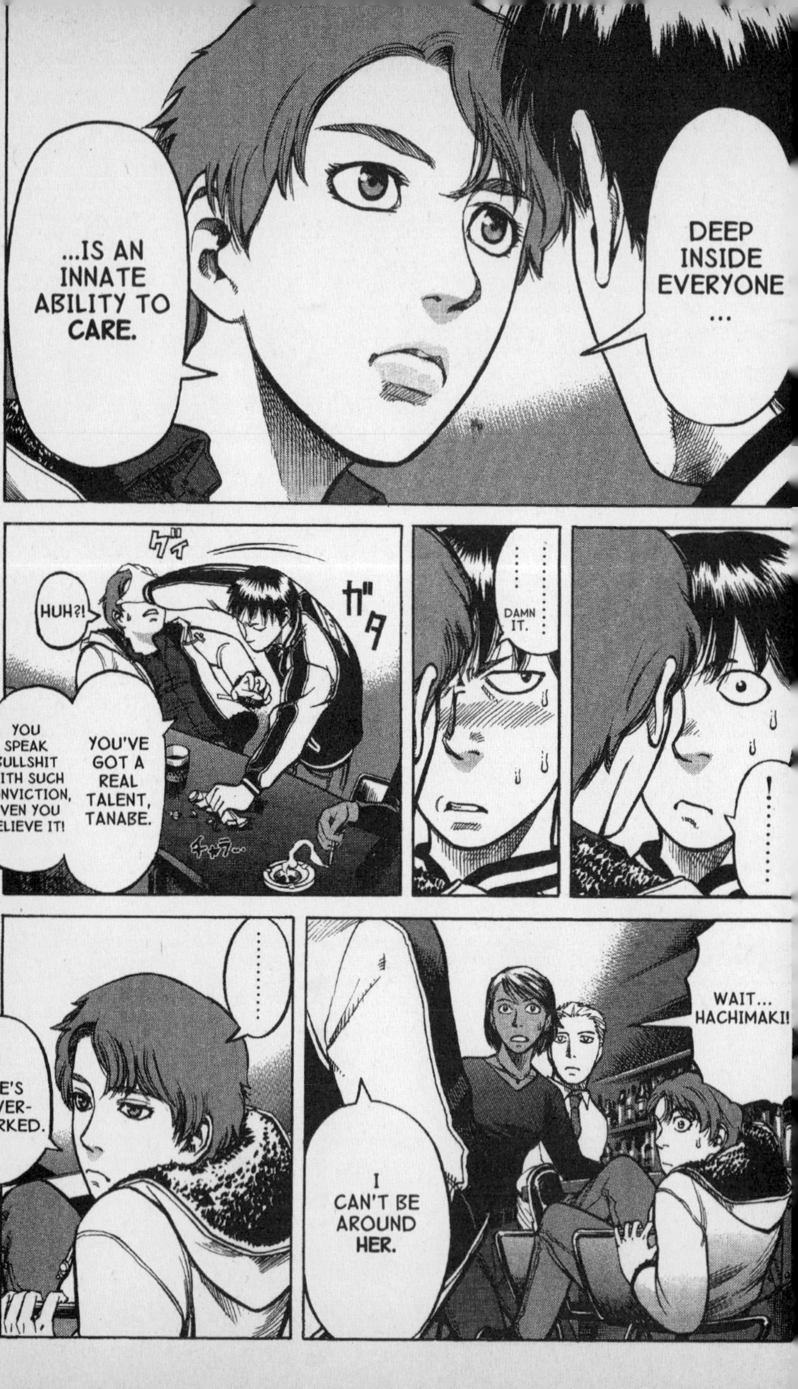
DEEP INSIDE EVERYONE ...
...IS AN INNATE ABILITY TO CARE.
!......
......
DAMN IT.
ガタ
グイ
HUH?!
YOU'VE GOT A REAL TALENT, TANABE.
YOU SPEAK BULLSHIT WITH SUCH CONVICTION, EVEN YOU BELIEVE IT!
チャラ…
WAIT... HACHIMAKI!
I CAN'T BE AROUND HER.
......
HE'S OVER-WORKED.

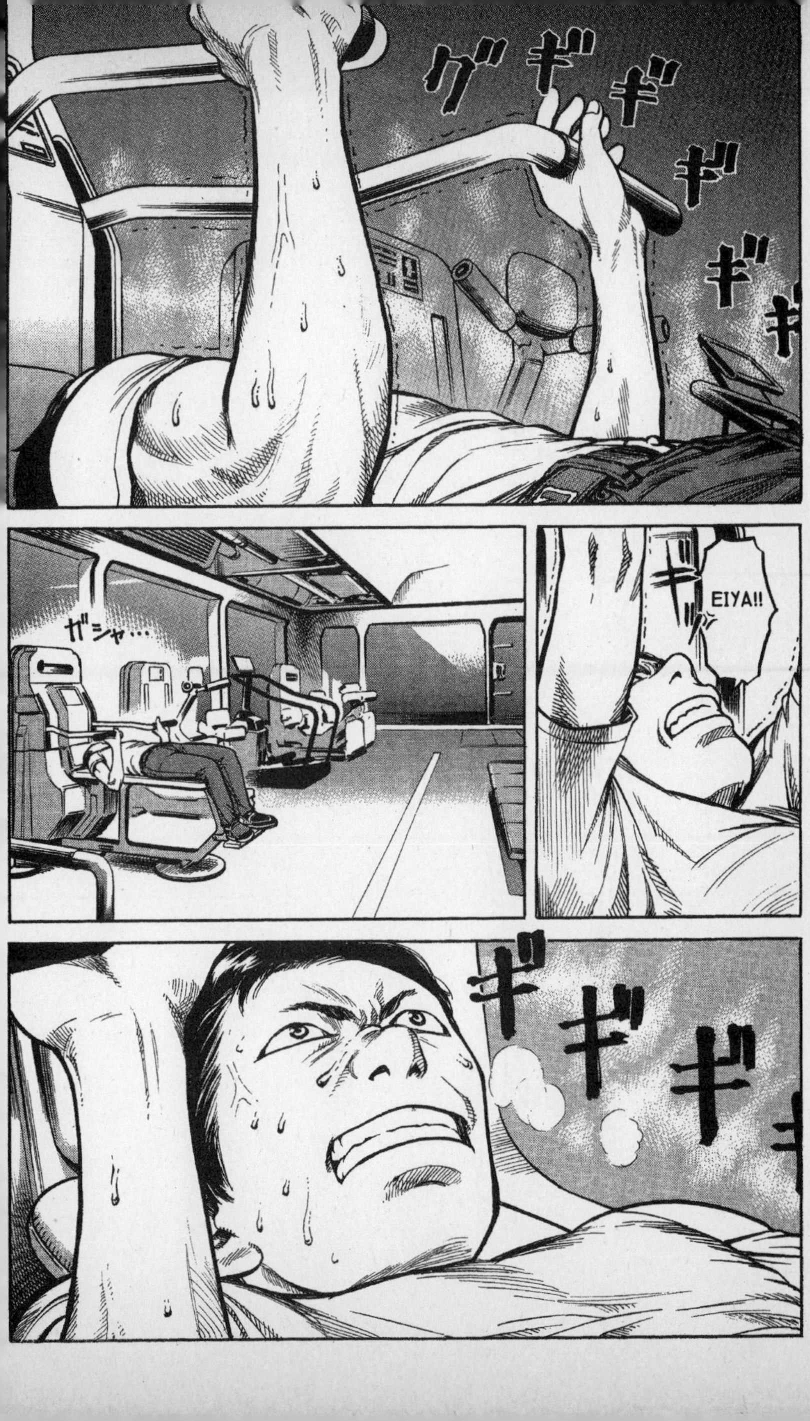
グギギギギギ
ギ
EIYA!!
ガシャ…
ギギギギ

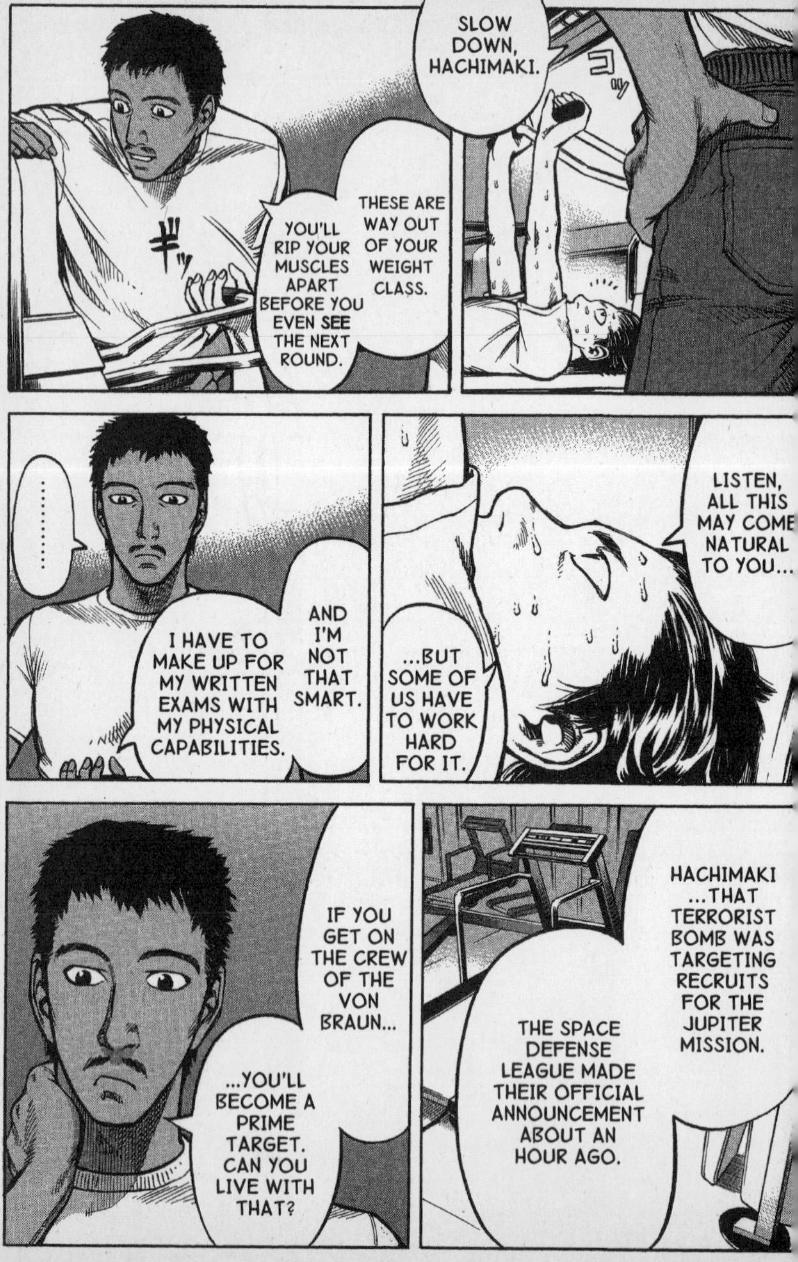
SLOW DOWN, HACHIMAKI.
コッ
THESE ARE WAY OUT OF YOUR WEIGHT CLASS.
YOU'LL RIP YOUR MUSCLES APART BEFORE YOU EVEN SEE THE NEXT ROUND.
ギッ
LISTEN, ALL THIS MAY COME NATURAL TO YOU...
...BUT SOME OF US HAVE TO WORK HARD FOR IT.
......
AND I'M NOT THAT SMART.
I HAVE TO MAKE UP FOR MY WRITTEN EXAMS WITH MY PHYSICAL CAPABILITIES.
HACHIMAKI ...THAT TERRORIST BOMB WAS TARGETING RECRUITS FOR THE JUPITER MISSION.
THE SPACE DEFENSE LEAGUE MADE THEIR OFFICIAL ANNOUNCEMENT ABOUT AN HOUR AGO.
IF YOU GET ON THE CREW OF THE VON BRAUN...
...YOU'LL BECOME A PRIME TARGET. CAN YOU LIVE WITH THAT?

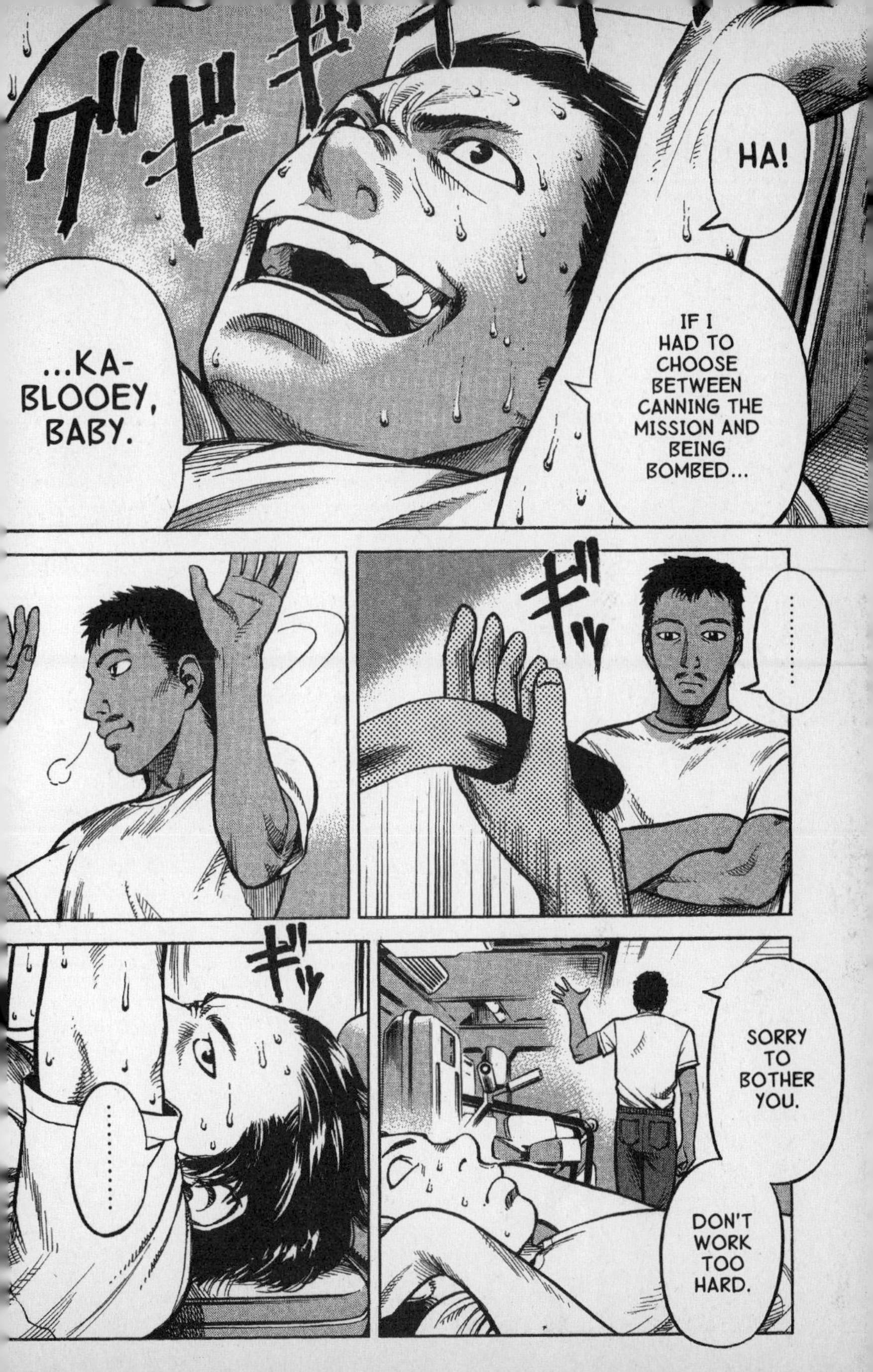
HA!
IF I HAD TO CHOOSE BETWEEN CANNING THE MISSION AND BEING BOMBED...
...KA-BLOOEY, BABY.
ギッ
......
SORRY TO BOTHER YOU.
DON'T WORK TOO HARD.
ギッ
......

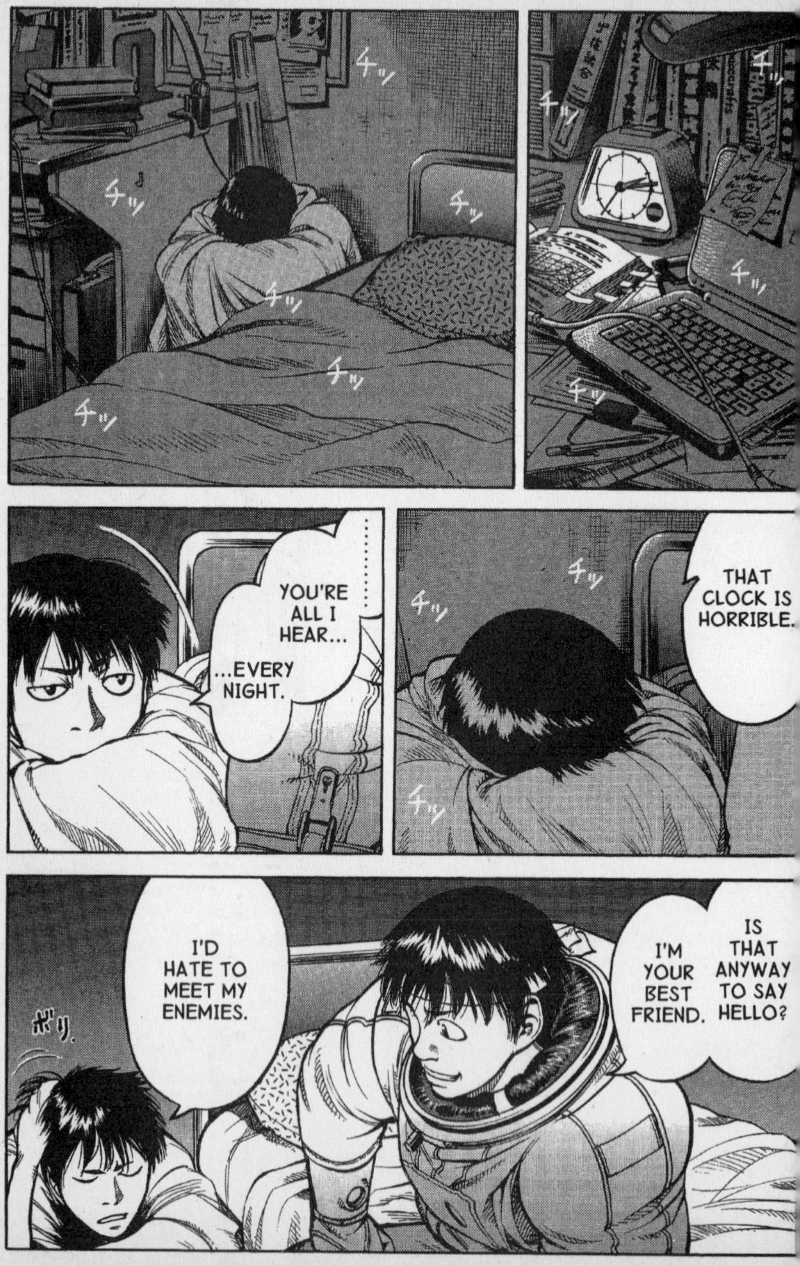
チッ
チッ
チッ
チッ
チッ
チッ
チッ
チッ
チッ
チッ
チッ
チッ
THAT CLOCK IS HORRIBLE.
チッ
チッ
チッ
......
YOU'RE ALL I HEAR...
...EVERY NIGHT.
IS THAT ANYWAY TO SAY HELLO?
I'M YOUR BEST FRIEND.
I'D HATE TO MEET MY ENEMIES.
ボリ.

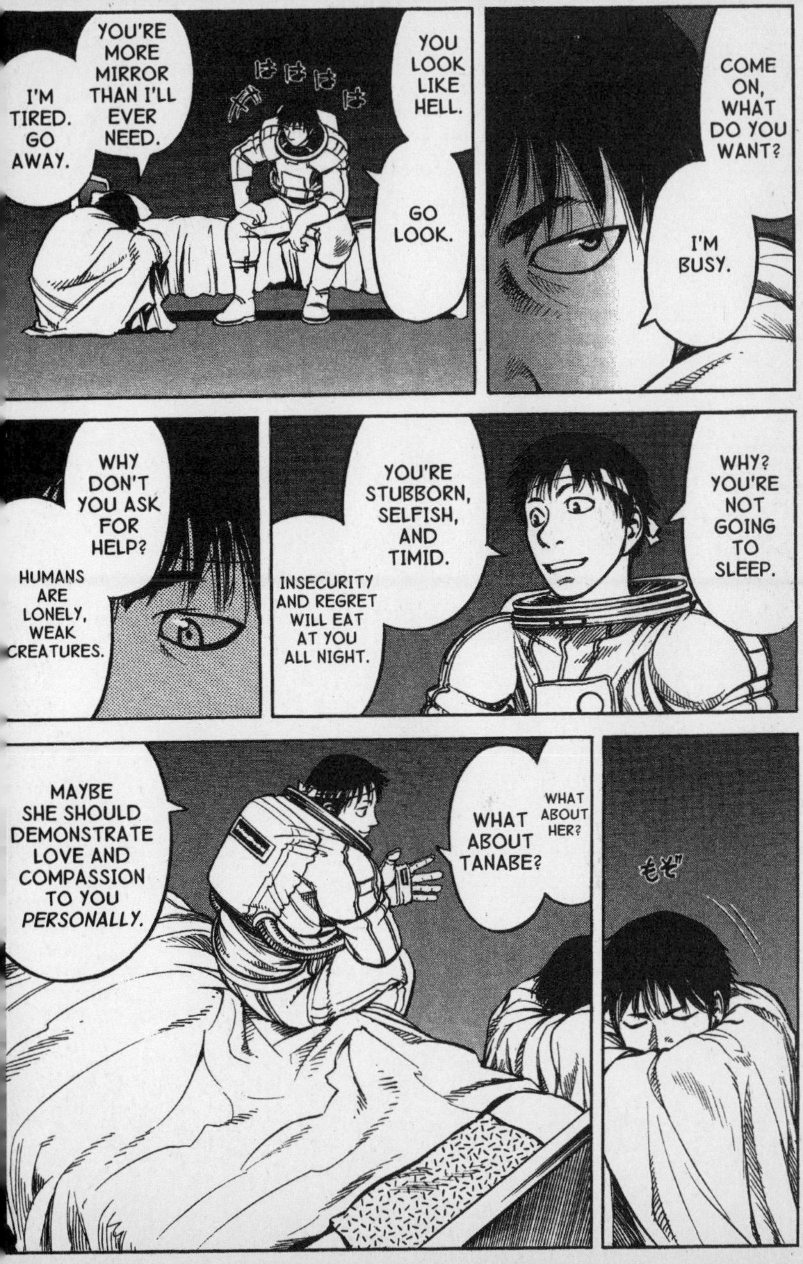
COME ON, WHAT DO YOU WANT?
I'M BUSY.
YOU LOOK LIKE HELL.
GO LOOK.
だはははは
YOU'RE MORE MIRROR THAN I'LL EVER NEED.
I'M TIRED. GO AWAY.
WHY? YOU'RE NOT GOING TO SLEEP.
YOU'RE STUBBORN, SELFISH, AND TIMID.
INSECURITY AND REGRET WILL EAT AT YOU ALL NIGHT.
WHY DON'T YOU ASK FOR HELP?
HUMANS ARE LONELY, WEAK CREATURES.
もぞ
WHAT ABOUT HER?
WHAT ABOUT TANABE?
MAYBE SHE SHOULD DEMONSTRATE LOVE AND COMPASSION TO YOU *PERSONALLY.*

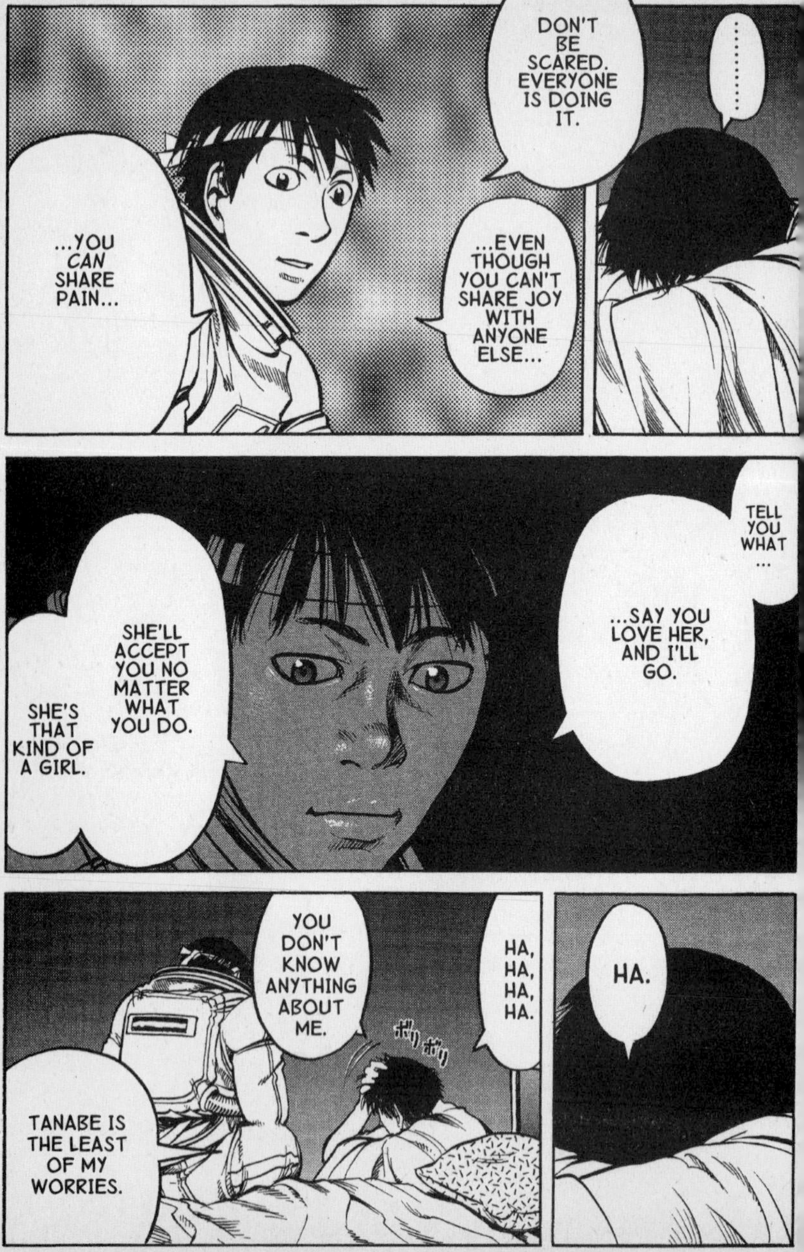
......
DON'T BE SCARED. EVERYONE IS DOING IT.
...EVEN THOUGH YOU CAN'T SHARE JOY WITH ANYONE ELSE...
...YOU *CAN* SHARE PAIN...
TELL YOU WHAT ...
...SAY YOU LOVE HER, AND I'LL GO.
SHE'LL ACCEPT YOU NO MATTER WHAT YOU DO.
SHE'S THAT KIND OF A GIRL.
HA.
HA, HA, HA, HA.
YOU DON'T KNOW ANYTHING ABOUT ME.
ポリ ポリ
TANABE IS THE LEAST OF MY WORRIES.

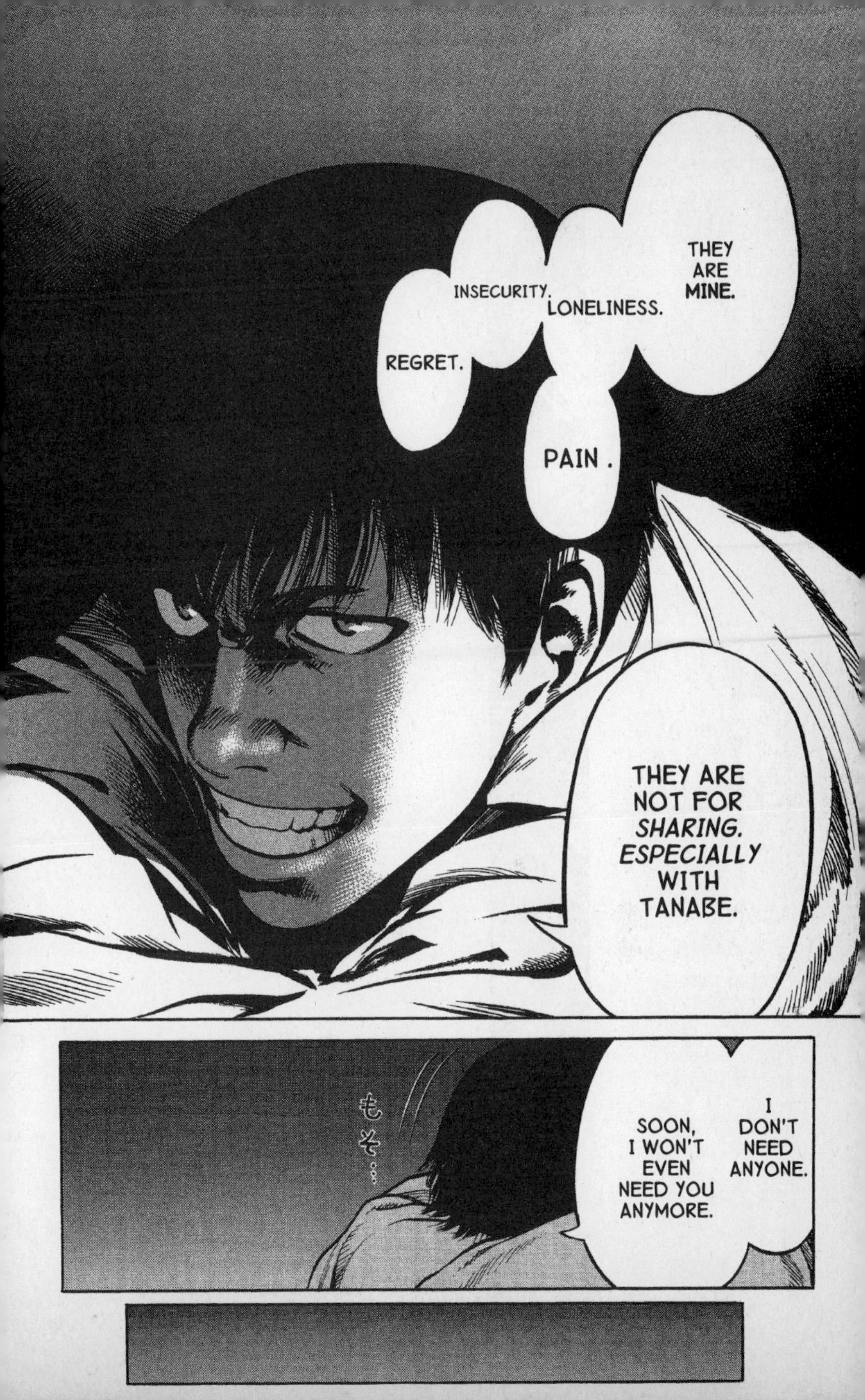
THEY ARE MINE.
LONELINESS.
INSECURITY.
REGRET.
PAIN .
THEY ARE NOT FOR *SHARING. ESPECIALLY* WITH TANABE.
I DON'T NEED ANYONE.
SOON, I WON'T EVEN NEED YOU ANYMORE.
もそ…

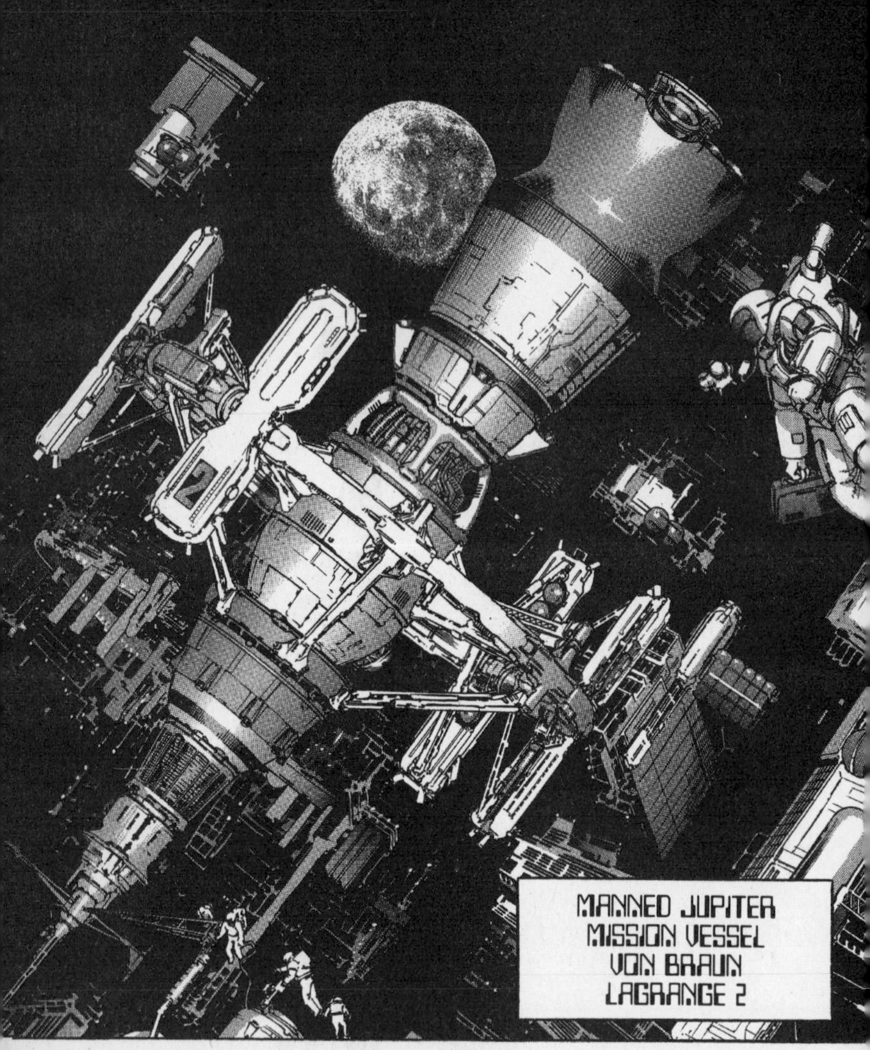
MANNED JUPITER
MISSION VESSEL
VON BRAUN
LAGRANGE 2

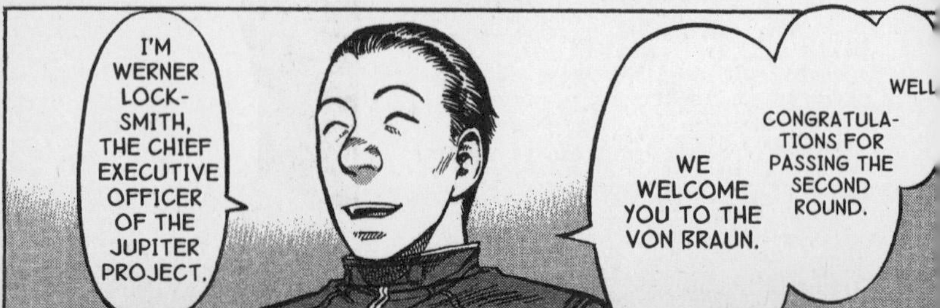
WELL
CONGRATULA-TIONS FOR PASSING THE SECOND ROUND.
WE WELCOME YOU TO THE VON BRAUN.
I'M WERNER LOCK-SMITH, THE CHIEF EXECUTIVE OFFICER OF THE JUPITER PROJECT.

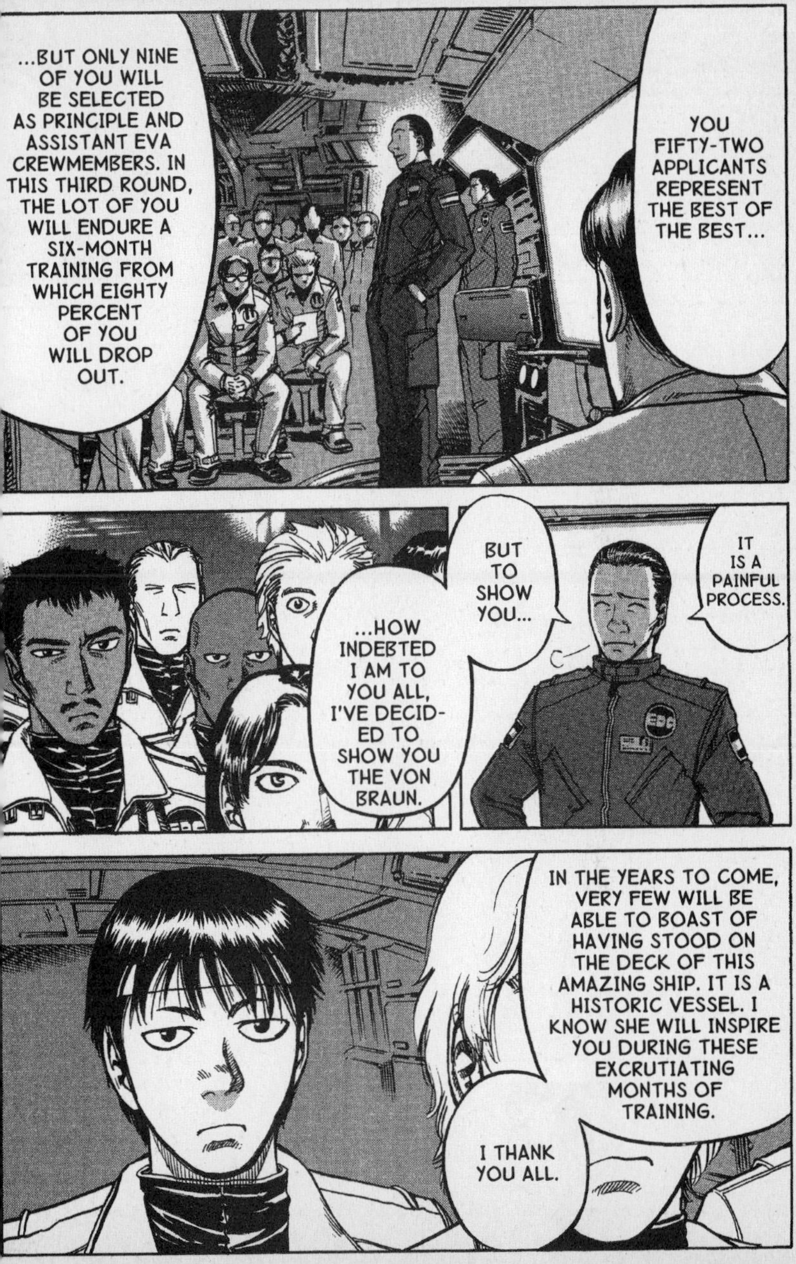
YOU FIFTY-TWO APPLICANTS REPRESENT THE BEST OF THE BEST...
...BUT ONLY NINE OF YOU WILL BE SELECTED AS PRINCIPLE AND ASSISTANT EVA CREWMEMBERS. IN THIS THIRD ROUND, THE LOT OF YOU WILL ENDURE A SIX-MONTH TRAINING FROM WHICH EIGHTY PERCENT OF YOU WILL DROP OUT.
IT IS A PAINFUL PROCESS.
BUT TO SHOW YOU...
...HOW INDEBTED I AM TO YOU ALL, I'VE DECIDED TO SHOW YOU THE VON BRAUN.
IN THE YEARS TO COME, VERY FEW WILL BE ABLE TO BOAST OF HAVING STOOD ON THE DECK OF THIS AMAZING SHIP. IT IS A HISTORIC VESSEL. I KNOW SHE WILL INSPIRE YOU DURING THESE EXCRUTIATING MONTHS OF TRAINING.
I THANK YOU ALL.

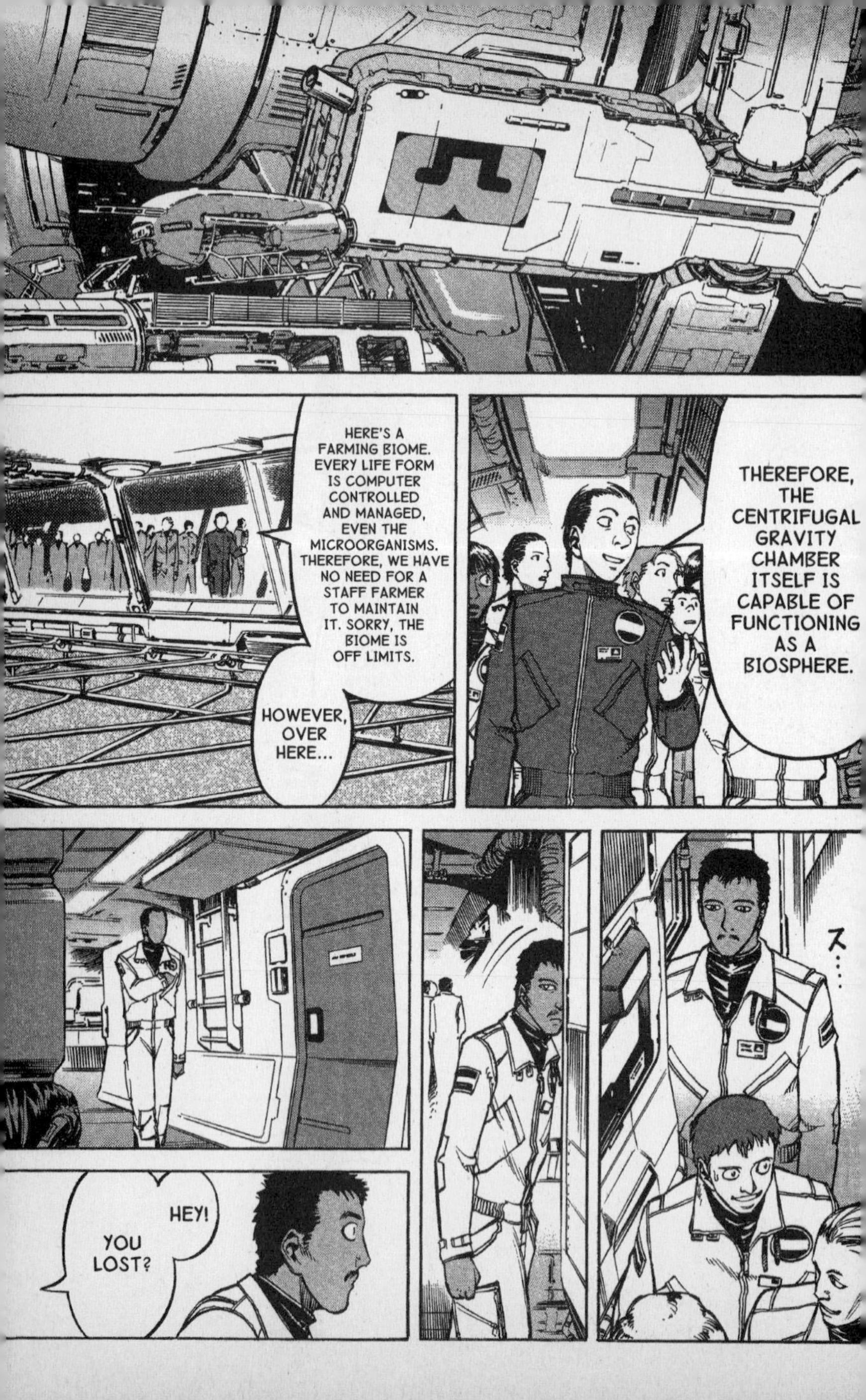
THEREFORE, THE CENTRIFUGAL GRAVITY CHAMBER ITSELF IS CAPABLE OF FUNCTIONING AS A BIOSPHERE.
HERE'S A FARMING BIOME. EVERY LIFE FORM IS COMPUTER CONTROLLED AND MANAGED, EVEN THE MICROORGANISMS. THEREFORE, WE HAVE NO NEED FOR A STAFF FARMER TO MAINTAIN IT. SORRY, THE BIOME IS OFF LIMITS.
HOWEVER, OVER HERE...
ス....
HEY!
YOU LOST?

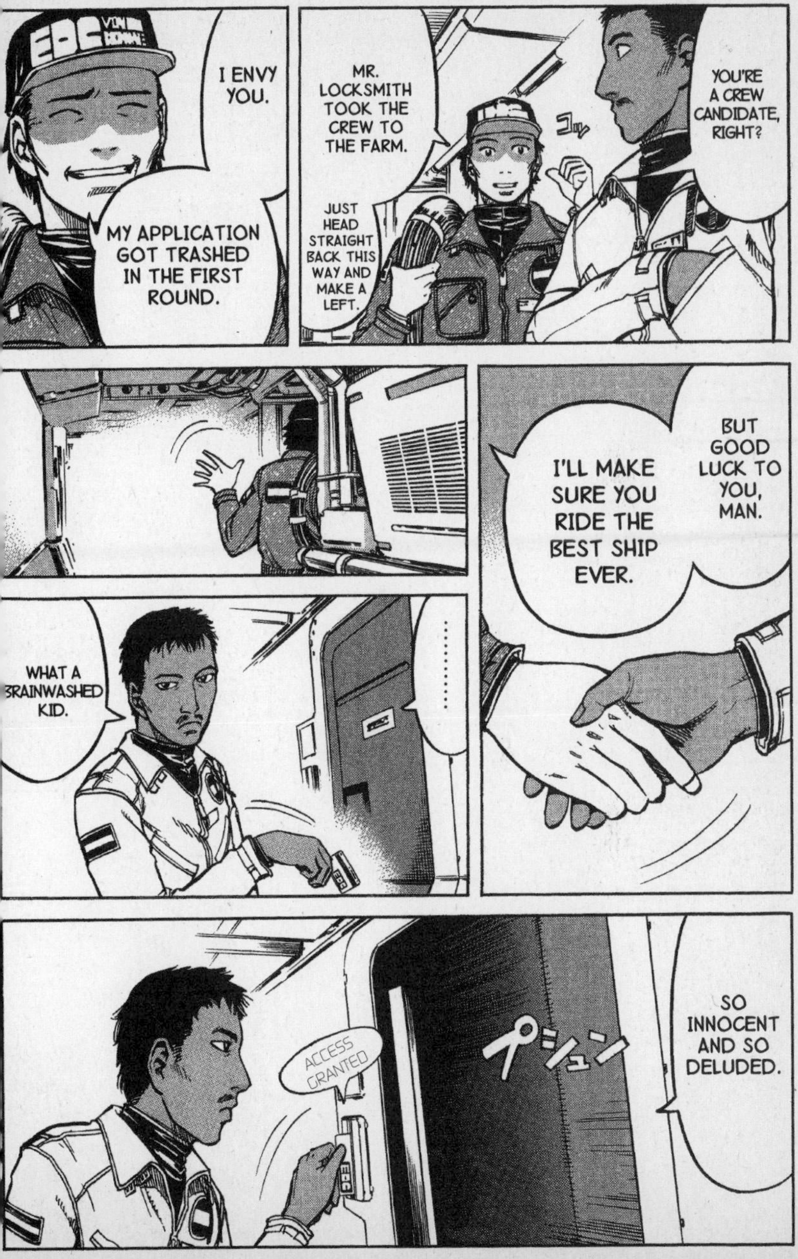
YOU'RE A CREW CANDIDATE, RIGHT?
MR. LOCKSMITH TOOK THE CREW TO THE FARM.
JUST HEAD STRAIGHT BACK THIS WAY AND MAKE A LEFT.
I ENVY YOU.
MY APPLICATION GOT TRASHED IN THE FIRST ROUND.
BUT GOOD LUCK TO YOU, MAN.
I'LL MAKE SURE YOU RIDE THE BEST SHIP EVER.
......
WHAT A BRAINWASHED KID.
SO INNOCENT AND SO DELUDED.
ACCESS GRANTED

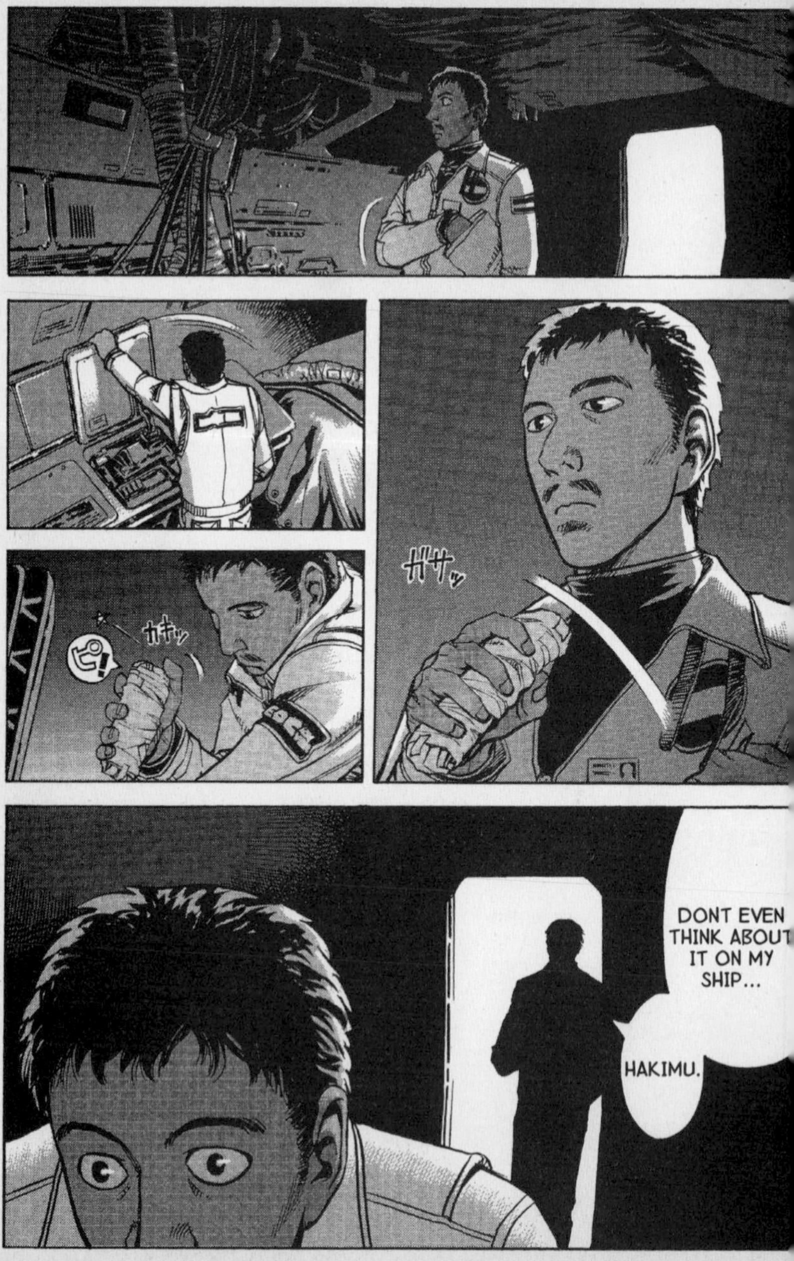
ガサッ
カキッ
ピ!
DONT EVEN THINK ABOUT IT ON MY SHIP...
HAKIMU.

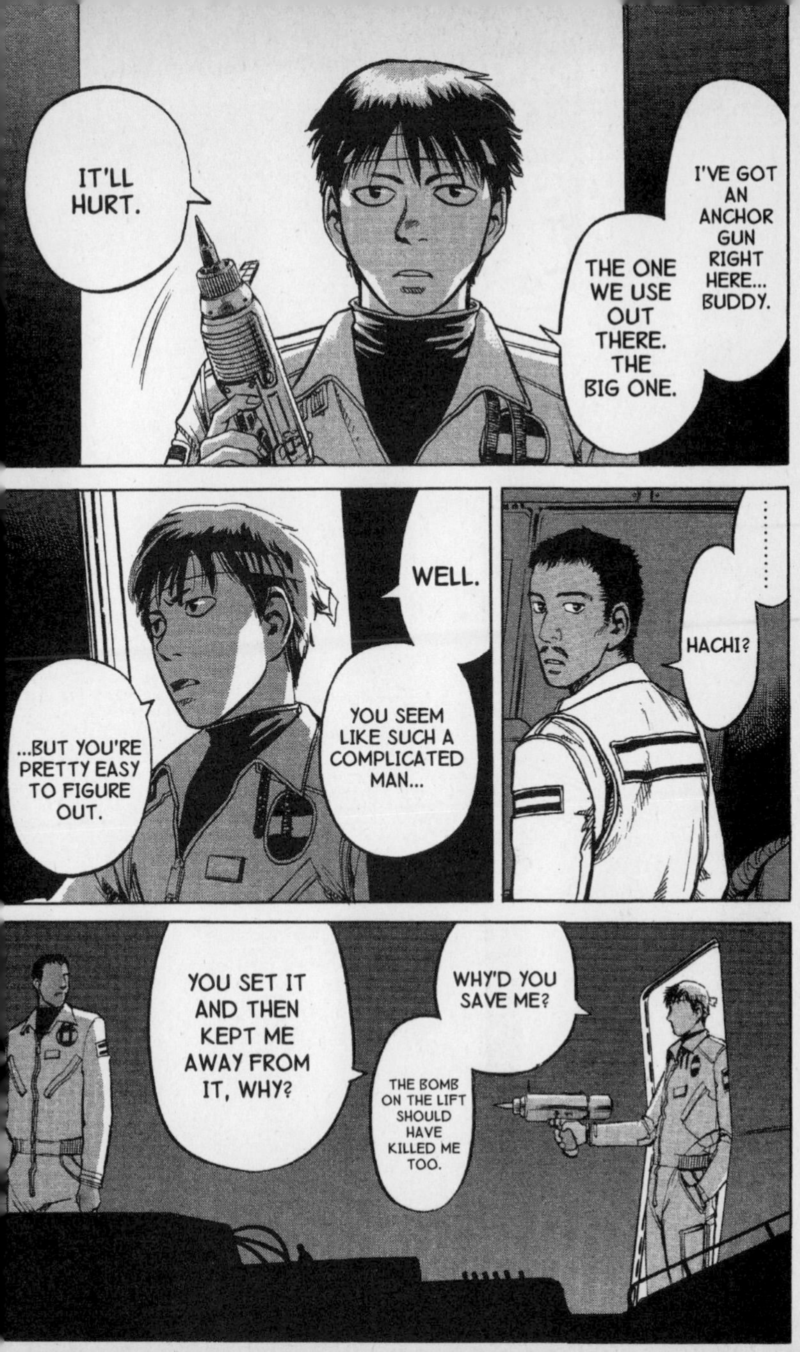
I'VE GOT AN ANCHOR GUN RIGHT HERE... BUDDY.
THE ONE WE USE OUT THERE. THE BIG ONE.
IT'LL HURT.
......
HACHI?
WELL.
YOU SEEM LIKE SUCH A COMPLICATED MAN...
...BUT YOU'RE PRETTY EASY TO FIGURE OUT.
WHY'D YOU SAVE ME?
THE BOMB ON THE LIFT SHOULD HAVE KILLED ME TOO.
YOU SET IT AND THEN KEPT ME AWAY FROM IT, WHY?

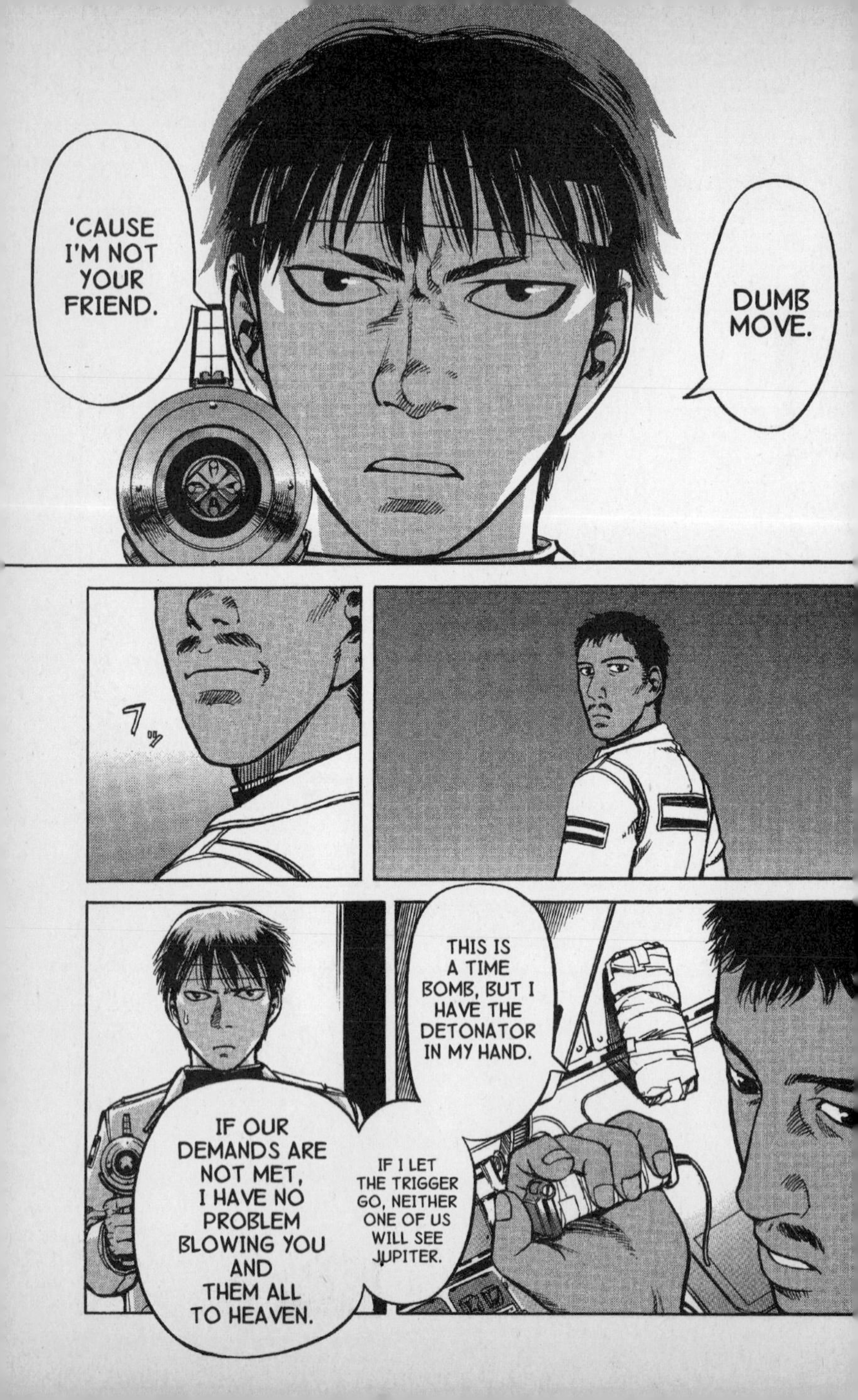
DUMB MOVE.
'CAUSE I'M NOT YOUR FRIEND.
フッ
THIS IS A TIME BOMB, BUT I HAVE THE DETONATOR IN MY HAND.
IF I LET THE TRIGGER GO, NEITHER ONE OF US WILL SEE JUPITER.
IF OUR DEMANDS ARE NOT MET, I HAVE NO PROBLEM BLOWING YOU AND THEM ALL TO HEAVEN.

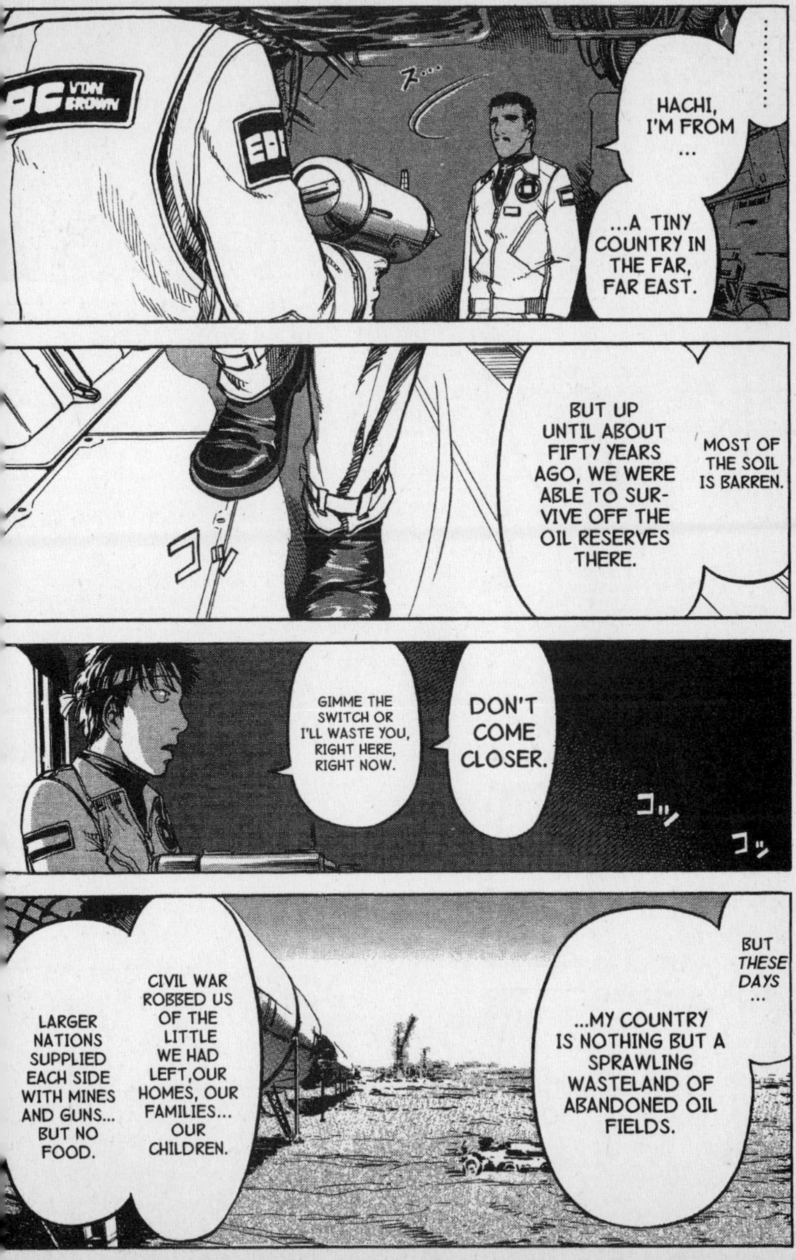
……
HACHI, I'M FROM ...
...A TINY COUNTRY IN THE FAR, FAR EAST.
MOST OF THE SOIL IS BARREN.
BUT UP UNTIL ABOUT FIFTY YEARS AGO, WE WERE ABLE TO SUR-VIVE OFF THE OIL RESERVES THERE.
コッ
DON'T COME CLOSER.
GIMME THE SWITCH OR I'LL WASTE YOU, RIGHT HERE, RIGHT NOW.
コッ
コッ
BUT *THESE* DAYS ...
...MY COUNTRY IS NOTHING BUT A SPRAWLING WASTELAND OF ABANDONED OIL FIELDS.
CIVIL WAR ROBBED US OF THE LITTLE WE HAD LEFT,OUR HOMES, OUR FAMILIES... OUR CHILDREN.
LARGER NATIONS SUPPLIED EACH SIDE WITH MINES AND GUNS... BUT NO FOOD.

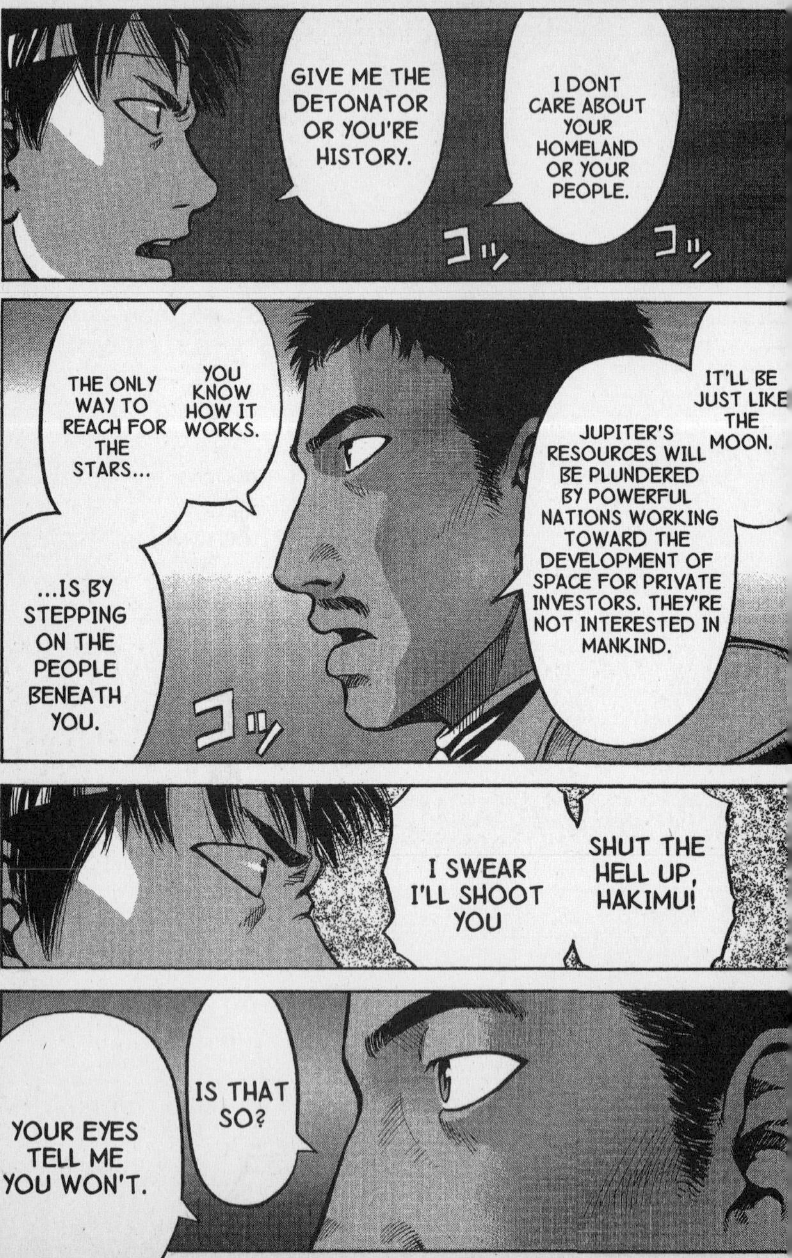
I DONT CARE ABOUT YOUR HOMELAND OR YOUR PEOPLE.
GIVE ME THE DETONATOR OR YOU'RE HISTORY.
コッ
コッ
IT'LL BE JUST LIKE THE MOON.
JUPITER'S RESOURCES WILL BE PLUNDERED BY POWERFUL NATIONS WORKING TOWARD THE DEVELOPMENT OF SPACE FOR PRIVATE INVESTORS. THEY'RE NOT INTERESTED IN MANKIND.
YOU KNOW HOW IT WORKS.
THE ONLY WAY TO REACH FOR THE STARS...
...IS BY STEPPING ON THE PEOPLE BENEATH YOU.
コッ
SHUT THE HELL UP, HAKIMU!
I SWEAR I'LL SHOOT YOU
IS THAT SO?
YOUR EYES TELL ME YOU WON'T.

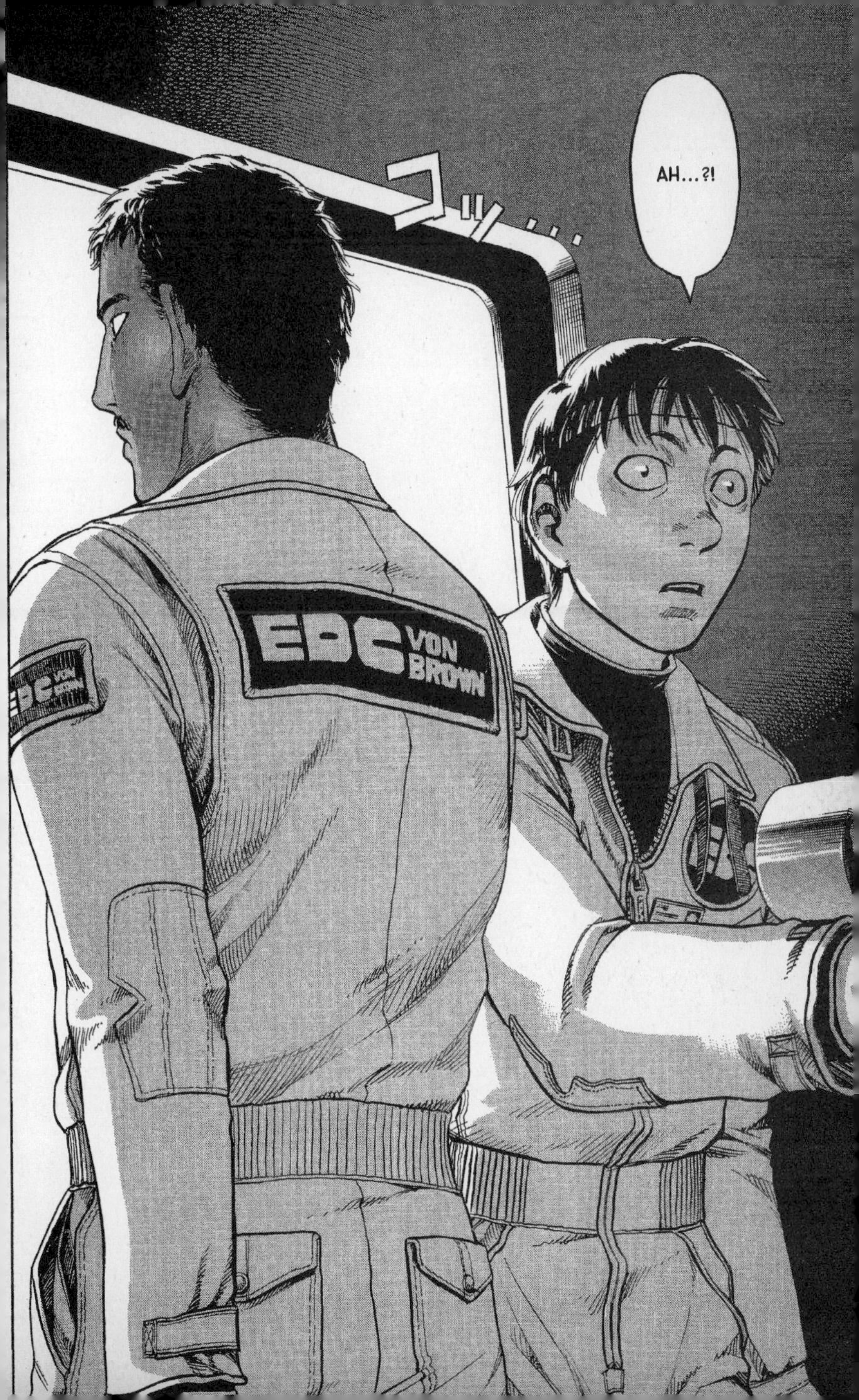
AH...?!
ゴッ...
EDC VON BROWN
EDC VON BROWN

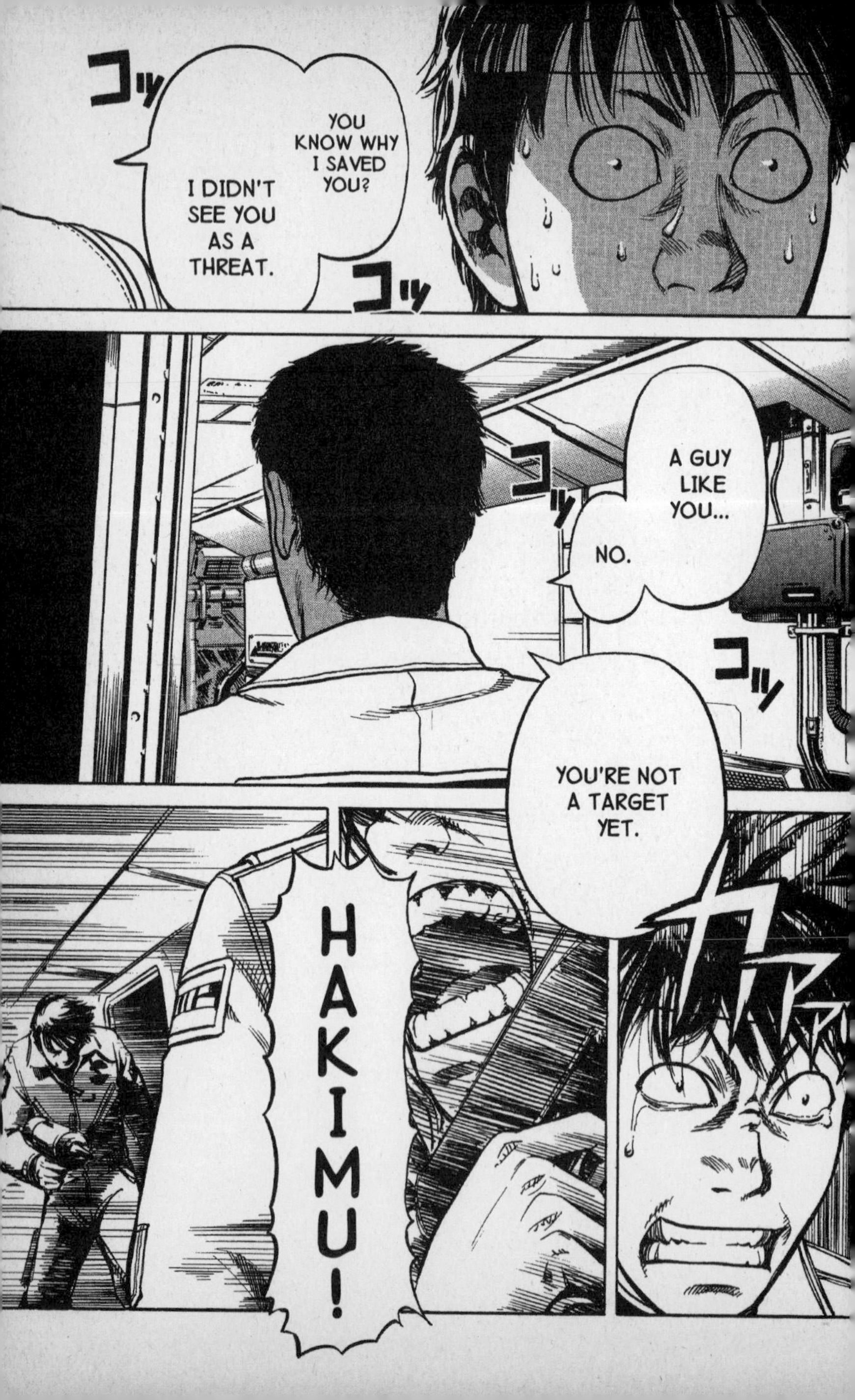
コッ
YOU KNOW WHY I SAVED YOU?
I DIDN'T SEE YOU AS A THREAT.
コッ
A GUY LIKE YOU...
NO.
コッ
コッ
YOU'RE NOT A TARGET YET.
HAKIMU!

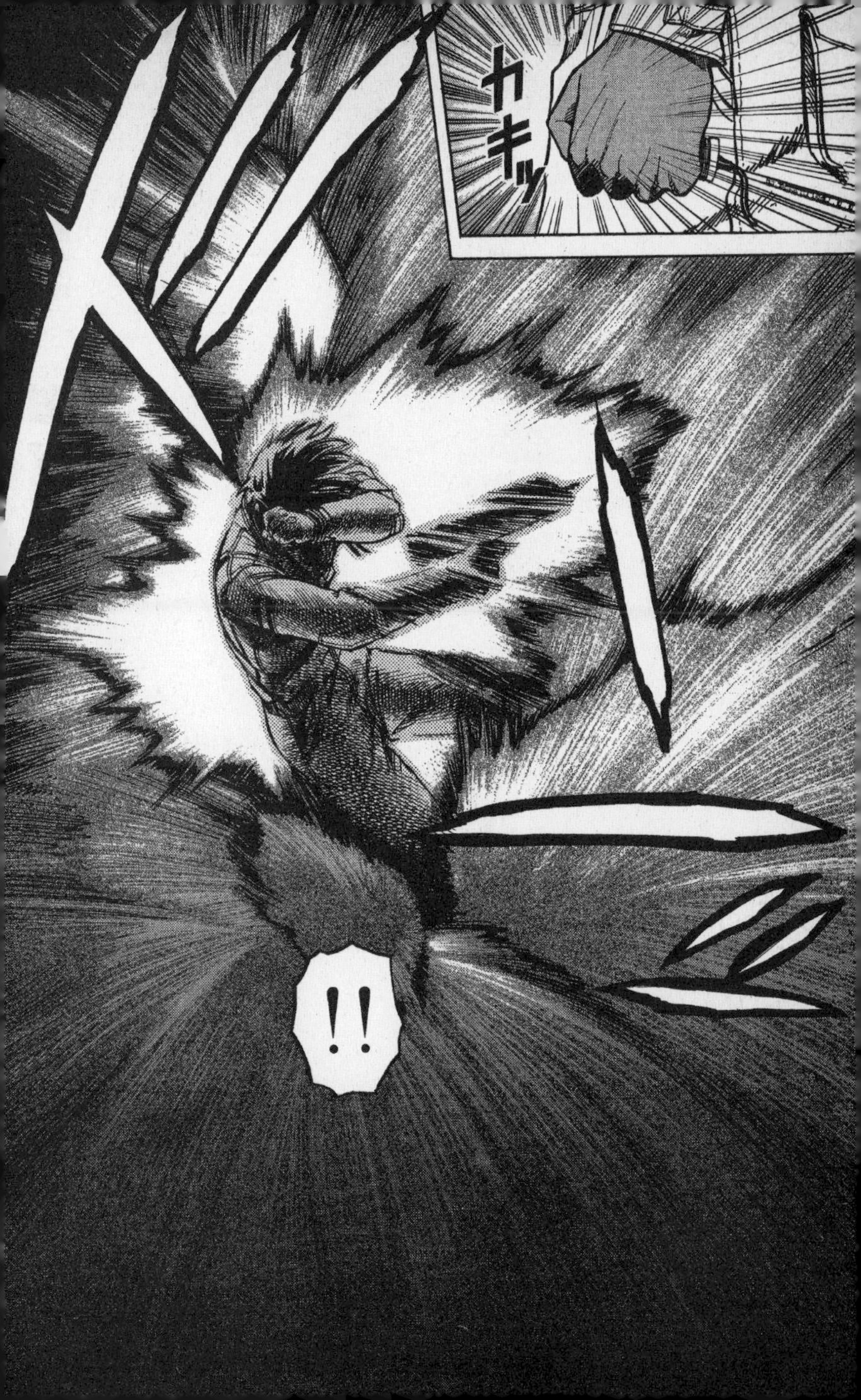
カキッ
!!

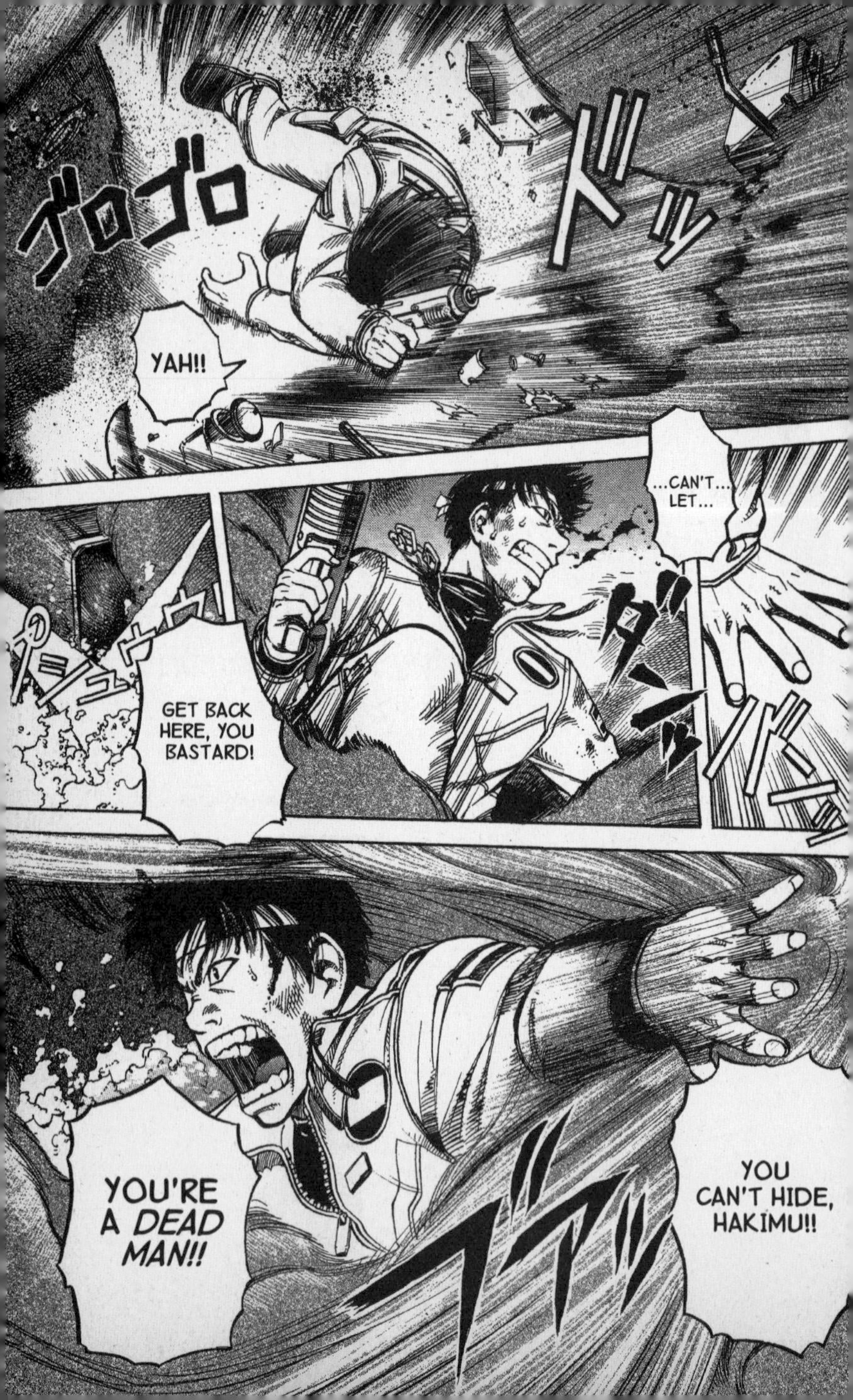
ドドッ
ゴロゴロ
YAH!!
...CAN'T... LET...
ダッ
GET BACK HERE, YOU BASTARD!
YOU CAN'T HIDE, HAKIMU!!
YOU'RE A DEAD MAN!!

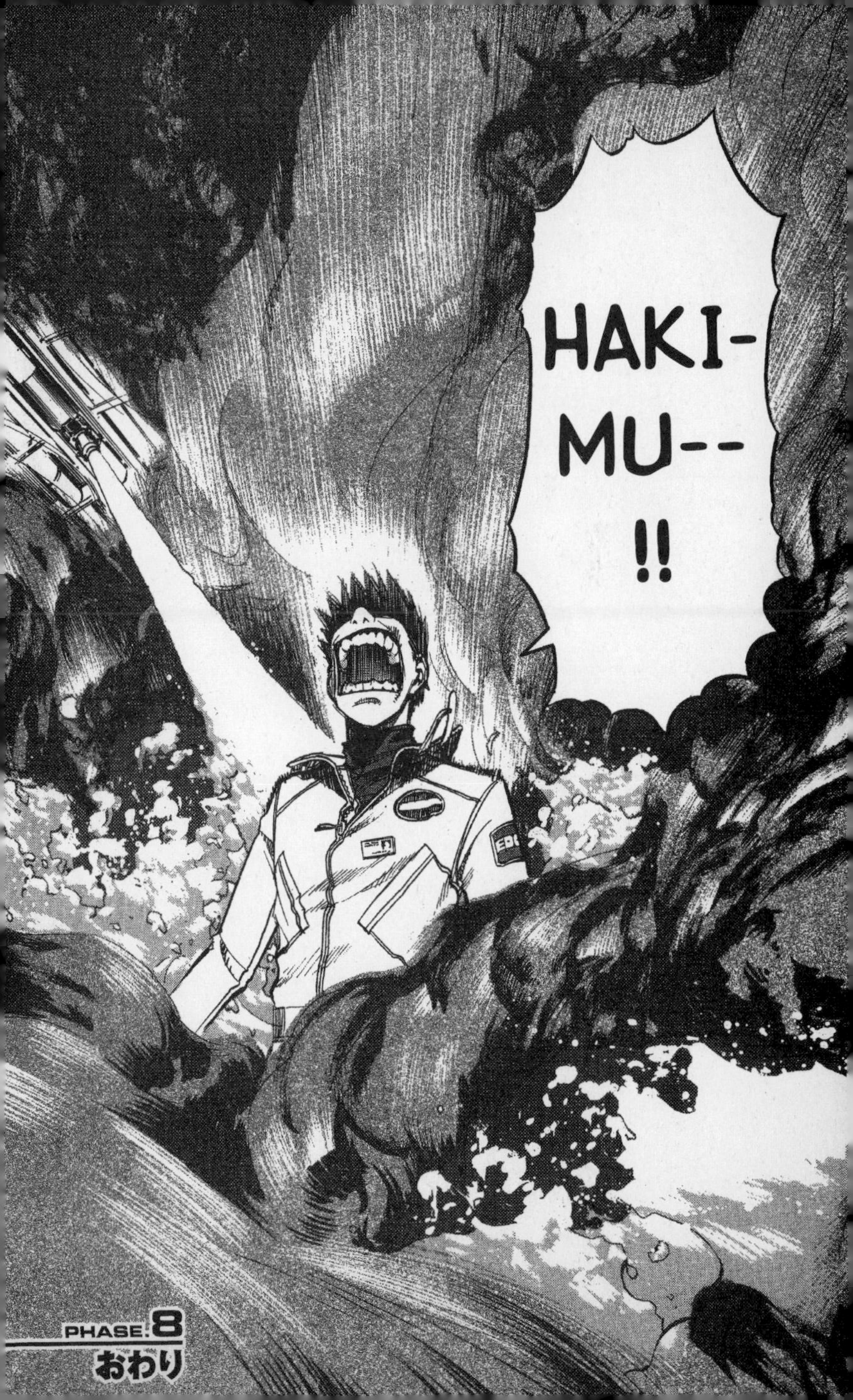
HAKI-
MU--
!!
EBC
PHASE.8
おわり

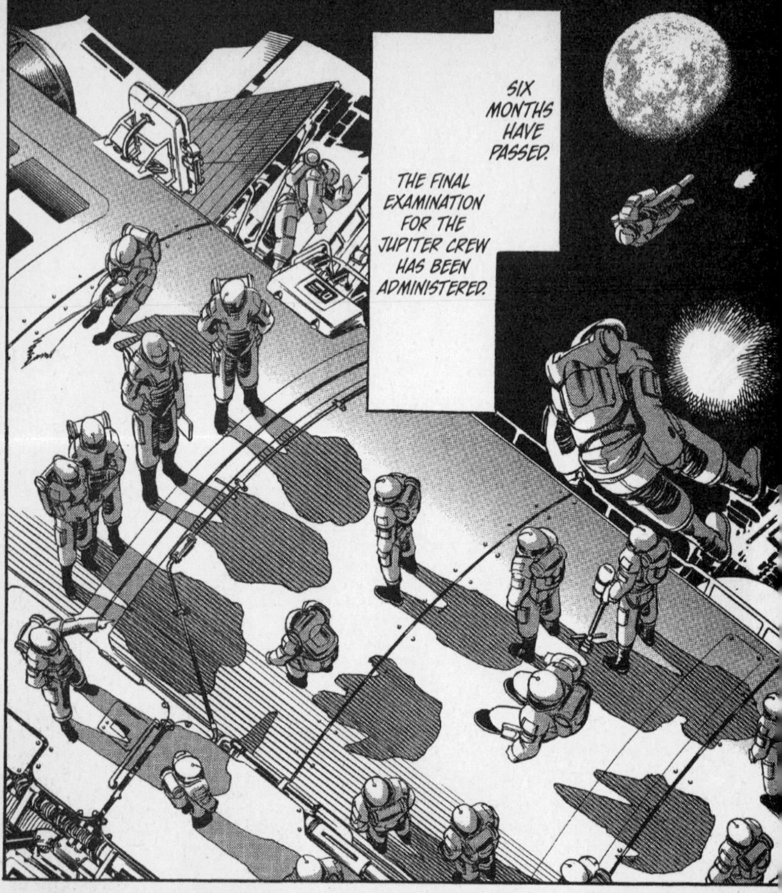
SIX MONTHS HAVE PASSED.
THE FINAL EXAMINATION FOR THE JUPITER CREW HAS BEEN ADMINISTERED.
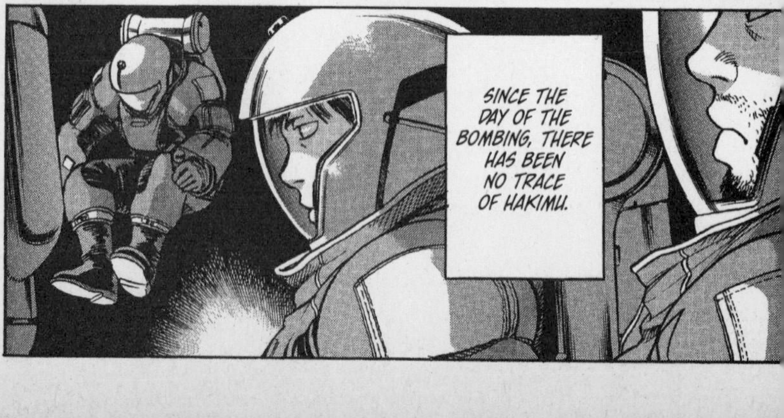
SINCE THE DAY OF THE BOMBING, THERE HAS BEEN NO TRACE OF HAKIMU.

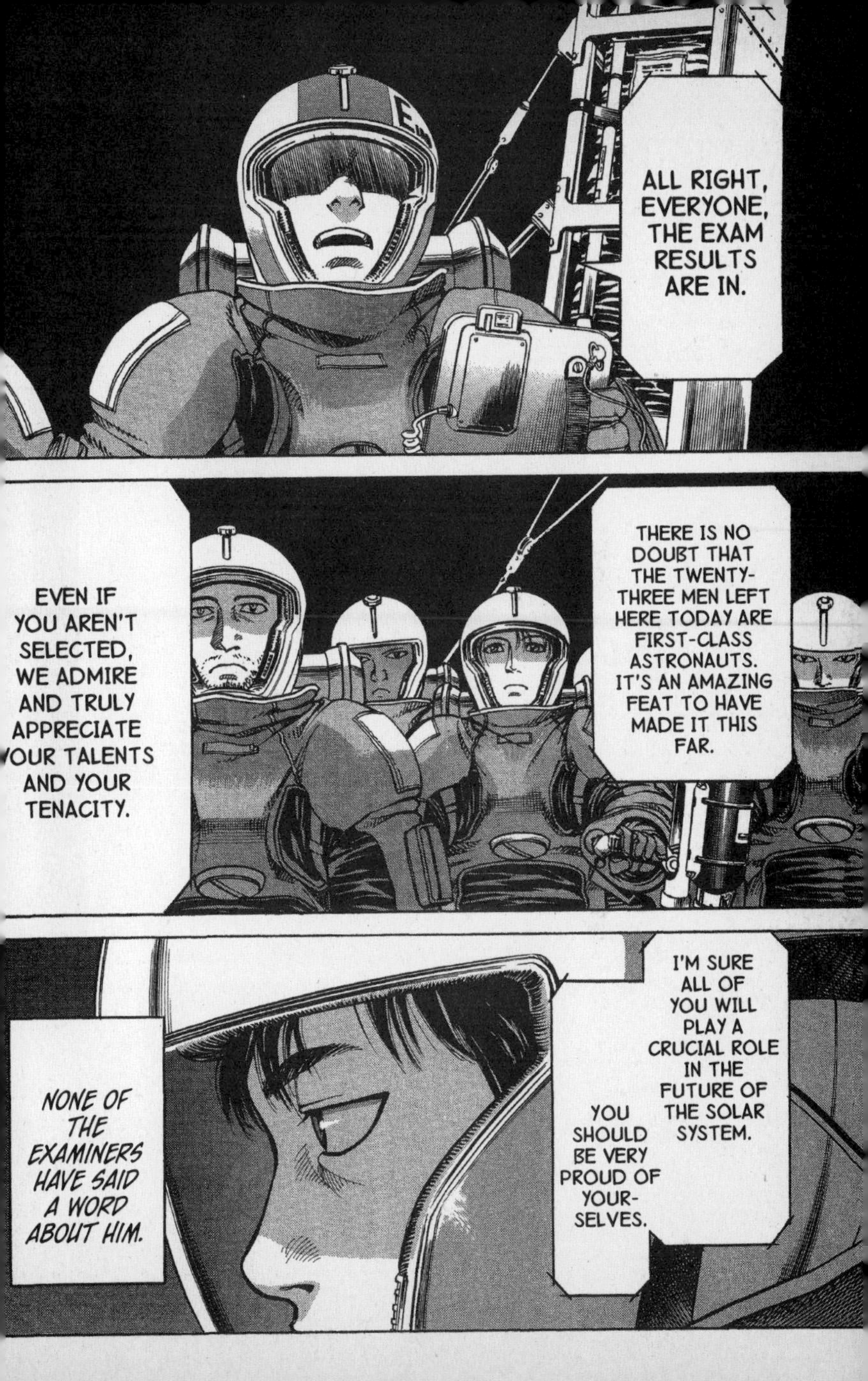
ALL RIGHT, EVERYONE, THE EXAM RESULTS ARE IN.
THERE IS NO DOUBT THAT THE TWENTY-THREE MEN LEFT HERE TODAY ARE FIRST-CLASS ASTRONAUTS. IT'S AN AMAZING FEAT TO HAVE MADE IT THIS FAR.
EVEN IF YOU AREN'T SELECTED, WE ADMIRE AND TRULY APPRECIATE YOUR TALENTS AND YOUR TENACITY.
I'M SURE ALL OF YOU WILL PLAY A CRUCIAL ROLE IN THE FUTURE OF THE SOLAR SYSTEM.
YOU SHOULD BE VERY PROUD OF YOURSELVES.
NONE OF THE EXAMINERS HAVE SAID A WORD ABOUT HIM.

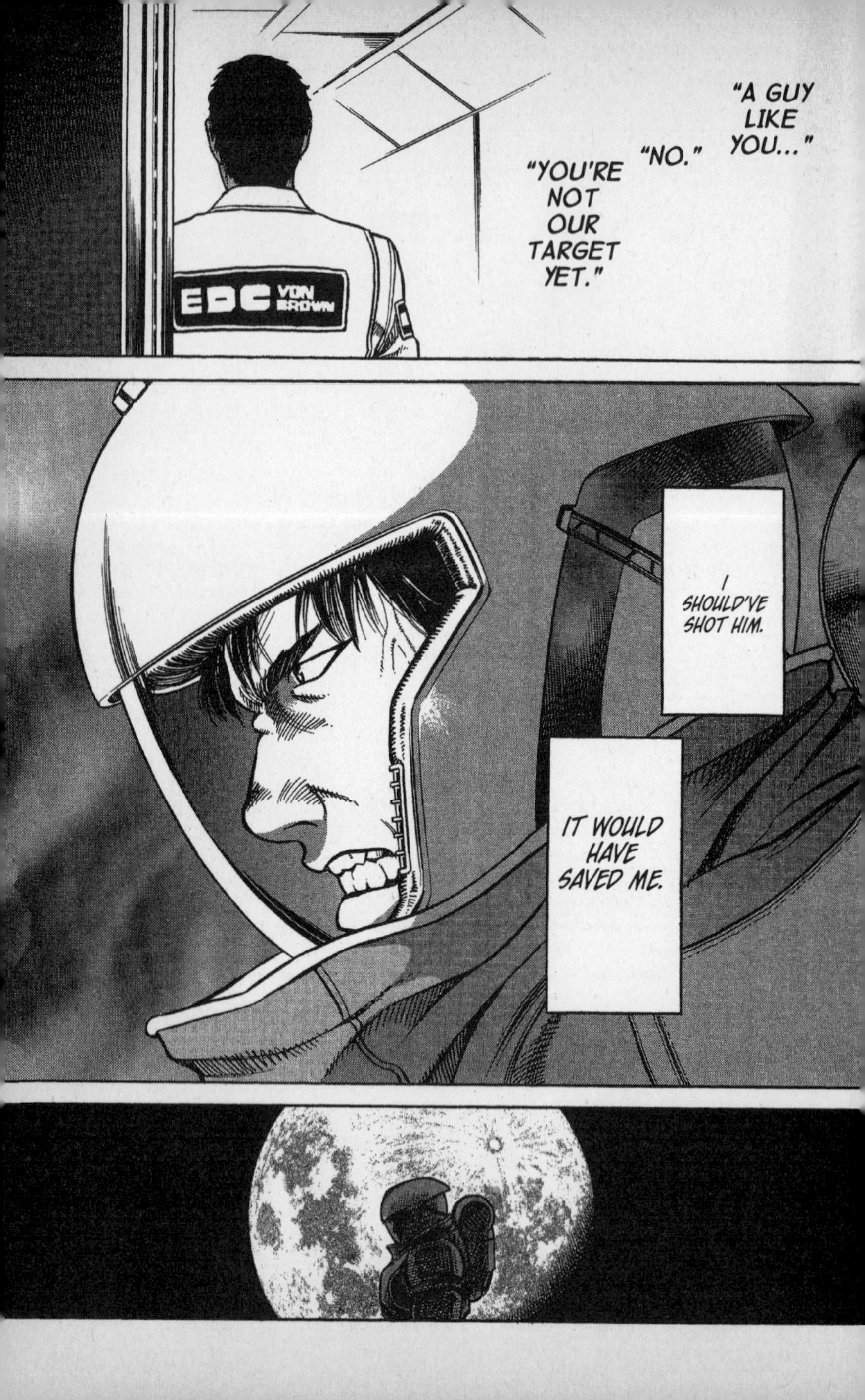
"A GUY LIKE YOU..."
"NO."
"YOU'RE NOT OUR TARGET YET."
EDC VON BROWN
I SHOULD'VE SHOT HIM.
IT WOULD HAVE SAVED ME.

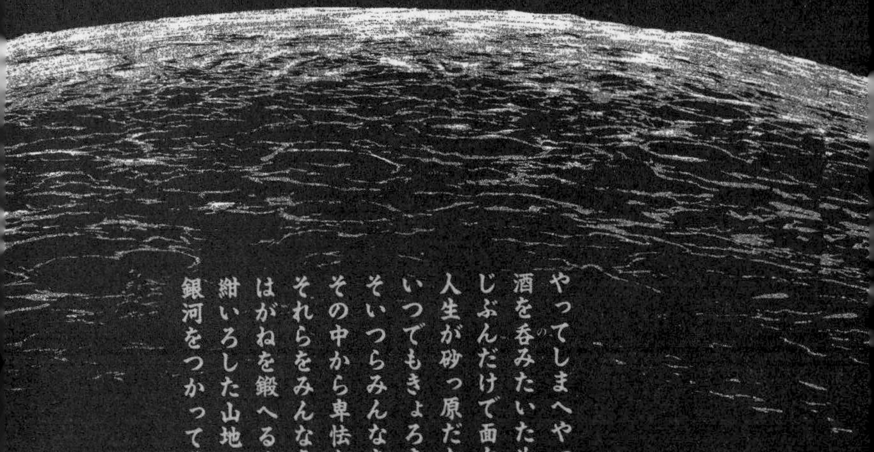

やってしまへやってしまへ
酒を呑(の)みたいために尤(もっと)もらしい波瀾(はらん)を起すやつも
じぶんだけで面白いことをしつくして
人生が砂っ原だなんていふにせ教師も
いつでもきょろきょろひとと自分とくらべるやつらも
そいつらみんなをびしゃびしゃに叩きつけて
その中から卑怯な鬼どもを追ひ払へ
それらをみんな魚や豚につかせてしまへ
はがねを鍛へるやうに新らしい世代は新らしい人間を鍛へる
紺いろした山地の稜をも砕け
銀河をつかって発電所もつくれ

宮沢賢二「サキノハカといふ黒い花といっしょに」より一部抜粋

PHASE.

9

A BLACK FLOWER NAMED SAKINOHAKA (PART 2)

A POEM BY KENJI MIYAZAWA

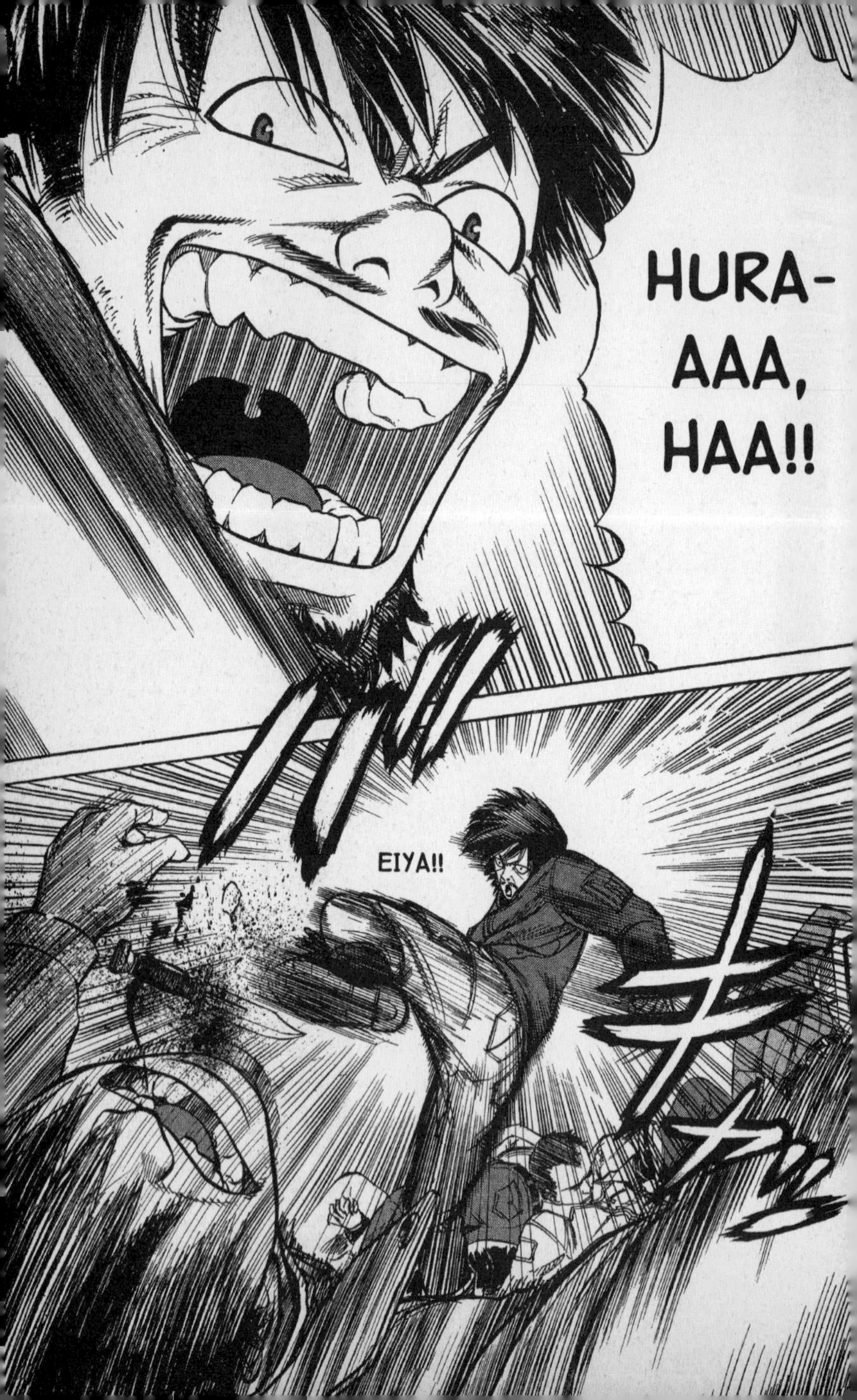
HURA-
AAA,
HAA!!
EIYA!!

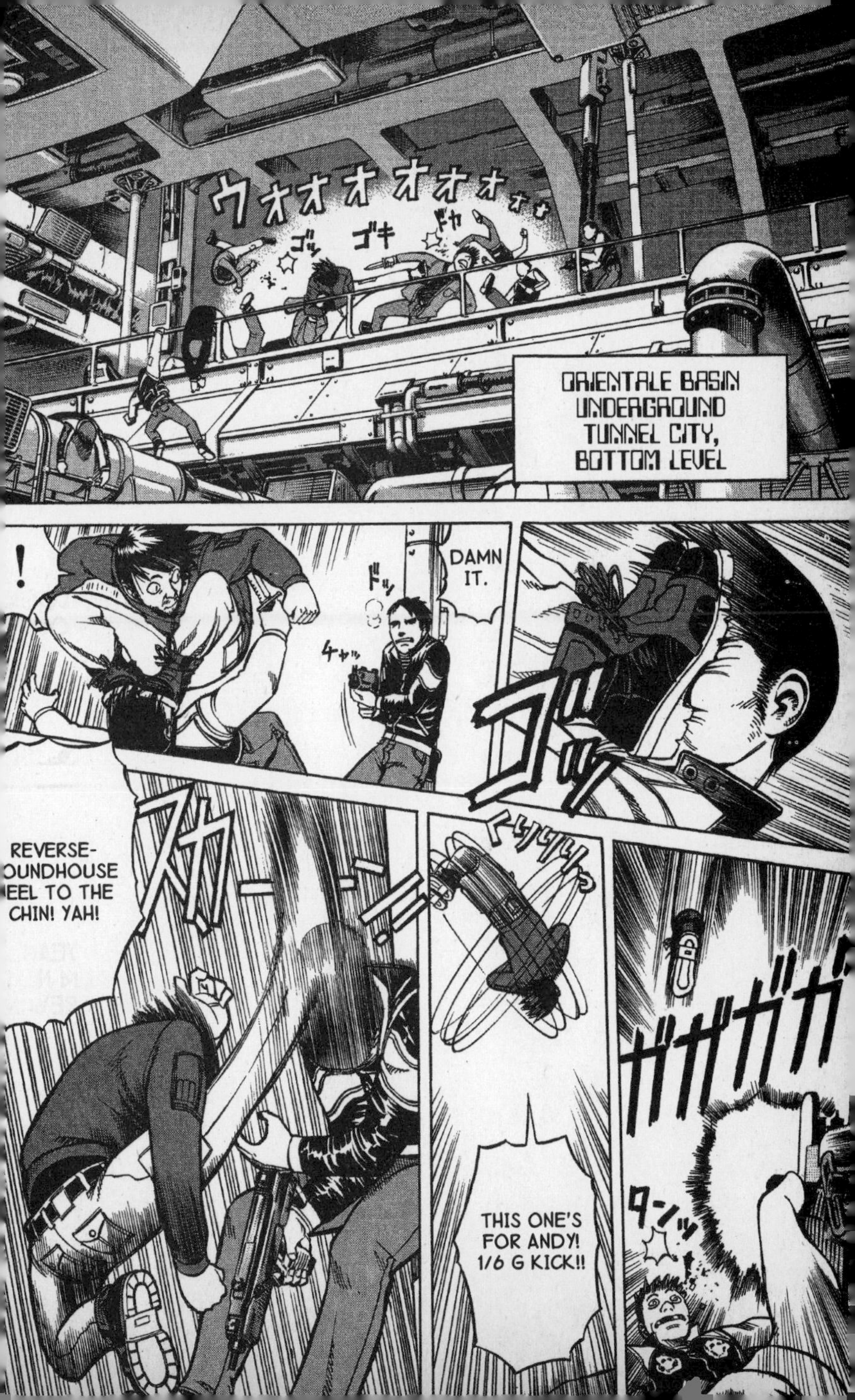
ORIENTALE BASIN UNDERGROUND TUNNEL CITY, BOTTOM LEVEL
DAMN IT.
!
THIS ONE'S FOR ANDY! 1/6 G KICK!!
REVERSE- OUNDHOUSE EEL TO THE CHIN! YAH!

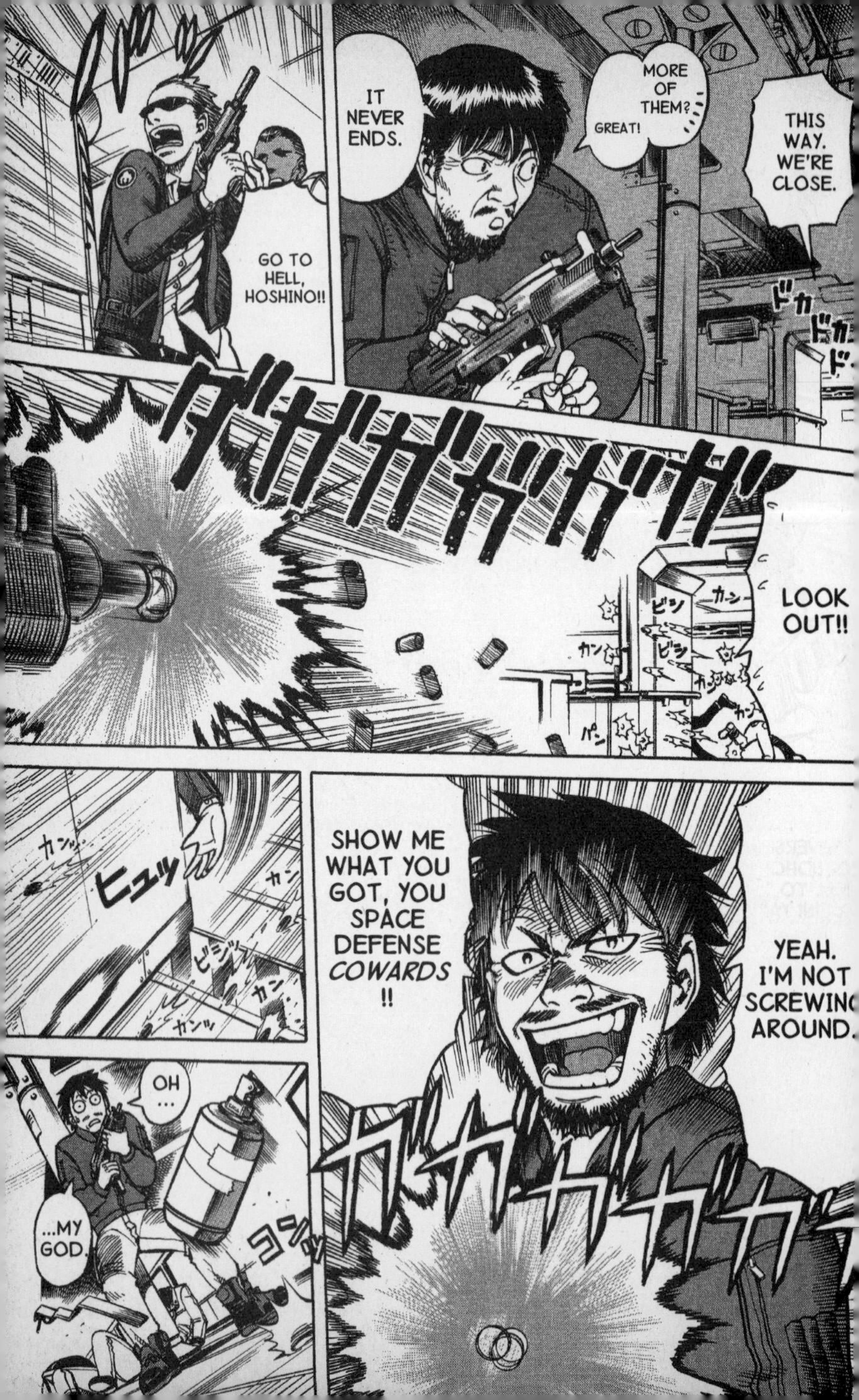
THIS WAY. WE'RE CLOSE.
MORE OF THEM? GREAT!
IT NEVER ENDS.
GO TO HELL, HOSHINO!!
LOOK OUT!!
YEAH. I'M NOT SCREWIN AROUND.
SHOW ME WHAT YOU GOT, YOU SPACE DEFENSE *COWARDS* !!
OH ...
...MY GOD.

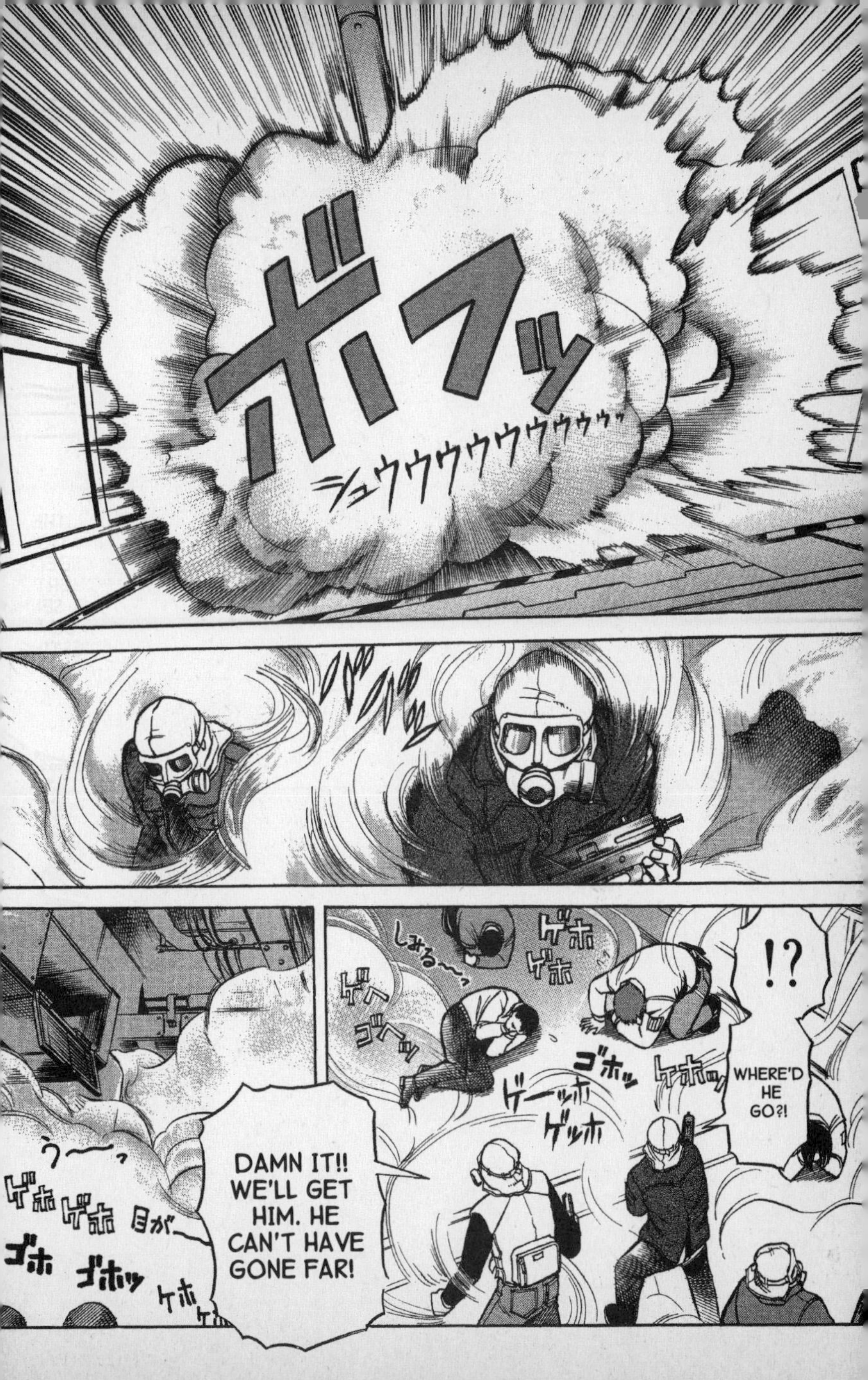
ボフッ
シュウウウウウウウゥッ
!?
WHERE'D HE GO?!
しみる〜っ
ゲホ ゲホ
ゲヘ ゴヘッ
ゴホッ
ケホッ
ゲーッホ ゲッホ
DAMN IT!! WE'LL GET HIM. HE CAN'T HAVE GONE FAR!
うーっ
ゲホ ゲホ
目が
ゴホ ゴホッ
ケホ

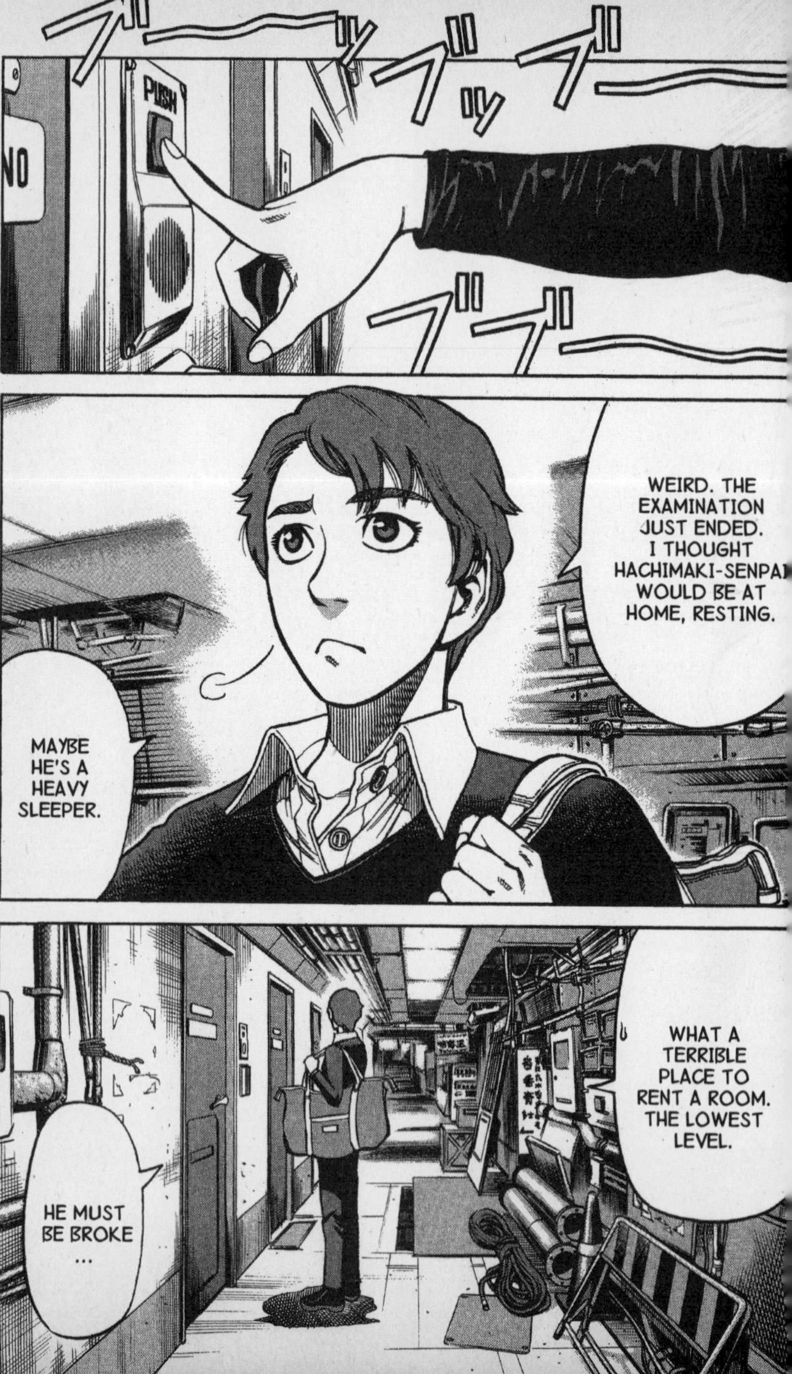
ブーーッ
ブッ
ブーー
ブブーー
WEIRD. THE EXAMINATION JUST ENDED. I THOUGHT HACHIMAKI-SENPAI WOULD BE AT HOME, RESTING.
MAYBE HE'S A HEAVY SLEEPER.
WHAT A TERRIBLE PLACE TO RENT A ROOM. THE LOWEST LEVEL.
HE MUST BE BROKE ...

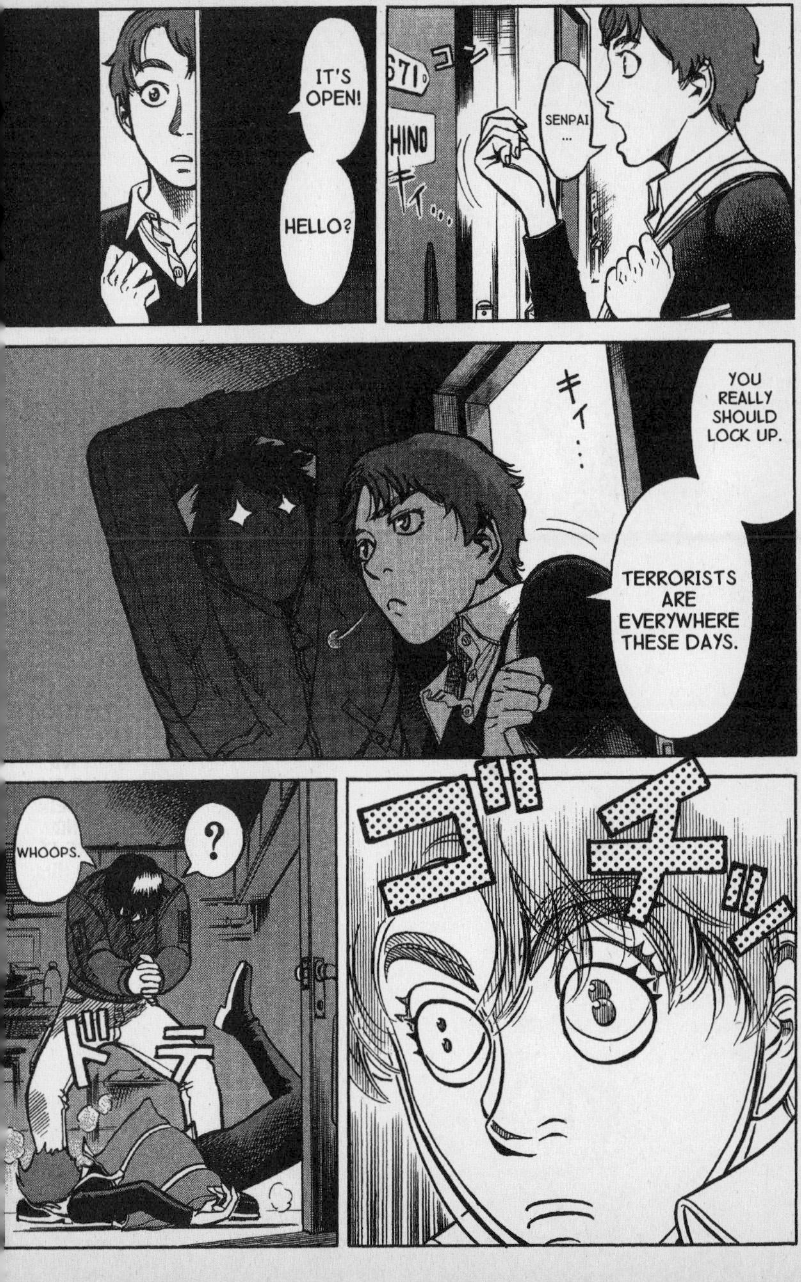

671
HINO
コン
キィ…
SENPAI …
IT'S OPEN!
HELLO?
キィ…
YOU REALLY SHOULD LOCK UP.
TERRORISTS ARE EVERYWHERE THESE DAYS.
ゴチッ
?
WHOOPS.
ドテ

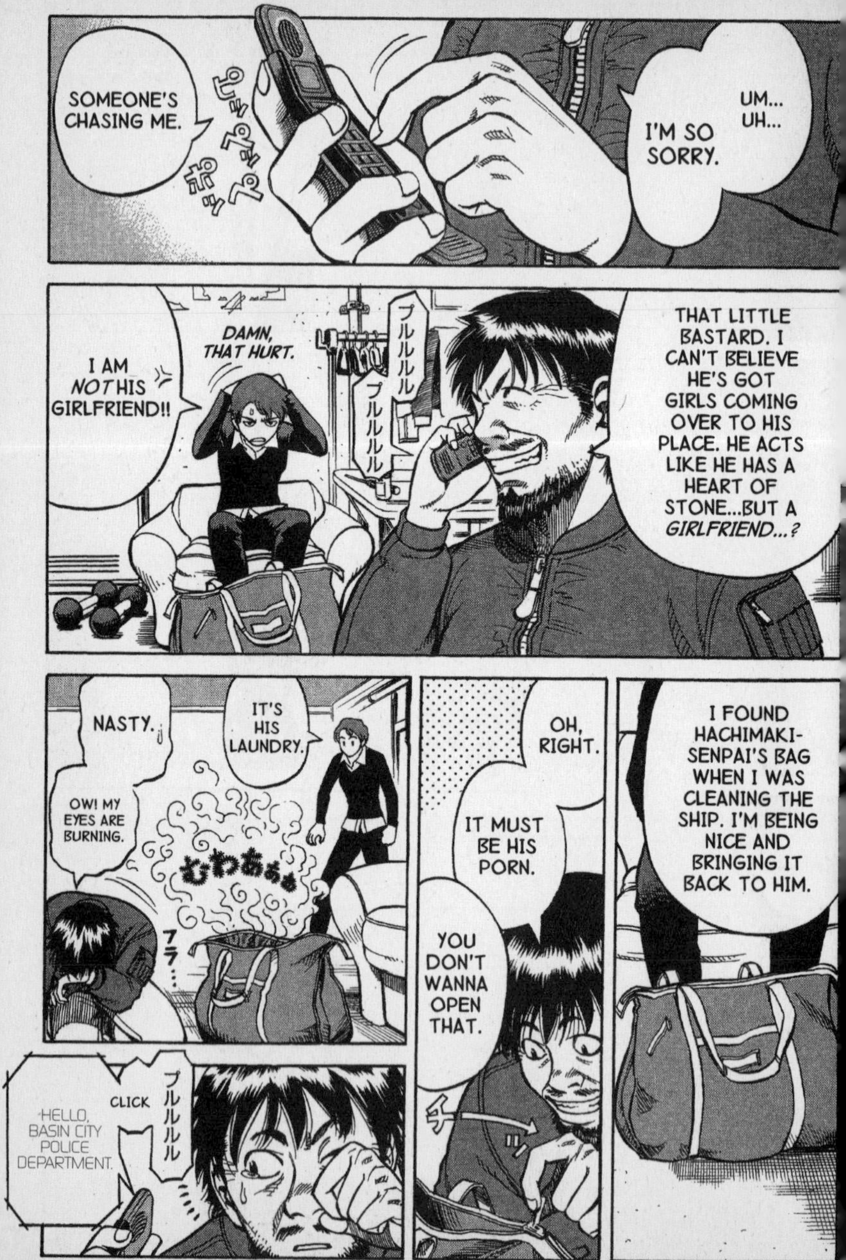
UM... UH...
I'M SO SORRY.
ピッポッポッ
SOMEONE'S CHASING ME.
THAT LITTLE BASTARD. I CAN'T BELIEVE HE'S GOT GIRLS COMING OVER TO HIS PLACE. HE ACTS LIKE HE HAS A HEART OF STONE...BUT A *GIRLFRIEND...?*
プルルルル
プルルルル
DAMN, THAT HURT.
I AM *NOT* HIS GIRLFRIEND!!
I FOUND HACHIMAKI-SENPAI'S BAG WHEN I WAS CLEANING THE SHIP. I'M BEING NICE AND BRINGING IT BACK TO HIM.
OH, RIGHT.
IT MUST BE HIS PORN.
YOU DON'T WANNA OPEN THAT.
チ
IT'S HIS LAUNDRY.
NASTY.
OW! MY EYES ARE BURNING.
むわぁぁぁ
フラ…
プルルルル
CLICK
HELLO, BASIN CITY POLICE DEPARTMENT.

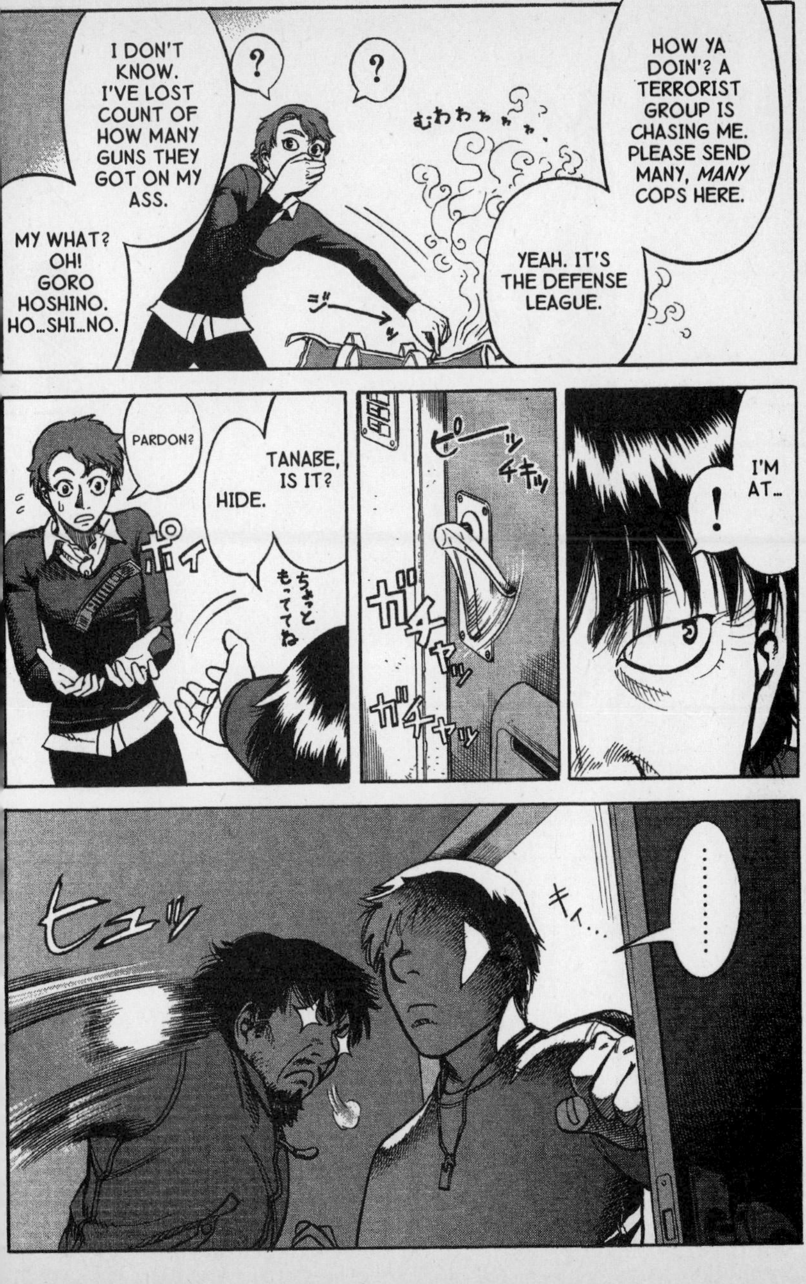
HOW YA DOIN'? A TERRORIST GROUP IS CHASING ME. PLEASE SEND MANY, *MANY* COPS HERE.
YEAH. IT'S THE DEFENSE LEAGUE.
?
?
むわわぁぁぁ
I DON'T KNOW. I'VE LOST COUNT OF HOW MANY GUNS THEY GOT ON MY ASS.
MY WHAT? OH! GORO HOSHINO. HO...SHI...NO.
ジー
ッ
I'M AT...
!
ピーッ
チキッ
ガチャッ
ガチャッ
TANABE, IS IT?
HIDE.
PARDON?
ちょっともっててね
ポイ
......
キィ...
ヒュッ

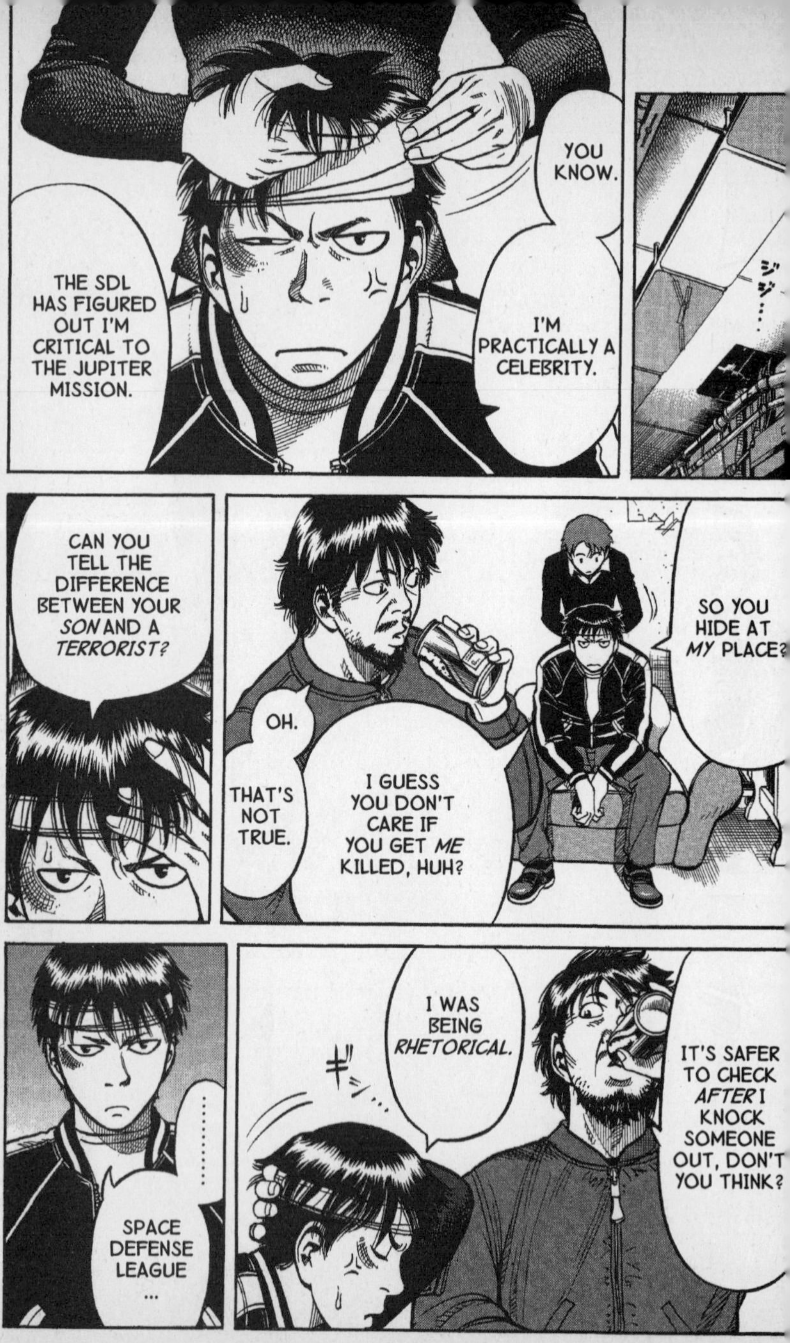

ジジ…
YOU KNOW.
I'M PRACTICALLY A CELEBRITY.
THE SDL HAS FIGURED OUT I'M CRITICAL TO THE JUPITER MISSION.
SO YOU HIDE AT *MY* PLACE?
OH.
THAT'S NOT TRUE.
I GUESS YOU DON'T CARE IF YOU GET *ME* KILLED, HUH?
CAN YOU TELL THE DIFFERENCE BETWEEN YOUR *SON* AND A *TERRORIST*?
IT'S SAFER TO CHECK *AFTER* I KNOCK SOMEONE OUT, DON'T YOU THINK?
I WAS BEING *RHETORICAL*.
ギシ…
......
SPACE DEFENSE LEAGUE ...

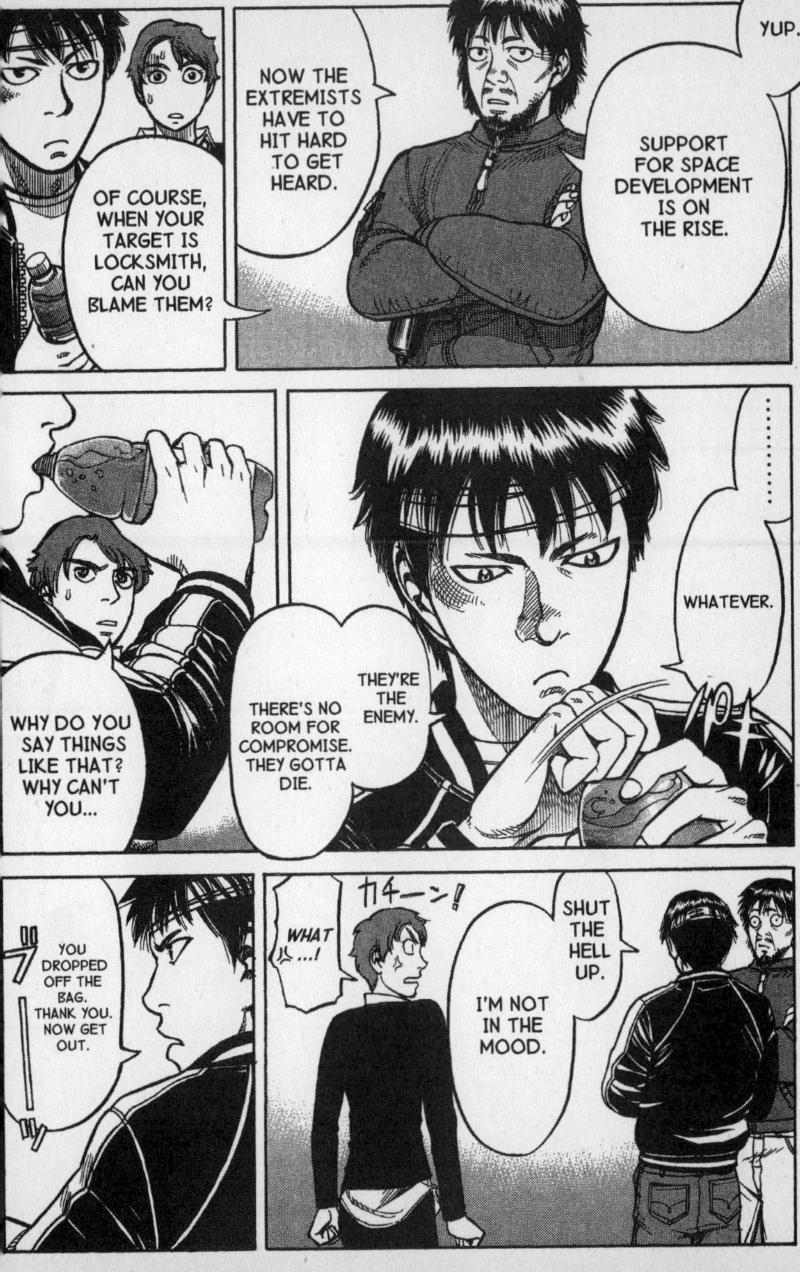
YUP.
SUPPORT FOR SPACE DEVELOPMENT IS ON THE RISE.
NOW THE EXTREMISTS HAVE TO HIT HARD TO GET HEARD.
OF COURSE, WHEN YOUR TARGET IS LOCKSMITH, CAN YOU BLAME THEM?
......
WHATEVER.
THEY'RE THE ENEMY.
THERE'S NO ROOM FOR COMPROMISE. THEY GOTTA DIE.
WHY DO YOU SAY THINGS LIKE THAT? WHY CAN'T YOU...
SHUT THE HELL UP.
I'M NOT IN THE MOOD.
カチーン!
WHAT ...!
YOU DROPPED OFF THE BAG. THANK YOU. NOW GET OUT.

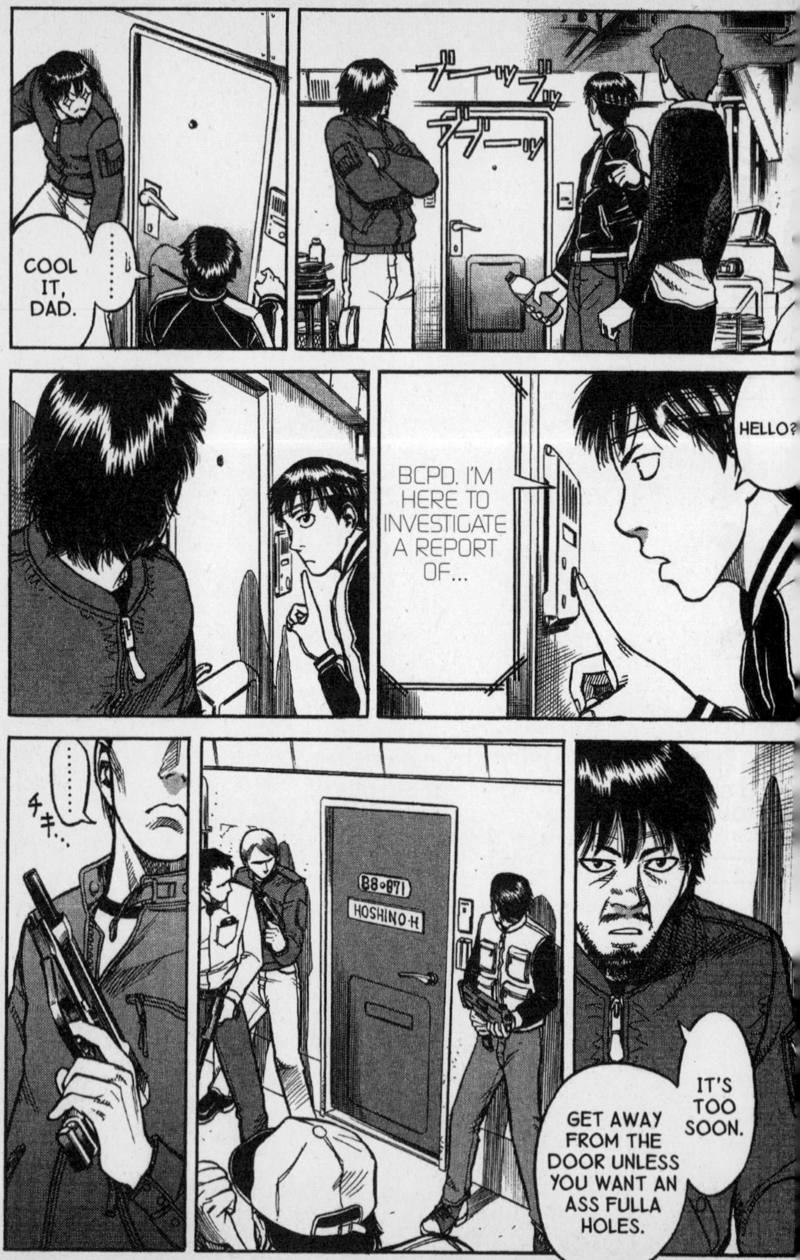
ブーッブッ
ブブーッ
......!
COOL IT, DAD.
HELLO?
BCPD. I'M HERE TO INVESTIGATE A REPORT OF...
IT'S TOO SOON.
GET AWAY FROM THE DOOR UNLESS YOU WANT AN ASS FULLA HOLES.
B8-871
HOSHINO·H
......
チキ...

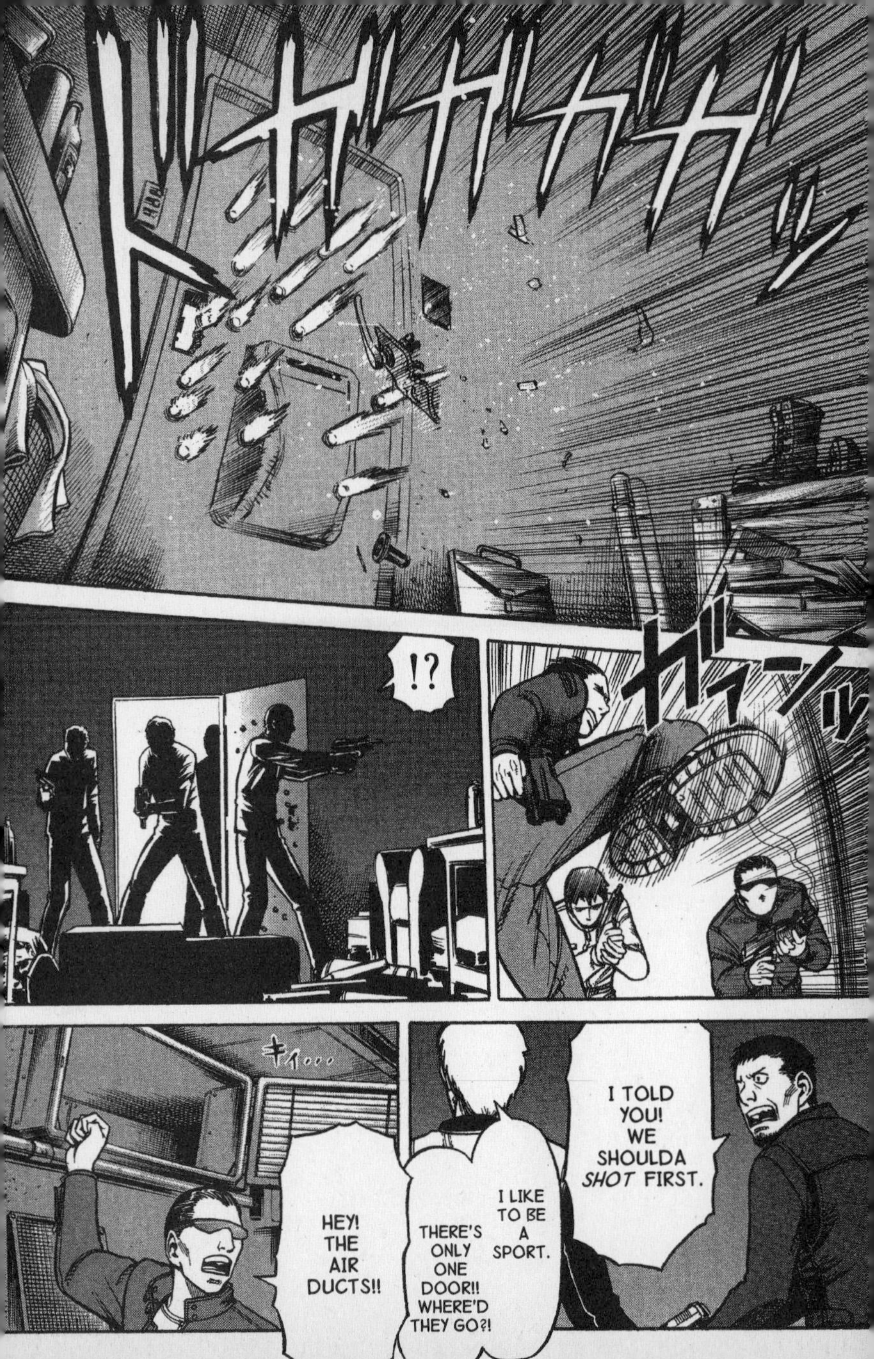
!?
I TOLD YOU! WE SHOULDA *SHOT* FIRST.
I LIKE TO BE A SPORT.
THERE'S ONLY ONE DOOR!! WHERE'D THEY GO?!
HEY! THE AIR DUCTS!!

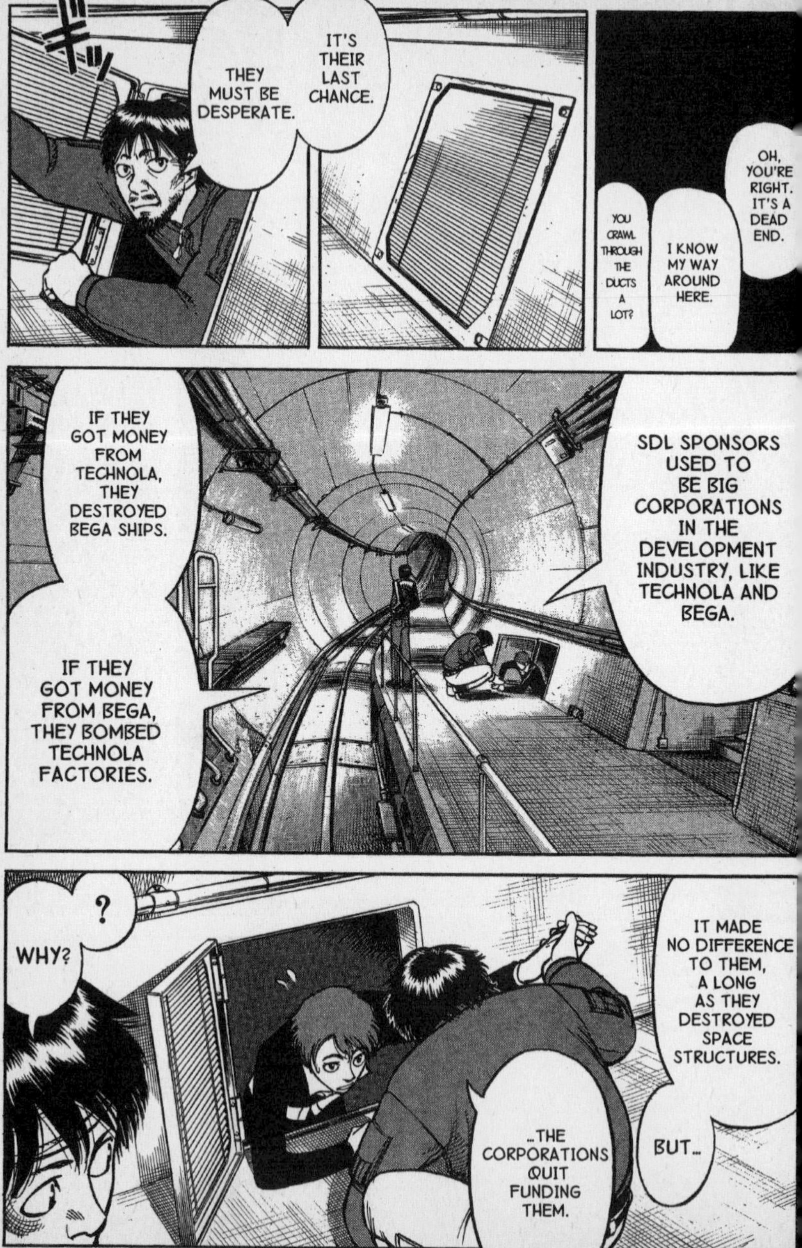
OH, YOU'RE RIGHT. IT'S A DEAD END.
I KNOW MY WAY AROUND HERE.
YOU CRAWL THROUGH THE DUCTS A LOT?
IT'S THEIR LAST CHANCE.
THEY MUST BE DESPERATE.
ギリ
SDL SPONSORS USED TO BE BIG CORPORATIONS IN THE DEVELOPMENT INDUSTRY, LIKE TECHNOLA AND BEGA.
IF THEY GOT MONEY FROM TECHNOLA, THEY DESTROYED BEGA SHIPS.
IF THEY GOT MONEY FROM BEGA, THEY BOMBED TECHNOLA FACTORIES.
IT MADE NO DIFFERENCE TO THEM, A LONG AS THEY DESTROYED SPACE STRUCTURES.
BUT...
...THE CORPORATIONS QUIT FUNDING THEM.
?
WHY?

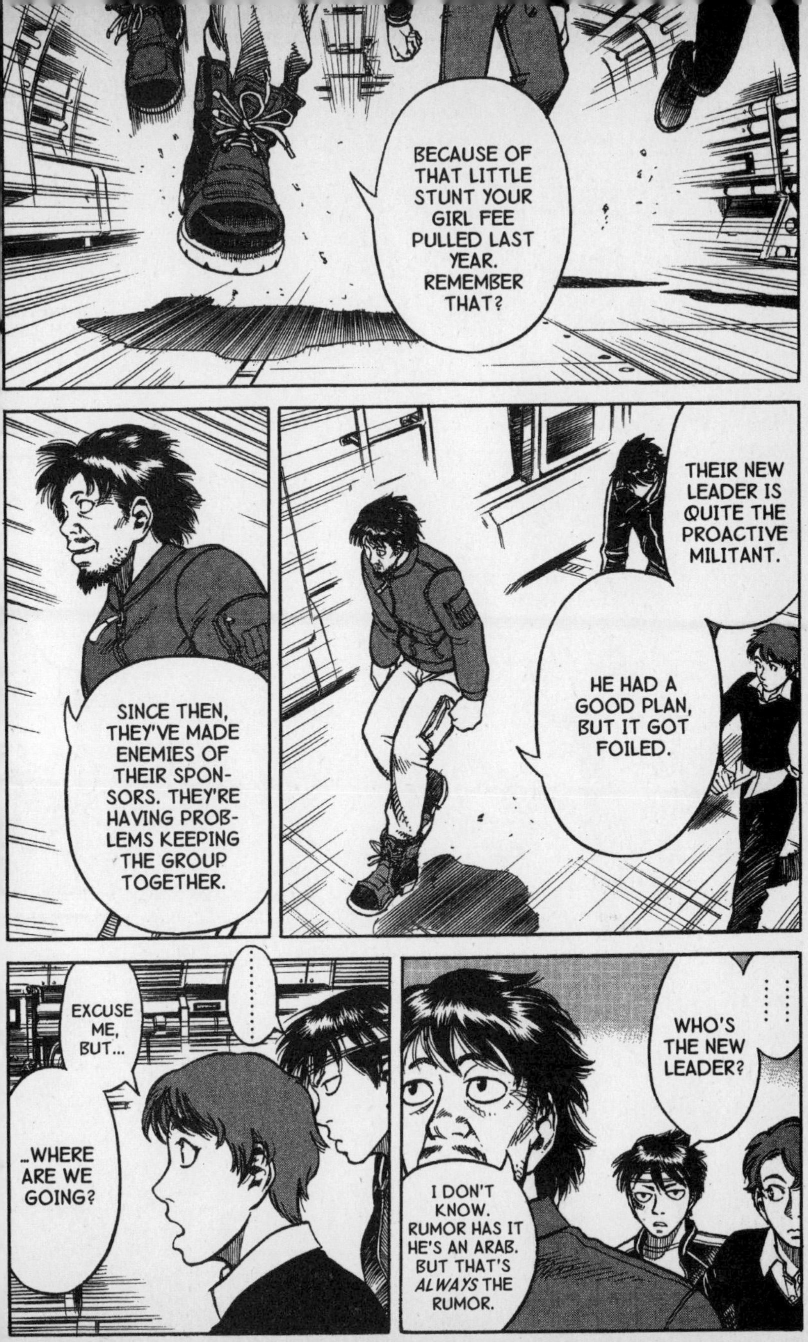
BECAUSE OF THAT LITTLE STUNT YOUR GIRL FEE PULLED LAST YEAR. REMEMBER THAT?
THEIR NEW LEADER IS QUITE THE PROACTIVE MILITANT.
HE HAD A GOOD PLAN, BUT IT GOT FOILED.
SINCE THEN, THEY'VE MADE ENEMIES OF THEIR SPONSORS. THEY'RE HAVING PROBLEMS KEEPING THE GROUP TOGETHER.
......
WHO'S THE NEW LEADER?
I DON'T KNOW. RUMOR HAS IT HE'S AN ARAB. BUT THAT'S *ALWAYS* THE RUMOR.
......
EXCUSE ME, BUT...
...WHERE ARE WE GOING?

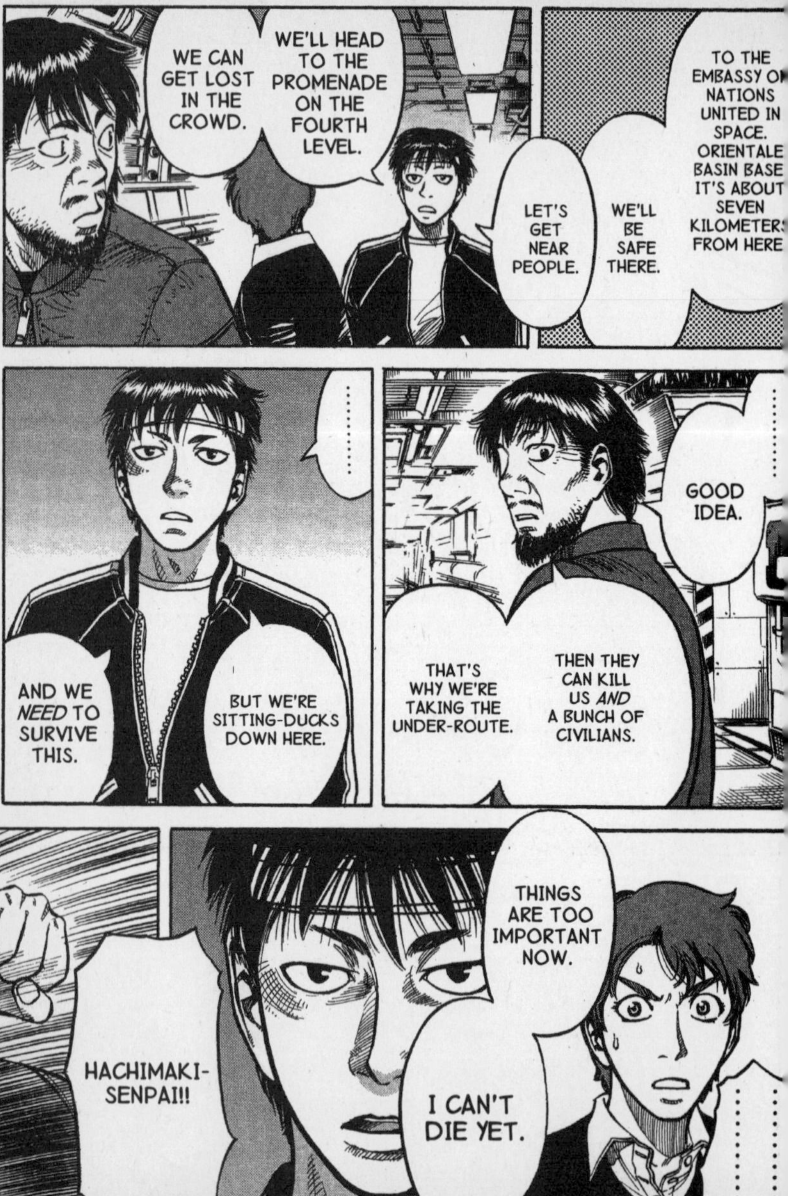
TO THE EMBASSY OF NATIONS UNITED IN SPACE. ORIENTALE BASIN BASE IT'S ABOUT SEVEN KILOMETERS FROM HERE
WE'LL BE SAFE THERE.
LET'S GET NEAR PEOPLE.
WE'LL HEAD TO THE PROMENADE ON THE FOURTH LEVEL.
WE CAN GET LOST IN THE CROWD.
......
GOOD IDEA.
THEN THEY CAN KILL US *AND* A BUNCH OF CIVILIANS.
THAT'S WHY WE'RE TAKING THE UNDER-ROUTE.
......
BUT WE'RE SITTING-DUCKS DOWN HERE.
AND WE *NEED* TO SURVIVE THIS.
......!!
THINGS ARE TOO IMPORTANT NOW.
I CAN'T DIE YET.
HACHIMAKI-SENPAI!!

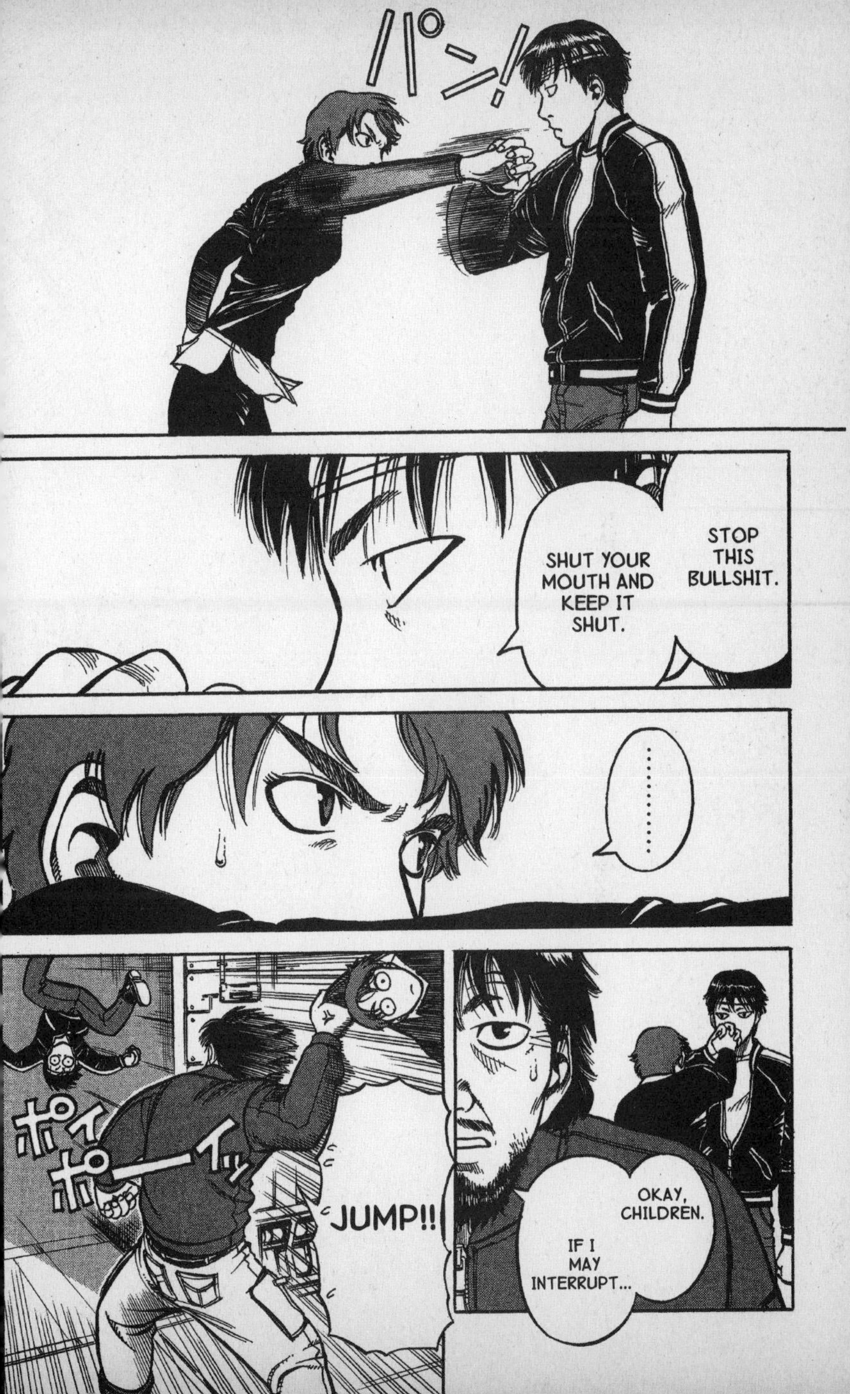
パーン!!
STOP THIS BULLSHIT.
SHUT YOUR MOUTH AND KEEP IT SHUT.
……
OKAY, CHILDREN.
IF I MAY INTERRUPT...
ポイ
ポーイッ
JUMP!!

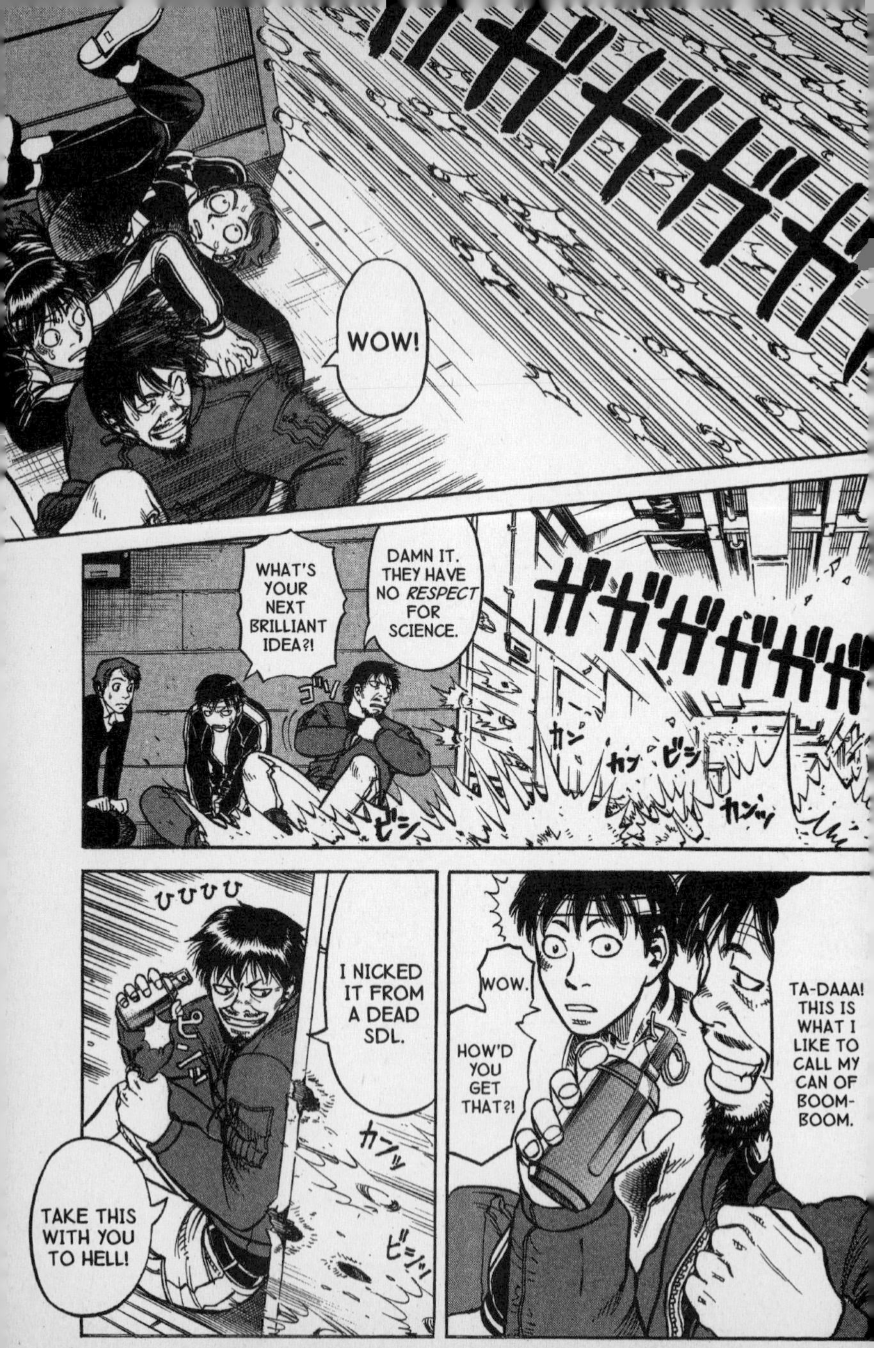
WOW!
DAMN IT. THEY HAVE NO *RESPECT* FOR SCIENCE.
WHAT'S YOUR NEXT BRILLIANT IDEA?!
TA-DAAA! THIS IS WHAT I LIKE TO CALL MY CAN OF BOOM-BOOM.
WOW.
HOW'D YOU GET THAT?!
I NICKED IT FROM A DEAD SDL.
TAKE THIS WITH YOU TO HELL!

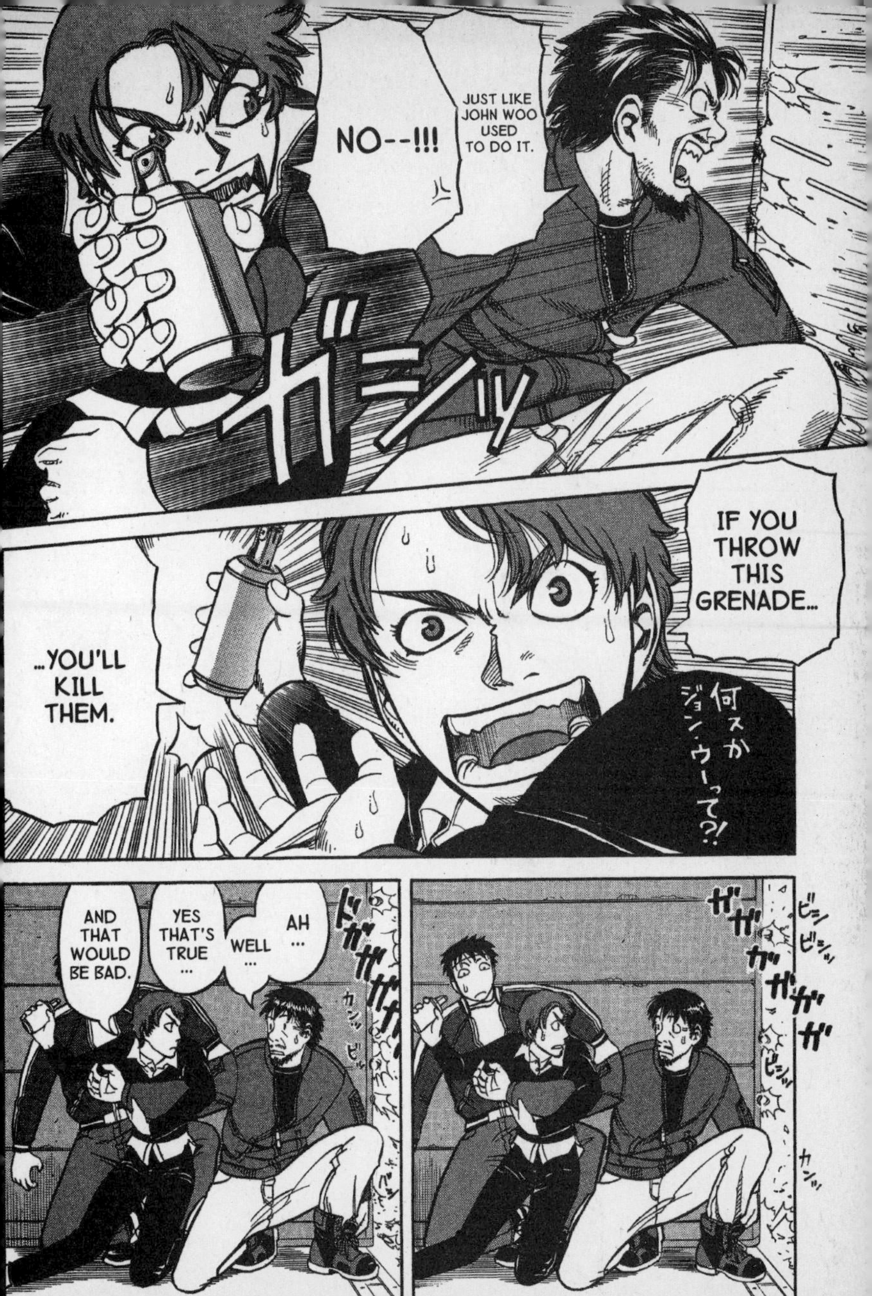
JUST LIKE JOHN WOO USED TO DO IT.
NO--!!!
ガシッ
IF YOU THROW THIS GRENADE...
何スかジョン・ウーって?!
...YOU'LL KILL THEM.
ガガガガガガ
ビシッ ビシッ
カンッ
AH...
WELL...
YES THAT'S TRUE...
AND THAT WOULD BE BAD.
ドガガガガ

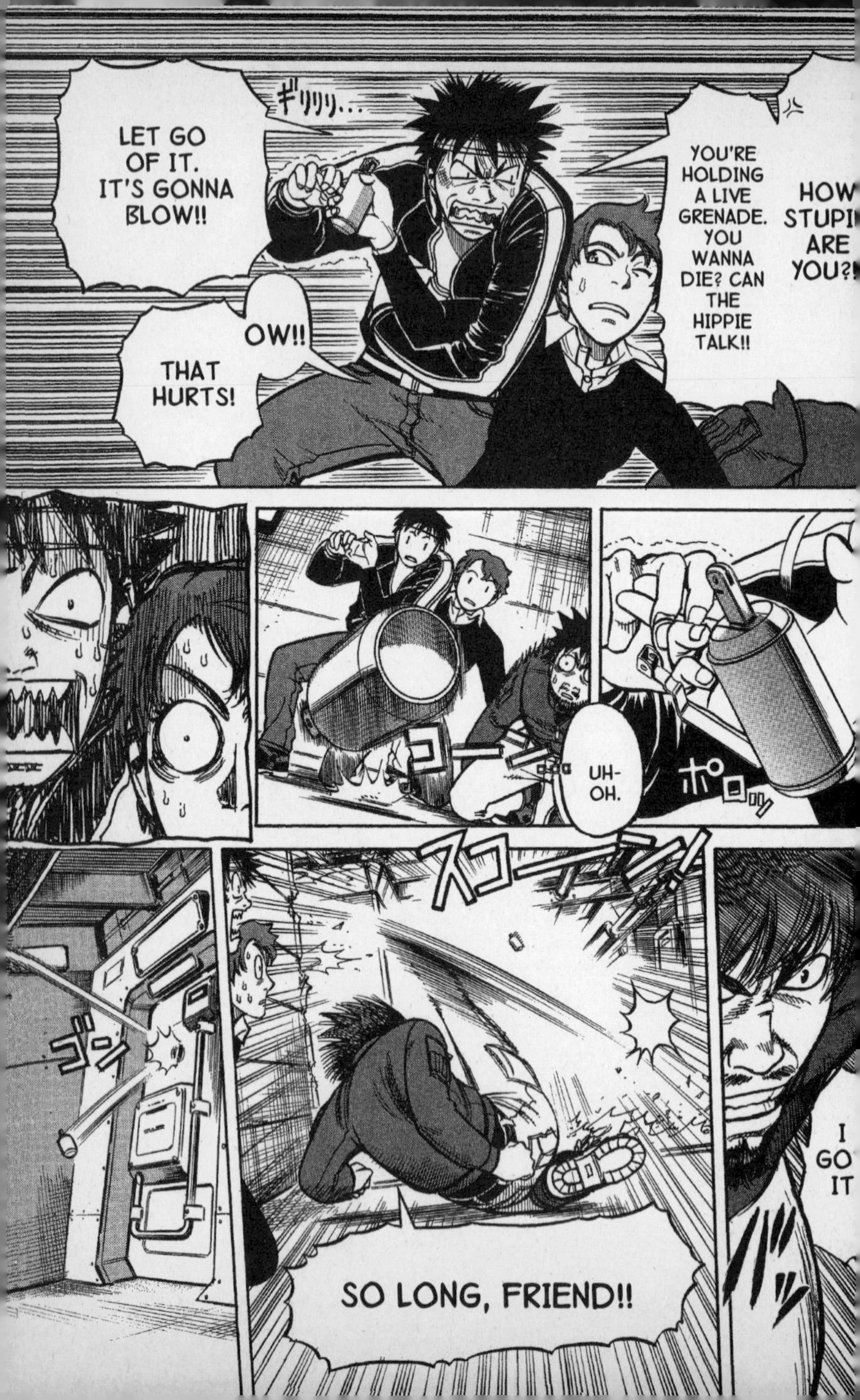
HOW STUPI ARE YOU?!
YOU'RE HOLDING A LIVE GRENADE. YOU WANNA DIE? CAN THE HIPPIE TALK!!
ギリリリ…
LET GO OF IT. IT'S GONNA BLOW!!
OW!!
THAT HURTS!
ポロッ
UH-OH.
I GO IT
スコーン
SO LONG, FRIEND!!

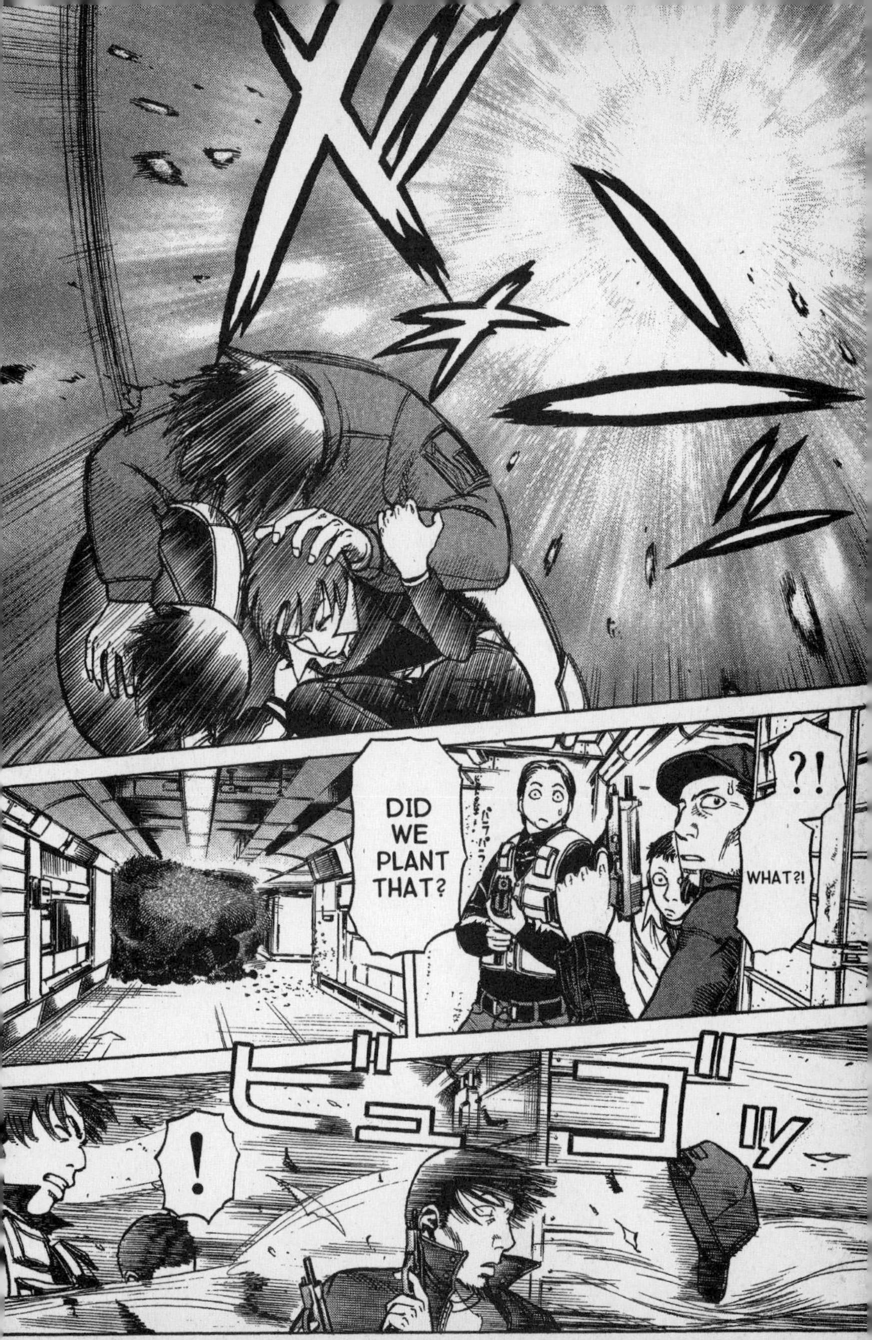
?!
WHAT?!
DID WE PLANT THAT?
ビュゴッ
!

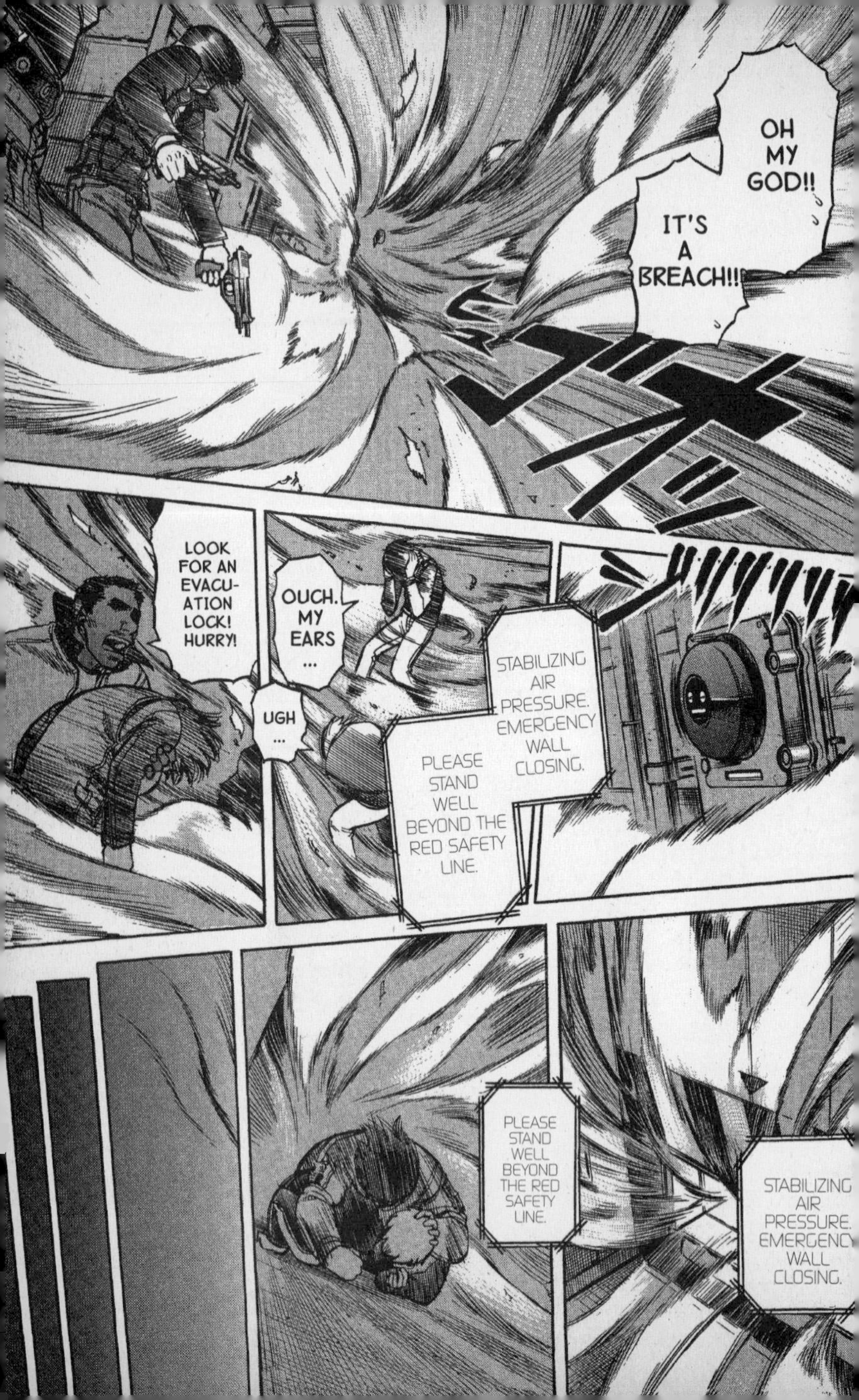
OH MY GOD!!
IT'S A BREACH!!!
STABILIZING AIR PRESSURE. EMERGENCY WALL CLOSING.
PLEASE STAND WELL BEYOND THE RED SAFETY LINE.
OUCH. MY EARS ...
UGH ...
LOOK FOR AN EVACU-ATION LOCK! HURRY!
STABILIZING AIR PRESSURE. EMERGENCY WALL CLOSING.
PLEASE STAND WELL BEYOND THE RED SAFETY LINE.

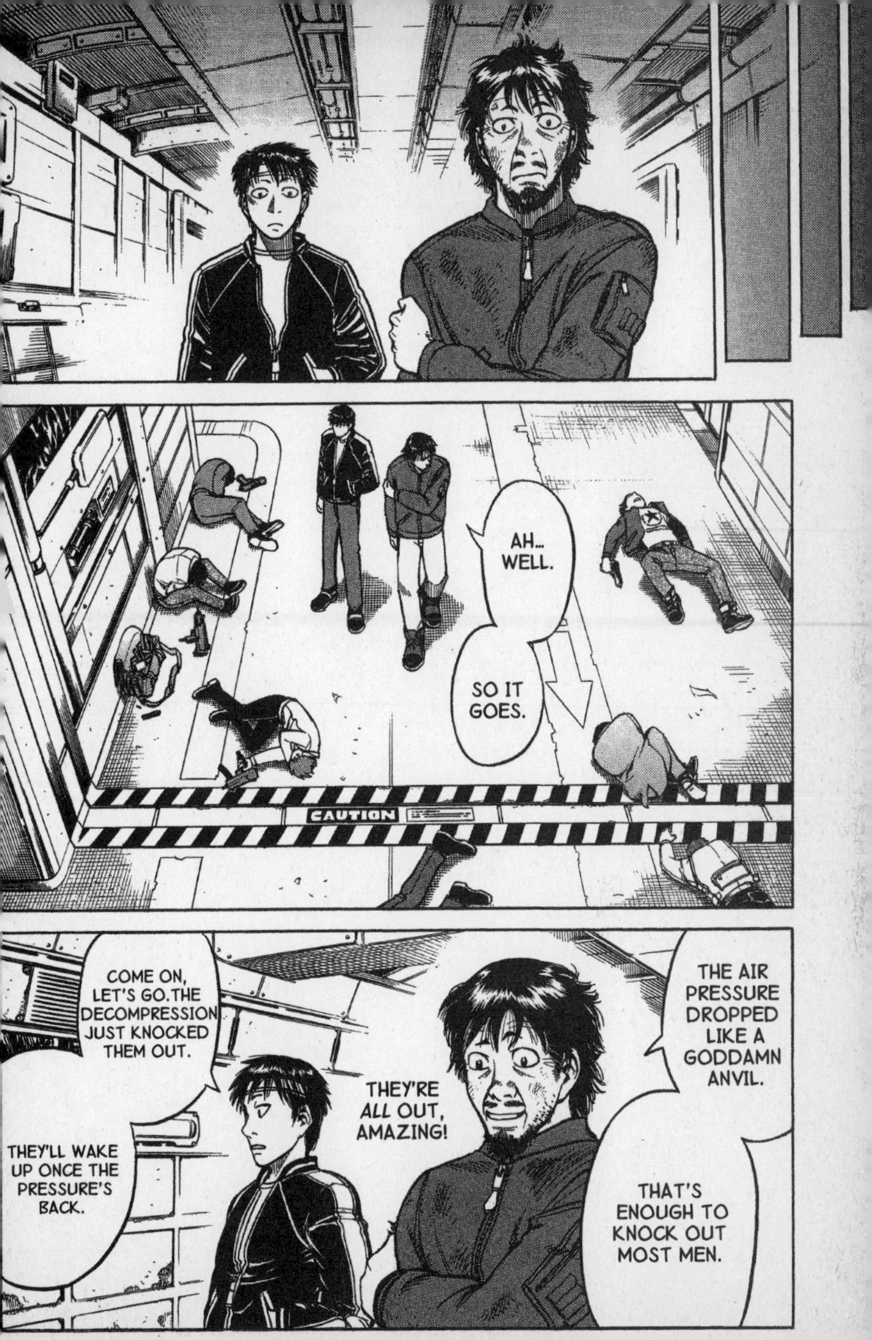
AH... WELL.
SO IT GOES.
THE AIR PRESSURE DROPPED LIKE A GODDAMN ANVIL.
THAT'S ENOUGH TO KNOCK OUT MOST MEN.
THEY'RE *ALL* OUT, AMAZING!
COME ON, LET'S GO. THE DECOMPRESSION JUST KNOCKED THEM OUT.
THEY'LL WAKE UP ONCE THE PRESSURE'S BACK.

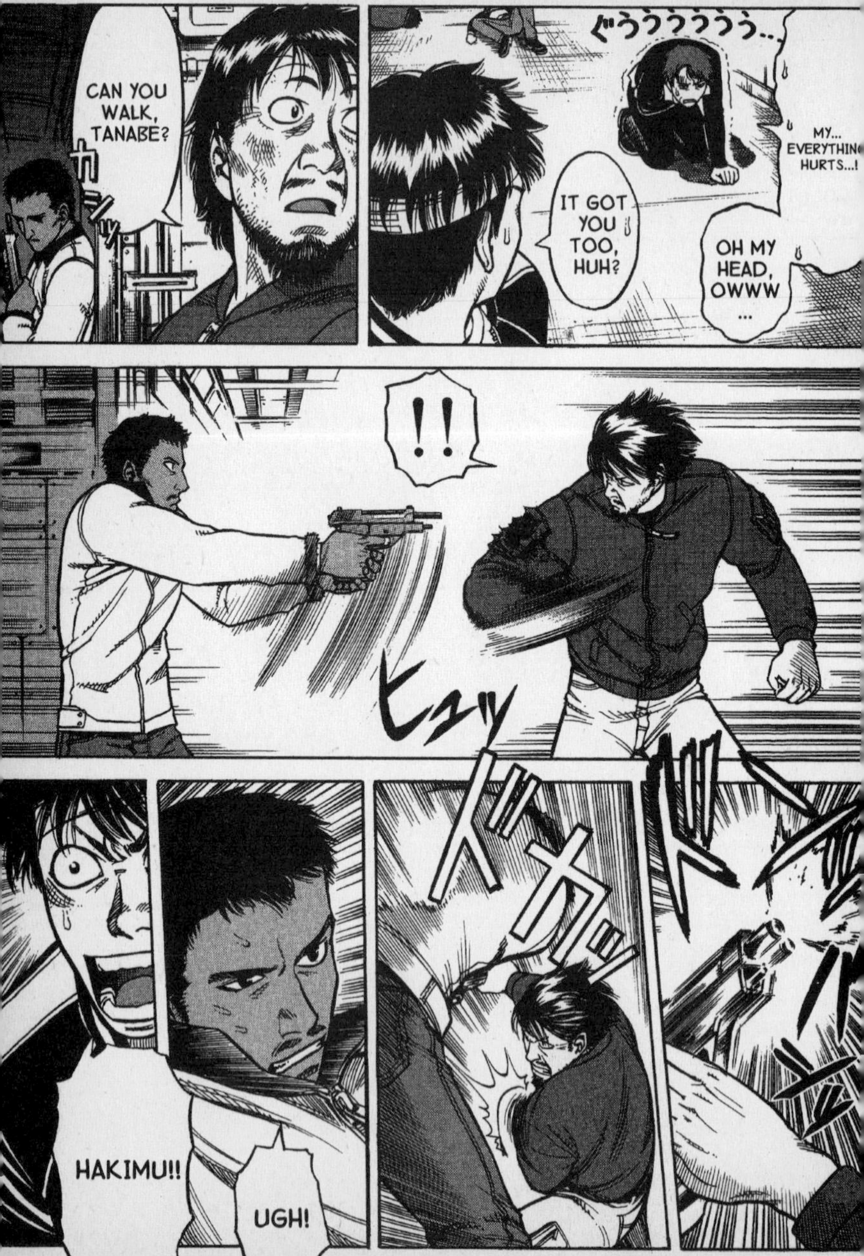
ぐううううううう...
MY... EVERYTHING HURTS...!
OH MY HEAD, OWWW...
IT GOT YOU TOO, HUH?
CAN YOU WALK, TANABE?
!!
ヒュッ
ドカッ
HAKIMU!!
UGH!

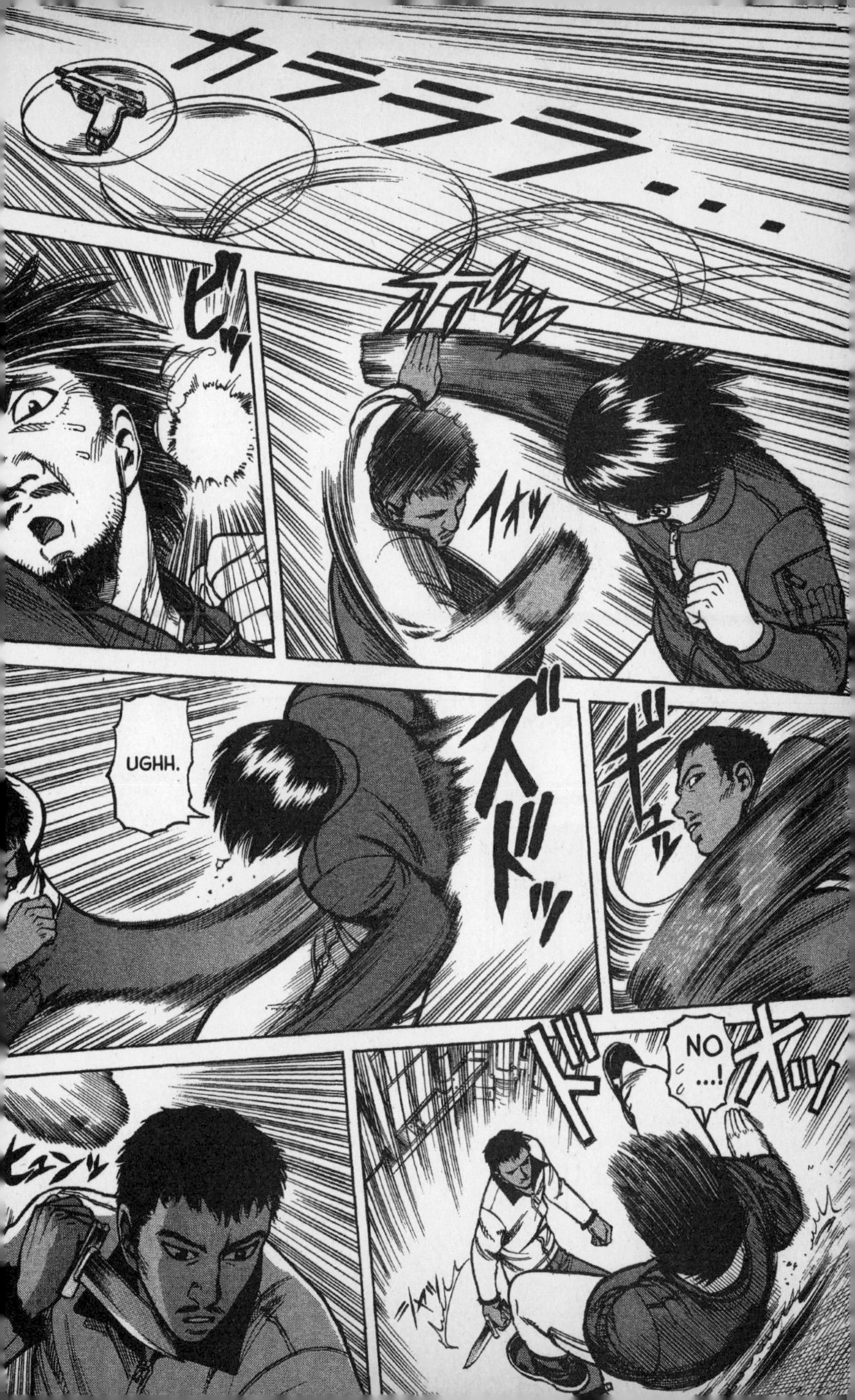
カラララ…
ビッ
UGHH.
NO ...!

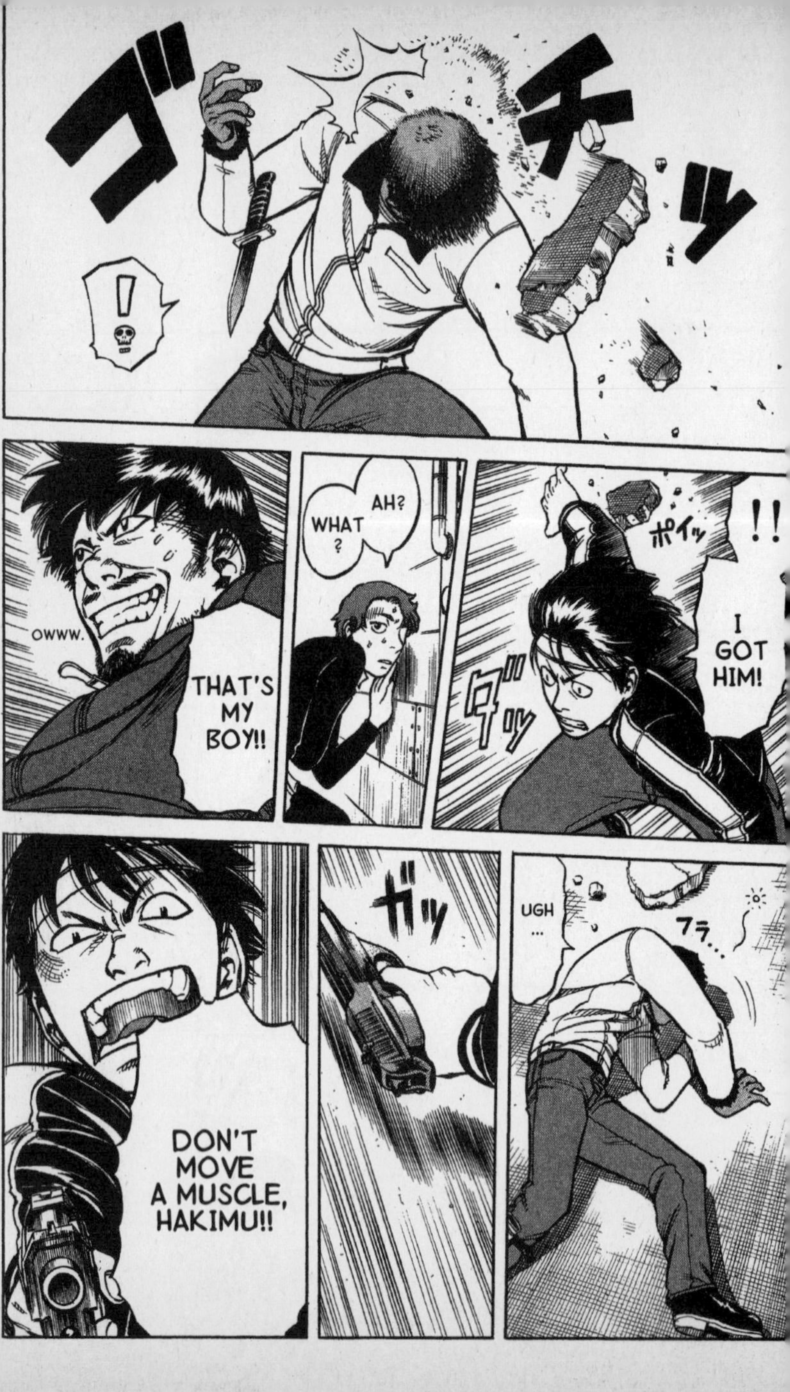
ゴチッ
!!
ポイッ
I GOT HIM!
ダッ
AH?
WHAT?
OWWW.
THAT'S MY BOY!!
UGH...
フラ...
ガッ
DON'T MOVE A MUSCLE, HAKIMU!!

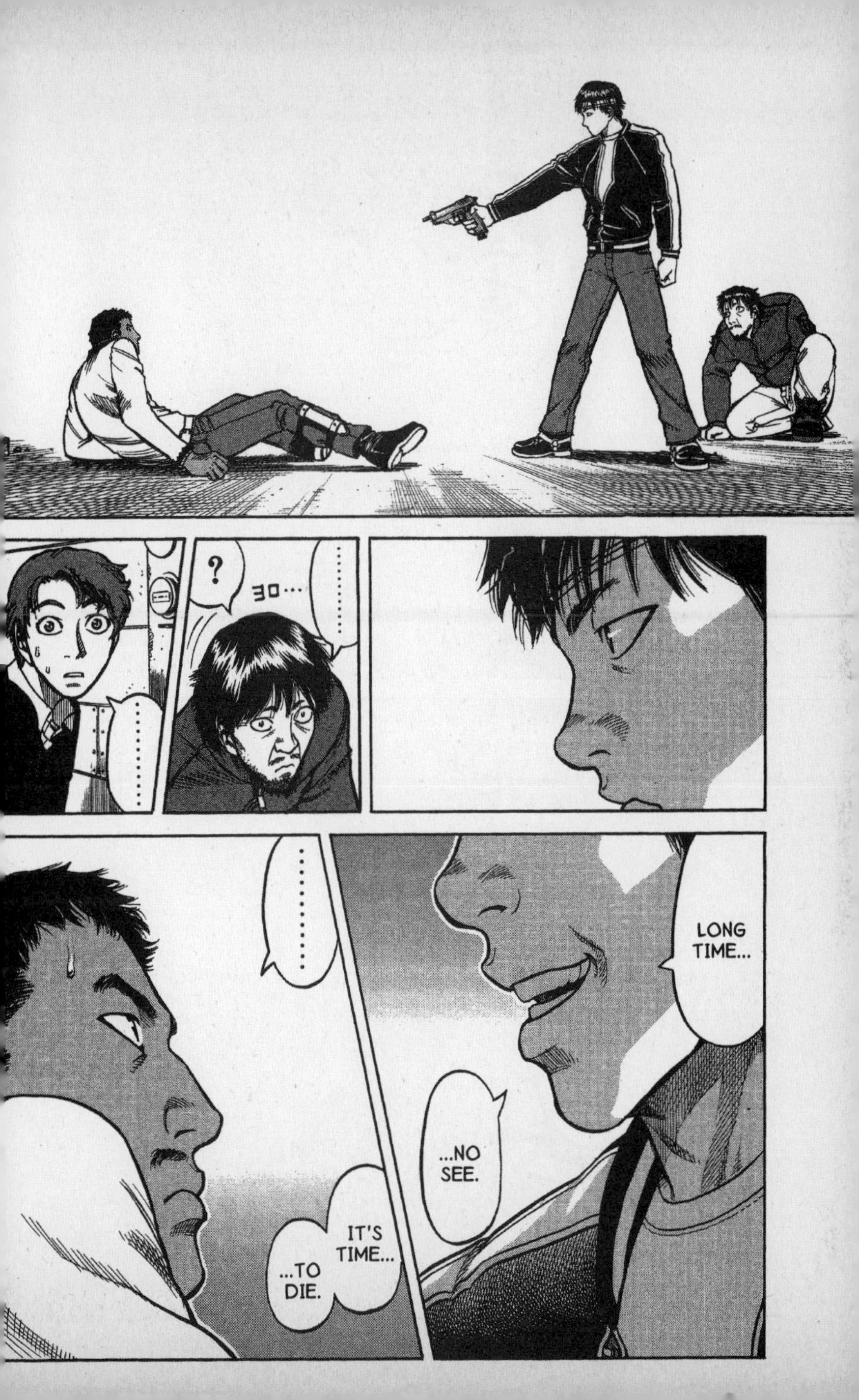

......
?
ヨロ…
......
LONG TIME...
...NO SEE.
......
IT'S TIME...
...TO DIE.

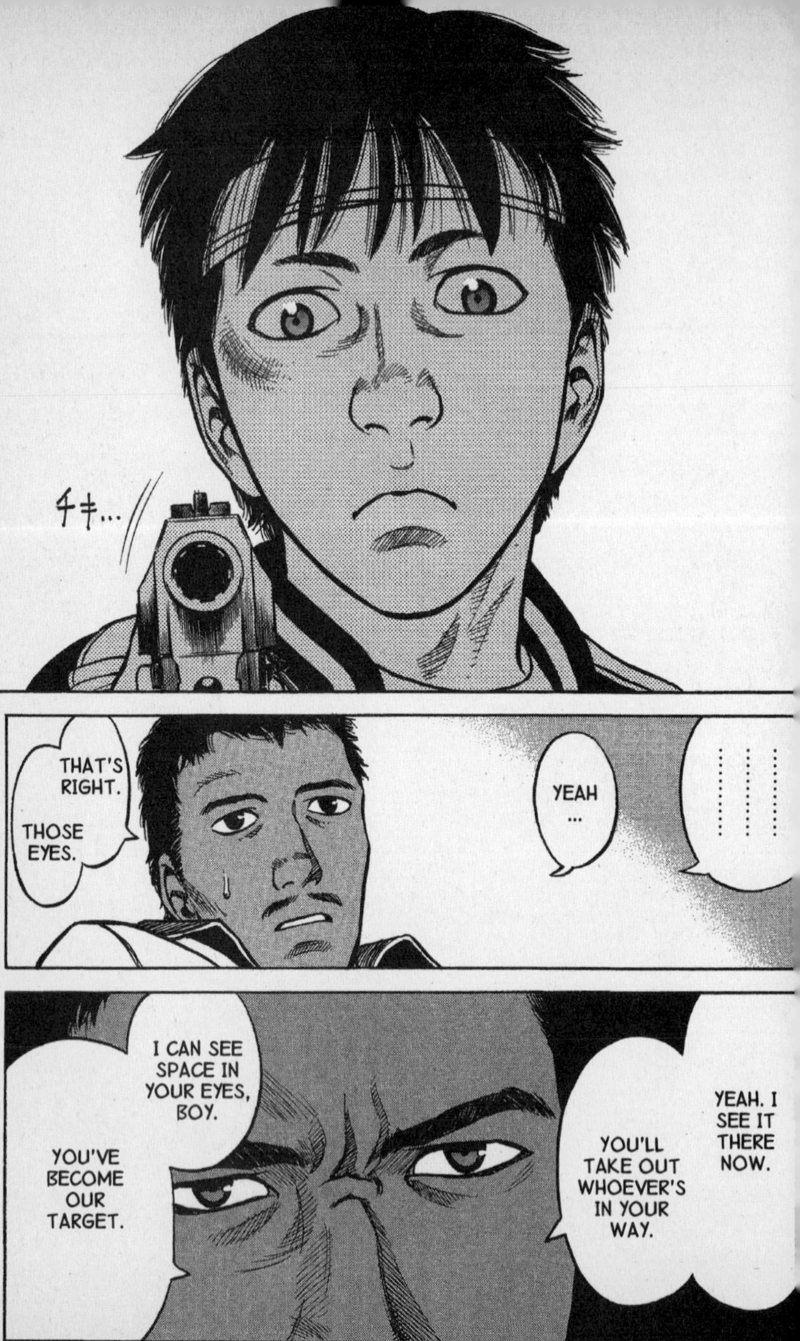
チキ…
……
YEAH …
THAT'S RIGHT.
THOSE EYES.
YEAH. I SEE IT THERE NOW.
YOU'LL TAKE OUT WHOEVER'S IN YOUR WAY.
I CAN SEE SPACE IN YOUR EYES, BOY.
YOU'VE BECOME OUR TARGET.

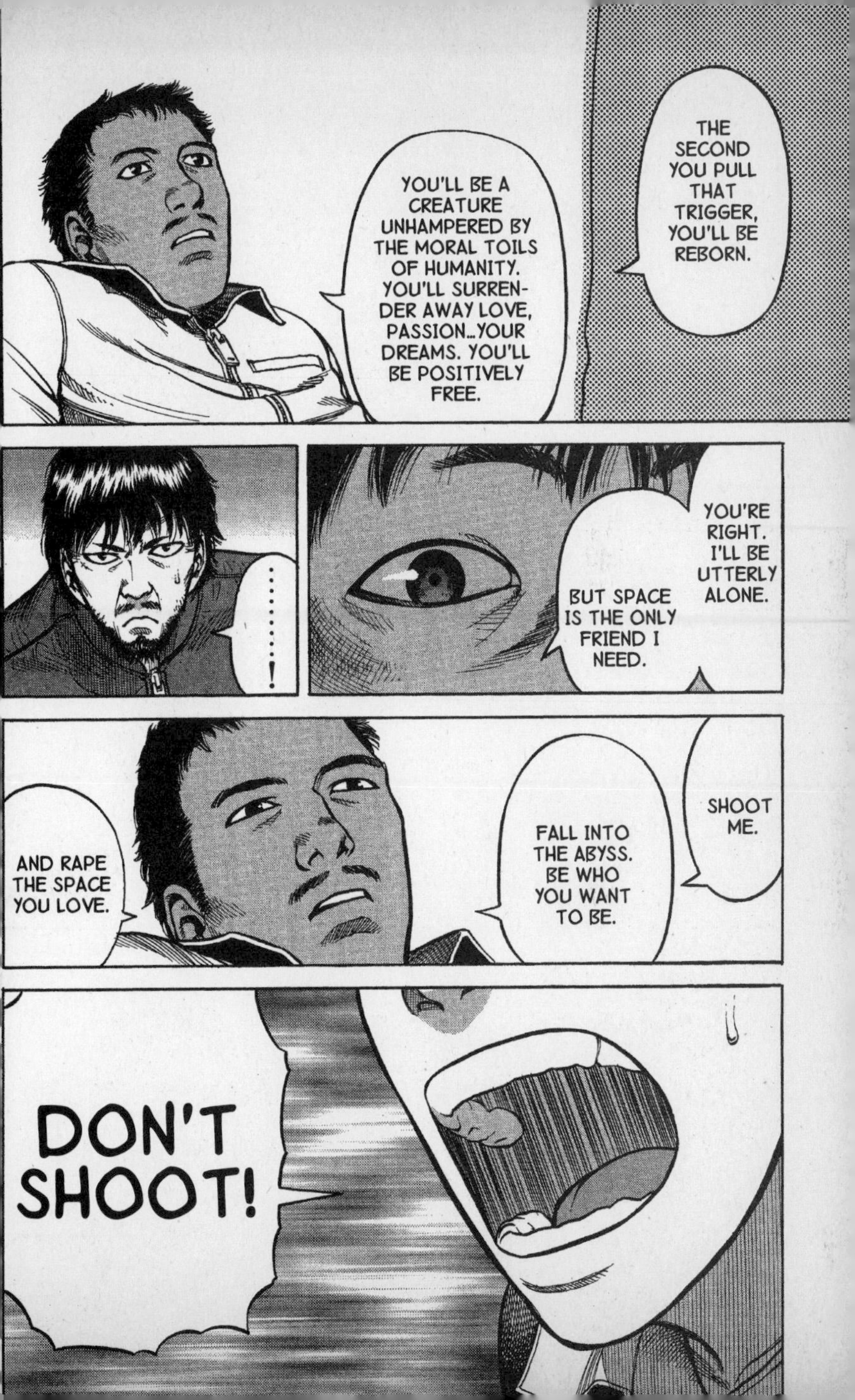
THE SECOND YOU PULL THAT TRIGGER, YOU'LL BE REBORN.
YOU'LL BE A CREATURE UNHAMPERED BY THE MORAL TOILS OF HUMANITY. YOU'LL SURREN-DER AWAY LOVE, PASSION...YOUR DREAMS. YOU'LL BE POSITIVELY FREE.
YOU'RE RIGHT. I'LL BE UTTERLY ALONE.
BUT SPACE IS THE ONLY FRIEND I NEED.
......!
SHOOT ME.
FALL INTO THE ABYSS. BE WHO YOU WANT TO BE.
AND RAPE THE SPACE YOU LOVE.
DON'T SHOOT!

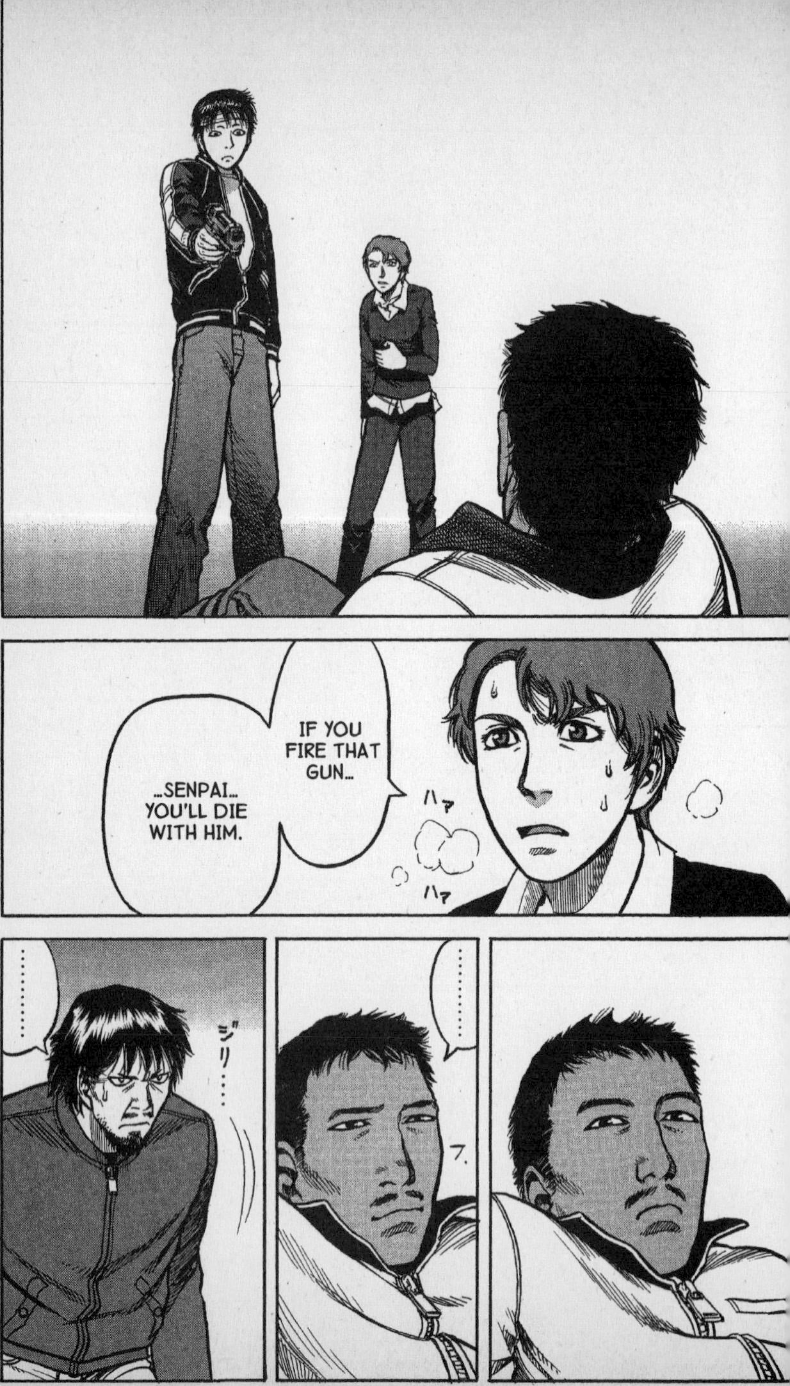
IF YOU FIRE THAT GUN…
…SENPAI… YOU'LL DIE WITH HIM.
ハァ
ハァ
……
フ.
……
ジリ….

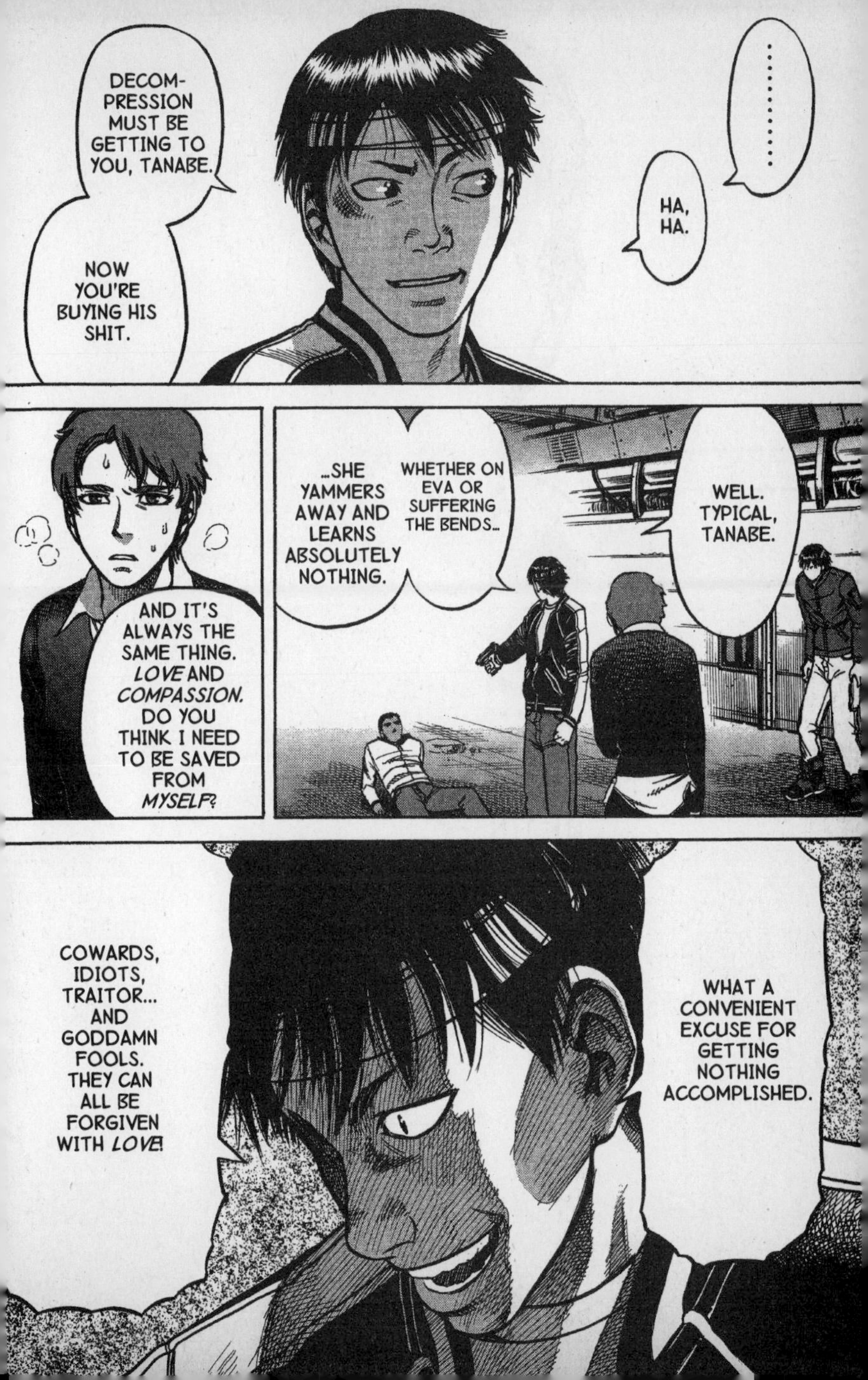
……
HA, HA.
DECOMPRESSION MUST BE GETTING TO YOU, TANABE.
NOW YOU'RE BUYING HIS SHIT.
WELL. TYPICAL, TANABE.
WHETHER ON EVA OR SUFFERING THE BENDS...
...SHE YAMMERS AWAY AND LEARNS ABSOLUTELY NOTHING.
AND IT'S ALWAYS THE SAME THING. LOVE AND COMPASSION. DO YOU THINK I NEED TO BE SAVED FROM MYSELF?
WHAT A CONVENIENT EXCUSE FOR GETTING NOTHING ACCOMPLISHED.
COWARDS, IDIOTS, TRAITOR... AND GODDAMN FOOLS. THEY CAN ALL BE FORGIVEN WITH LOVE!

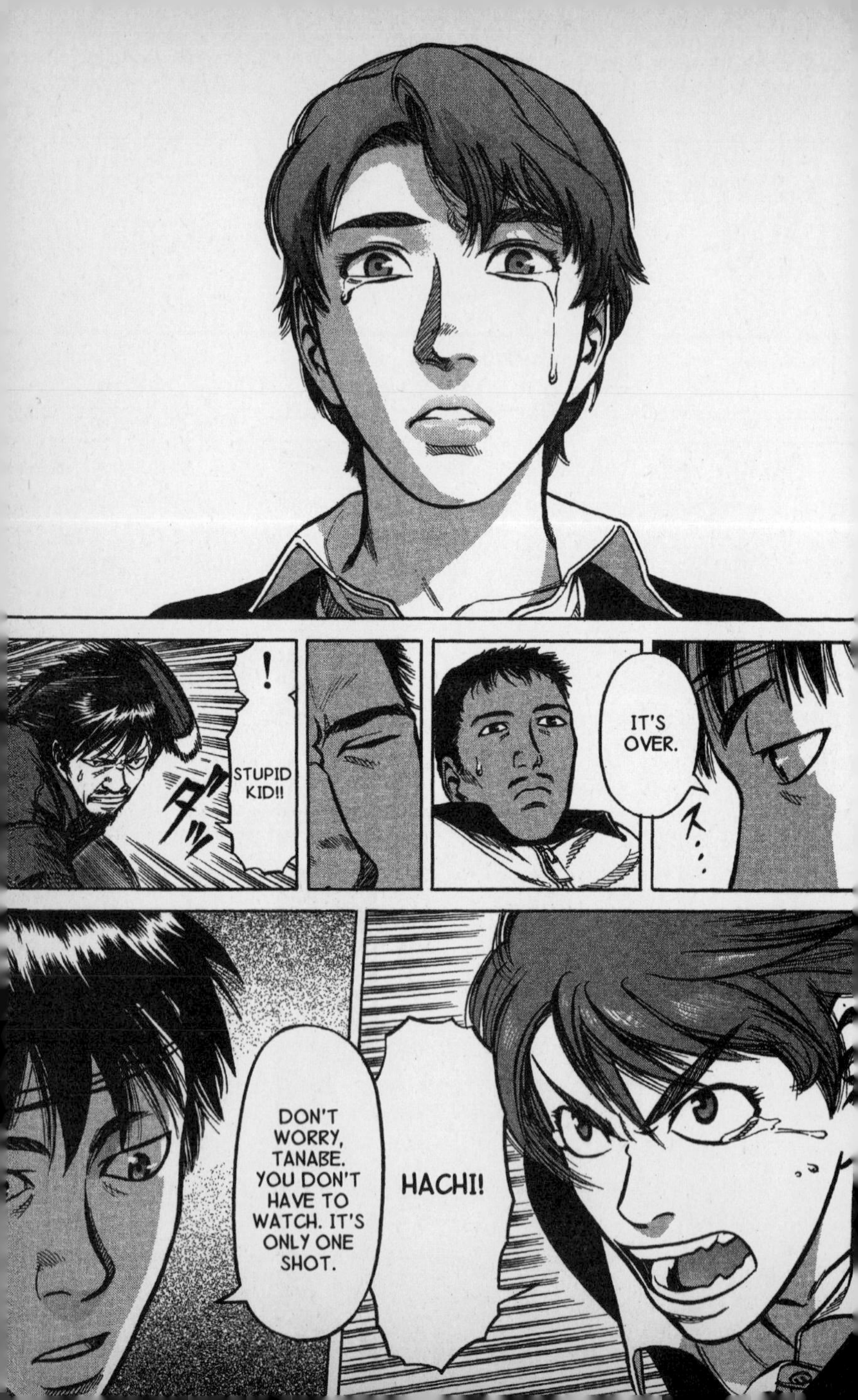

IT'S OVER.
ス…
!
STUPID KID!!
ダッ
HACHI!
DON'T WORRY, TANABE. YOU DON'T HAVE TO WATCH. IT'S ONLY ONE SHOT.

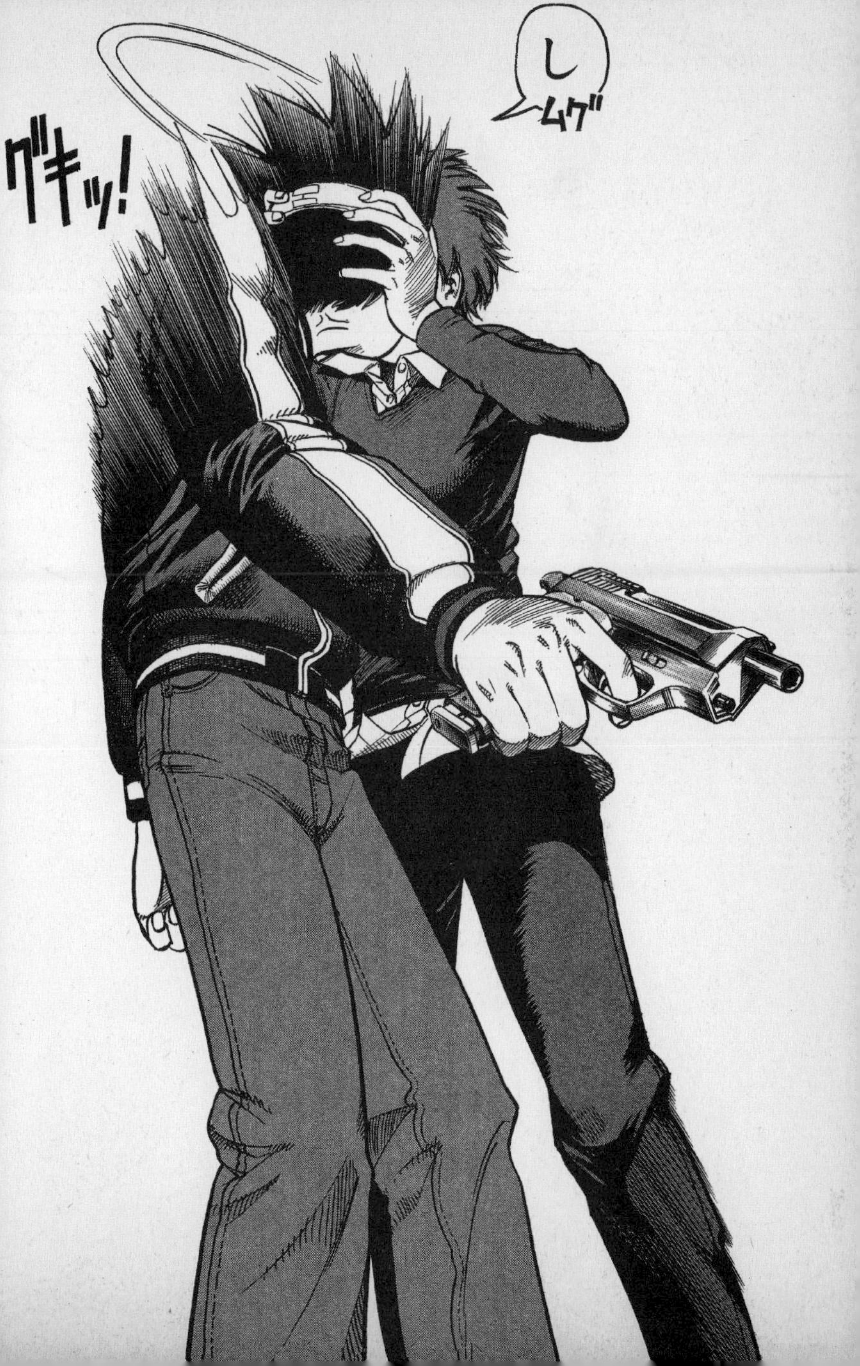
グキッ!
しムグ

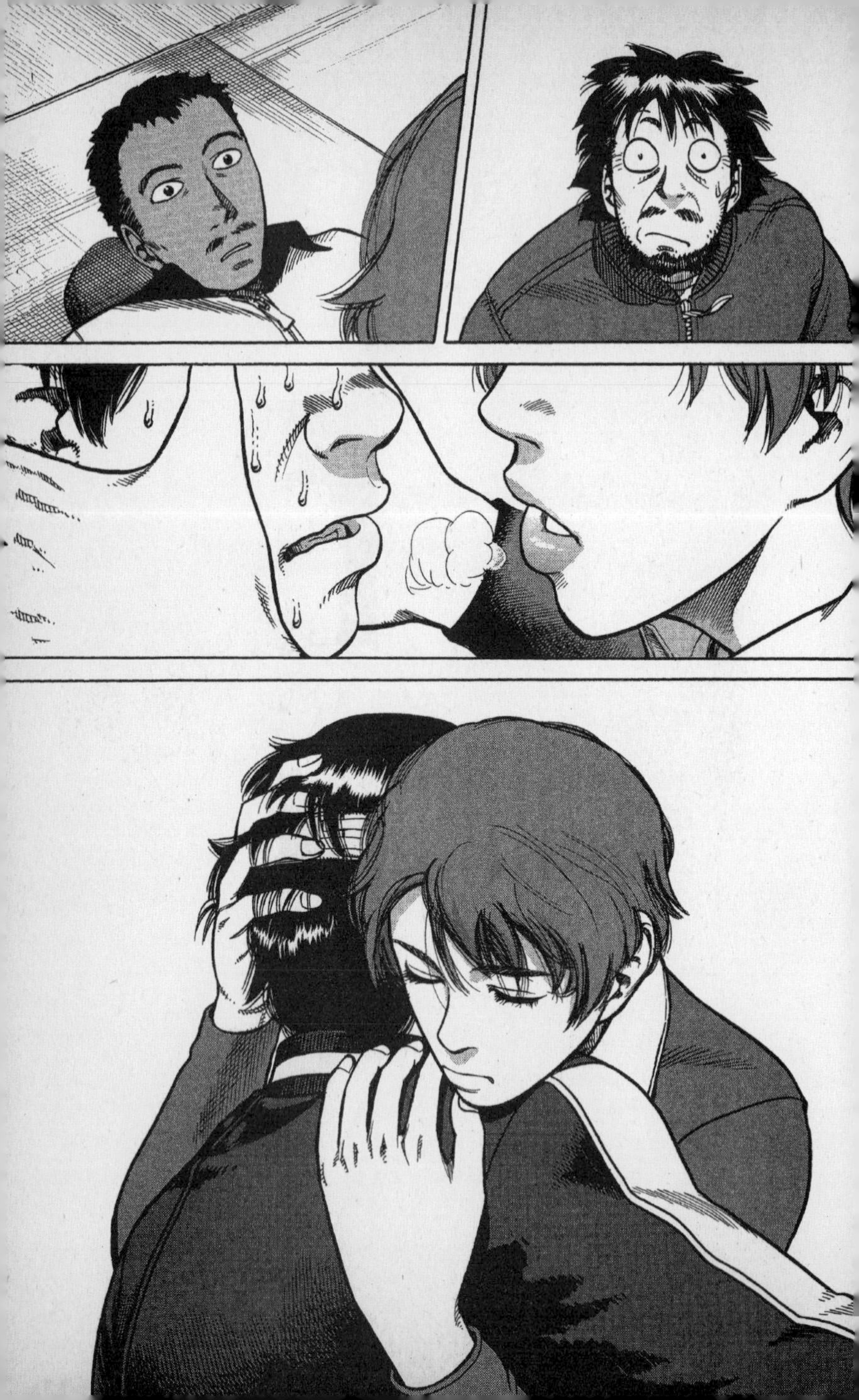

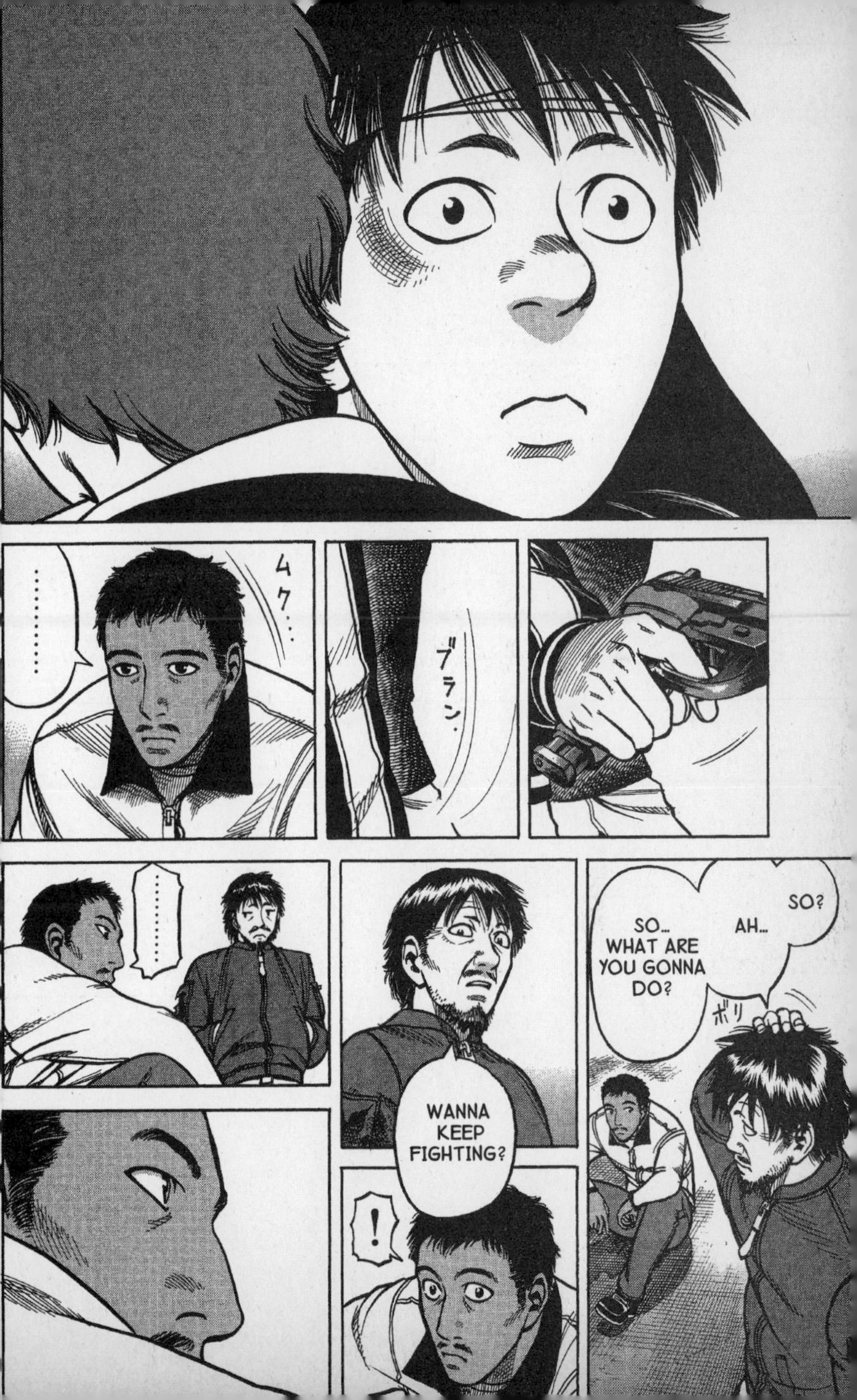

ブラン・
ムク…
……
SO?
AH...
SO... WHAT ARE YOU GONNA DO?
ボリ
WANNA KEEP FIGHTING?
!
……

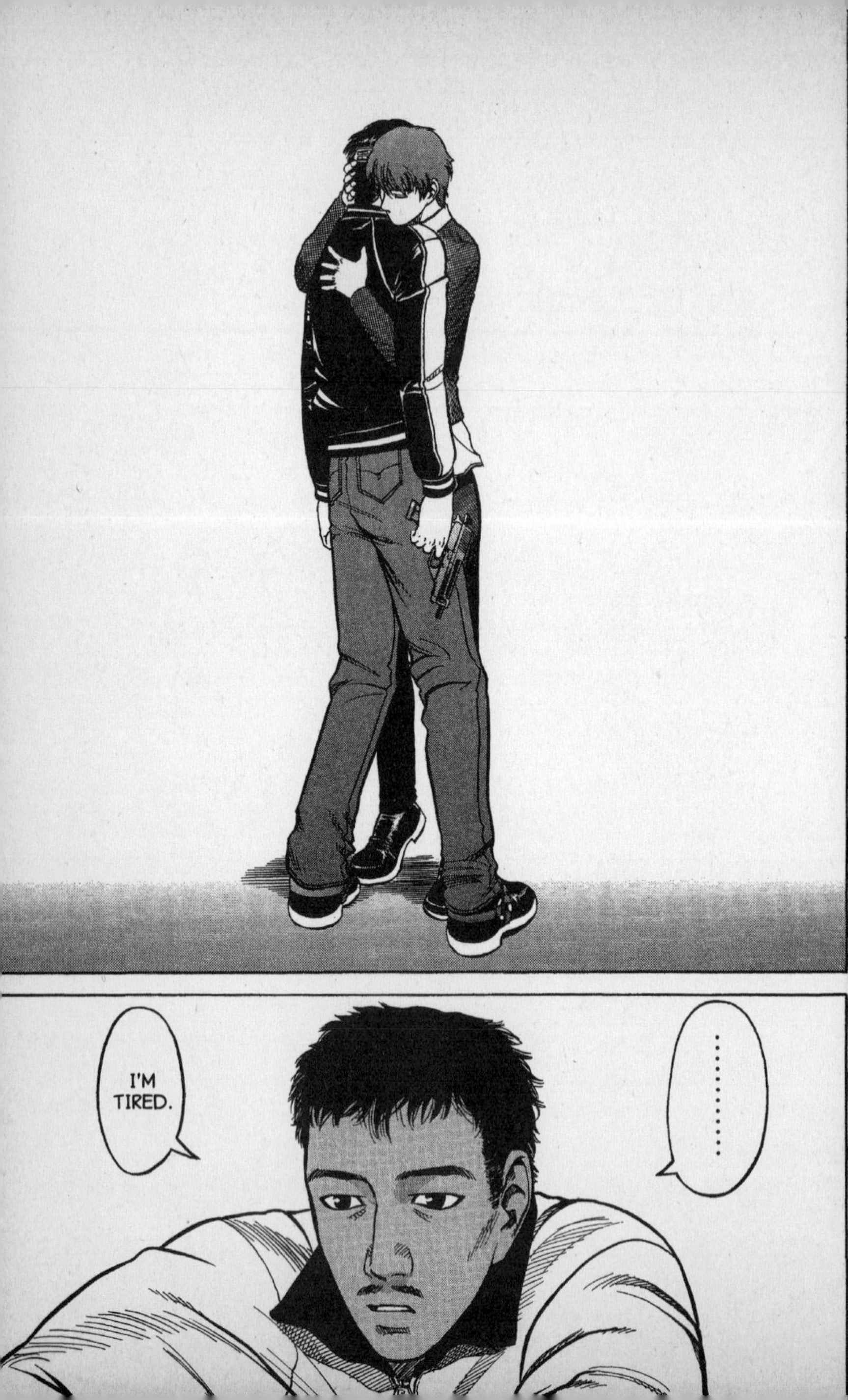
....
I'M TIRED.

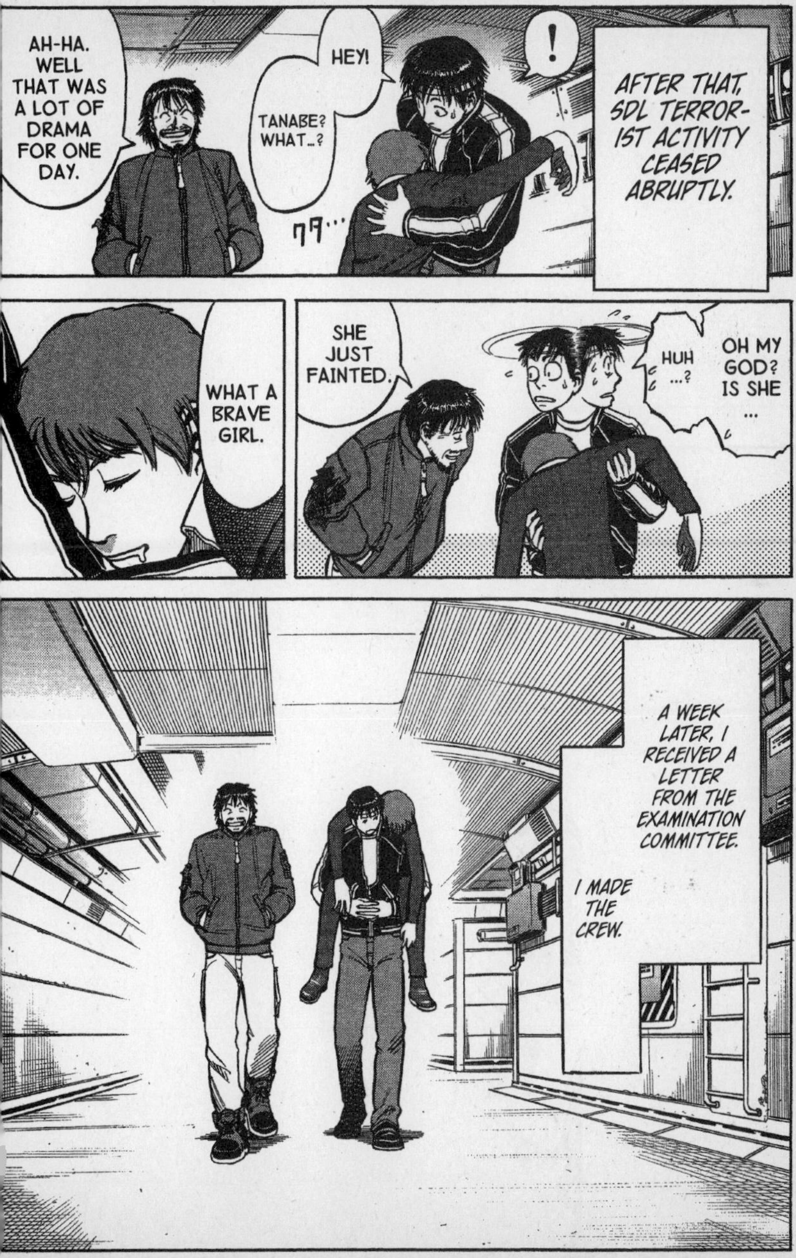
AFTER THAT, SDL TERROR-IST ACTIVITY CEASED ABRUPTLY.
!
HEY!
TANABE? WHAT...?
クタ…
AH-HA. WELL THAT WAS A LOT OF DRAMA FOR ONE DAY.
OH MY GOD? IS SHE ...
HUH ...?
SHE JUST FAINTED.
WHAT A BRAVE GIRL.
A WEEK LATER, I RECEIVED A LETTER FROM THE EXAMINATION COMMITTEE.
I MADE THE CREW.

PHASE.9
おわり

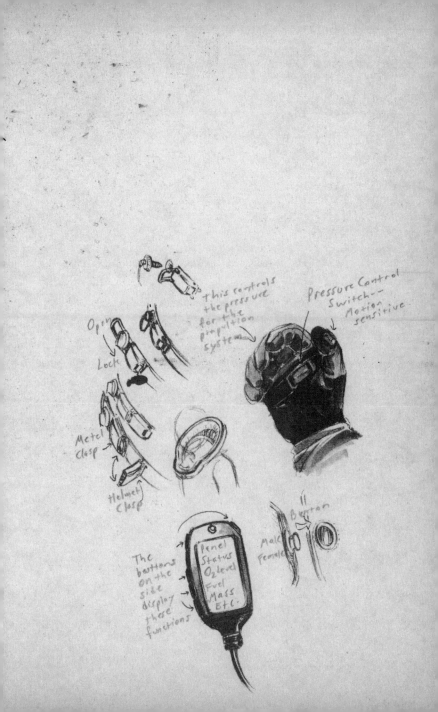

This controls the pressure for the propulsion system

Pressure Control Switch-- Motion sensitive

Open

Lock

Metal Clasp

Helmet Clasp

The buttons on the side display these functions

Panel Status O₂ level Fuel Mass Etc.

Male Female

Button

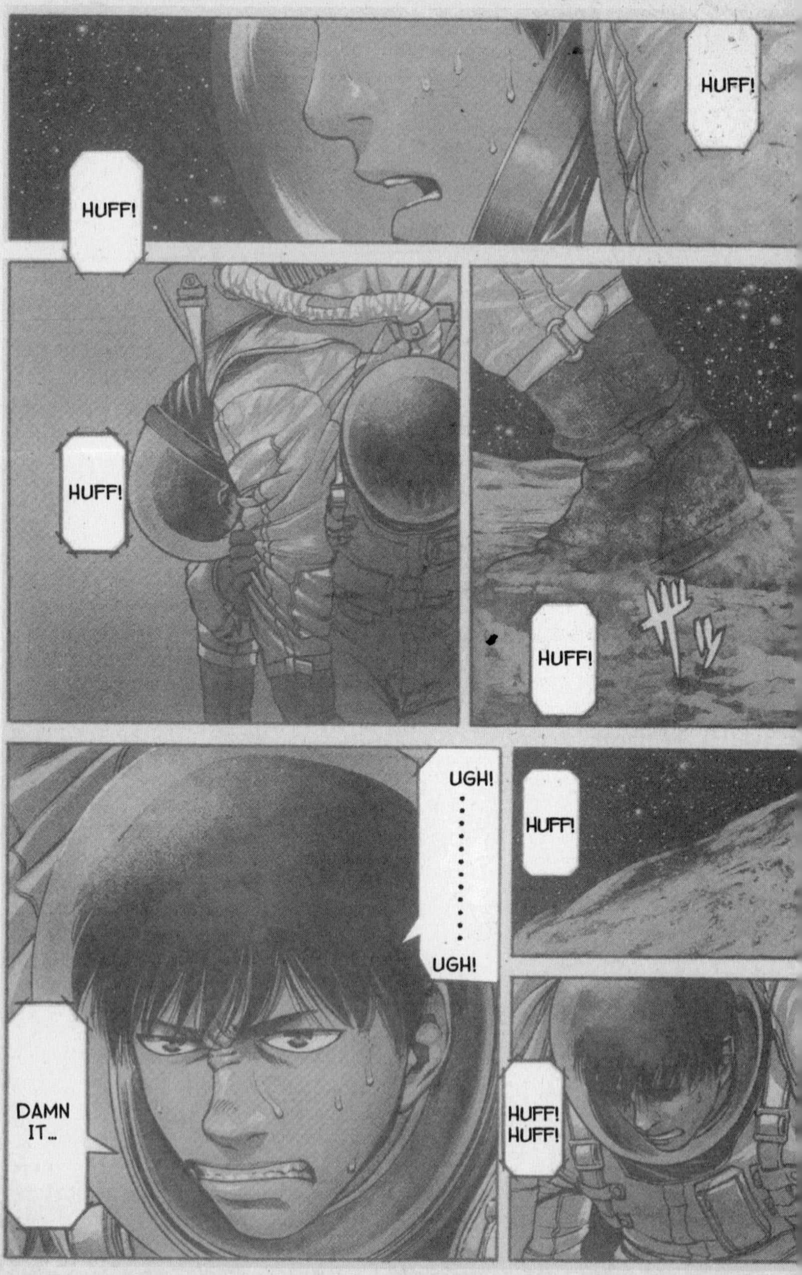
HUFF!
HUFF!
HUFF!
HUFF!
HUFF!
HUFF! HUFF!
UGH! .... UGH!
DAMN IT...

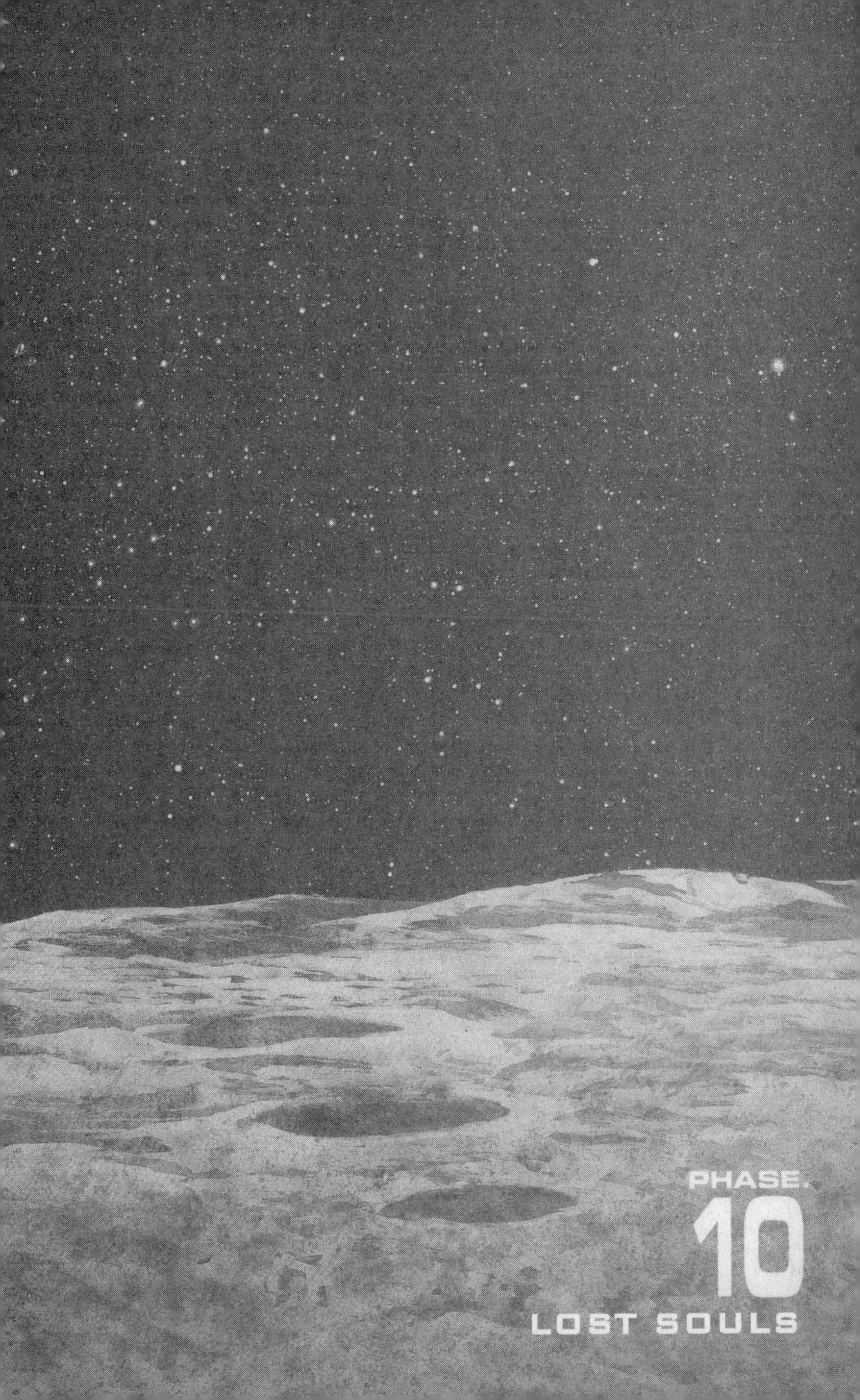
PHASE.
10
LOST SOULS

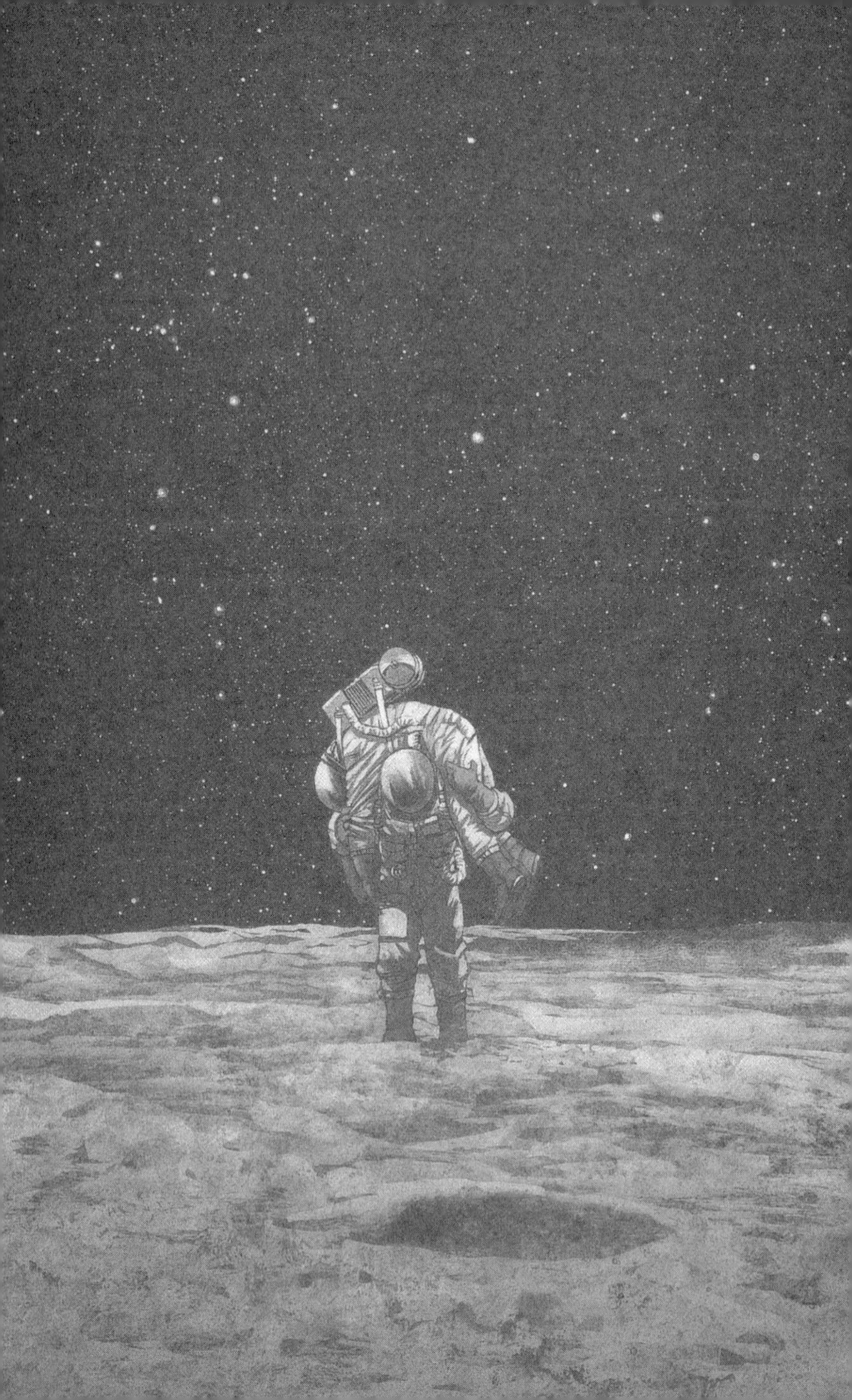

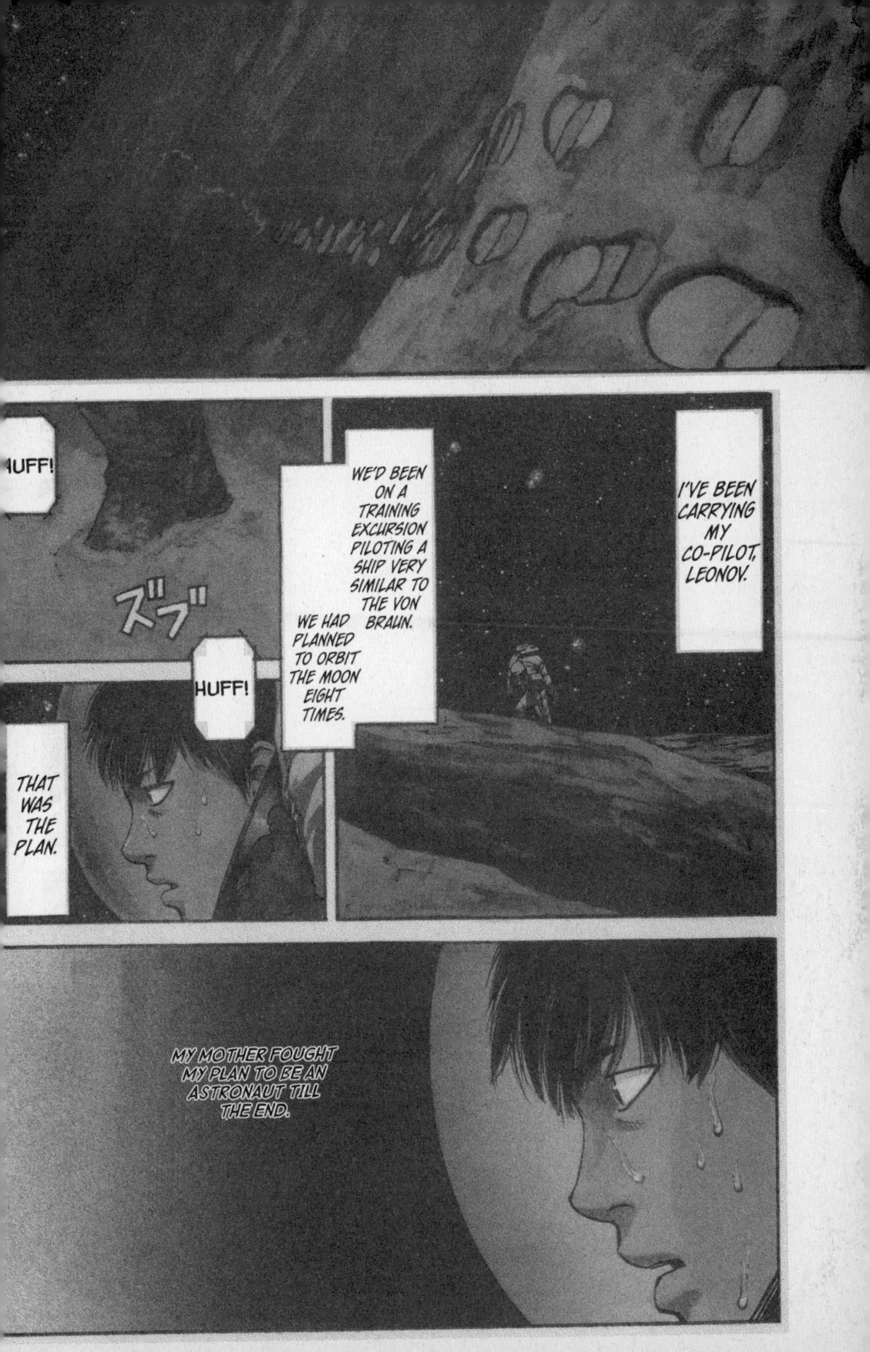

I'VE BEEN CARRYING MY CO-PILOT, LEONOV.
WE'D BEEN ON A TRAINING EXCURSION PILOTING A SHIP VERY SIMILAR TO THE VON BRAUN.
WE HAD PLANNED TO ORBIT THE MOON EIGHT TIMES.
HUFF!
ズブ
HUFF!
THAT WAS THE PLAN.
MY MOTHER FOUGHT MY PLAN TO BE AN ASTRONAUT TILL THE END.

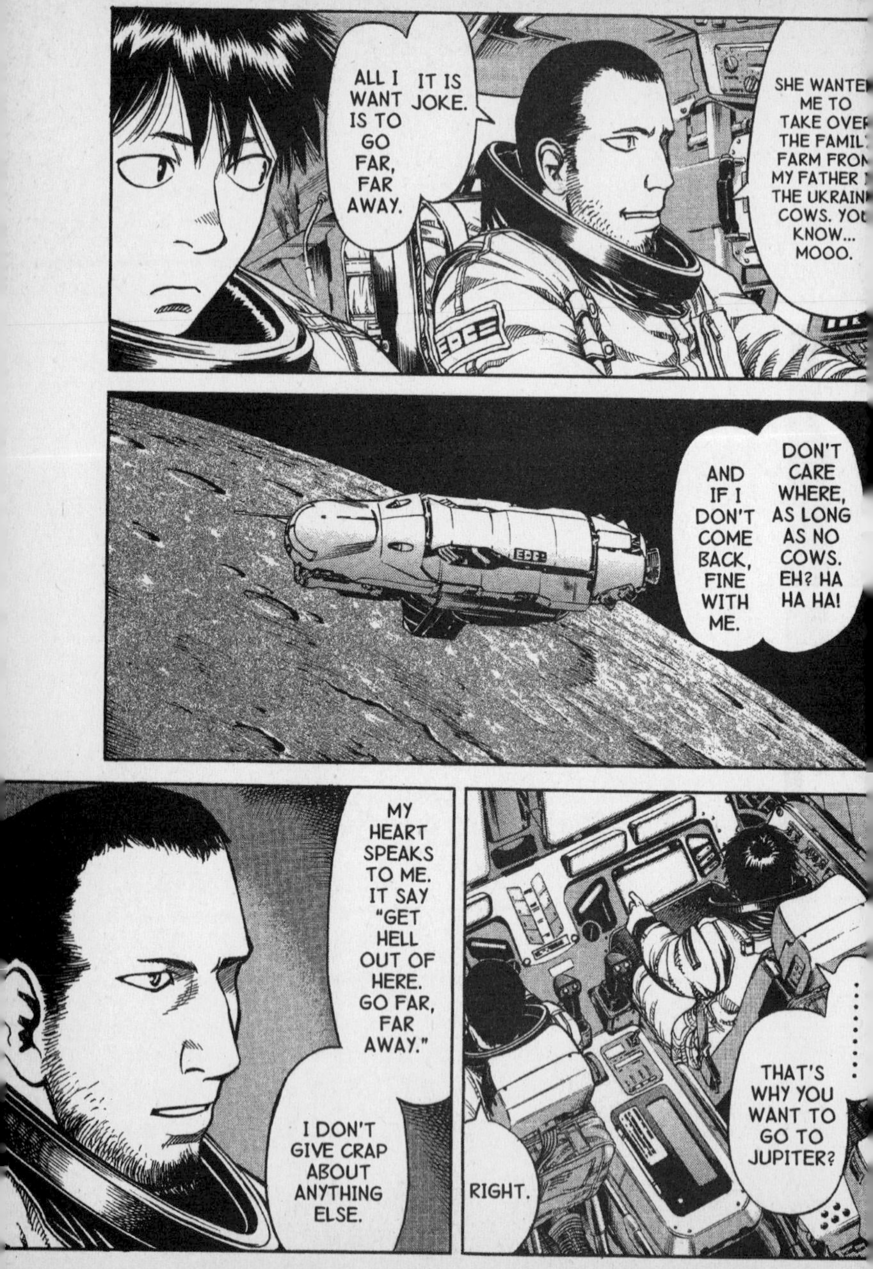
SHE WANTE ME TO TAKE OVE THE FAMIL FARM FRO MY FATHER THE UKRAI COWS. YO KNOW... MOOO.
IT IS JOKE.
ALL I WANT IS TO GO FAR, FAR AWAY.
DON'T CARE WHERE, AS LONG AS NO COWS. EH? HA HA HA!
AND IF I DON'T COME BACK, FINE WITH ME.
THAT'S WHY YOU WANT TO GO TO JUPITER?
RIGHT.
MY HEART SPEAKS TO ME. IT SAY "GET HELL OUT OF HERE. GO FAR, FAR AWAY."
I DON'T GIVE CRAP ABOUT ANYTHING ELSE.

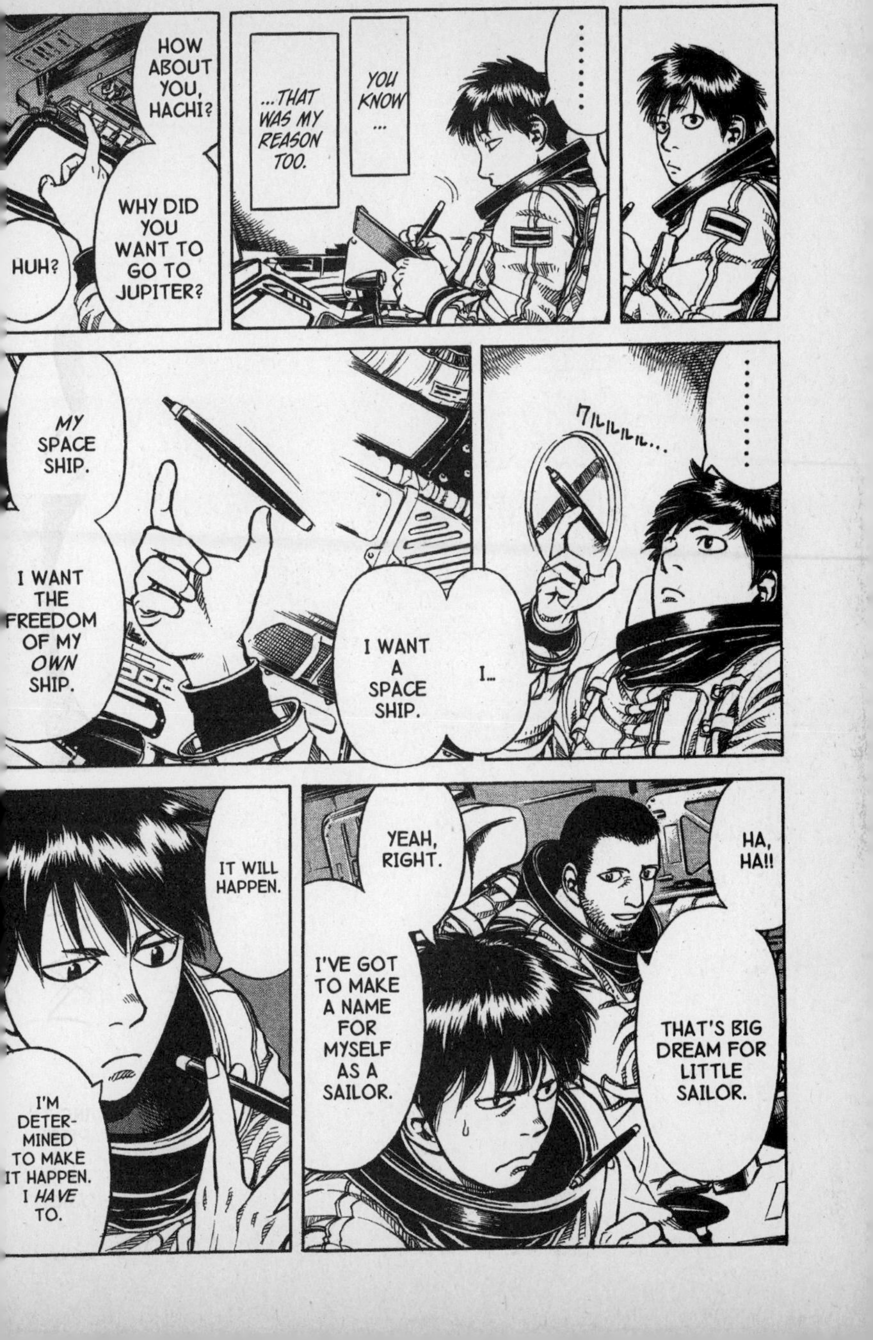

......
YOU KNOW ...
...THAT WAS MY REASON TOO.
HOW ABOUT YOU, HACHI?
WHY DID YOU WANT TO GO TO JUPITER?
HUH?
......
クルルルル...
I...
I WANT A SPACE SHIP.
MY SPACE SHIP.
I WANT THE FREEDOM OF MY *OWN* SHIP.
HA, HA!!
YEAH, RIGHT.
THAT'S BIG DREAM FOR LITTLE SAILOR.
I'VE GOT TO MAKE A NAME FOR MYSELF AS A SAILOR.
IT WILL HAPPEN.
I'M DETER-MINED TO MAKE IT HAPPEN. I *HAVE* TO.

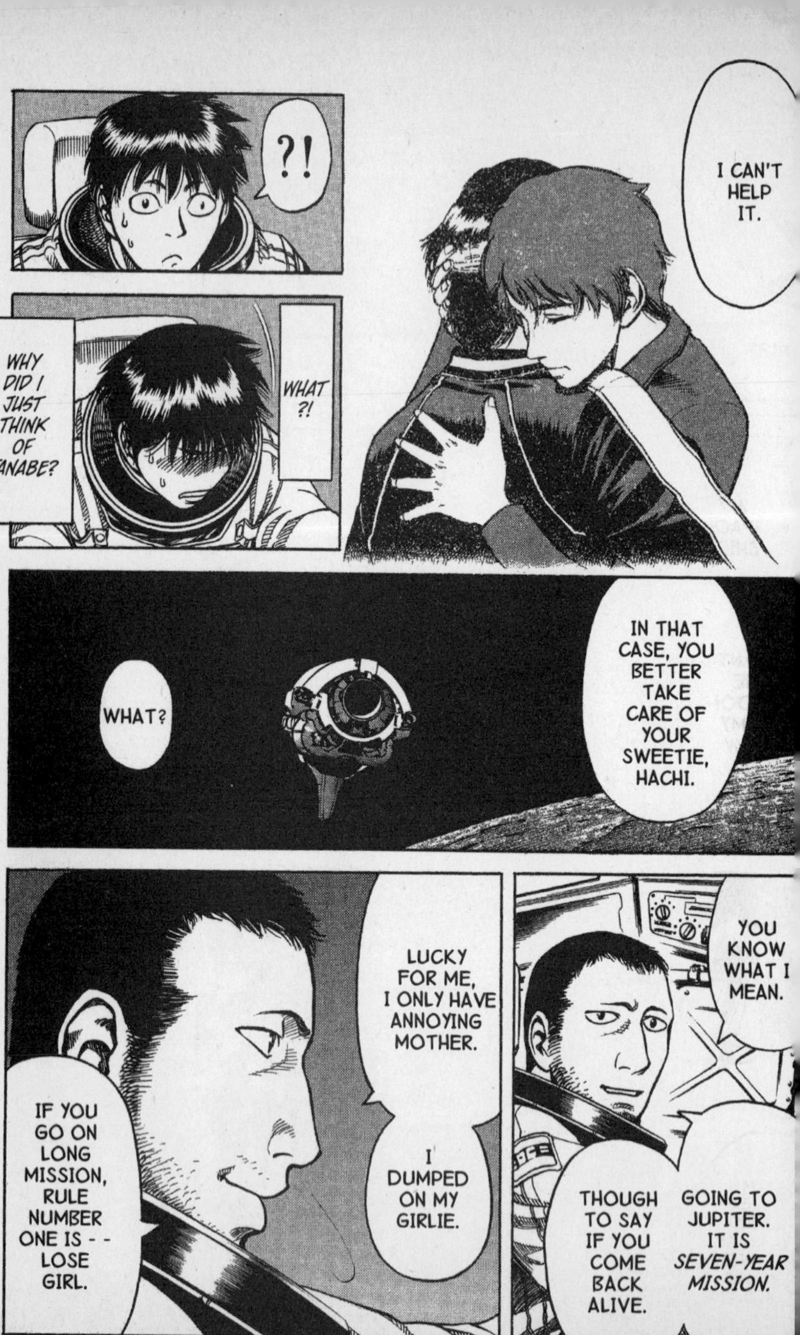
I CAN'T HELP IT.
?!
WHAT ?!
WHY DID I JUST THINK OF TANABE?
IN THAT CASE, YOU BETTER TAKE CARE OF YOUR SWEETIE, HACHI.
WHAT?
YOU KNOW WHAT I MEAN.
GOING TO JUPITER. IT IS *SEVEN-YEAR MISSION.*
THOUGH TO SAY IF YOU COME BACK ALIVE.
LUCKY FOR ME, I ONLY HAVE ANNOYING MOTHER.
I DUMPED ON MY GIRLIE.
IF YOU GO ON LONG MISSION, RULE NUMBER ONE IS - - LOSE GIRL.

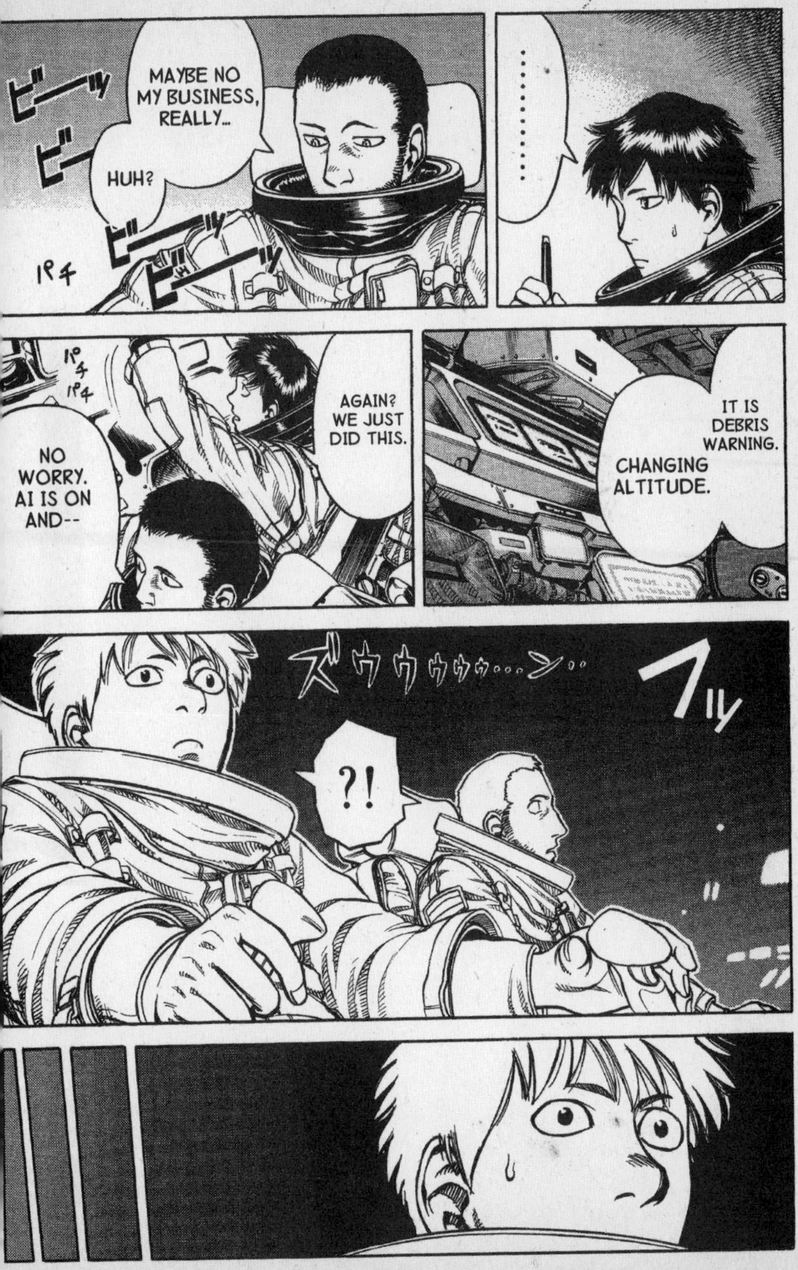

......
MAYBE NO MY BUSINESS, REALLY...
ビーーッ
ビー
HUH?
ビーーッ
ビーーッ
パチ
IT IS DEBRIS WARNING.
CHANGING ALTITUDE.
AGAIN? WE JUST DID THIS.
パチパチ
NO WORRY. AI IS ON AND--
ヘッ
ズウウウウウ...ン..
?!

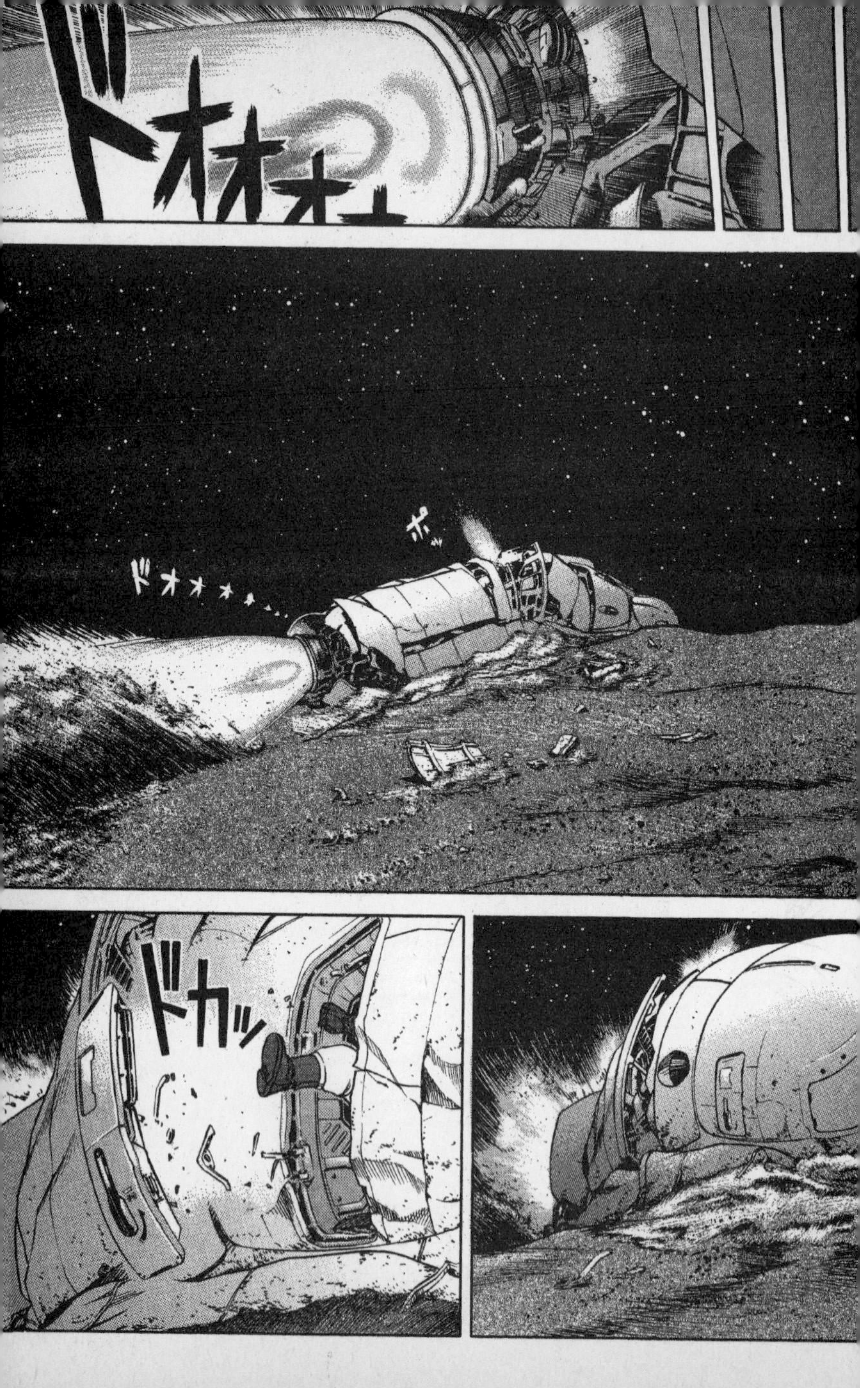
ドオオオォ
ボッ
ドオオオォ…
ドカッ

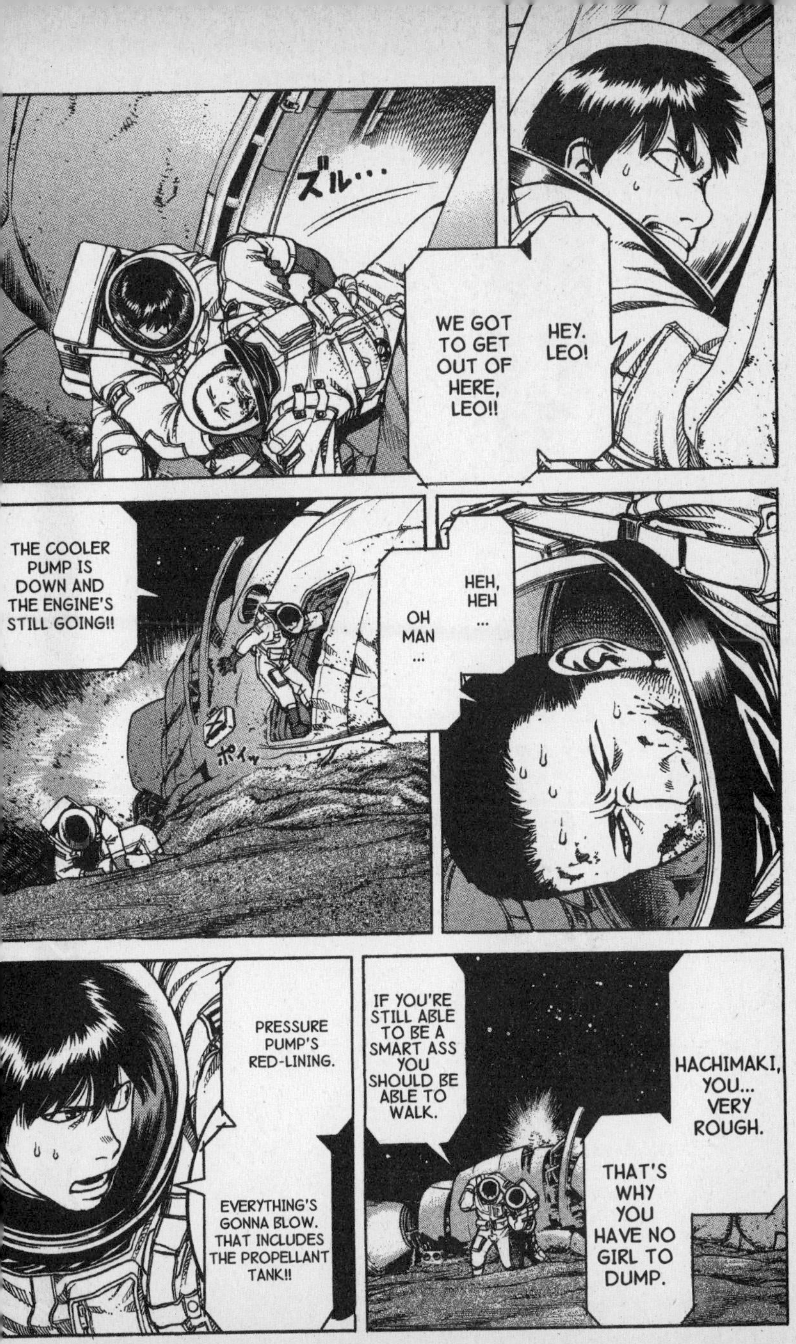
HEY. LEO!
WE GOT TO GET OUT OF HERE, LEO!!
ズル・・・
HEH, HEH ...
OH MAN ...
THE COOLER PUMP IS DOWN AND THE ENGINE'S STILL GOING!!
ポイッ
IF YOU'RE STILL ABLE TO BE A SMART ASS YOU SHOULD BE ABLE TO WALK.
HACHIMAKI, YOU... VERY ROUGH.
THAT'S WHY YOU HAVE NO GIRL TO DUMP.
PRESSURE PUMP'S RED-LINING.
EVERYTHING'S GONNA BLOW. THAT INCLUDES THE PROPELLANT TANK!!

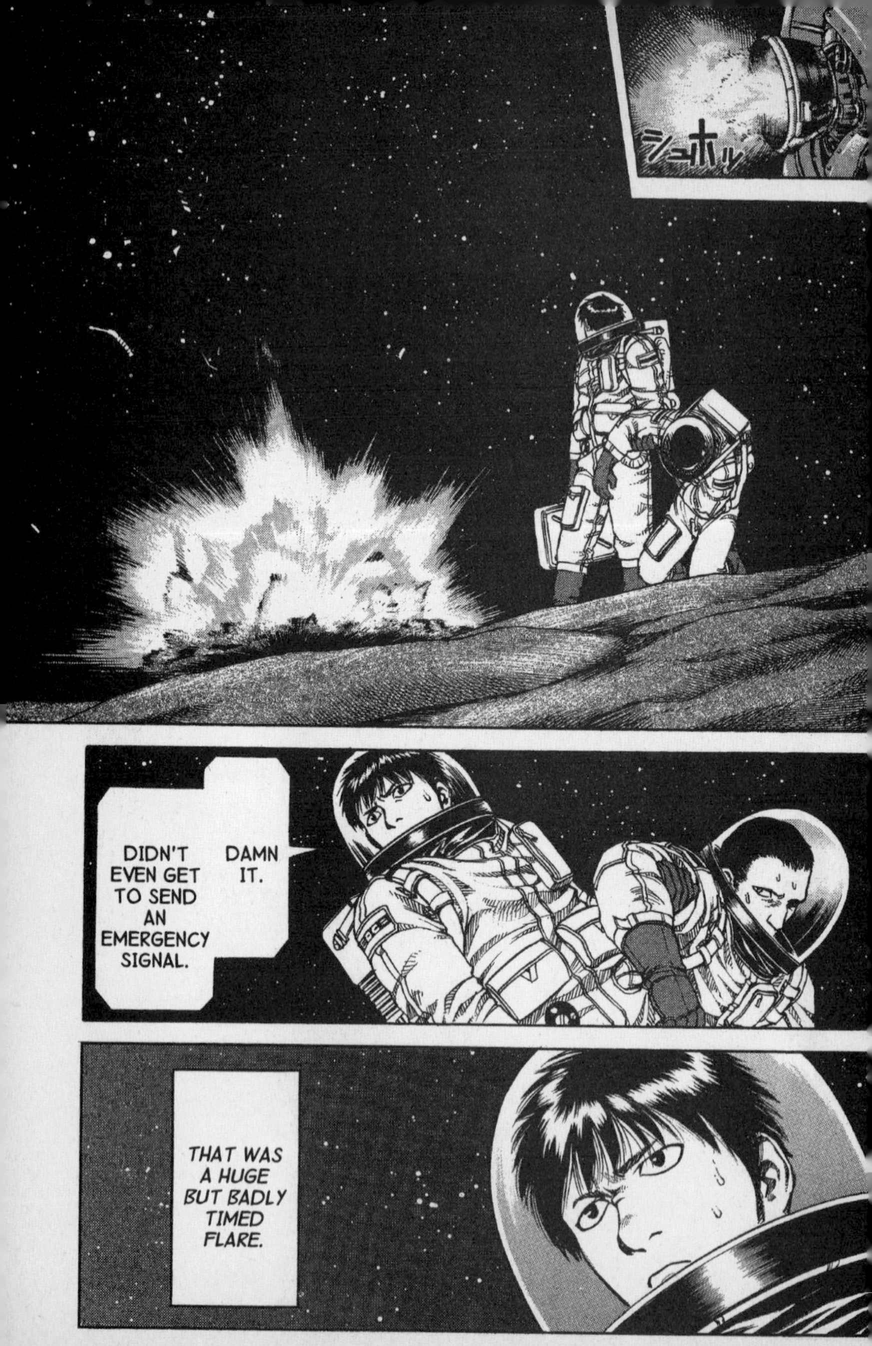
シュホッ
DAMN IT.
DIDN'T EVEN GET TO SEND AN EMERGENCY SIGNAL.
THAT WAS A HUGE BUT BADLY TIMED FLARE.

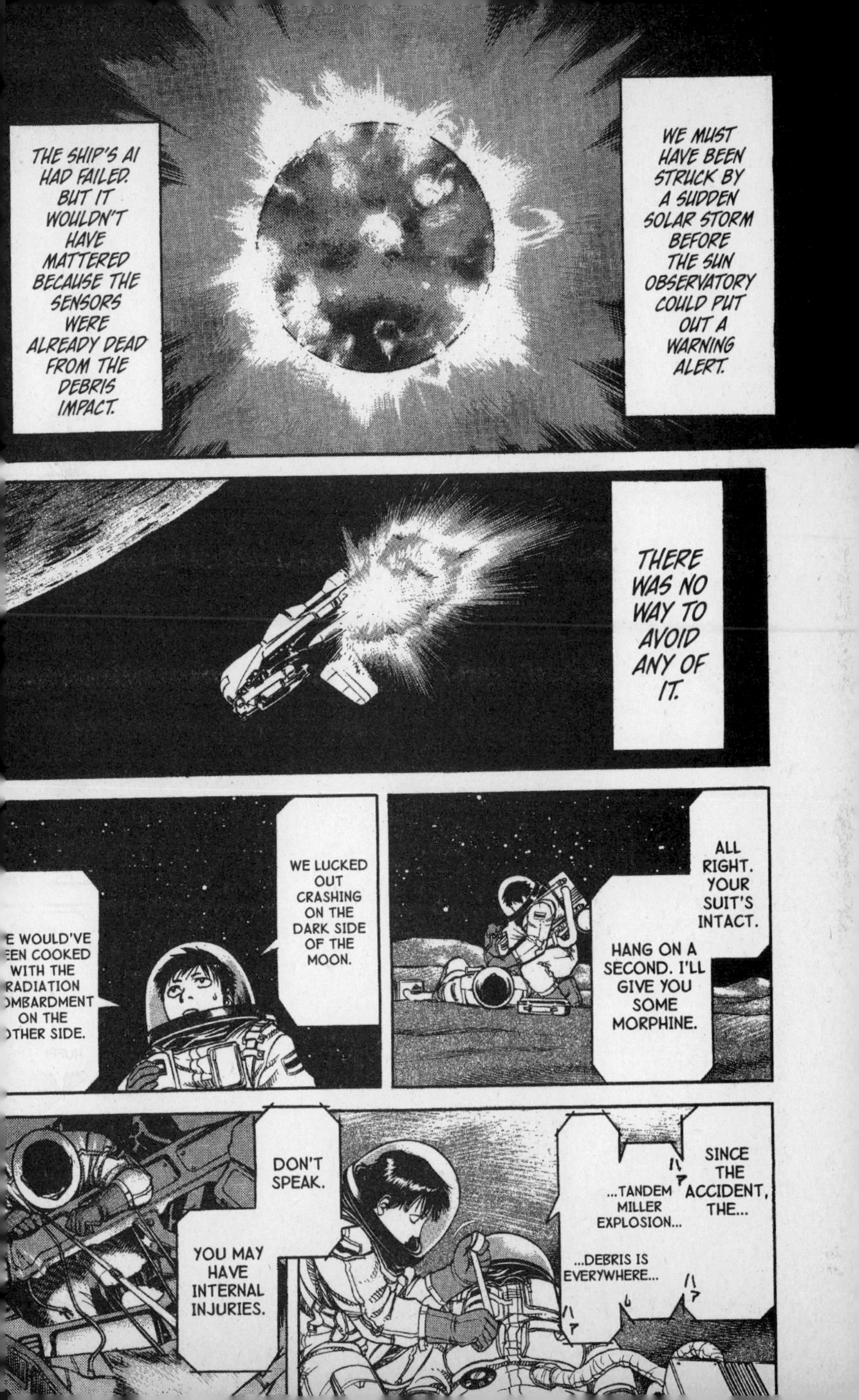

WE MUST HAVE BEEN STRUCK BY A SUDDEN SOLAR STORM BEFORE THE SUN OBSERVATORY COULD PUT OUT A WARNING ALERT.
THE SHIP'S AI HAD FAILED. BUT IT WOULDN'T HAVE MATTERED BECAUSE THE SENSORS WERE ALREADY DEAD FROM THE DEBRIS IMPACT.
THERE WAS NO WAY TO AVOID ANY OF IT.
ALL RIGHT. YOUR SUIT'S INTACT.
HANG ON A SECOND. I'LL GIVE YOU SOME MORPHINE.
WE LUCKED OUT CRASHING ON THE DARK SIDE OF THE MOON.
E WOULD'VE EEN COOKED WITH THE RADIATION OMBARDMENT ON THE OTHER SIDE.
SINCE THE ACCIDENT, THE...
...TANDEM MILLER EXPLOSION...
...DEBRIS IS EVERYWHERE...
ハァ
ハァ
ハァ
DON'T SPEAK.
YOU MAY HAVE INTERNAL INJURIES.

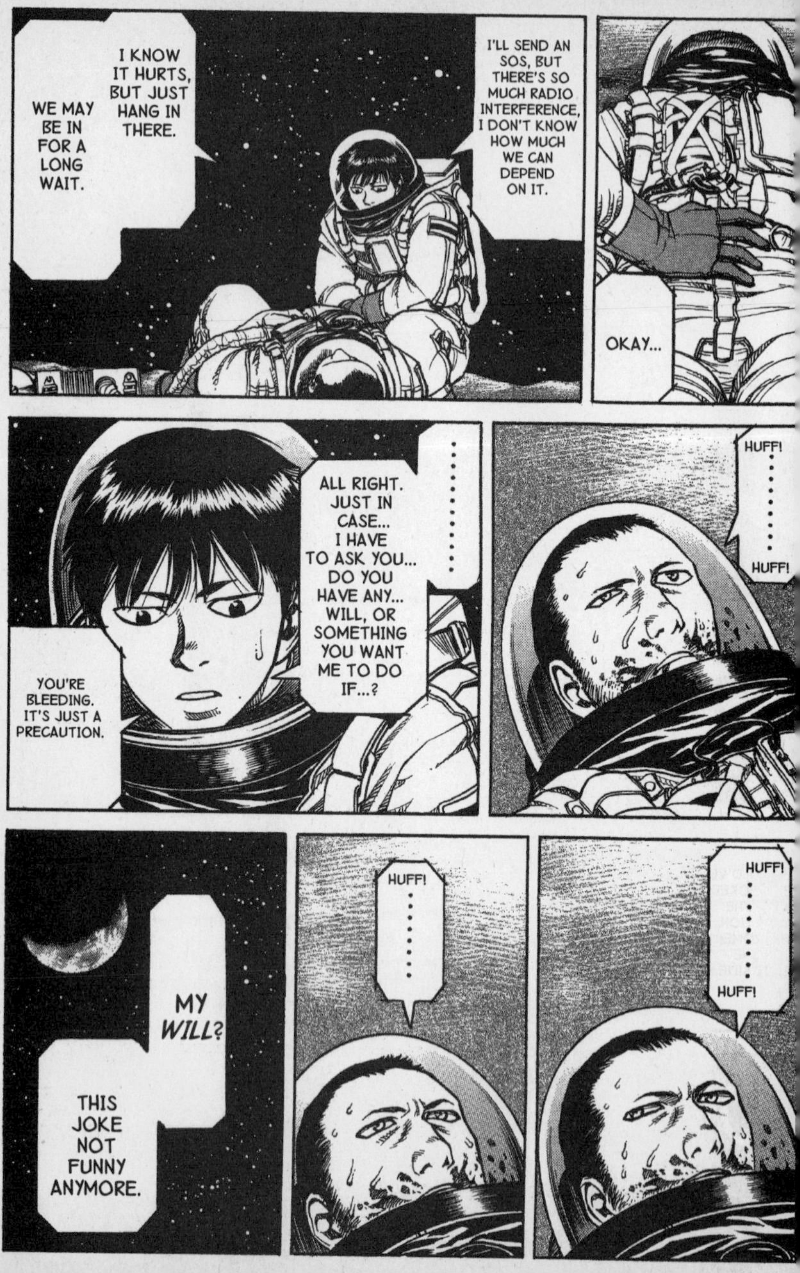
OKAY...
I'LL SEND AN SOS, BUT THERE'S SO MUCH RADIO INTERFERENCE, I DON'T KNOW HOW MUCH WE CAN DEPEND ON IT.
I KNOW IT HURTS, BUT JUST HANG IN THERE.
WE MAY BE IN FOR A LONG WAIT.
HUFF! ...... HUFF!
......
ALL RIGHT. JUST IN CASE... I HAVE TO ASK YOU... DO YOU HAVE ANY... WILL, OR SOMETHING YOU WANT ME TO DO IF...?
YOU'RE BLEEDING. IT'S JUST A PRECAUTION.
HUFF! ...... HUFF!
HUFF! ......
MY *WILL*?
THIS JOKE NOT FUNNY ANYMORE.

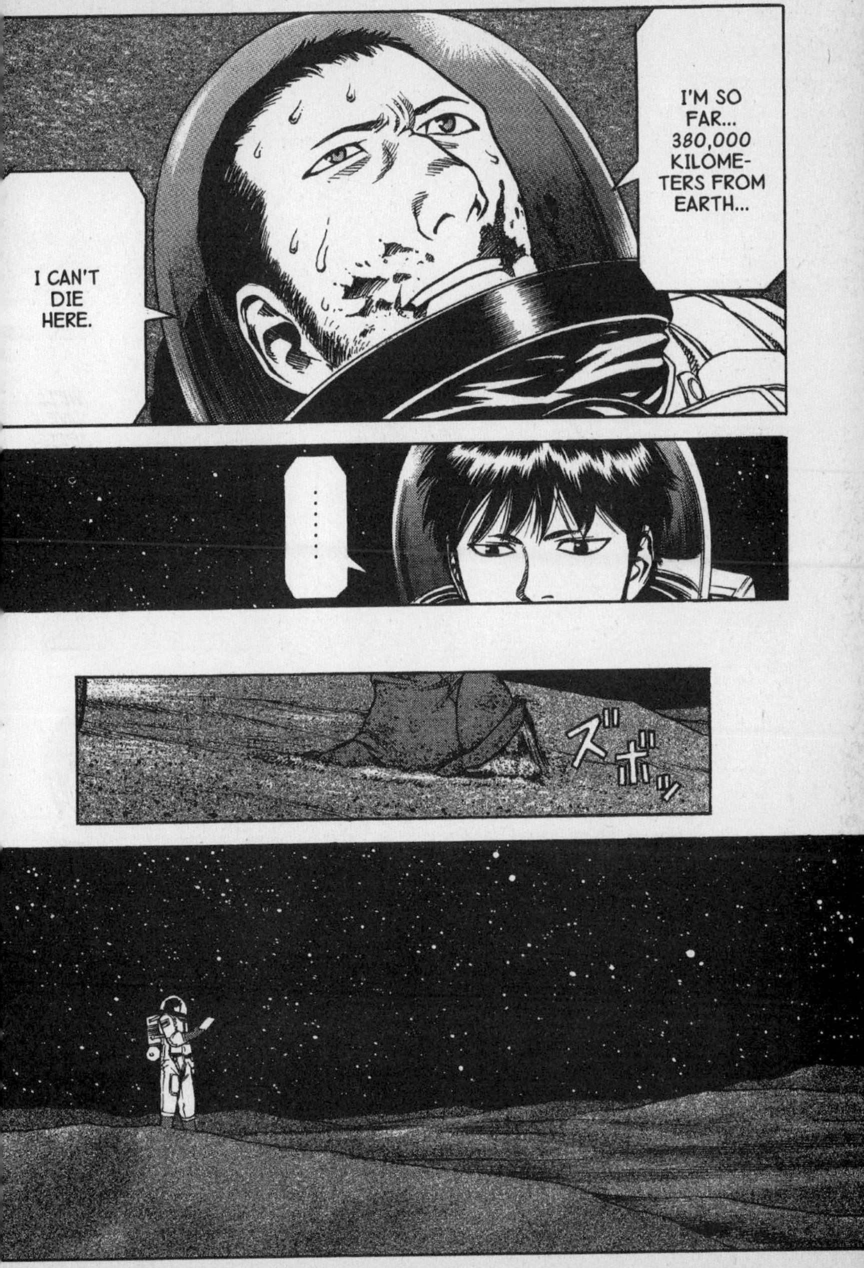
I'M SO FAR... 380,000 KILOMETERS FROM EARTH...
I CAN'T DIE HERE.
......
ズボッ

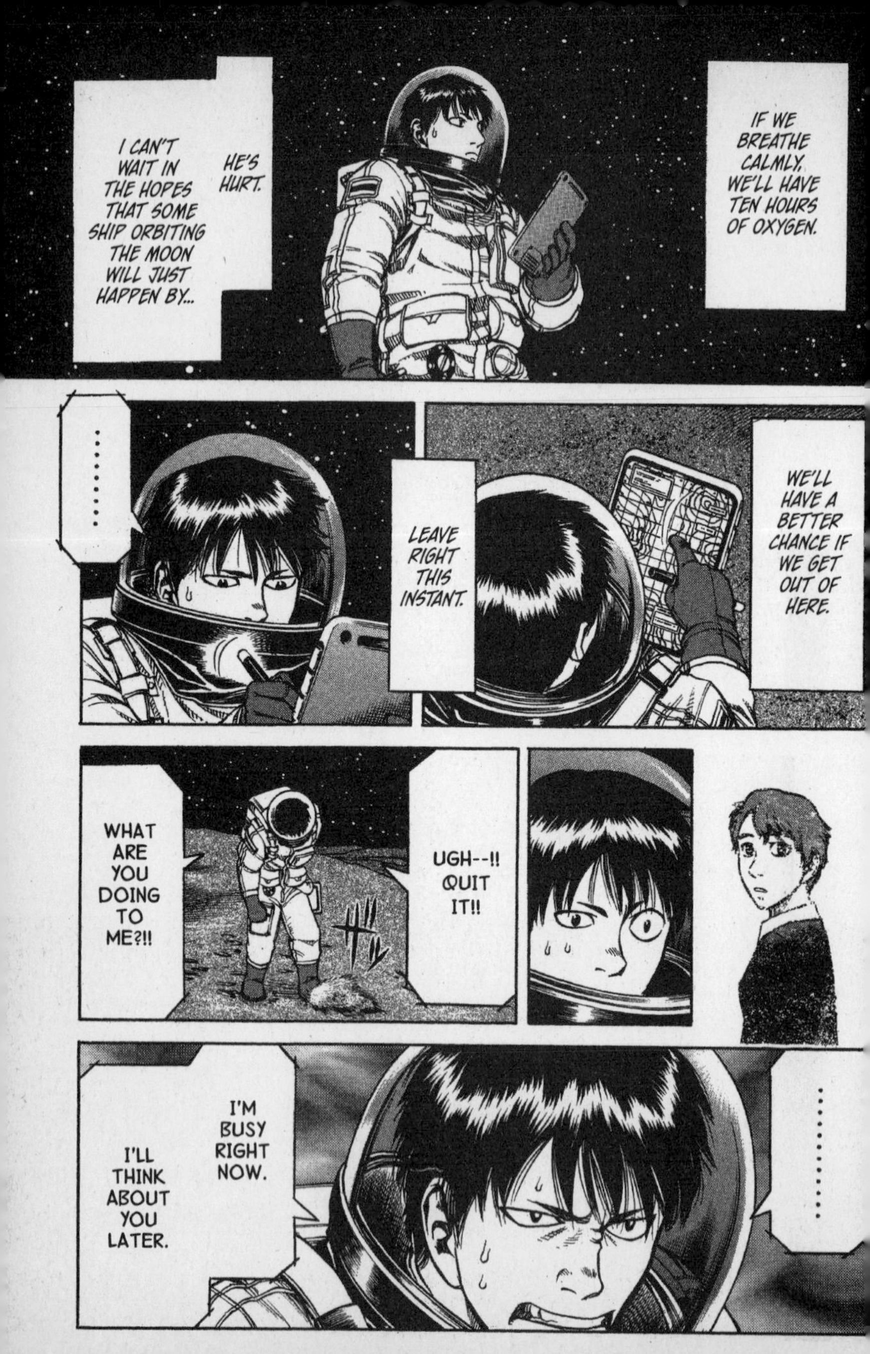
IF WE BREATHE CALMLY, WE'LL HAVE TEN HOURS OF OXYGEN.
HE'S HURT.
I CAN'T WAIT IN THE HOPES THAT SOME SHIP ORBITING THE MOON WILL JUST HAPPEN BY...
WE'LL HAVE A BETTER CHANCE IF WE GET OUT OF HERE.
LEAVE RIGHT THIS INSTANT.
....
UGH--!! QUIT IT!!
WHAT ARE YOU DOING TO ME?!!
....
I'M BUSY RIGHT NOW.
I'LL THINK ABOUT YOU LATER.

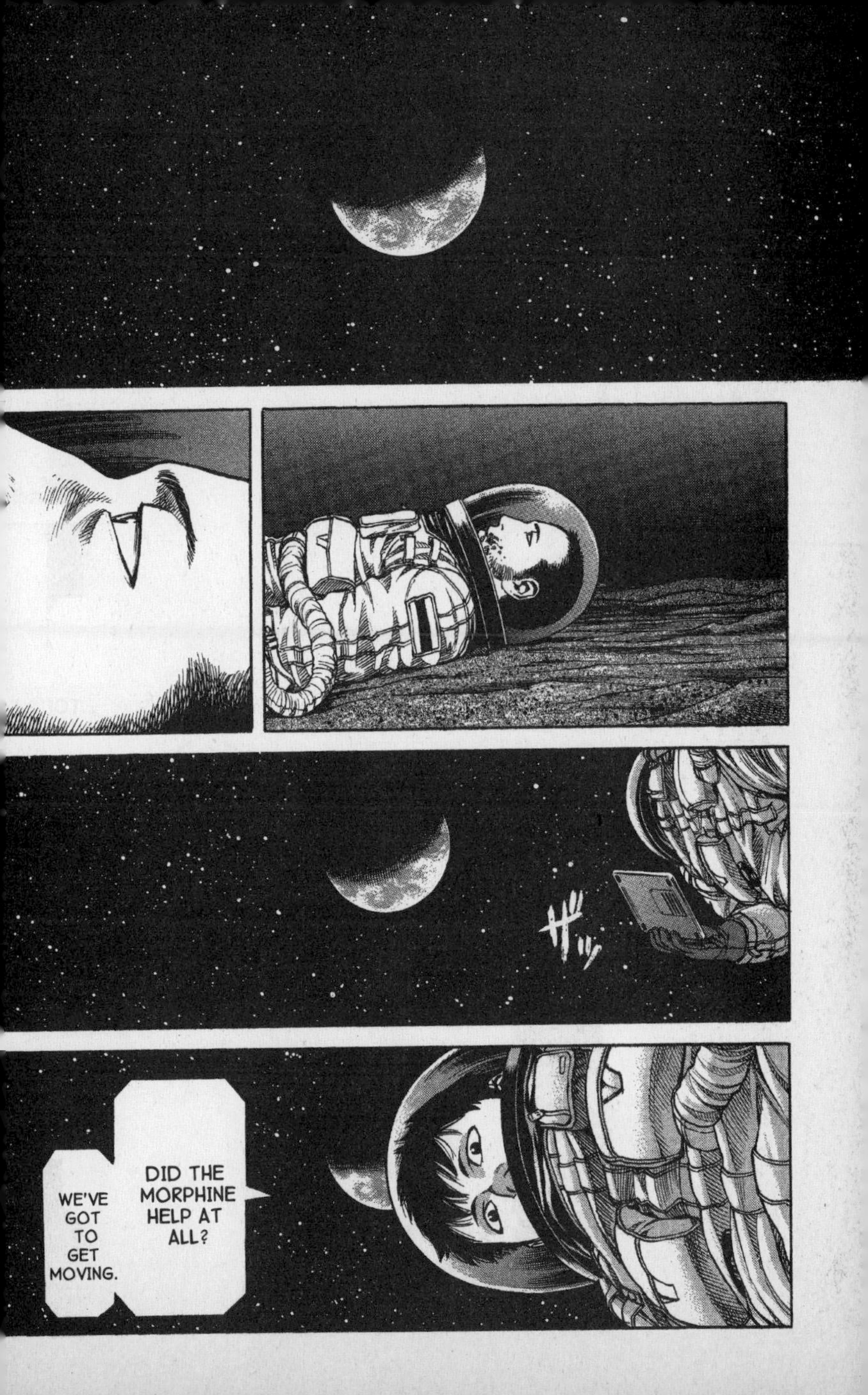
DID THE MORPHINE HELP AT ALL?
WE'VE GOT TO GET MOVING.

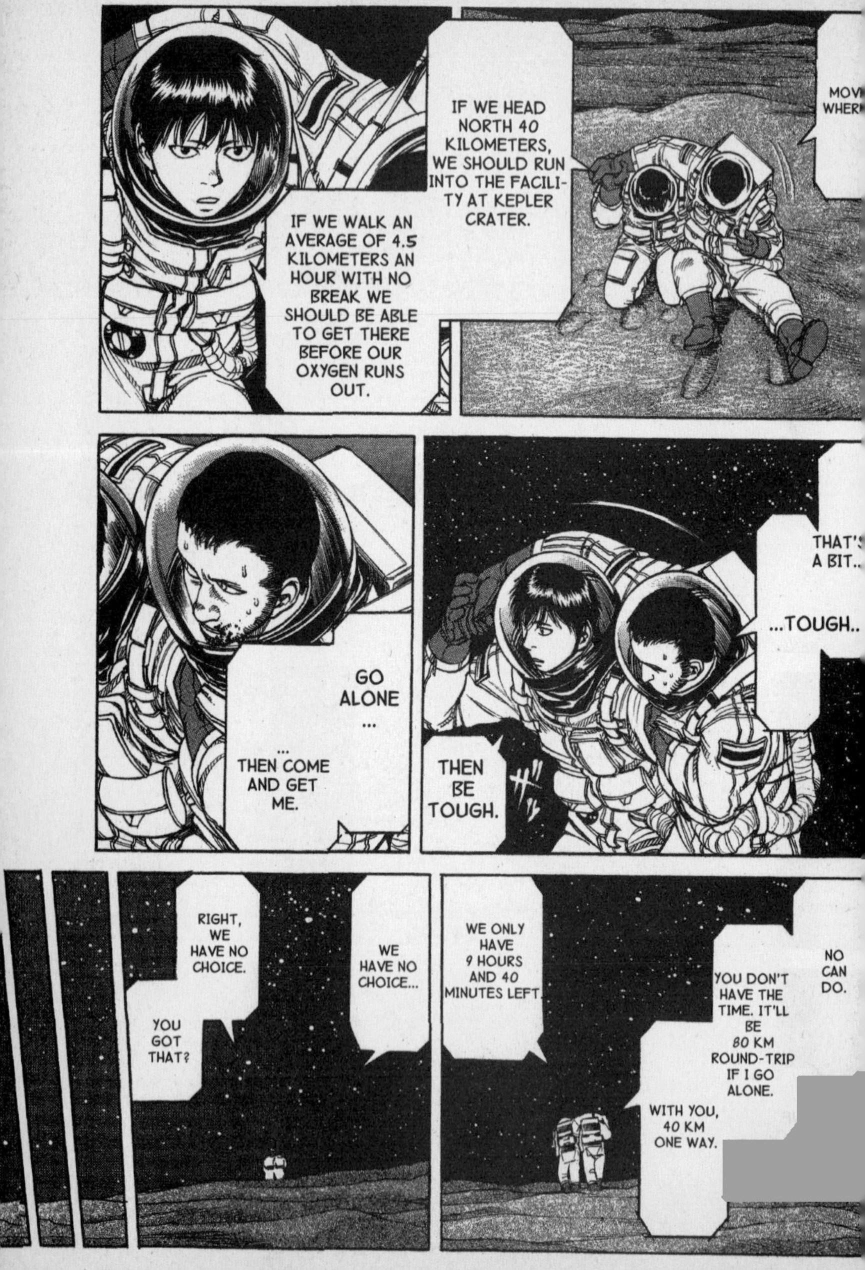
IF WE HEAD NORTH 40 KILOMETERS, WE SHOULD RUN INTO THE FACILITY AT KEPLER CRATER.
IF WE WALK AN AVERAGE OF 4.5 KILOMETERS AN HOUR WITH NO BREAK WE SHOULD BE ABLE TO GET THERE BEFORE OUR OXYGEN RUNS OUT.
THAT'S A BIT...
...TOUGH..
THEN BE TOUGH.
GO ALONE ...
... THEN COME AND GET ME.
NO CAN DO.
YOU DON'T HAVE THE TIME. IT'LL BE 80 KM ROUND-TRIP IF I GO ALONE.
WITH YOU, 40 KM ONE WAY.
WE ONLY HAVE 9 HOURS AND 40 MINUTES LEFT.
WE HAVE NO CHOICE...
RIGHT, WE HAVE NO CHOICE.
YOU GOT THAT?

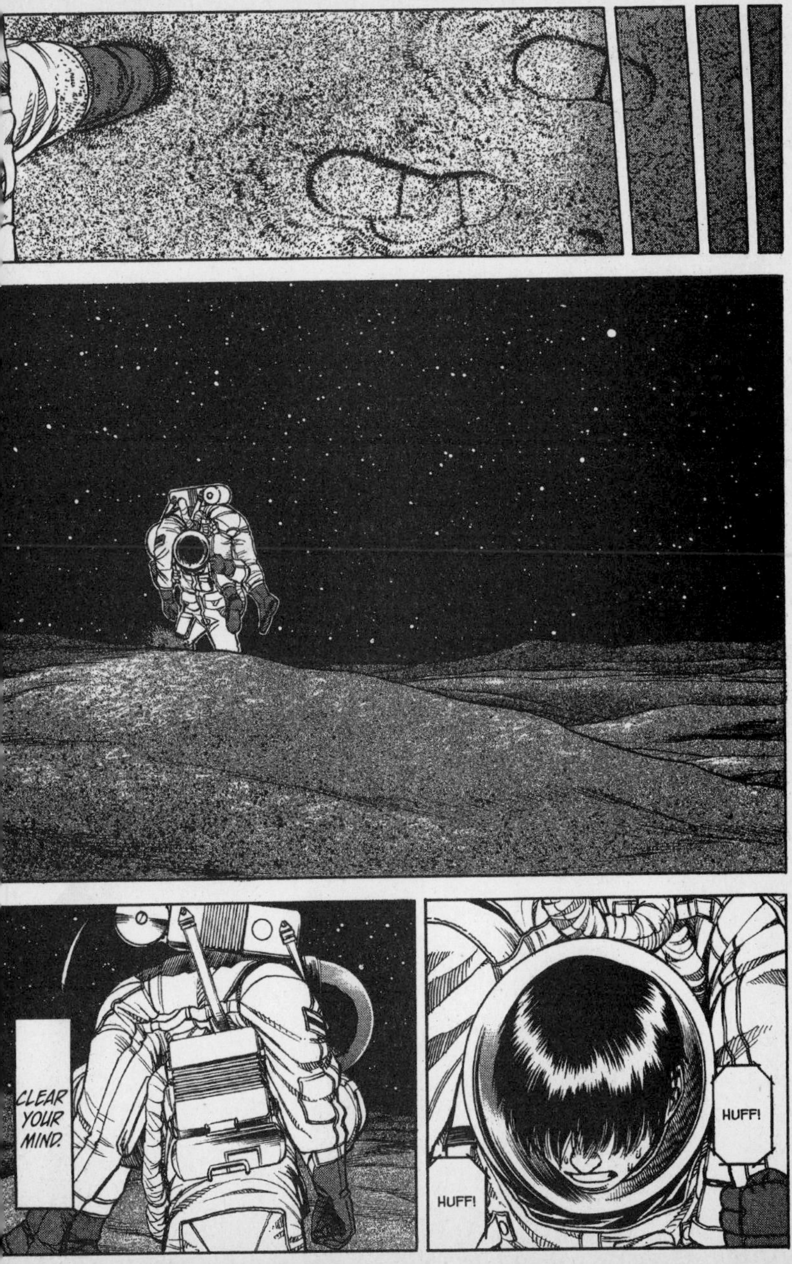
HUFF!
HUFF!
CLEAR YOUR MIND.

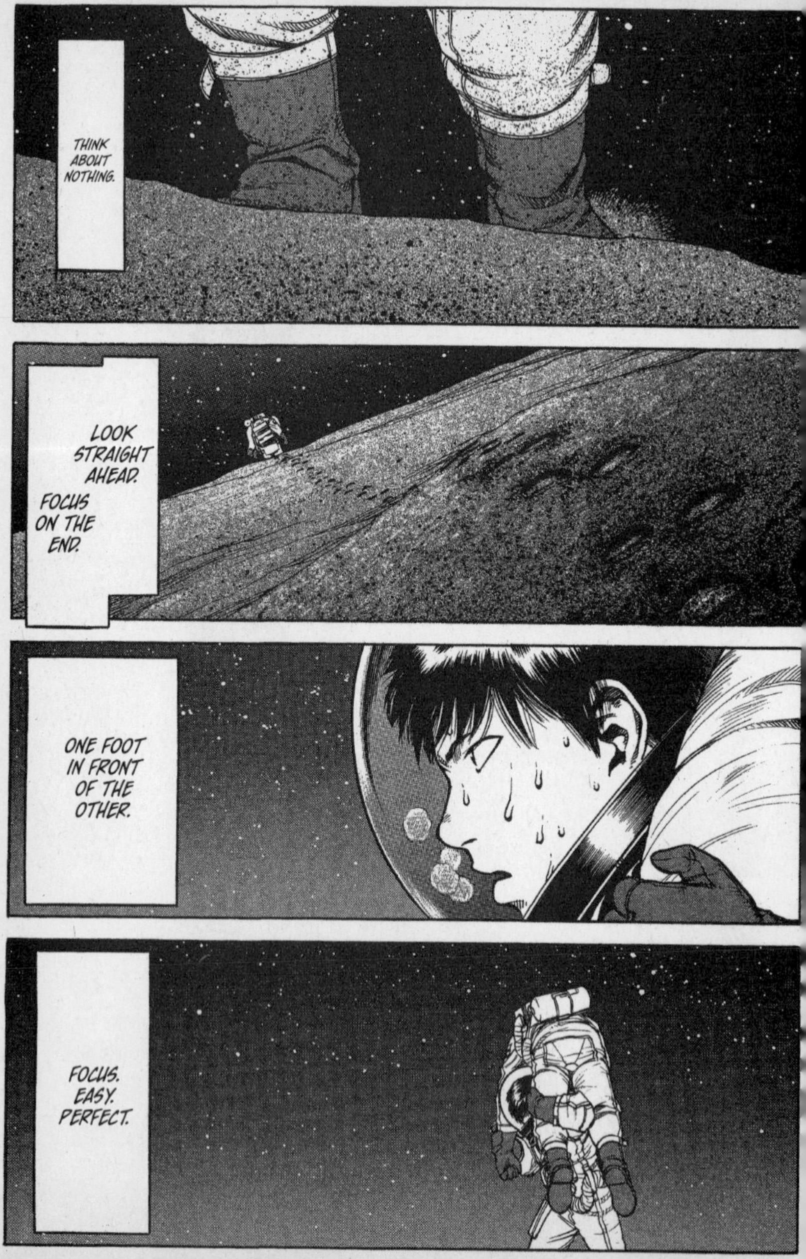
THINK ABOUT NOTHING.
LOOK STRAIGHT AHEAD.
FOCUS ON THE END.
ONE FOOT IN FRONT OF THE OTHER.
FOCUS. EASY. PERFECT.

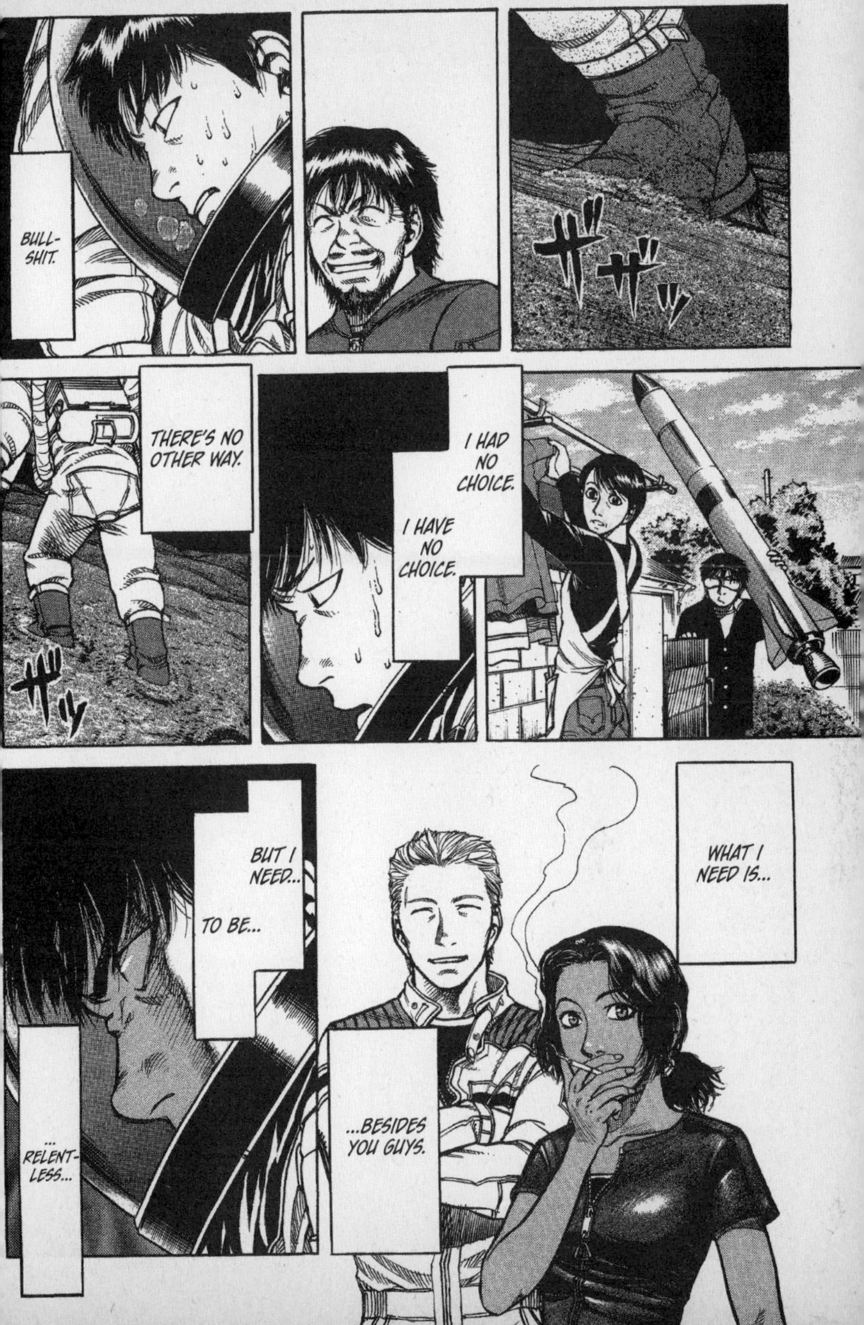
ザザッ
BULL-SHIT.
I HAD NO CHOICE.
I HAVE NO CHOICE.
THERE'S NO OTHER WAY.
ザッ
WHAT I NEED IS...
...BESIDES YOU GUYS.
BUT I NEED...
TO BE...
...RELENTLESS...

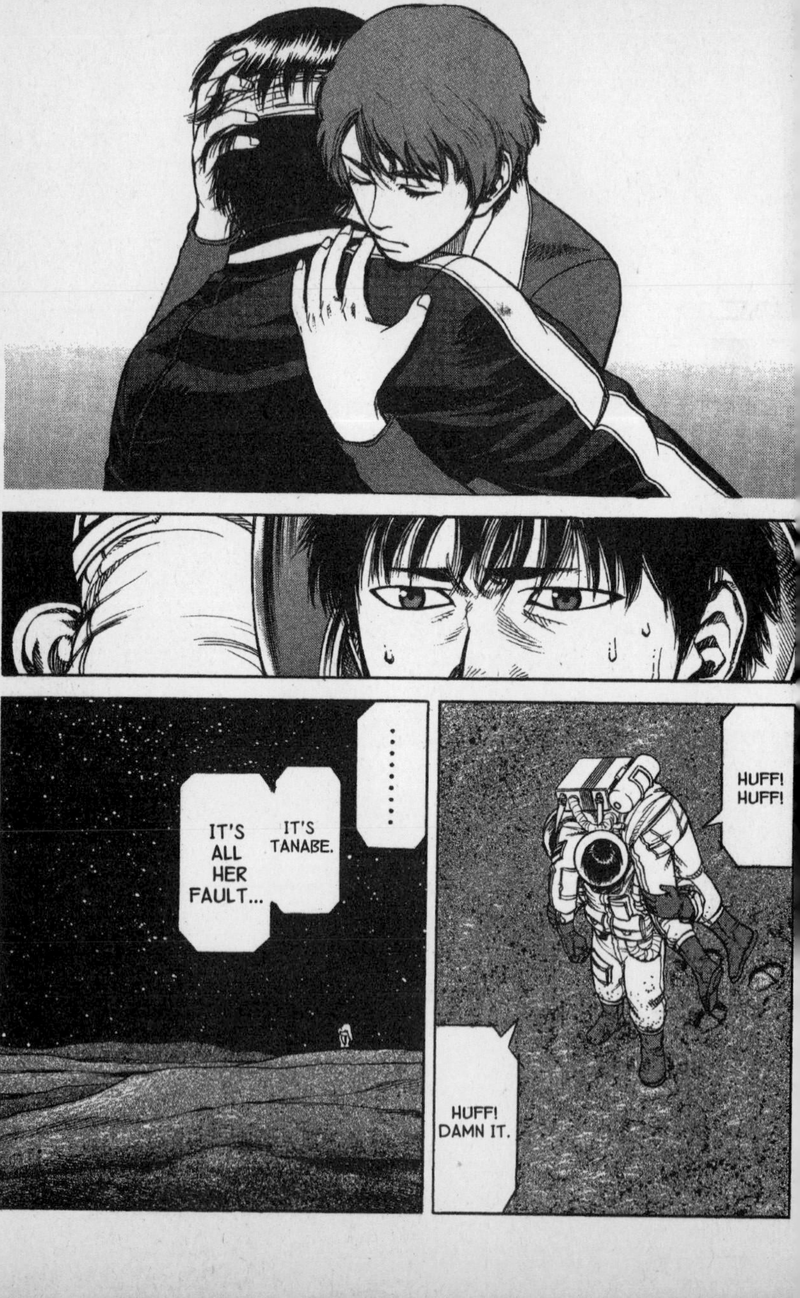
HUFF! HUFF!
HUFF! DAMN IT.
......
IT'S TANABE.
IT'S ALL HER FAULT...

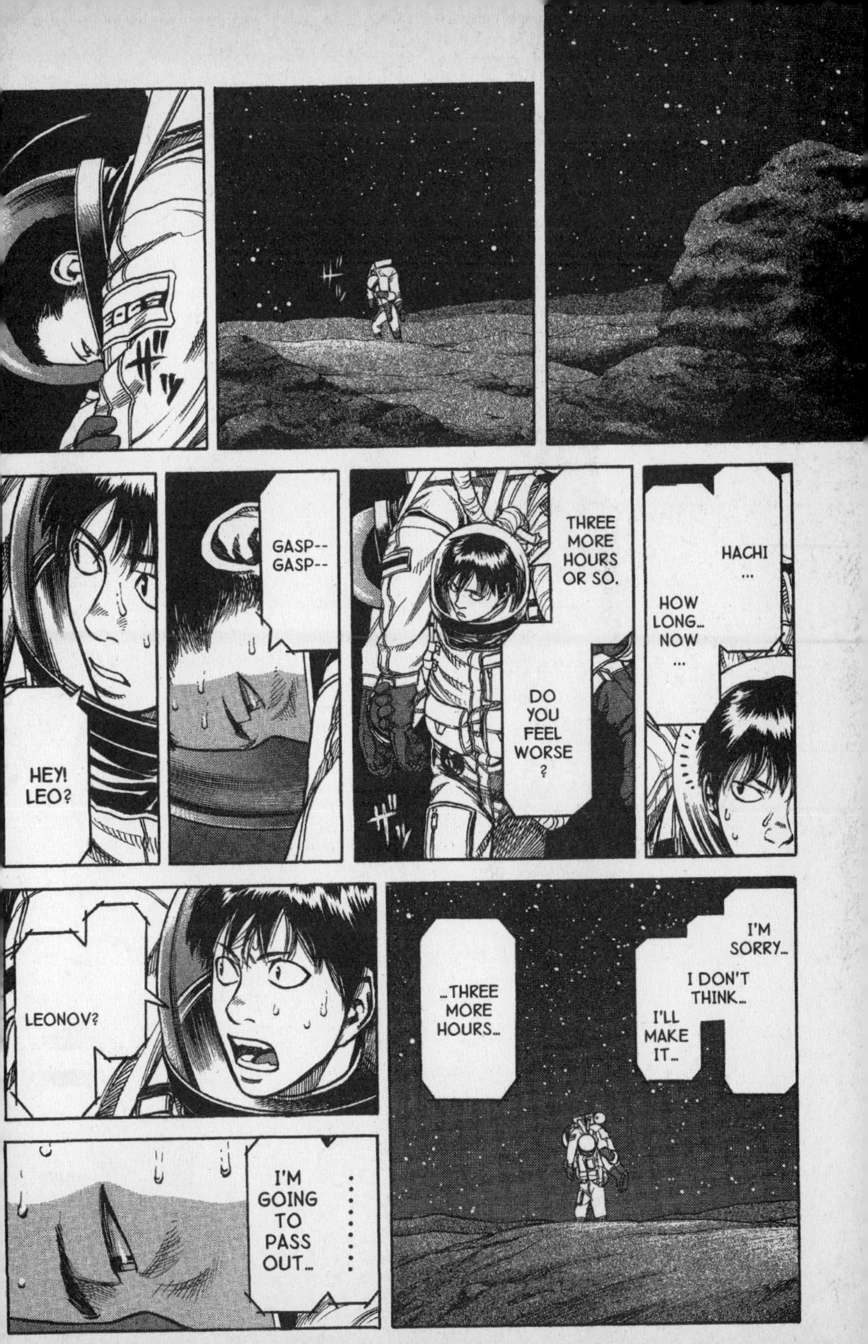
HACHI ... HOW LONG... NOW ...
THREE MORE HOURS OR SO.
DO YOU FEEL WORSE ?
GASP-- GASP--
HEY! LEO?
I'M SORRY... I DON'T THINK... I'LL MAKE IT...
...THREE MORE HOURS...
LEONOV?
I'M GOING TO PASS OUT... ......

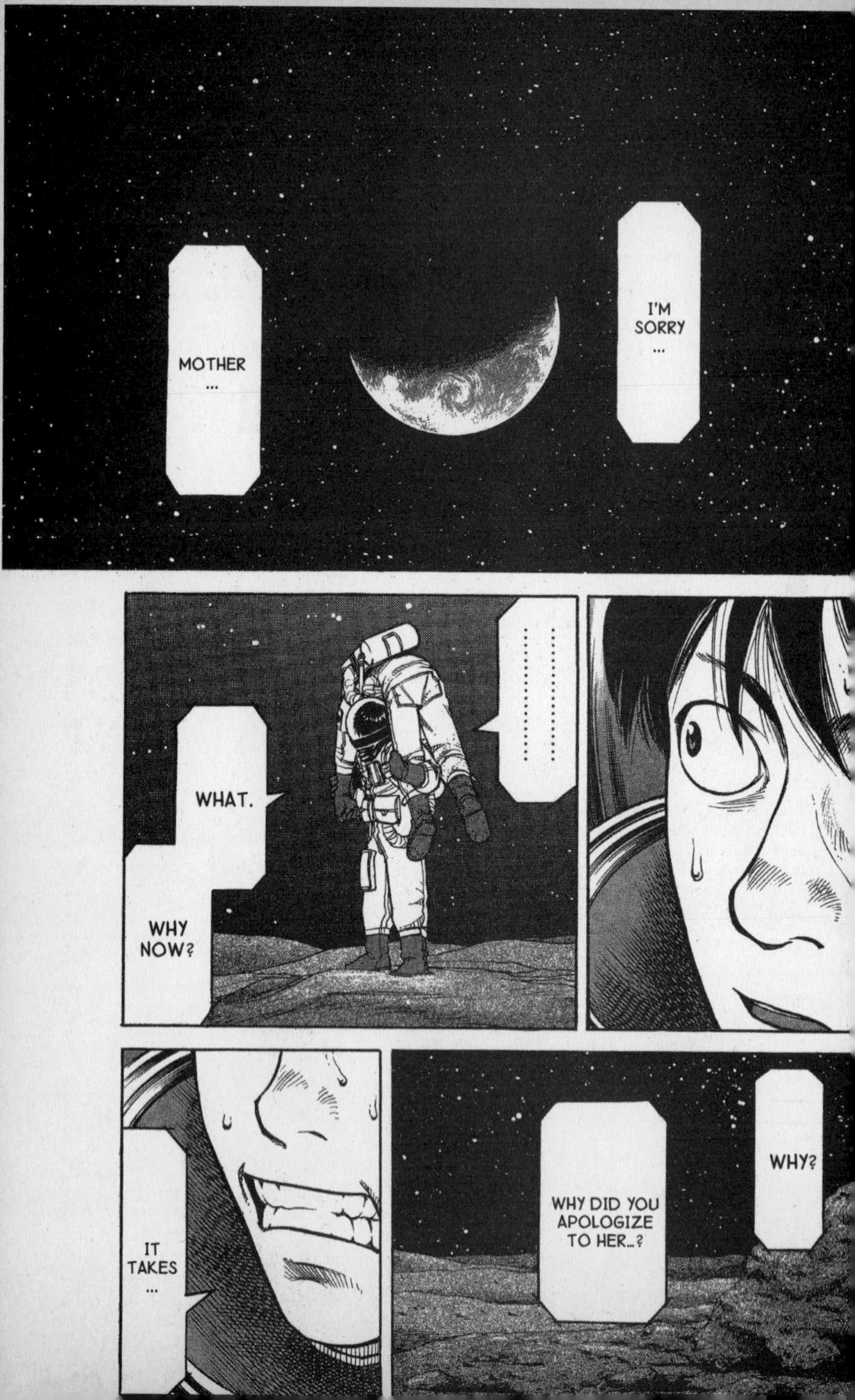
I'M SORRY ...
MOTHER ...
......
WHAT.
WHY NOW?
WHY?
WHY DID YOU APOLOGIZE TO HER...?
IT TAKES ...

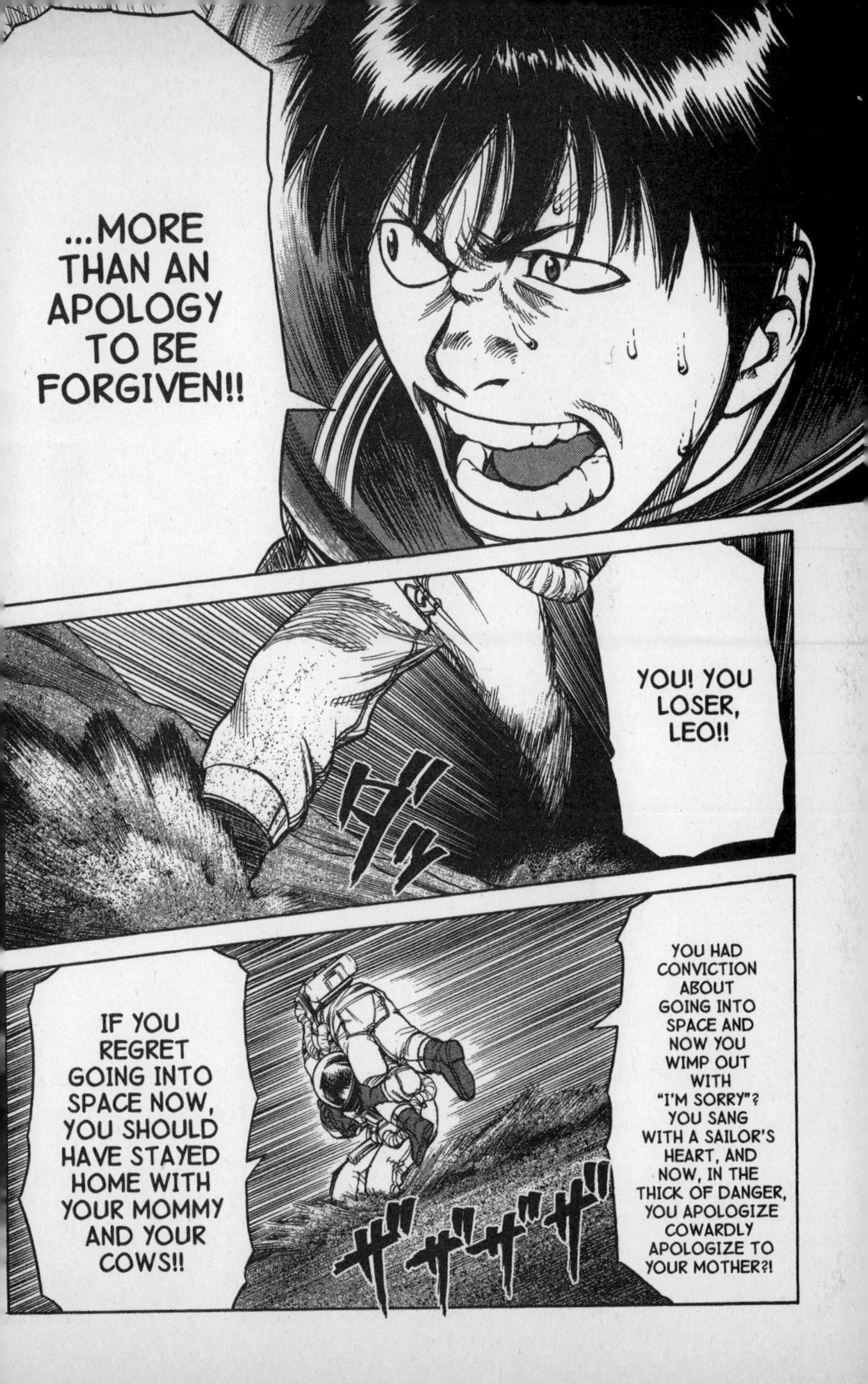
...MORE THAN AN APOLOGY TO BE FORGIVEN!!
YOU! YOU LOSER, LEO!!
YOU HAD CONVICTION ABOUT GOING INTO SPACE AND NOW YOU WIMP OUT WITH "I'M SORRY"? YOU SANG WITH A SAILOR'S HEART, AND NOW, IN THE THICK OF DANGER, YOU APOLOGIZE COWARDLY APOLOGIZE TO YOUR MOTHER?!
IF YOU REGRET GOING INTO SPACE NOW, YOU SHOULD HAVE STAYED HOME WITH YOUR MOMMY AND YOUR COWS!!

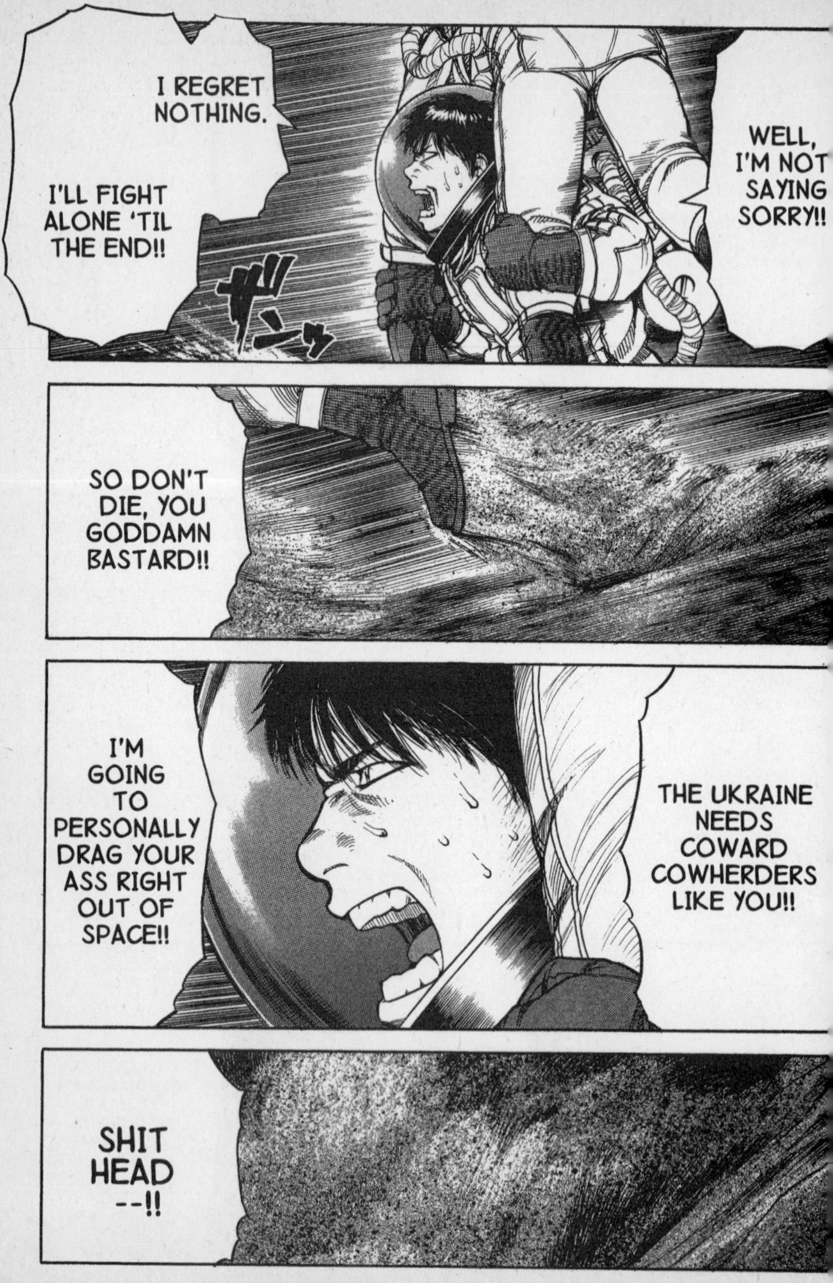
WELL, I'M NOT SAYING SORRY!!
I REGRET NOTHING.
I'LL FIGHT ALONE 'TIL THE END!!
ザンッ
SO DON'T DIE, YOU GODDAMN BASTARD!!
THE UKRAINE NEEDS COWARD COWHERDERS LIKE YOU!!
I'M GOING TO PERSONALLY DRAG YOUR ASS RIGHT OUT OF SPACE!!
SHIT HEAD --!!

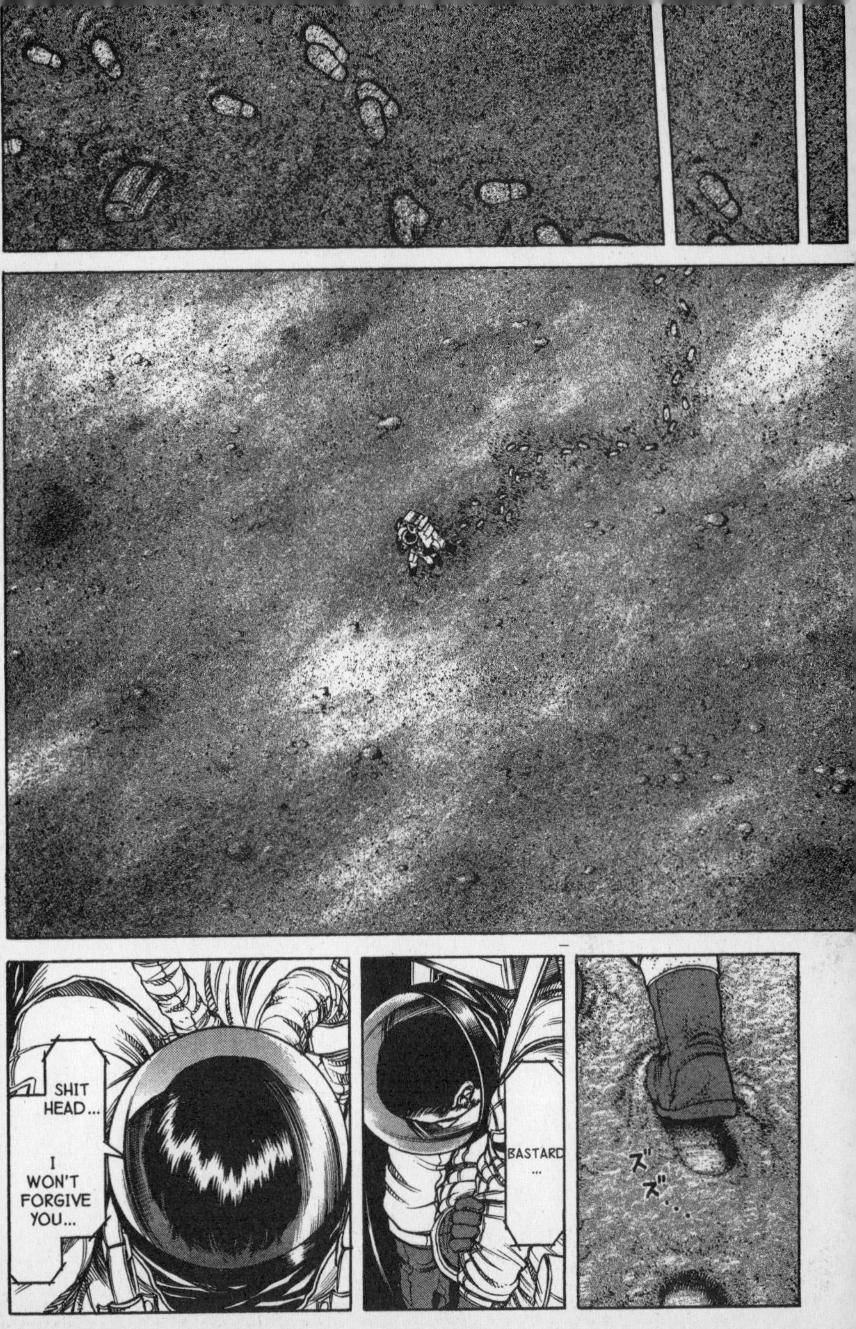
ズズ..
BASTARD ...
SHIT HEAD...
I WON'T FORGIVE YOU...

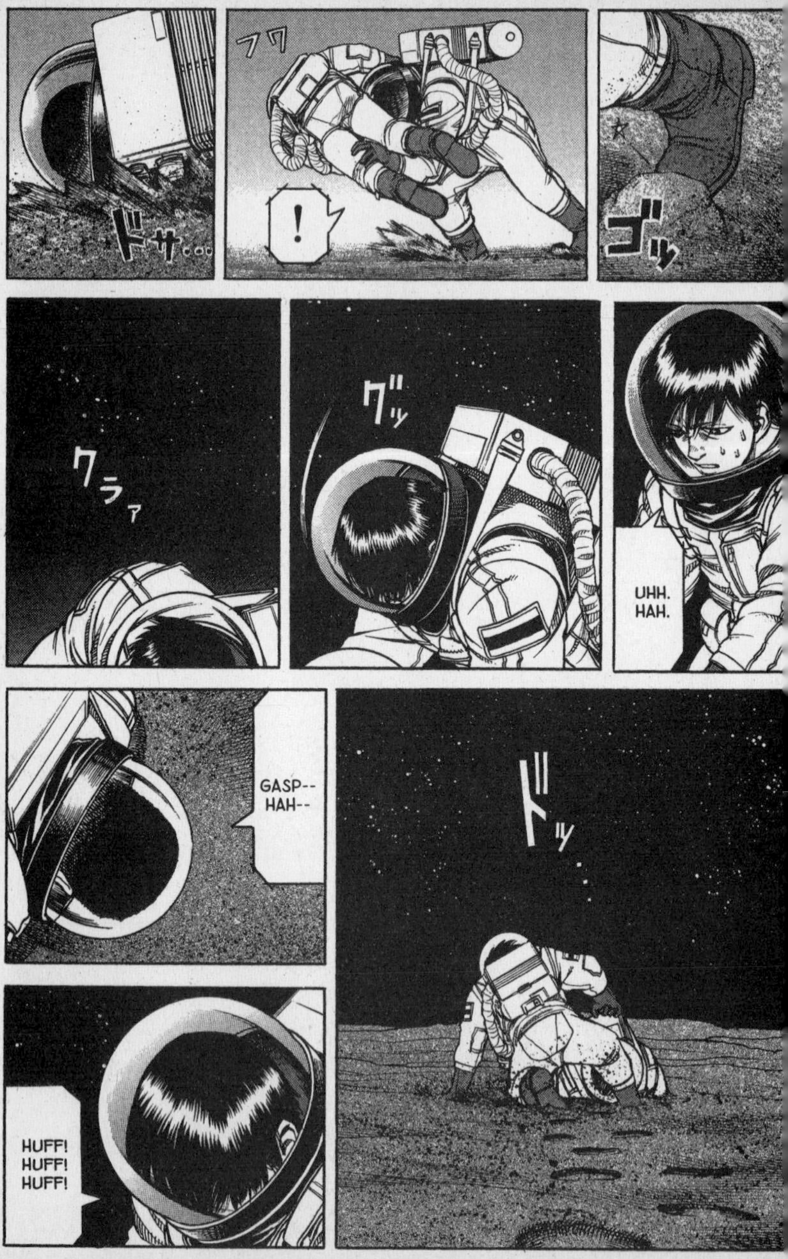
ゴッ
フワ
!
ドサ…
UHH. HAH.
グッ
クラァ
ドッ
GASP-- HAH--
HUFF! HUFF! HUFF!

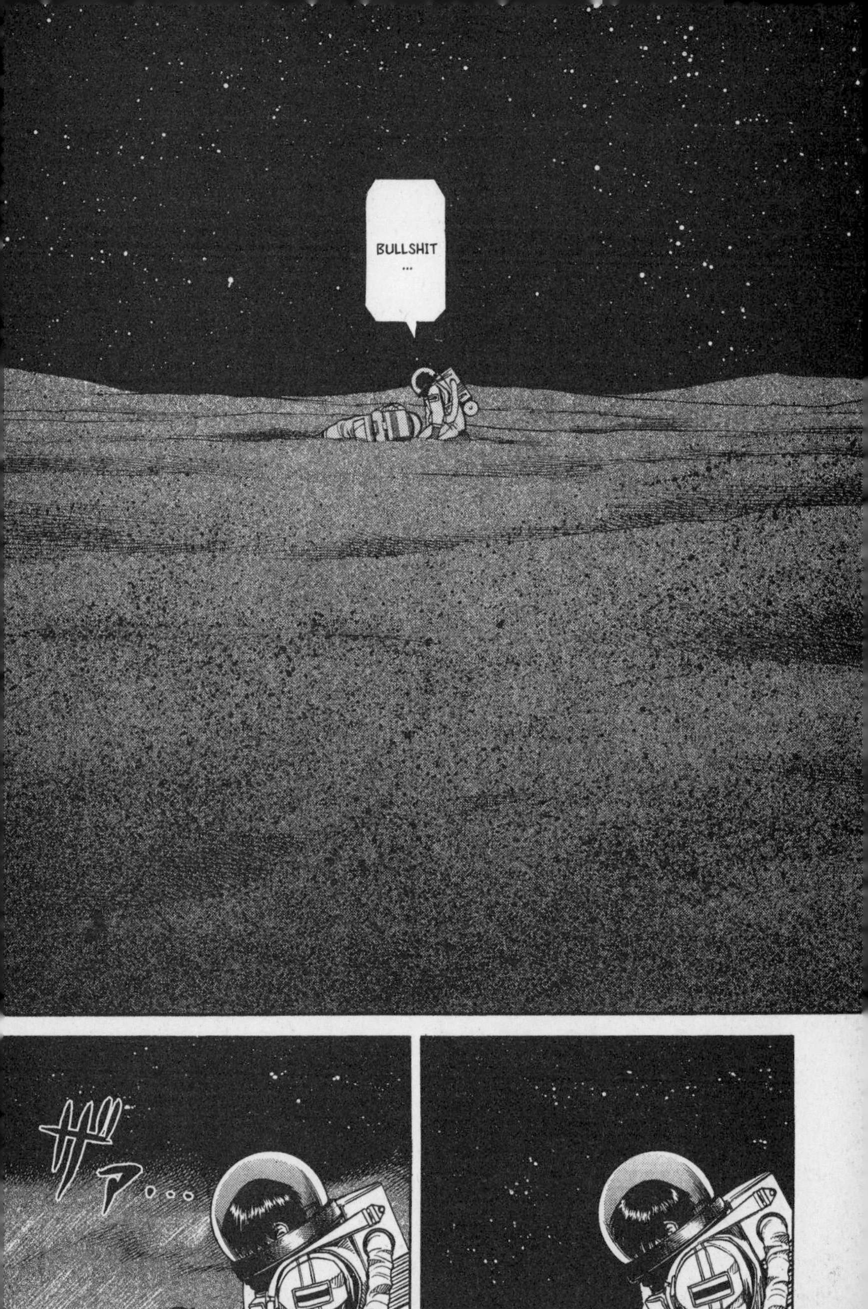
BULLSHIT ...
ザァ...

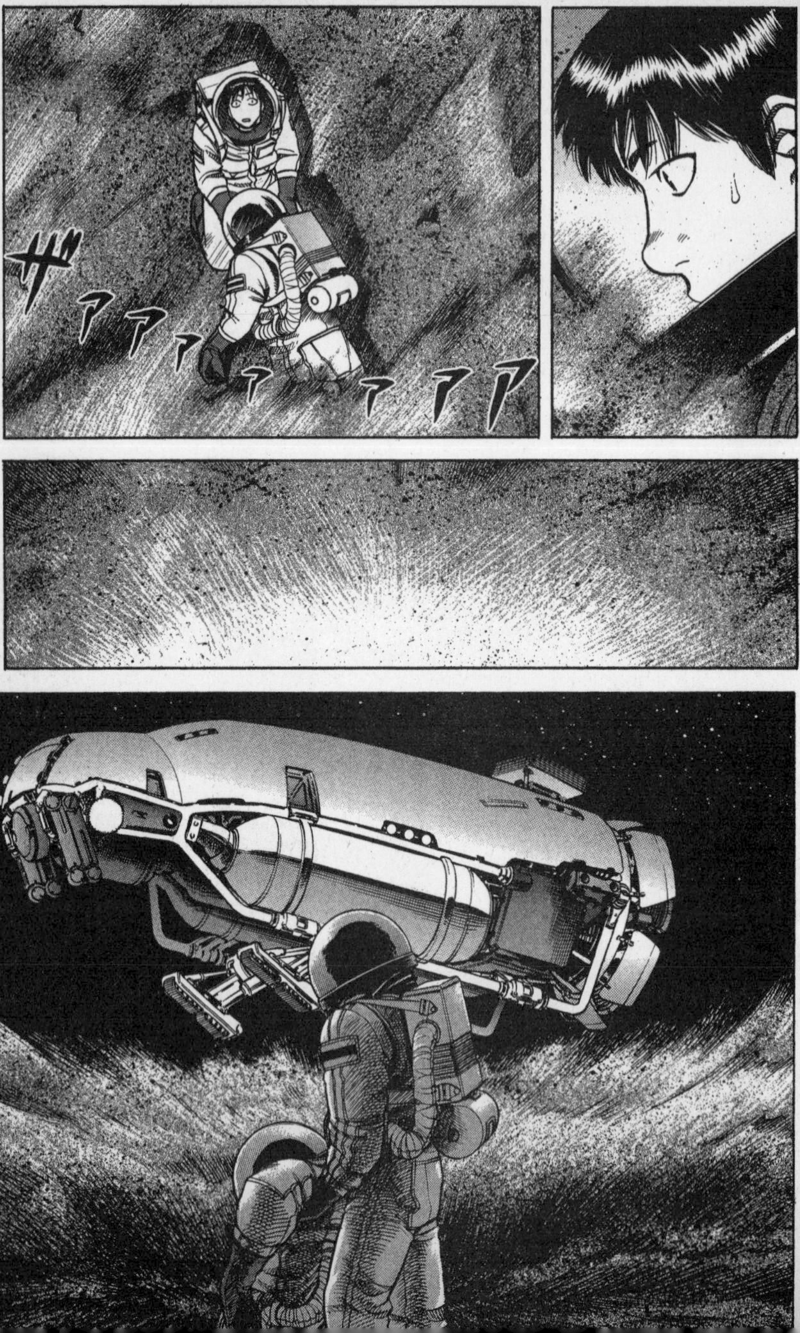
ザアアアアアアア

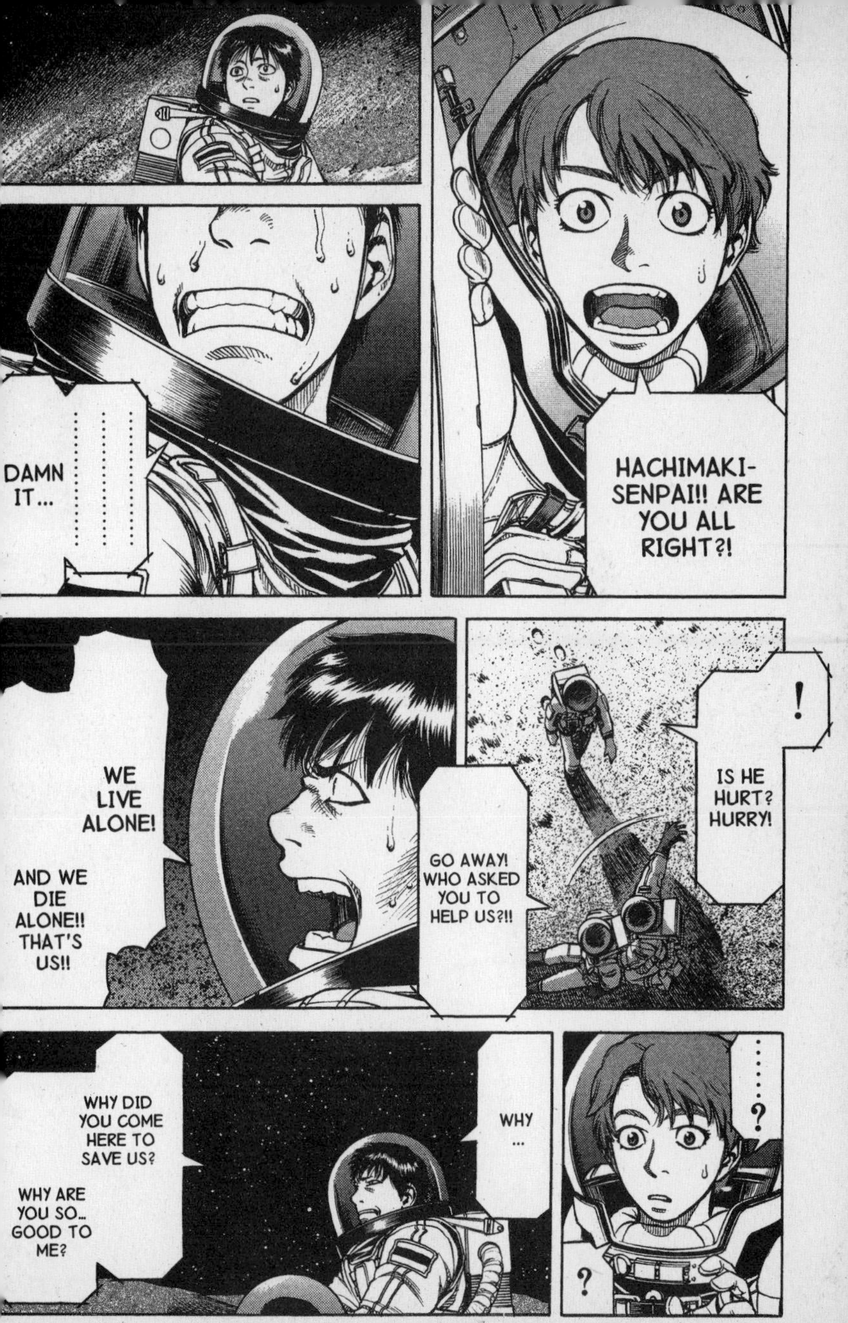
HACHIMAKI-SENPAI!! ARE YOU ALL RIGHT?!
......
DAMN IT...
!
IS HE HURT? HURRY!
GO AWAY! WHO ASKED YOU TO HELP US?!!
WE LIVE ALONE!
AND WE DIE ALONE!! THAT'S US!!
......?
?
WHY ...
WHY DID YOU COME HERE TO SAVE US?
WHY ARE YOU SO... GOOD TO ME?

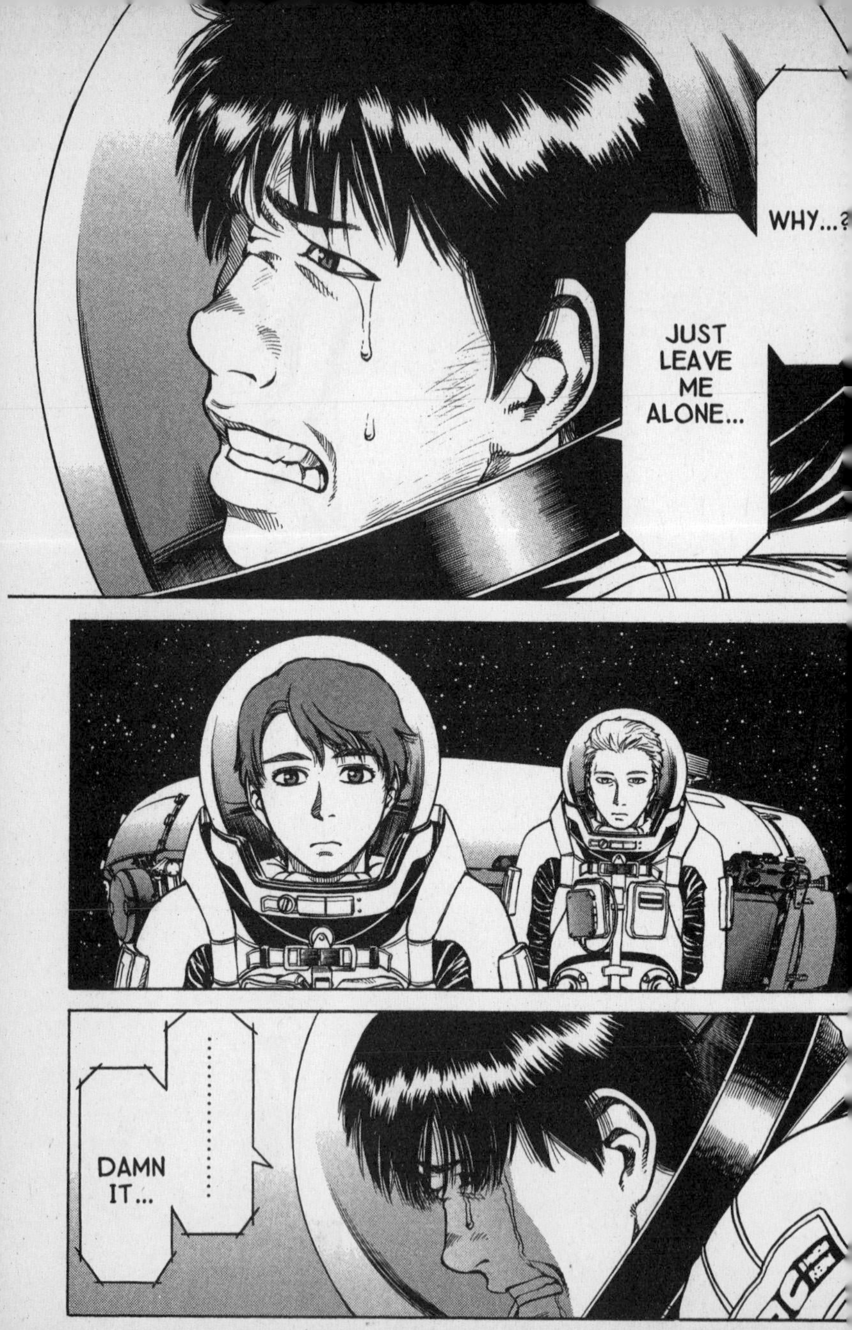
WHY...?
JUST LEAVE ME ALONE...
......
DAMN IT...

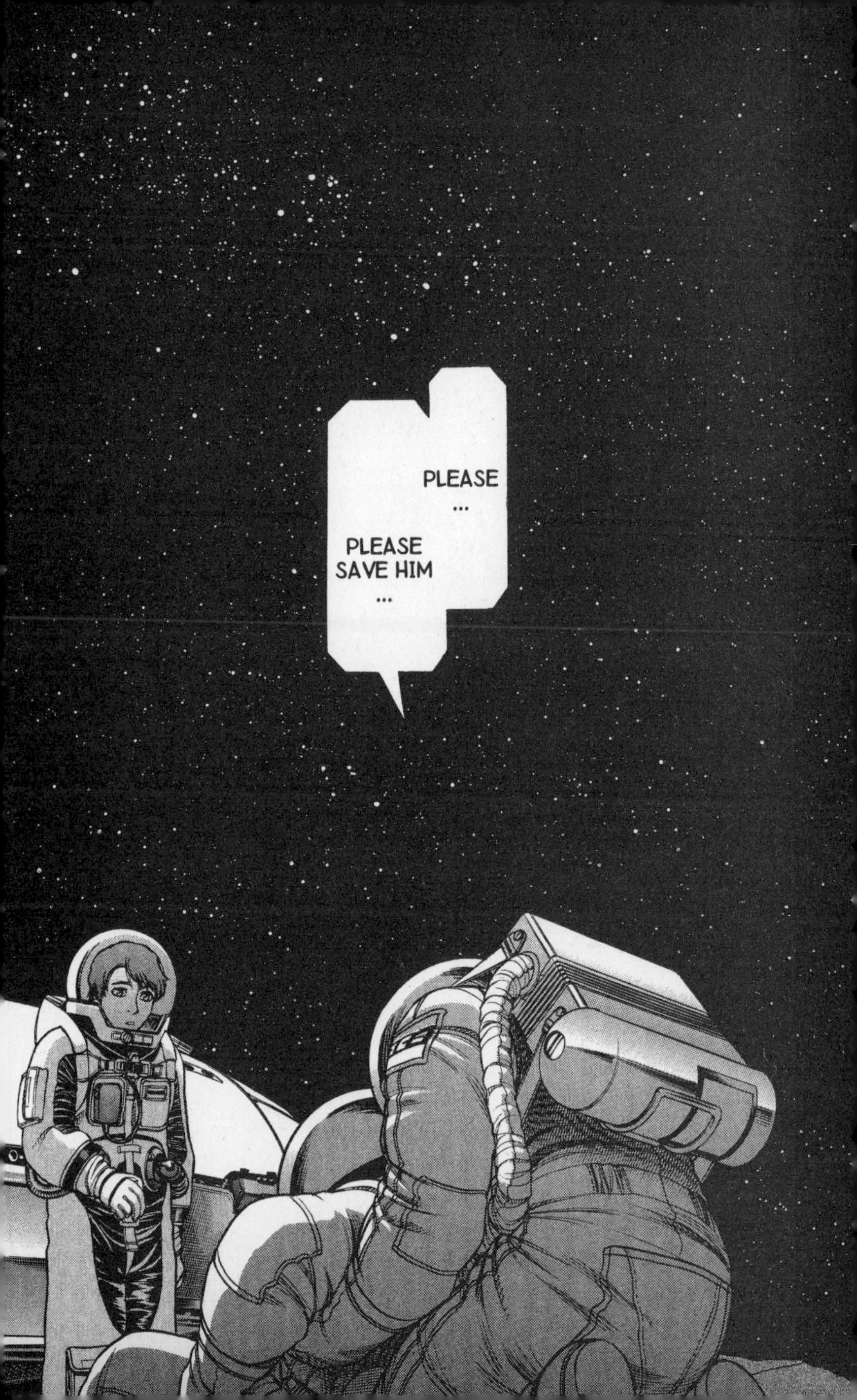
PLEASE ... PLEASE SAVE HIM ...

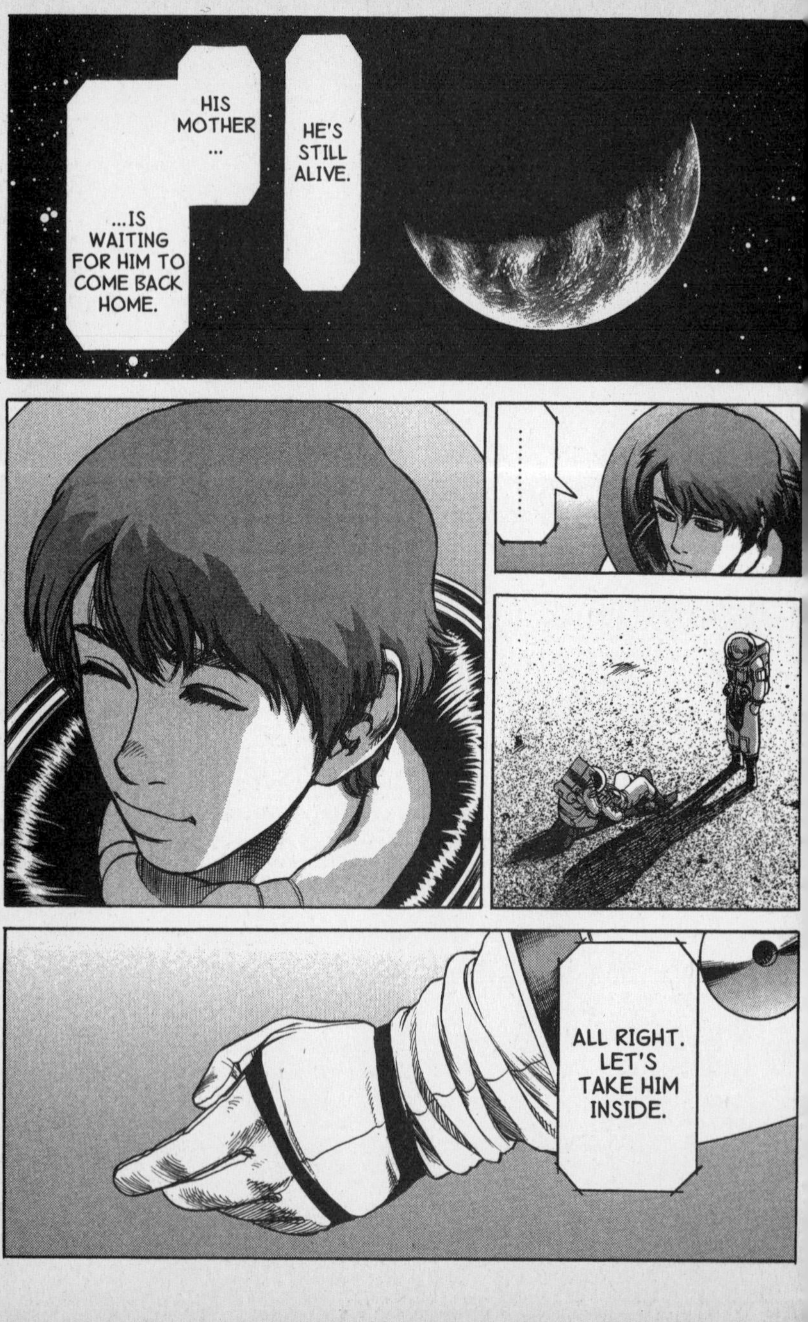
HE'S STILL ALIVE.
HIS MOTHER ...
...IS WAITING FOR HIM TO COME BACK HOME.
....
ALL RIGHT. LET'S TAKE HIM INSIDE.

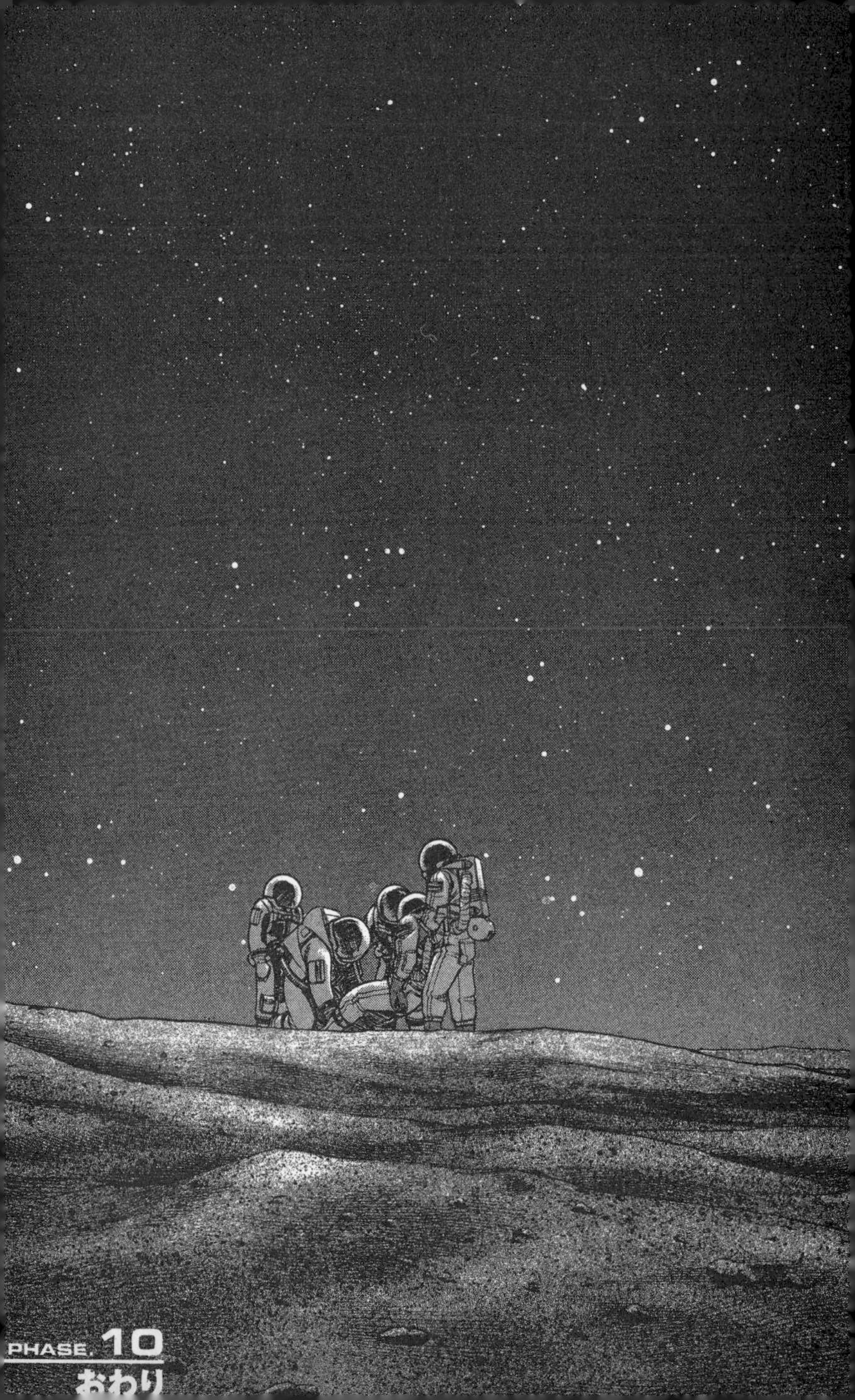
PHASE. 10
おわり

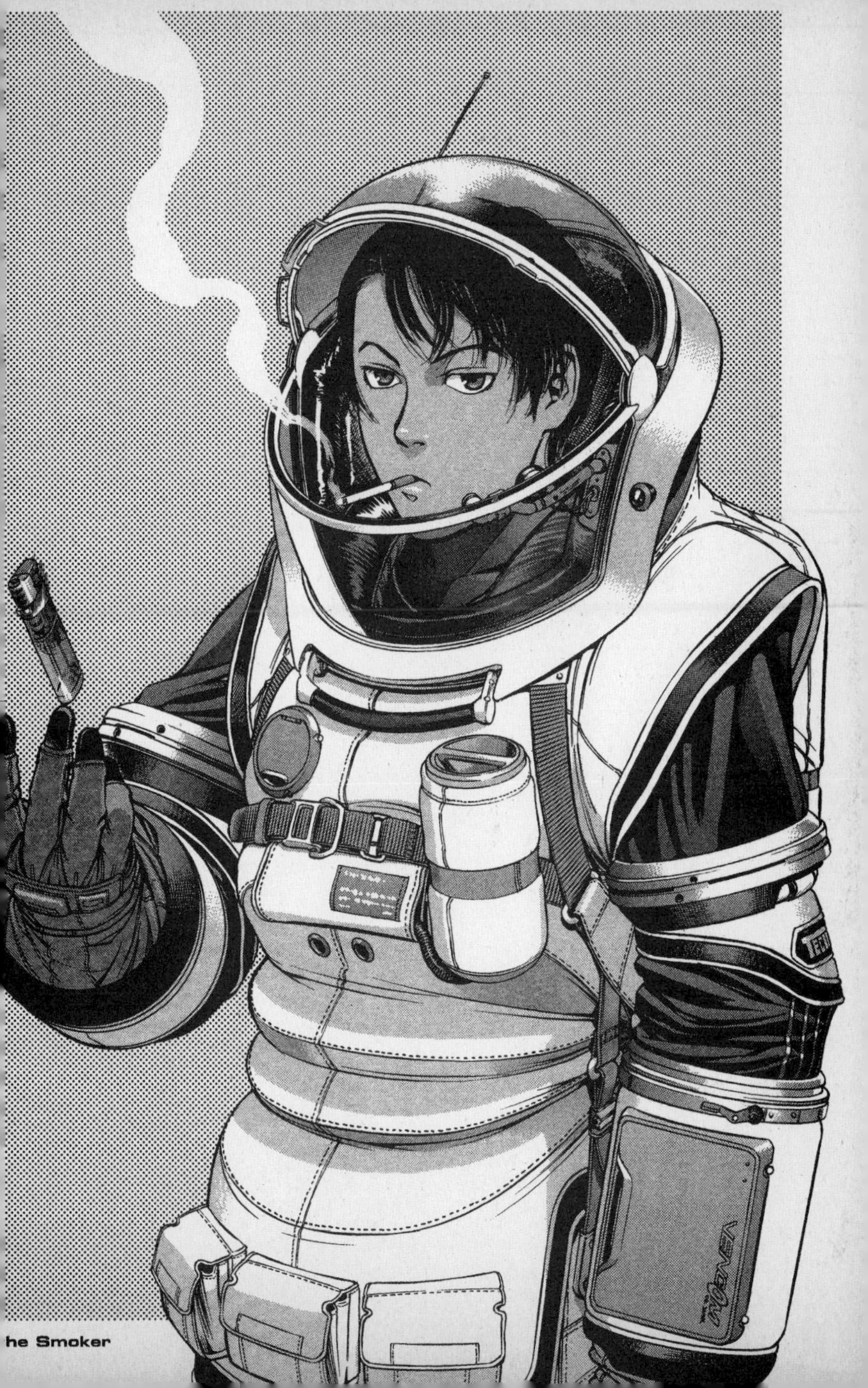

he Smoker

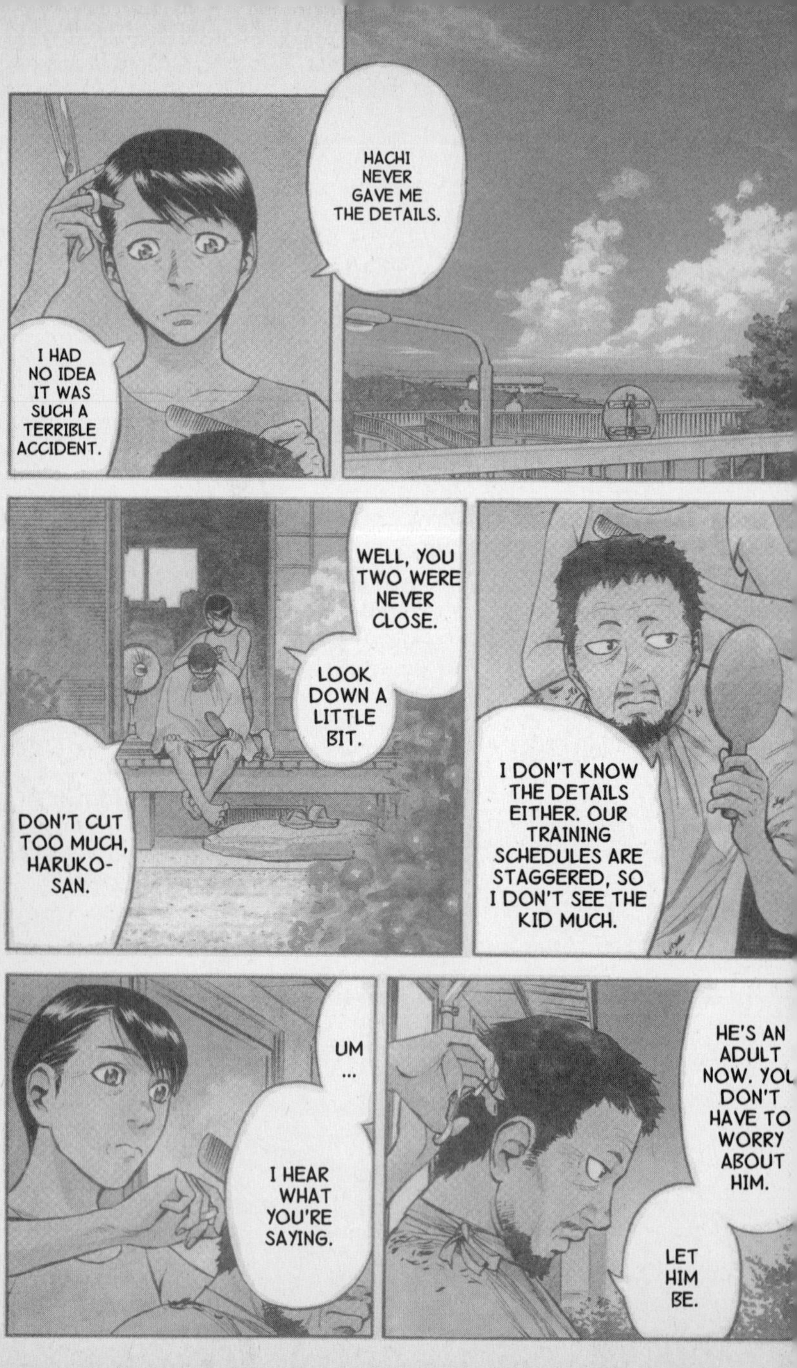
HACHI NEVER GAVE ME THE DETAILS.
I HAD NO IDEA IT WAS SUCH A TERRIBLE ACCIDENT.
I DON'T KNOW THE DETAILS EITHER. OUR TRAINING SCHEDULES ARE STAGGERED, SO I DON'T SEE THE KID MUCH.
WELL, YOU TWO WERE NEVER CLOSE.
LOOK DOWN A LITTLE BIT.
DON'T CUT TOO MUCH, HARUKO-SAN.
HE'S AN ADULT NOW. YOU DON'T HAVE TO WORRY ABOUT HIM.
LET HIM BE.
UM ...
I HEAR WHAT YOU'RE SAYING.

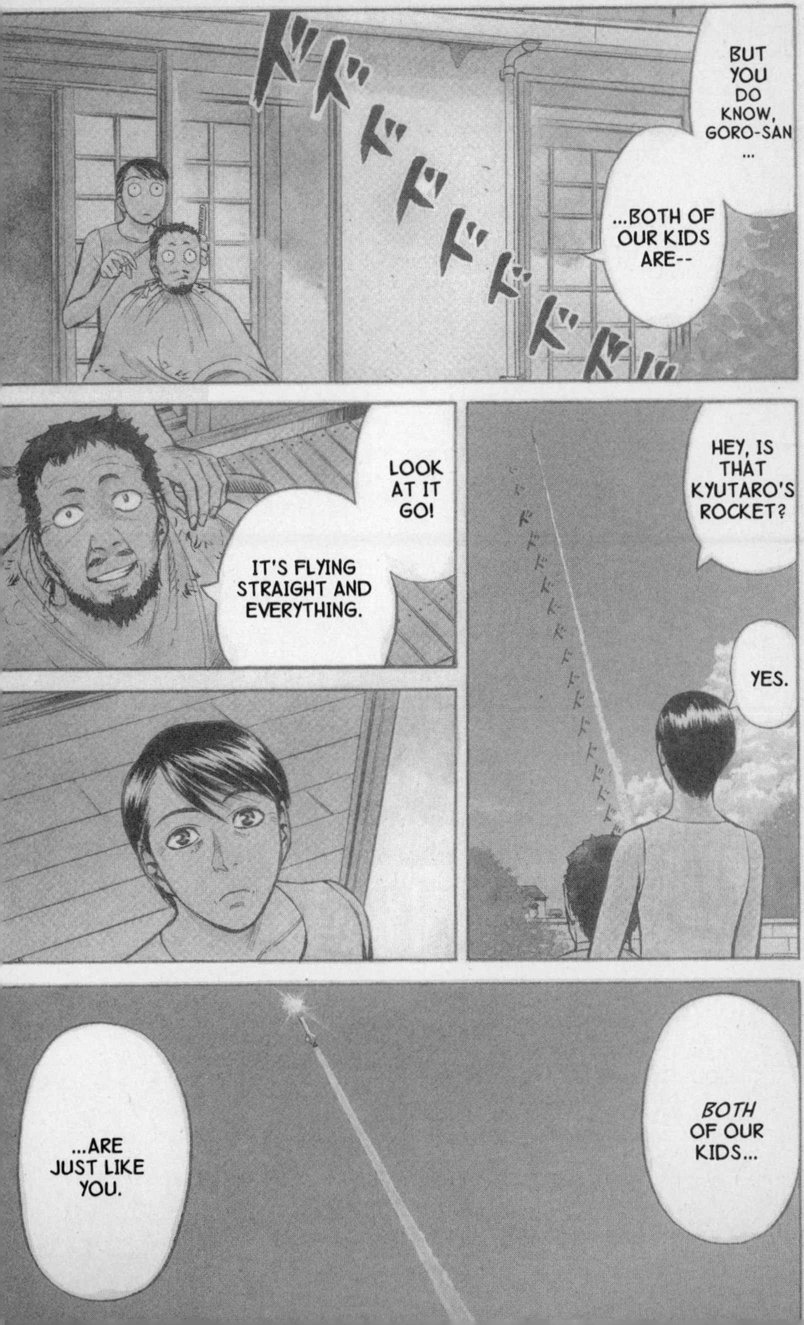
BUT YOU DO KNOW, GORO-SAN ...
...BOTH OF OUR KIDS ARE--
HEY, IS THAT KYUTARO'S ROCKET?
YES.
LOOK AT IT GO!
IT'S FLYING STRAIGHT AND EVERYTHING.
BOTH OF OUR KIDS...
...ARE JUST LIKE YOU.

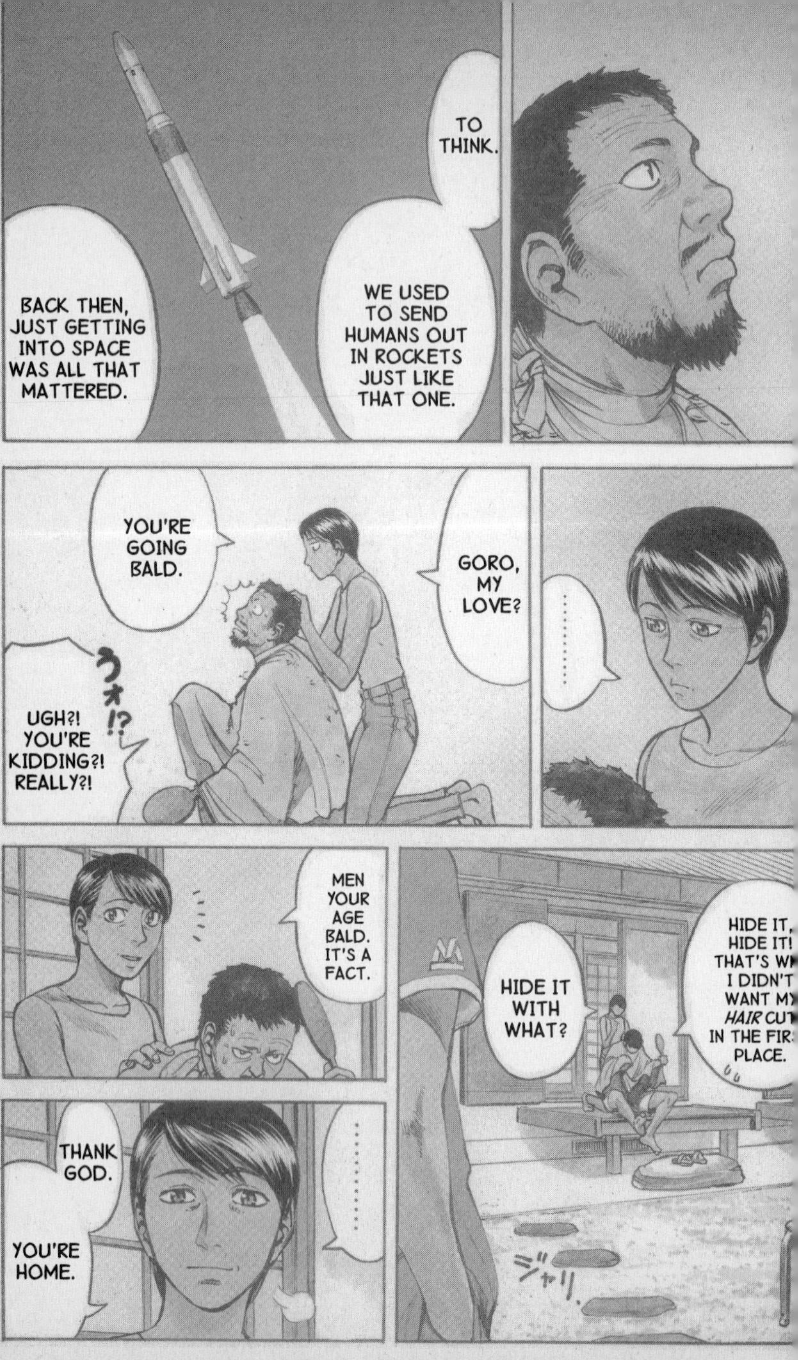
TO THINK.
WE USED TO SEND HUMANS OUT IN ROCKETS JUST LIKE THAT ONE.
BACK THEN, JUST GETTING INTO SPACE WAS ALL THAT MATTERED.
......
GORO, MY LOVE?
YOU'RE GOING BALD.
うォ!?
UGH?! YOU'RE KIDDING?! REALLY?!
HIDE IT, HIDE IT! THAT'S W I DIDN'T WANT MY *HAIR* CUT IN THE FIR PLACE.
HIDE IT WITH WHAT?
ジャリ
MEN YOUR AGE BALD. IT'S A FACT.
......
THANK GOD.
YOU'RE HOME.

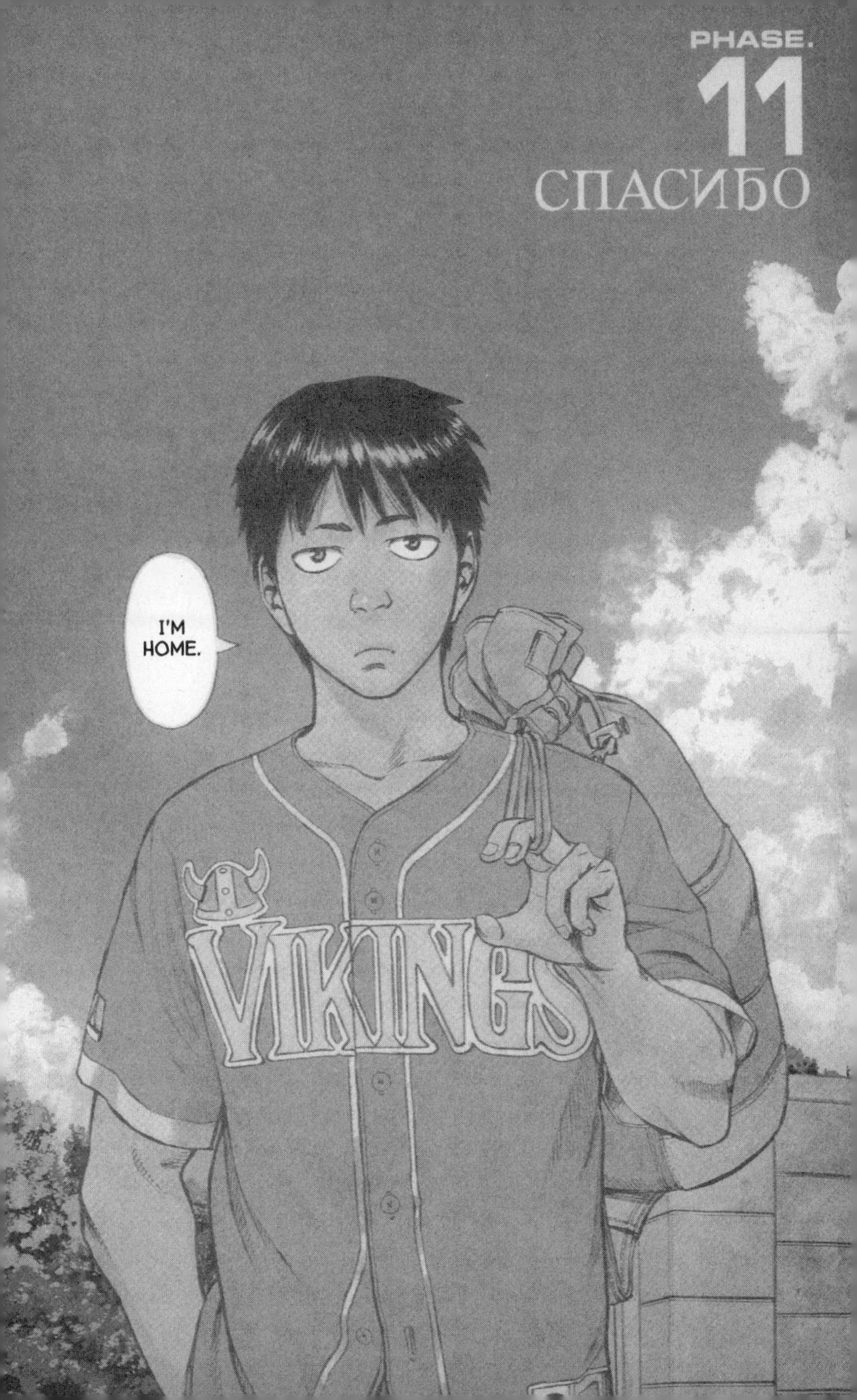
PHASE.
11
СПАСИБО
I'M HOME.
VIKINGS

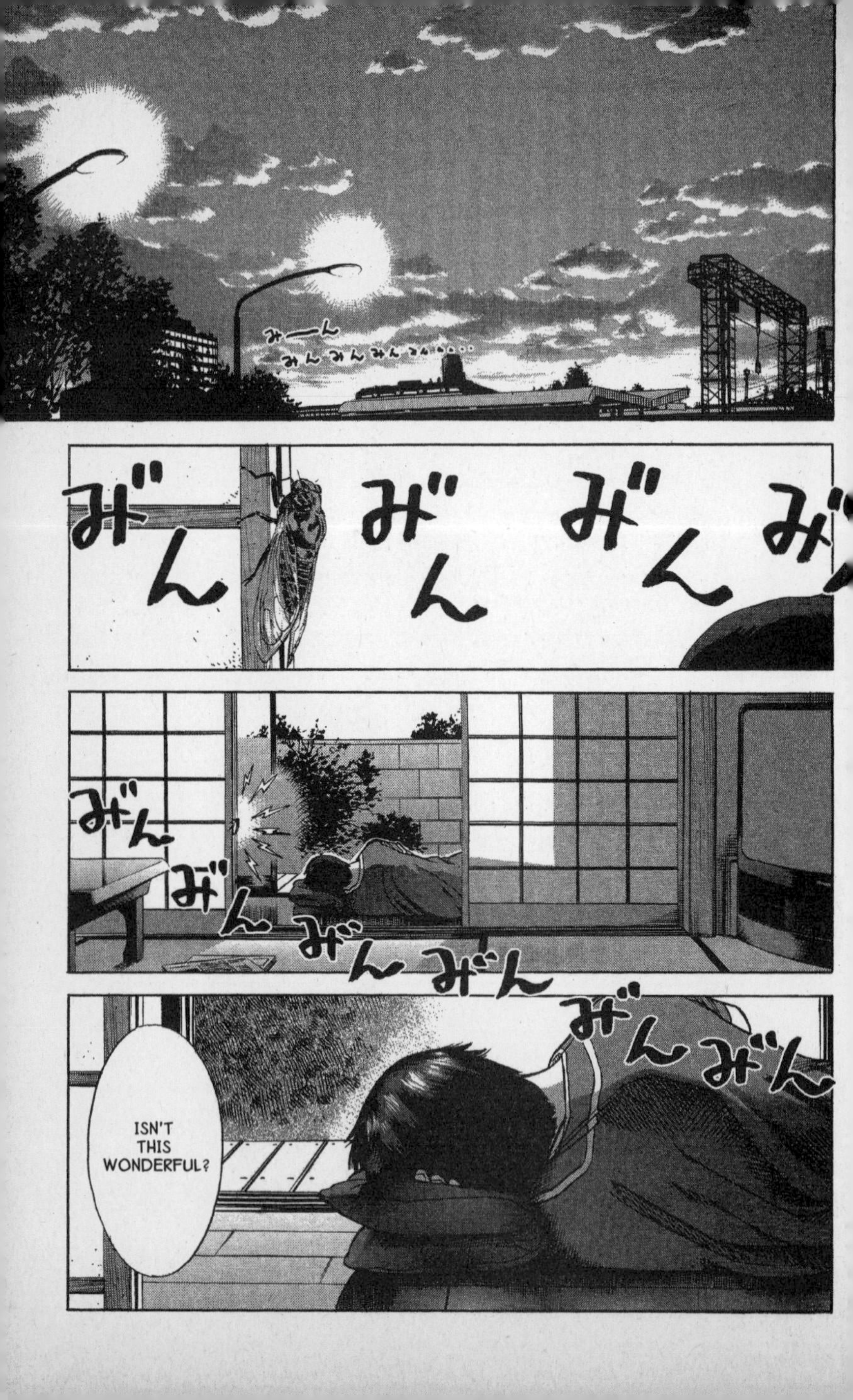
みーん
みんみんみんみん・・・
み゛ん み゛ん み゛ん み゛ん
み゛ん み゛ん み゛ん み゛ん
み゛ん み゛ん
ISN'T THIS WONDERFUL?

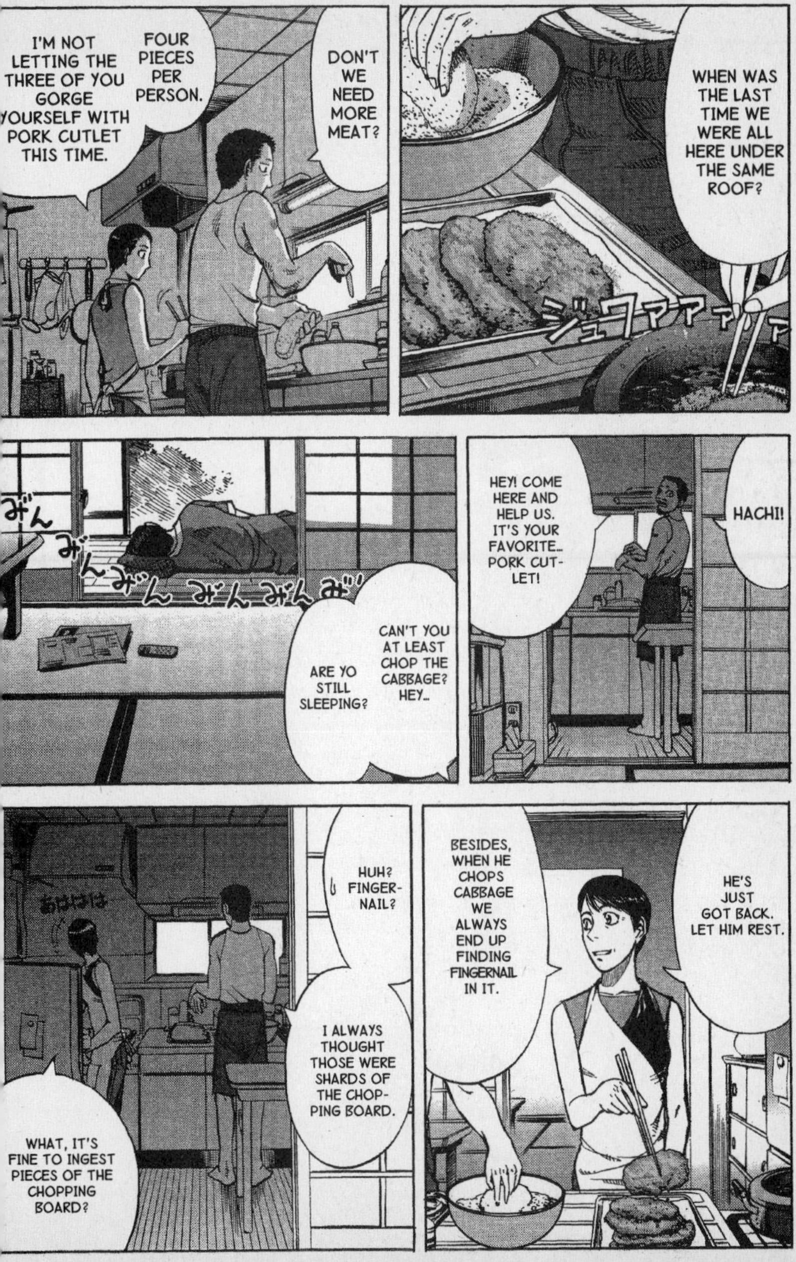

WHEN WAS THE LAST TIME WE WERE ALL HERE UNDER THE SAME ROOF?
ジュワアアァァ
DON'T WE NEED MORE MEAT?
FOUR PIECES PER PERSON.
I'M NOT LETTING THE THREE OF YOU GORGE YOURSELF WITH PORK CUTLET THIS TIME.
HACHI!
HEY! COME HERE AND HELP US. IT'S YOUR FAVORITE... PORK CUT-LET!
みん みん みん みん みん みん
CAN'T YOU AT LEAST CHOP THE CABBAGE? HEY...
ARE YO STILL SLEEPING?
HE'S JUST GOT BACK. LET HIM REST.
BESIDES, WHEN HE CHOPS CABBAGE WE ALWAYS END UP FINDING FINGERNAIL IN IT.
HUH? FINGER-NAIL?
あははは
I ALWAYS THOUGHT THOSE WERE SHARDS OF THE CHOP-PING BOARD.
WHAT, IT'S FINE TO INGEST PIECES OF THE CHOPPING BOARD?

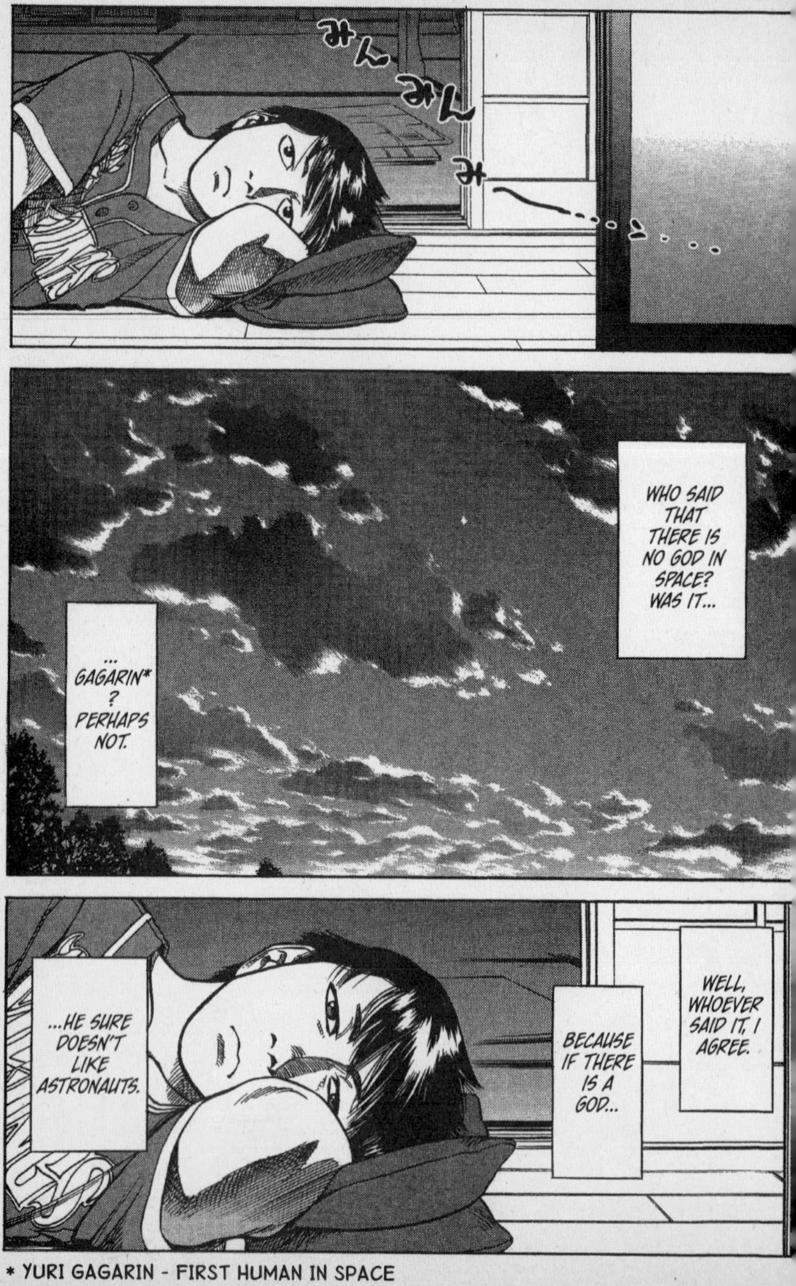
WHO SAID THAT THERE IS NO GOD IN SPACE? WAS IT...
... GAGARIN* ? PERHAPS NOT.
WELL, WHOEVER SAID IT, I AGREE.
BECAUSE IF THERE IS A GOD...
...HE SURE DOESN'T LIKE ASTRONAUTS.

* YURI GAGARIN - FIRST HUMAN IN SPACE

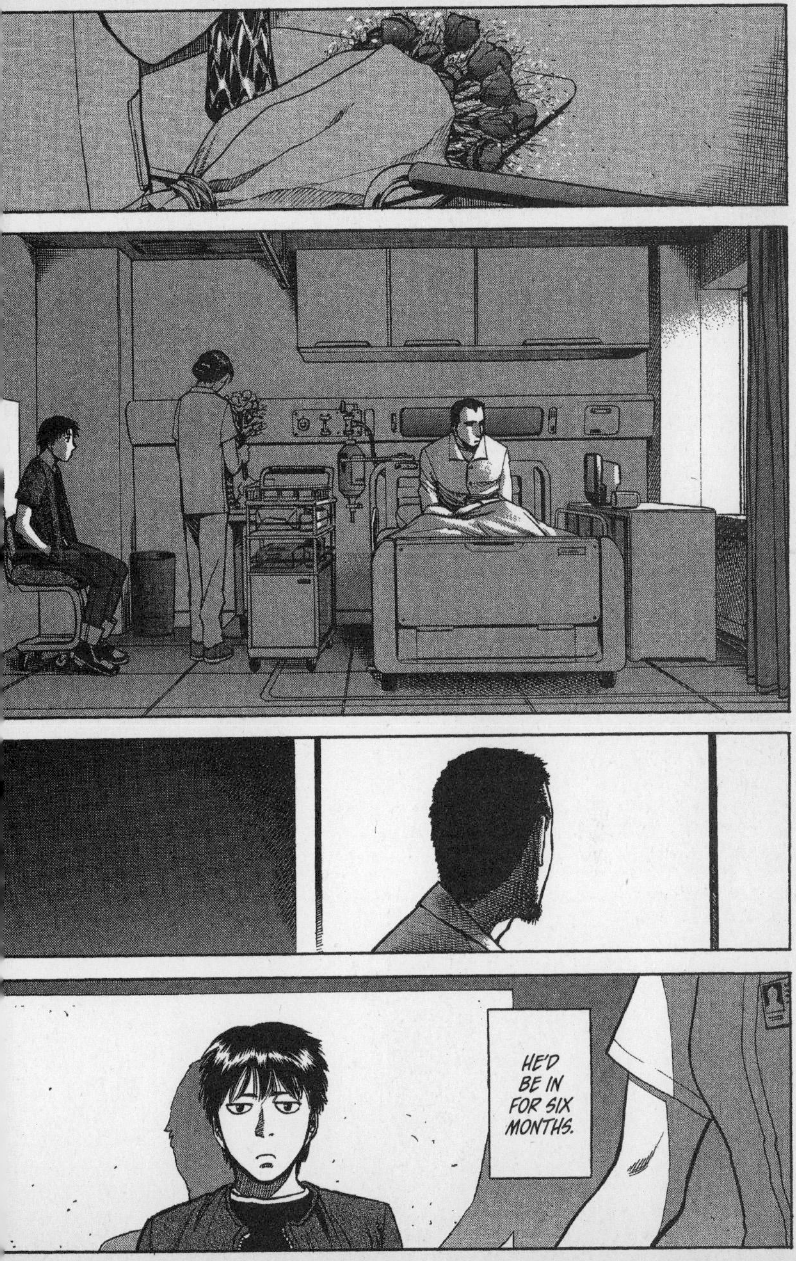
HE'D BE IN FOR SIX MONTHS.

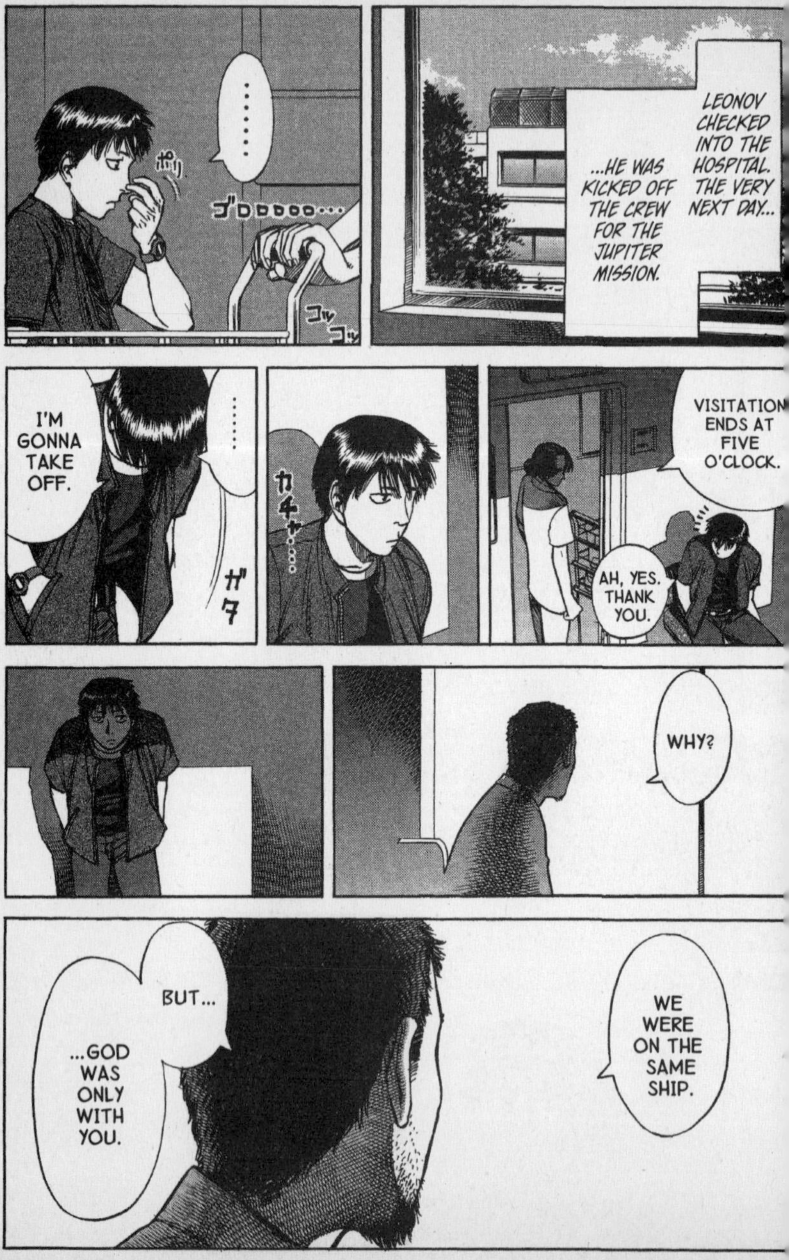
LEONOV CHECKED INTO THE HOSPITAL. THE VERY NEXT DAY...
...HE WAS KICKED OFF THE CREW FOR THE JUPITER MISSION.
....
ポリ
ゴロロロロロ・・・
コッ コッ
VISITATION ENDS AT FIVE O'CLOCK.
AH, YES. THANK YOU.
カチャ・・・
......
I'M GONNA TAKE OFF.
ガタ
WHY?
WE WERE ON THE SAME SHIP.
BUT...
...GOD WAS ONLY WITH YOU.

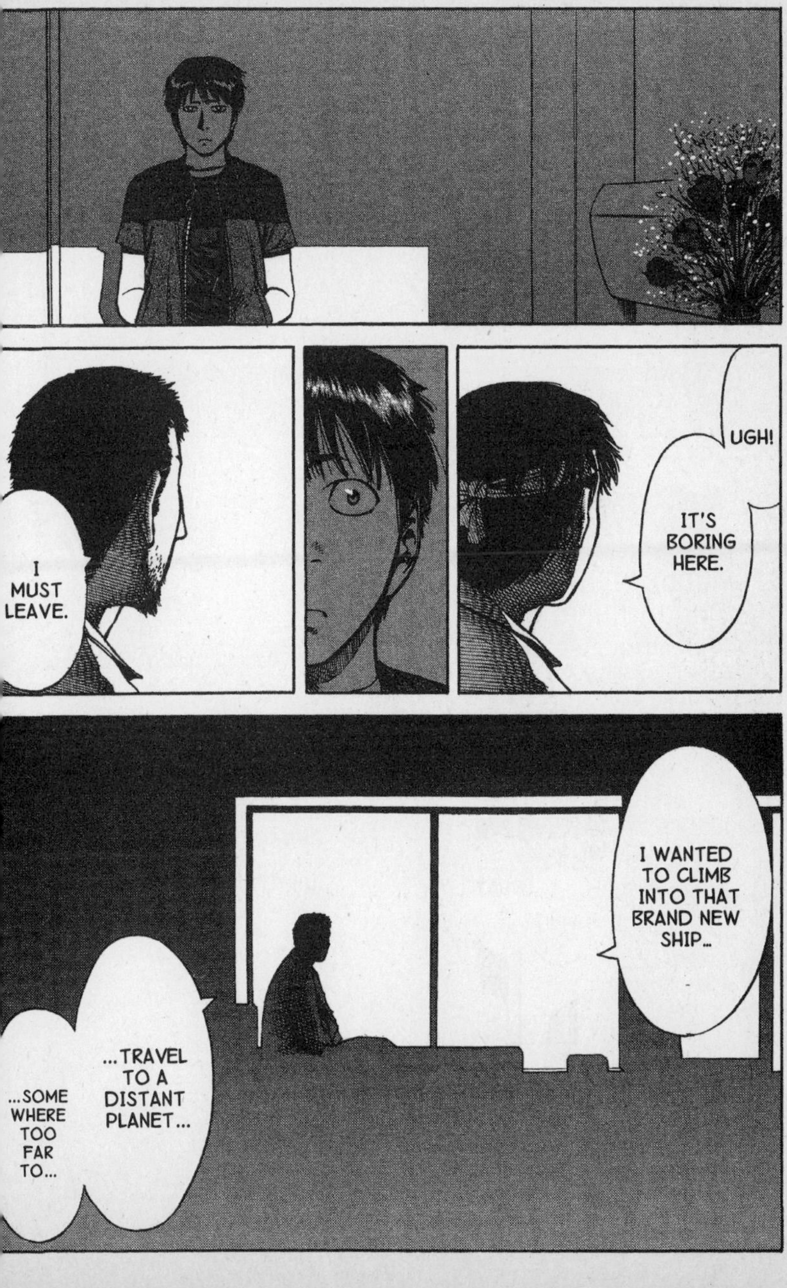
UGH!
IT'S BORING HERE.
I MUST LEAVE.
I WANTED TO CLIMB INTO THAT BRAND NEW SHIP...
...TRAVEL TO A DISTANT PLANET...
...SOME WHERE TOO FAR TO...

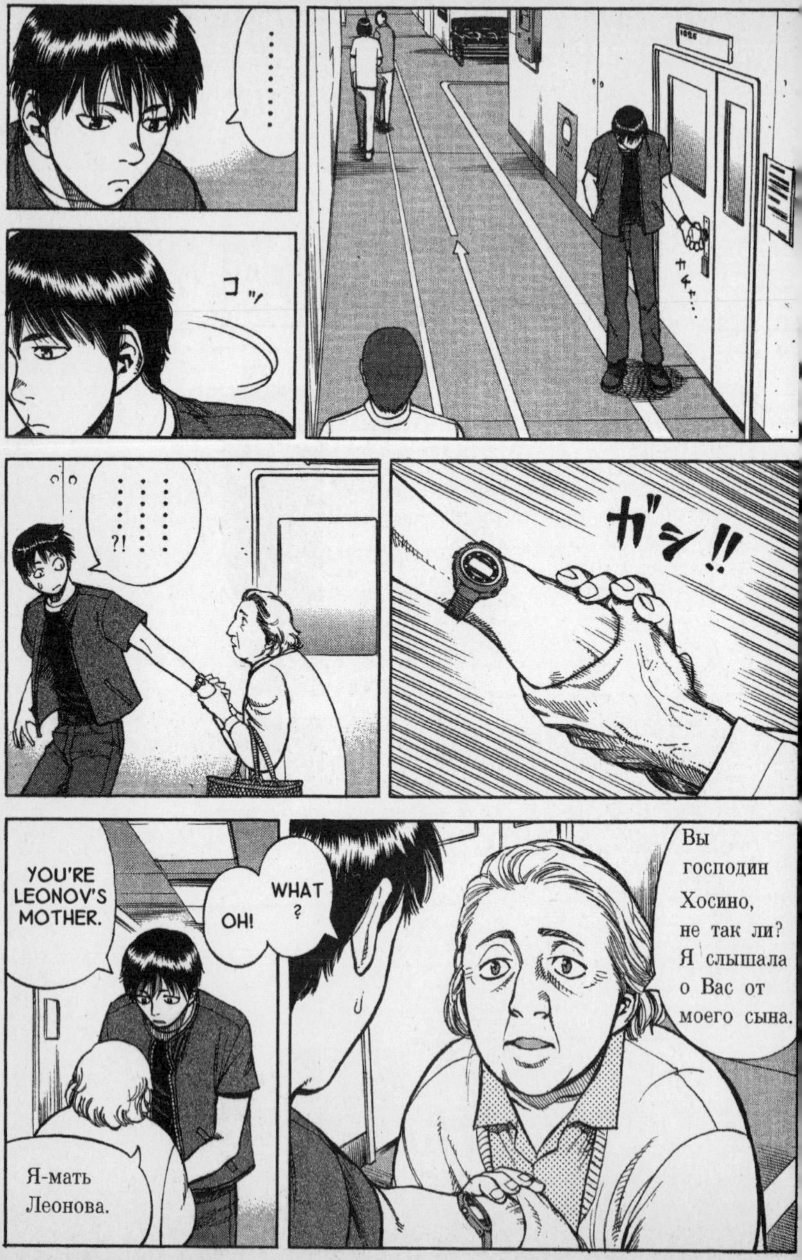
カチャ…
……
コッ
ガシ!!
…… ?!
Вы господин Хосино, не так ли? Я слышала о Вас от моего сына.
WHAT ?
OH!
YOU'RE LEONOV'S MOTHER.
Я-мать Леонова.

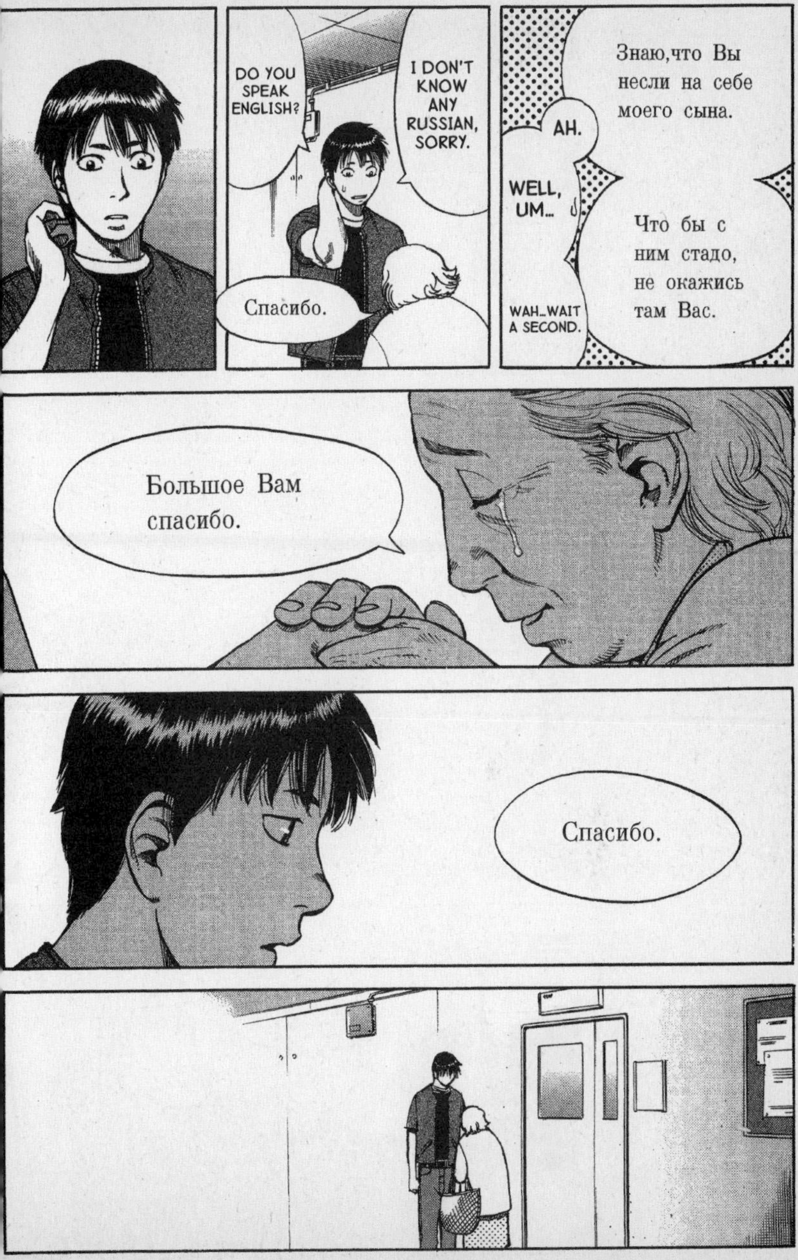
Знаю,что Вы несли на себе моего сына.
AH.
Что бы с ним стадо, не окажись там Вас.
WELL, UM...
WAH...WAIT A SECOND.
I DON'T KNOW ANY RUSSIAN, SORRY.
DO YOU SPEAK ENGLISH?
Спасибо.
Большое Вам спасибо.
Спасибо.

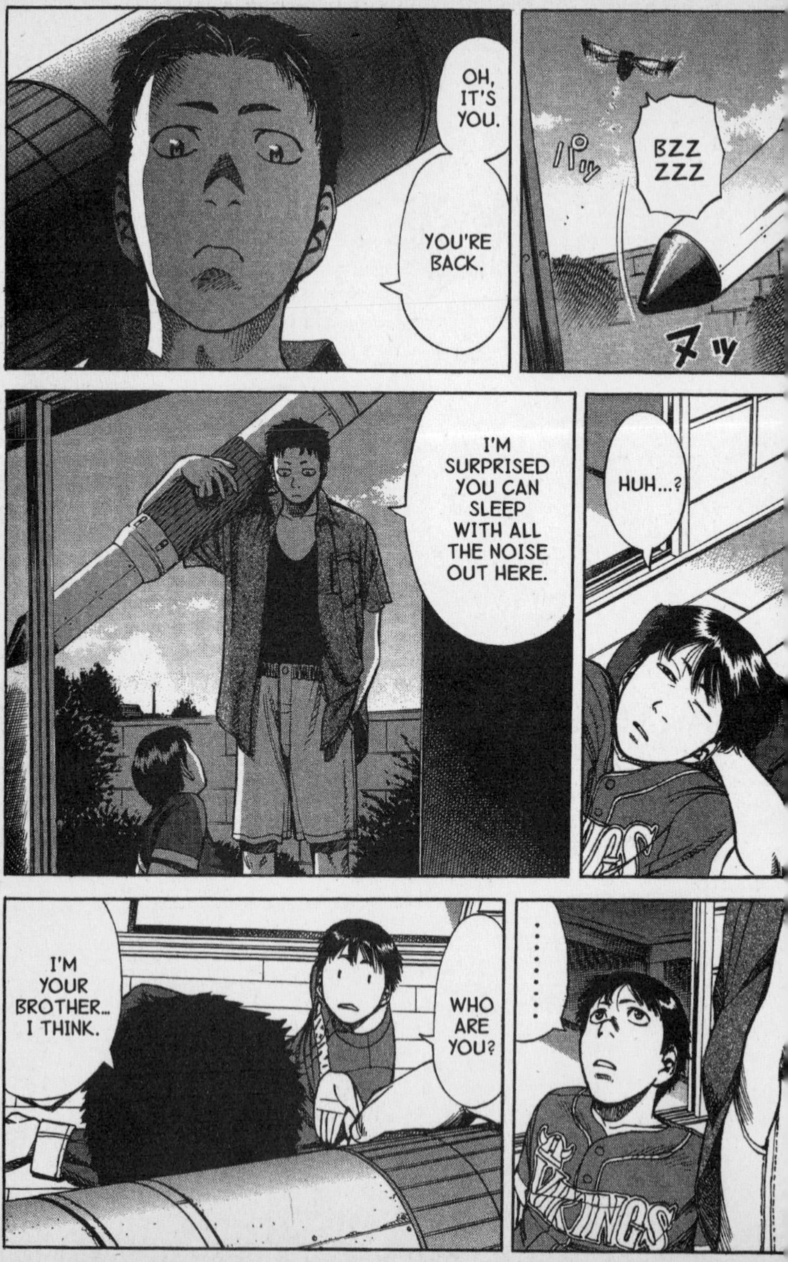
BZZ ZZZ
パッ
OH, IT'S YOU.
YOU'RE BACK.
HUH...?
I'M SURPRISED YOU CAN SLEEP WITH ALL THE NOISE OUT HERE.
......
WHO ARE YOU?
I'M YOUR BROTHER... I THINK.

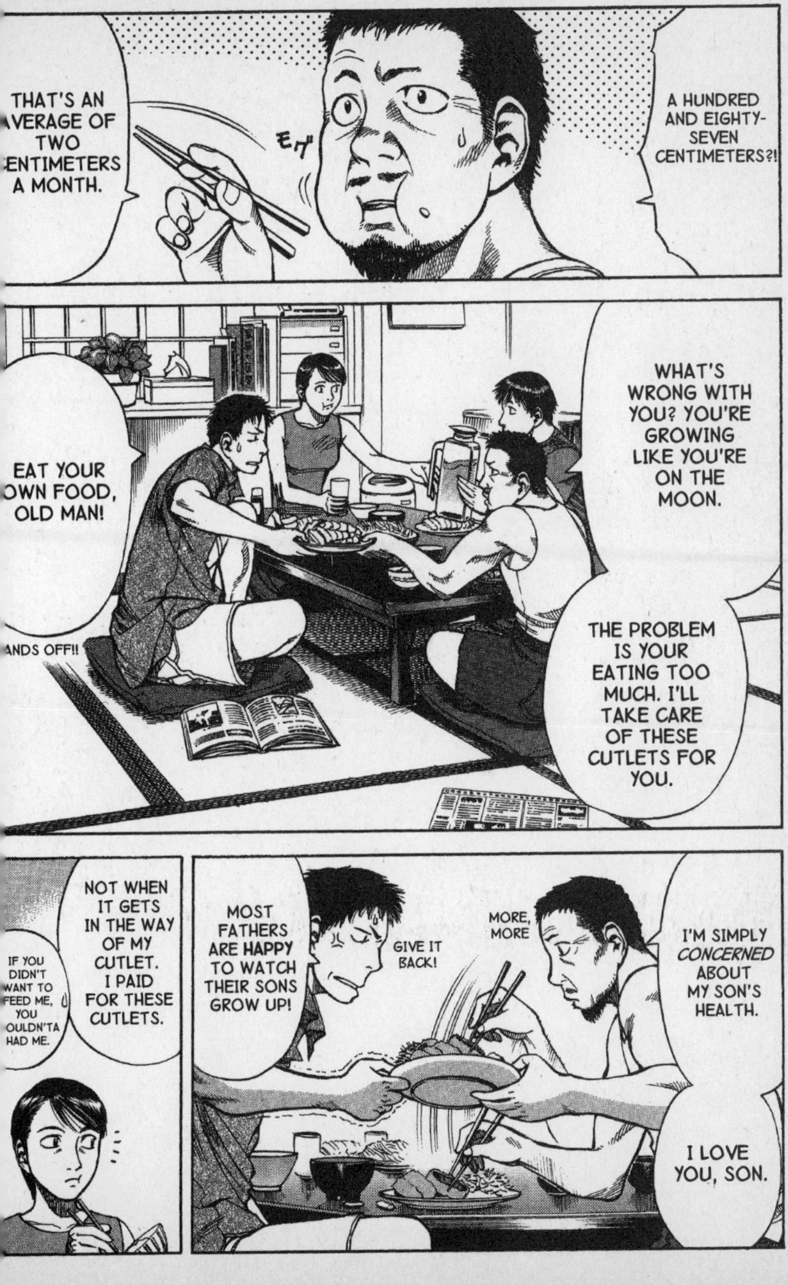
A HUNDRED AND EIGHTY-SEVEN CENTIMETERS?!
THAT'S AN VERAGE OF TWO ENTIMETERS A MONTH.
WHAT'S WRONG WITH YOU? YOU'RE GROWING LIKE YOU'RE ON THE MOON.
THE PROBLEM IS YOUR EATING TOO MUCH. I'LL TAKE CARE OF THESE CUTLETS FOR YOU.
EAT YOUR WN FOOD, OLD MAN!
ANDS OFF!!
I'M SIMPLY *CONCERNED* ABOUT MY SON'S HEALTH.
I LOVE YOU, SON.
MORE, MORE
GIVE IT BACK!
MOST FATHERS ARE **HAPPY** TO WATCH THEIR SONS GROW UP!
NOT WHEN IT GETS IN THE WAY OF MY CUTLET. I PAID FOR THESE CUTLETS.
IF YOU DIDN'T WANT TO FEED ME, YOU OULDN'TA HAD ME.

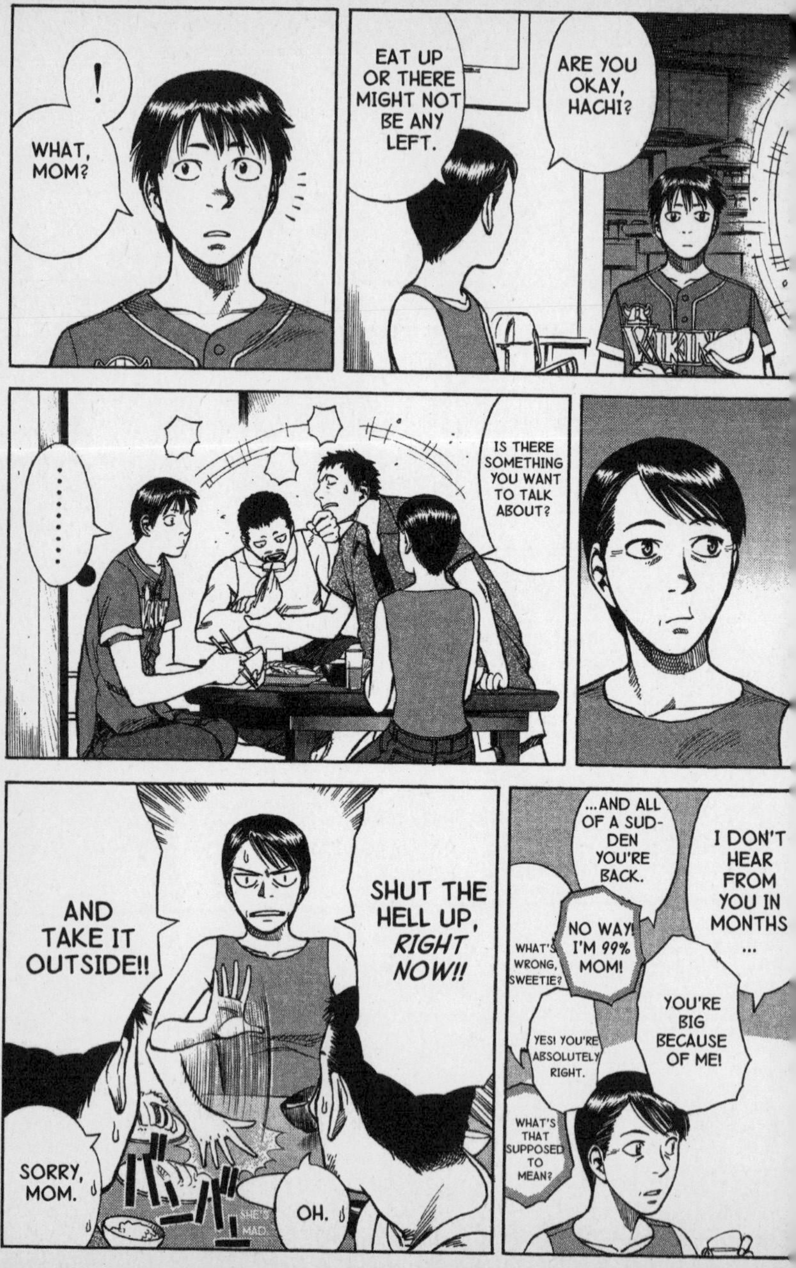
ARE YOU OKAY, HACHI?
EAT UP OR THERE MIGHT NOT BE ANY LEFT.
!
WHAT, MOM?
IS THERE SOMETHING YOU WANT TO TALK ABOUT?
......
I DON'T HEAR FROM YOU IN MONTHS ...
...AND ALL OF A SUDDEN YOU'RE BACK.
YOU'RE BIG BECAUSE OF ME!
NO WAY! I'M 99% MOM!
WHAT'S WRONG, SWEETIE?
YES! YOU'RE ABSOLUTELY RIGHT.
WHAT'S THAT SUPPOSED TO MEAN?
SHUT THE HELL UP, *RIGHT NOW!!*
AND TAKE IT OUTSIDE!!
OH.
SHE'S MAD.
SORRY, MOM.

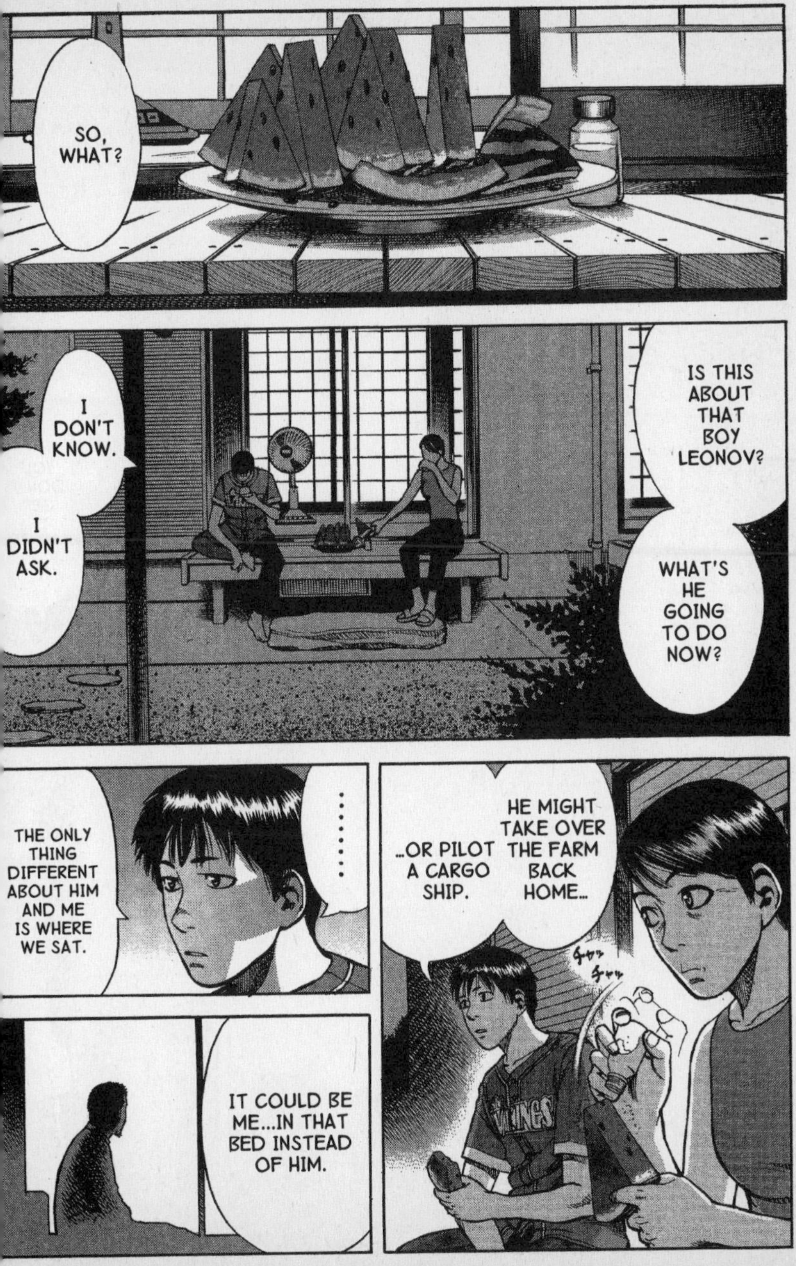
SO, WHAT?
IS THIS ABOUT THAT BOY LEONOV?
WHAT'S HE GOING TO DO NOW?
I DON'T KNOW.
I DIDN'T ASK.
HE MIGHT TAKE OVER THE FARM BACK HOME...
...OR PILOT A CARGO SHIP.
......
THE ONLY THING DIFFERENT ABOUT HIM AND ME IS WHERE WE SAT.
IT COULD BE ME...IN THAT BED INSTEAD OF HIM.

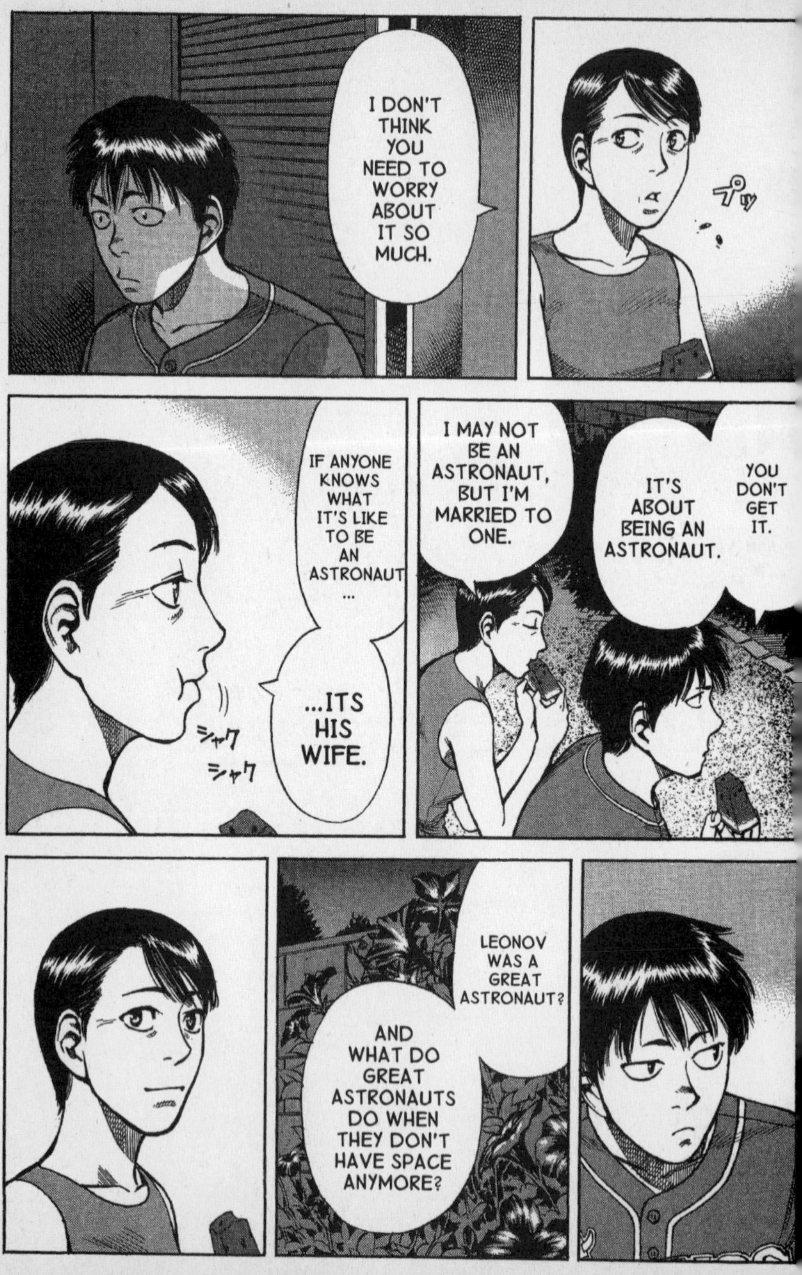
I DON'T THINK YOU NEED TO WORRY ABOUT IT SO MUCH.
YOU DON'T GET IT.
IT'S ABOUT BEING AN ASTRONAUT.
I MAY NOT BE AN ASTRONAUT, BUT I'M MARRIED TO ONE.
IF ANYONE KNOWS WHAT IT'S LIKE TO BE AN ASTRONAUT...
...ITS HIS WIFE.
シャク
シャク
LEONOV WAS A GREAT ASTRONAUT?
AND WHAT DO GREAT ASTRONAUTS DO WHEN THEY DON'T HAVE SPACE ANYMORE?

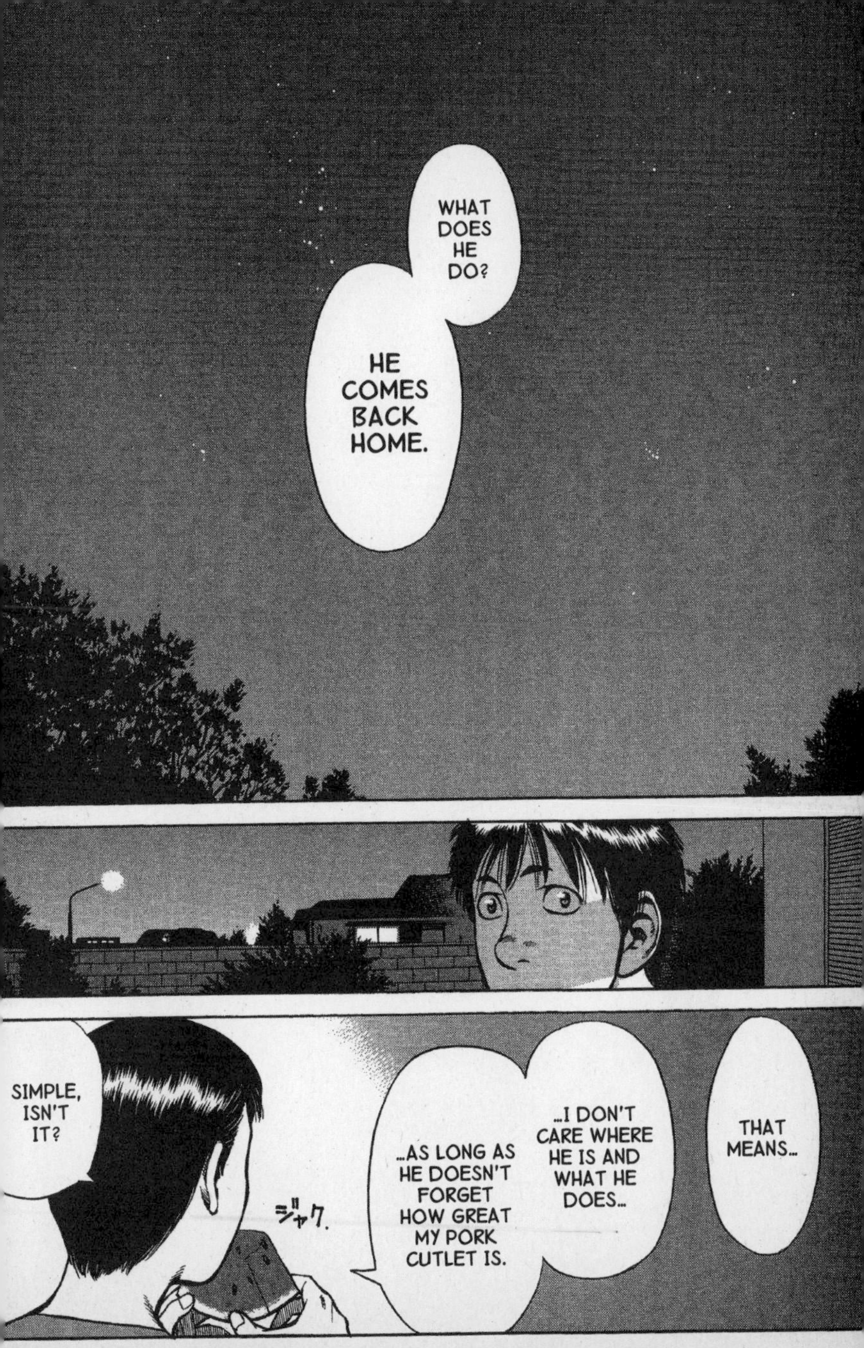
WHAT DOES HE DO?
HE COMES BACK HOME.
THAT MEANS...
...I DON'T CARE WHERE HE IS AND WHAT HE DOES...
...AS LONG AS HE DOESN'T FORGET HOW GREAT MY PORK CUTLET IS.
ジャク.
SIMPLE, ISN'T IT?

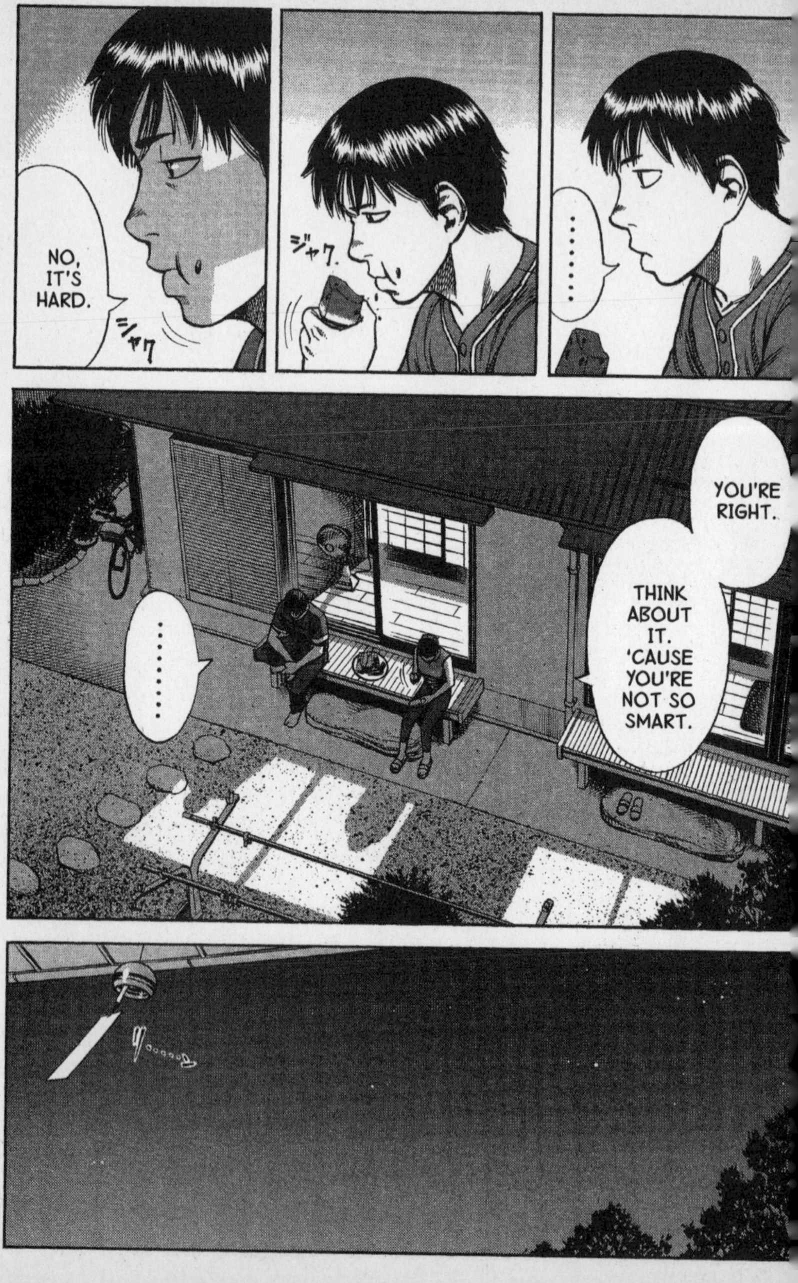
....
ジャク
NO, IT'S HARD.
ジャク
YOU'RE RIGHT.
THINK ABOUT IT. 'CAUSE YOU'RE NOT SO SMART.
....

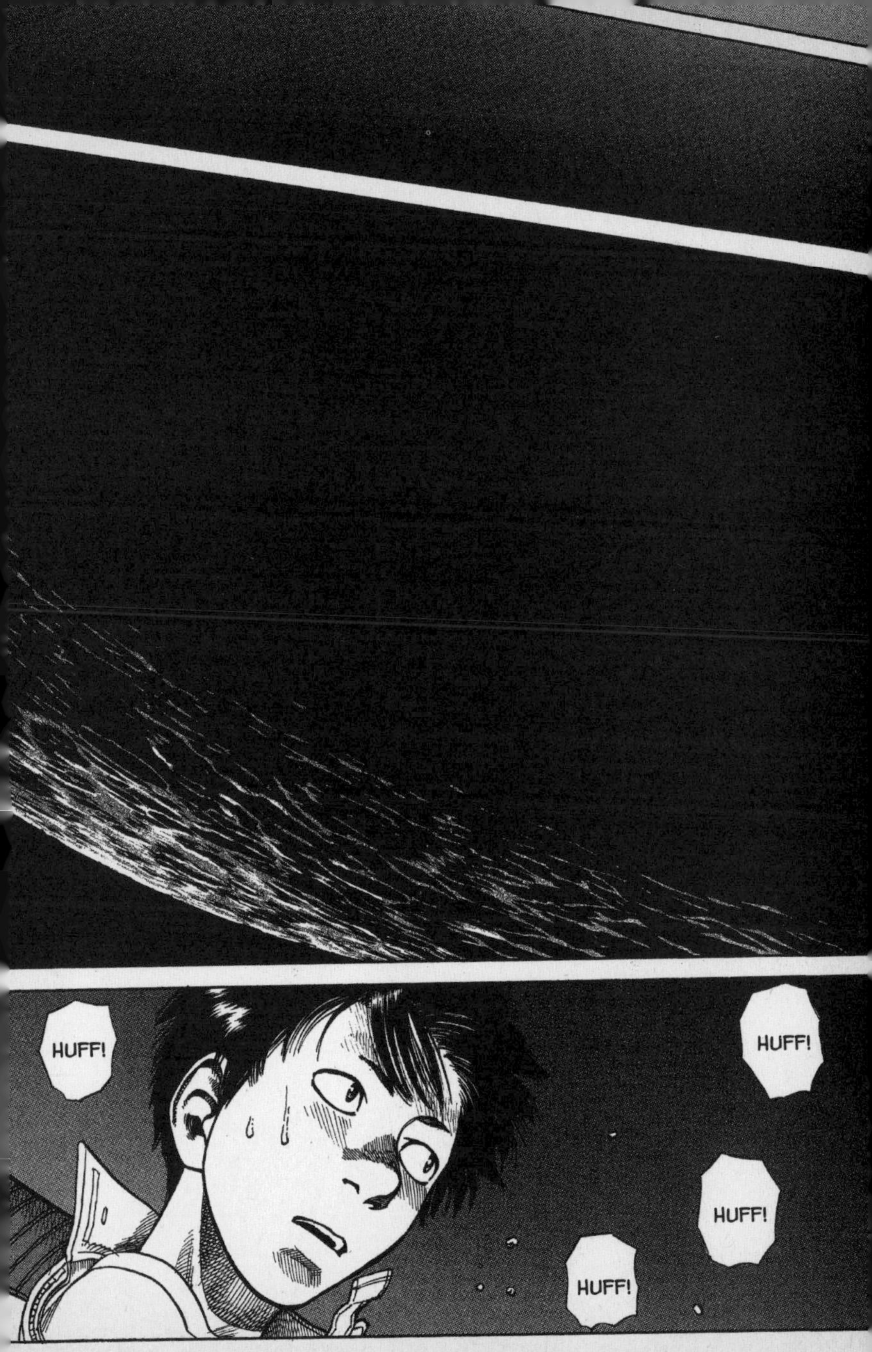
HUFF!
HUFF!
HUFF!
HUFF!

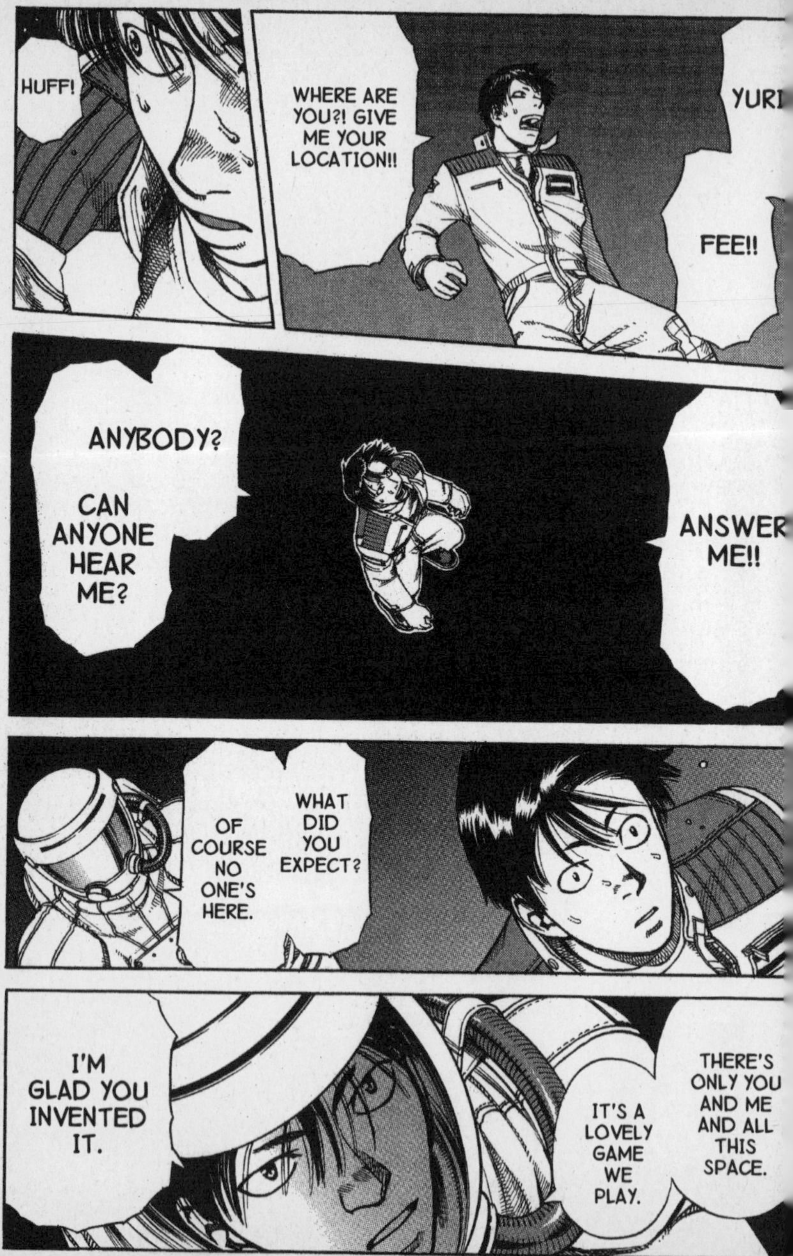
YURI
FEE!!
WHERE ARE YOU?! GIVE ME YOUR LOCATION!!
HUFF!
ANYBODY?
CAN ANYONE HEAR ME?
ANSWER ME!!
WHAT DID YOU EXPECT?
OF COURSE NO ONE'S HERE.
THERE'S ONLY YOU AND ME AND ALL THIS SPACE.
IT'S A LOVELY GAME WE PLAY.
I'M GLAD YOU INVENTED IT.

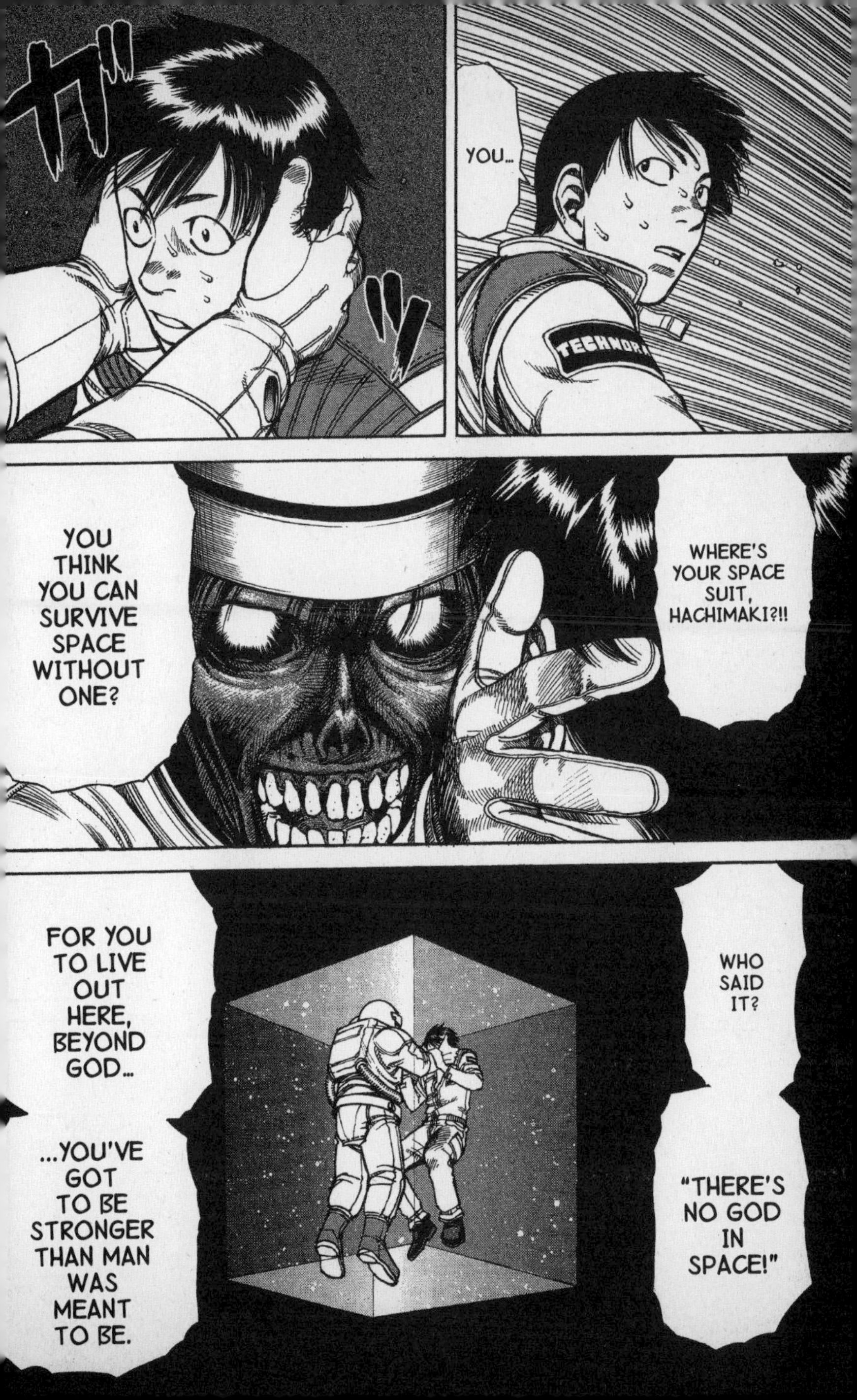

YOU...
ガッ
WHERE'S YOUR SPACE SUIT, HACHIMAKI?!!
YOU THINK YOU CAN SURVIVE SPACE WITHOUT ONE?
WHO SAID IT?
FOR YOU TO LIVE OUT HERE, BEYOND GOD...
"THERE'S NO GOD IN SPACE!"
...YOU'VE GOT TO BE STRONGER THAN MAN WAS MEANT TO BE.

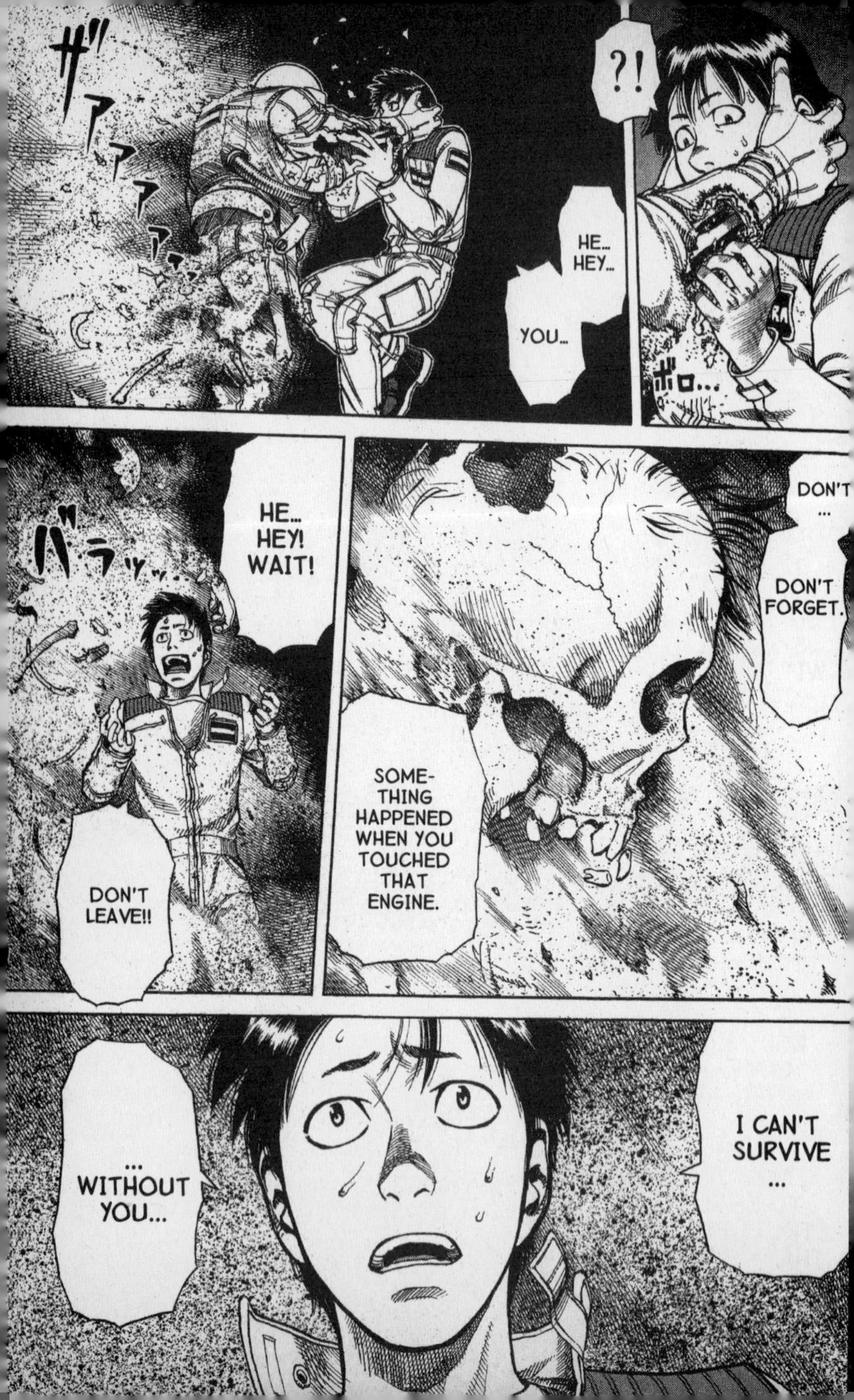
?!
HE.. HEY...
YOU...
ボロ...
ザァァァァ
DON'T ... DON'T FORGET.
SOME-THING HAPPENED WHEN YOU TOUCHED THAT ENGINE.
HE... HEY! WAIT!
バラッ...
DON'T LEAVE!!
I CAN'T SURVIVE ...
... WITHOUT YOU...

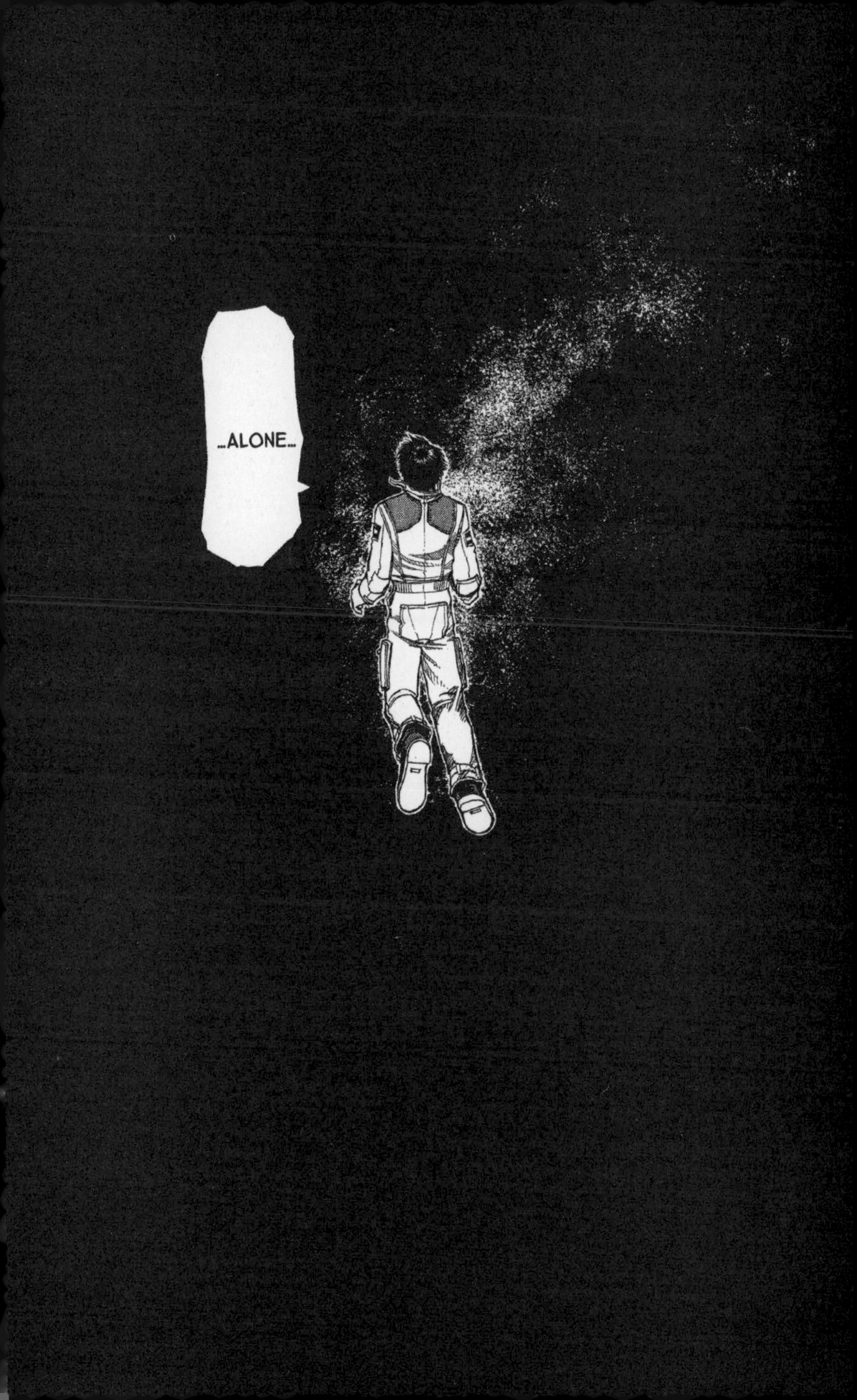
...ALONE...

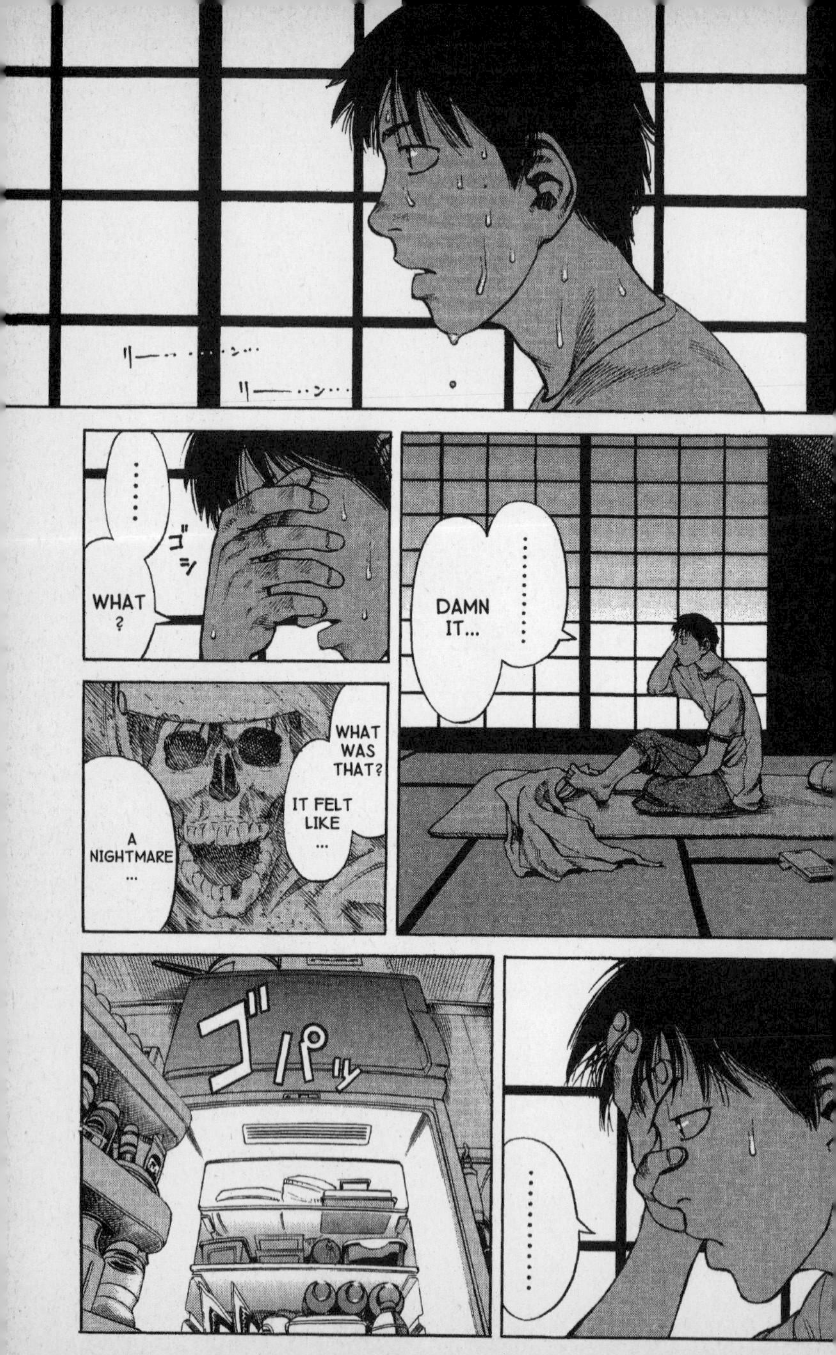

リー…・…ン…
リー…ン…
……
DAMN IT...
……
ゴシ
WHAT ?
WHAT WAS THAT?
IT FELT LIKE ...
A NIGHTMARE ...
……
ゴパッ

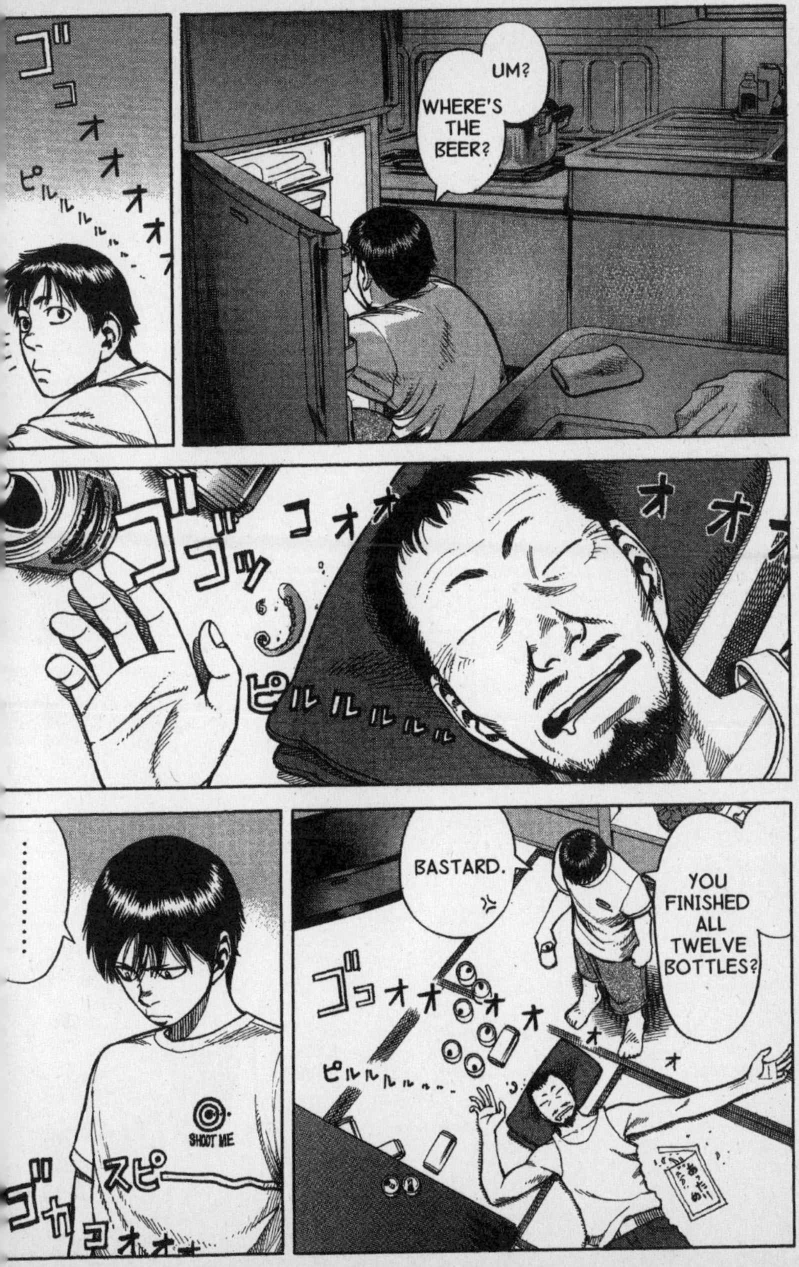
UM?
WHERE'S THE BEER?
ゴォオオオオオ
ピルルルル…
ゴゴッ
コオオ
オオ
ピルルルルル
YOU FINISHED ALL TWELVE BOTTLES?
BASTARD.
ゴォオオオオオ
ピルルルル…
……
SHOOT ME
スピー
ゴォォオオ

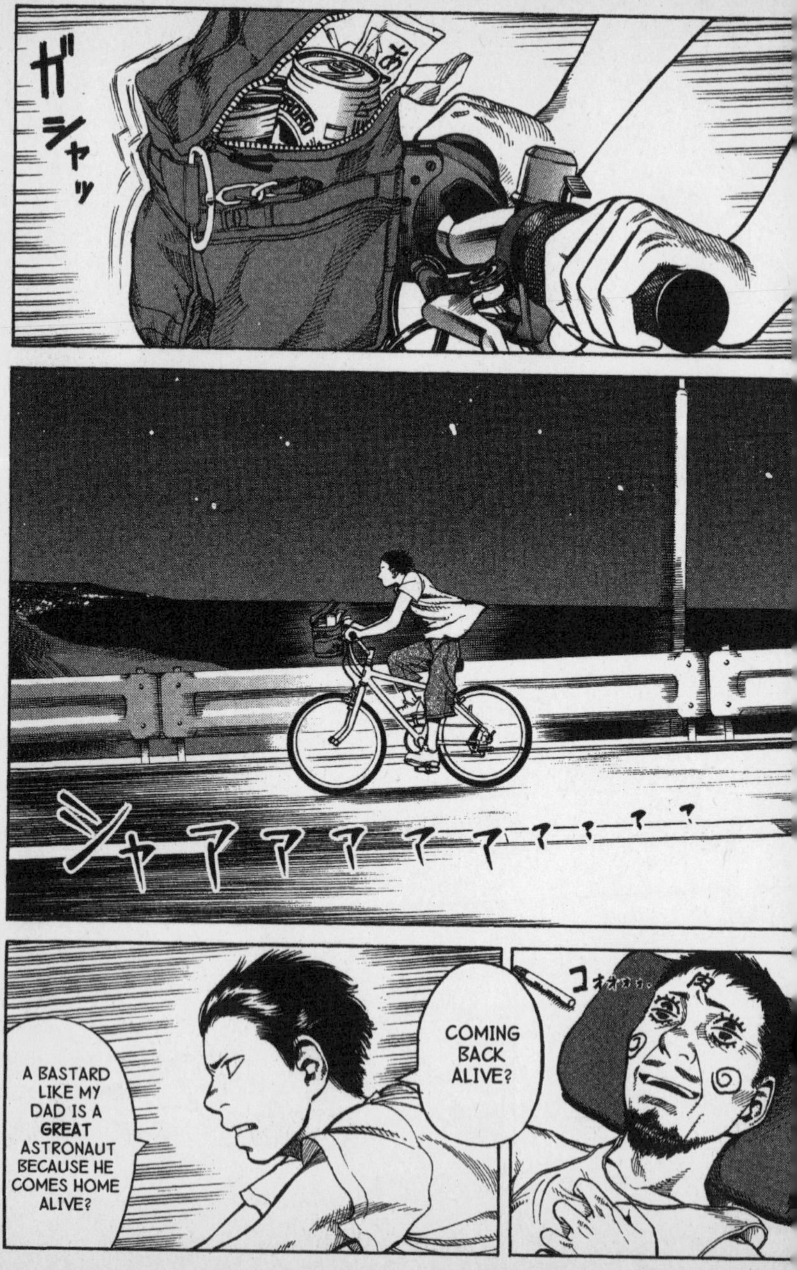
ガシャッ
シャアアアアアアアアア
COMING BACK ALIVE?
A BASTARD LIKE MY DAD IS A **GREAT** ASTRONAUT BECAUSE HE COMES HOME ALIVE?

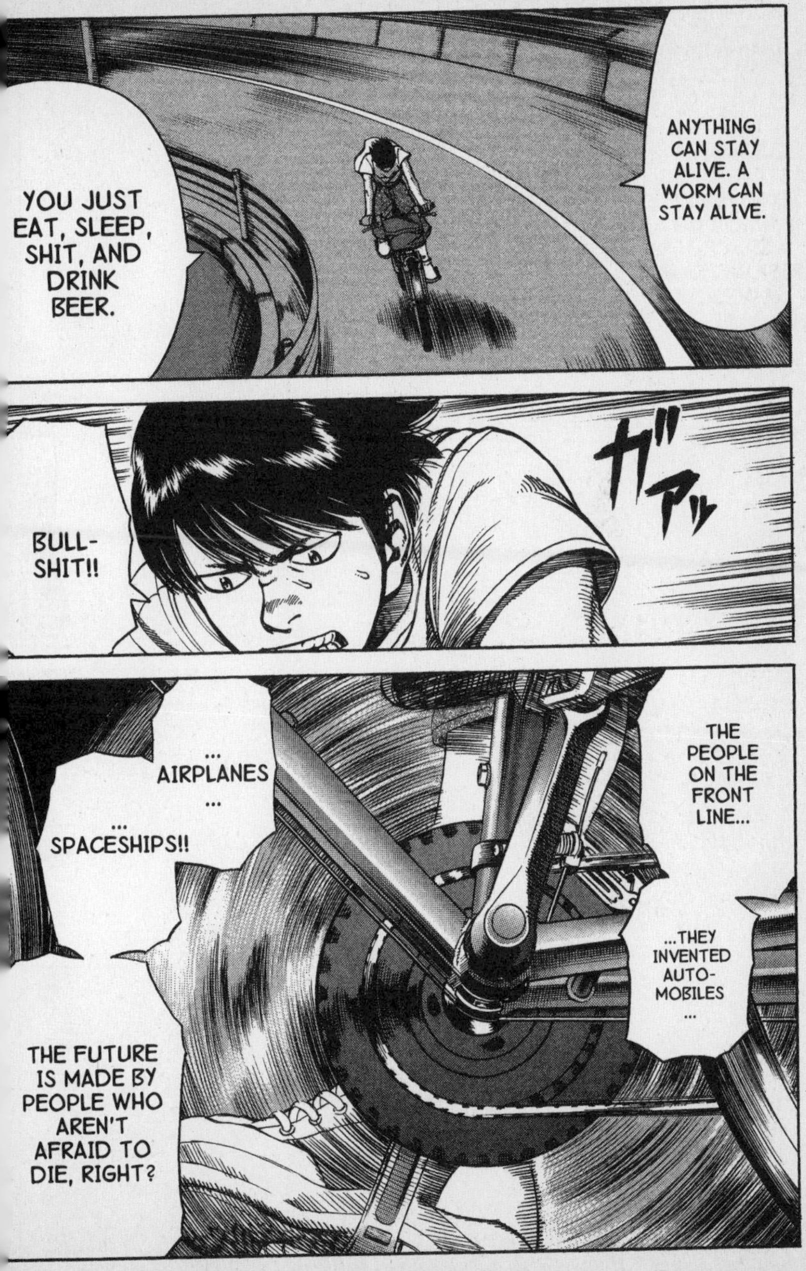
ANYTHING CAN STAY ALIVE. A WORM CAN STAY ALIVE.
YOU JUST EAT, SLEEP, SHIT, AND DRINK BEER.
ガアッ
BULL-SHIT!!
THE PEOPLE ON THE FRONT LINE...
...THEY INVENTED AUTO-MOBILES ...
... AIRPLANES ... ... SPACESHIPS!!
THE FUTURE IS MADE BY PEOPLE WHO AREN'T AFRAID TO DIE, RIGHT?

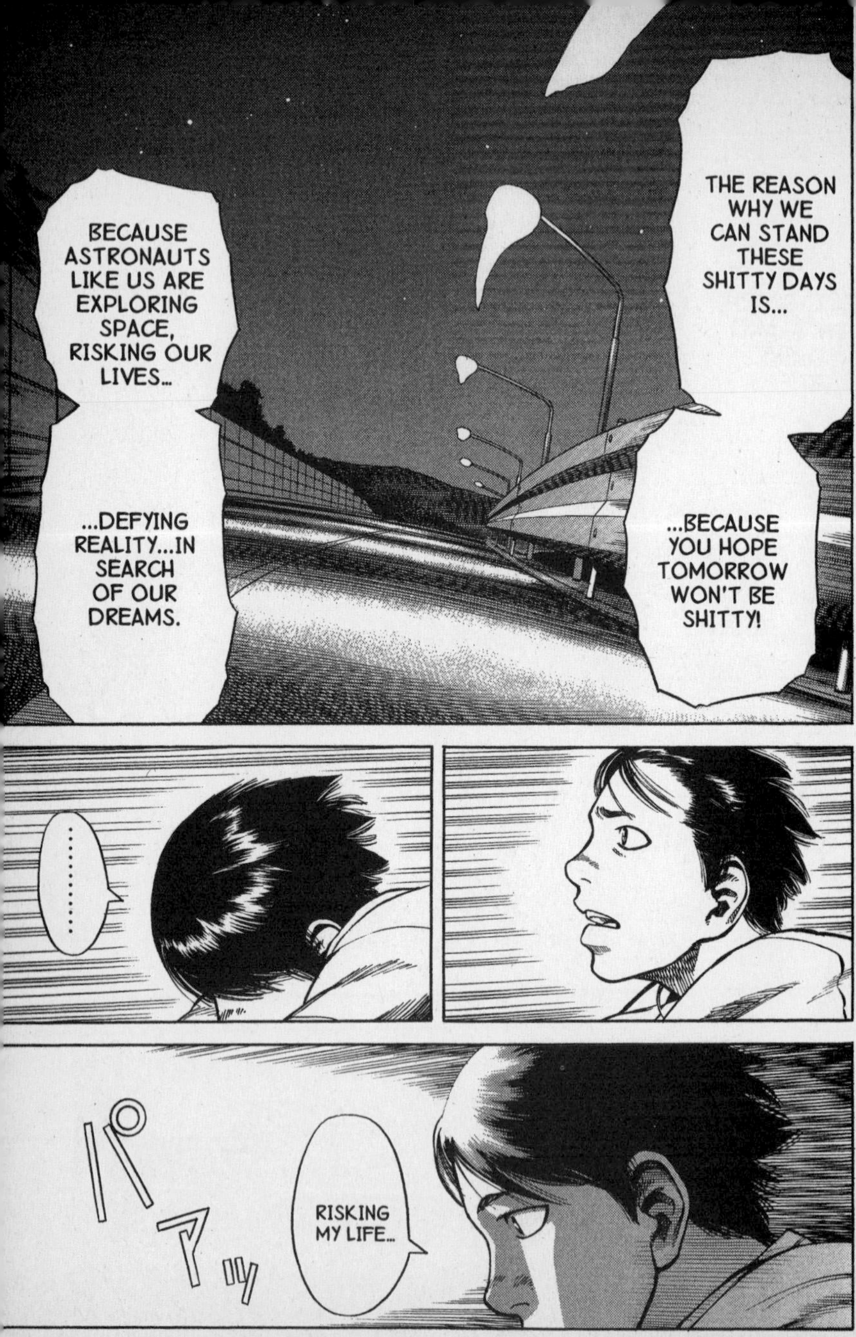
THE REASON WHY WE CAN STAND THESE SHITTY DAYS IS...
...BECAUSE YOU HOPE TOMORROW WON'T BE SHITTY!
BECAUSE ASTRONAUTS LIKE US ARE EXPLORING SPACE, RISKING OUR LIVES...
...DEFYING REALITY...IN SEARCH OF OUR DREAMS.
....
RISKING MY LIFE...
パァッ

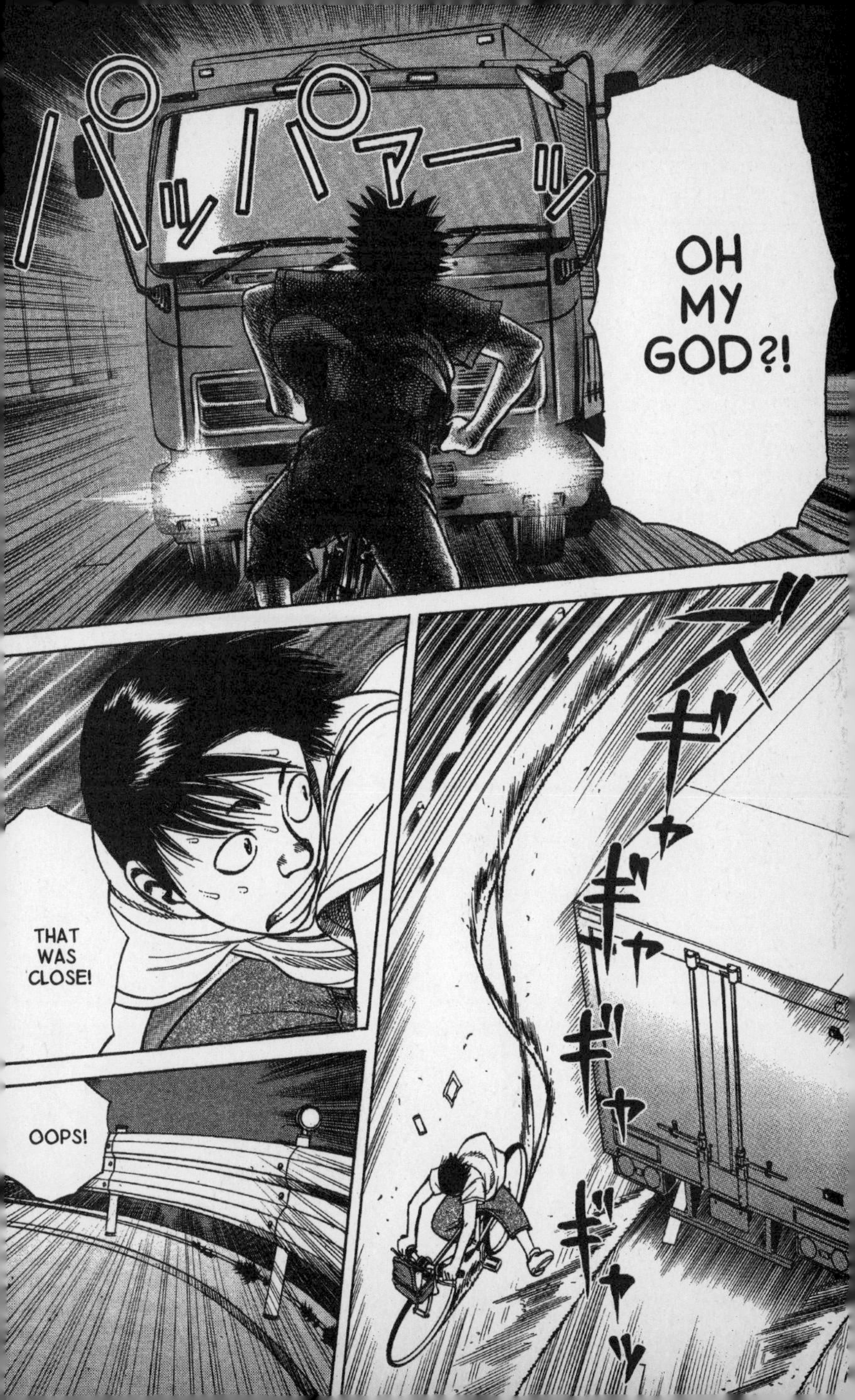
パッパアーーッ
OH MY GOD?!
ズギャギャギャギャギャッ
THAT WAS CLOSE!
OOPS!

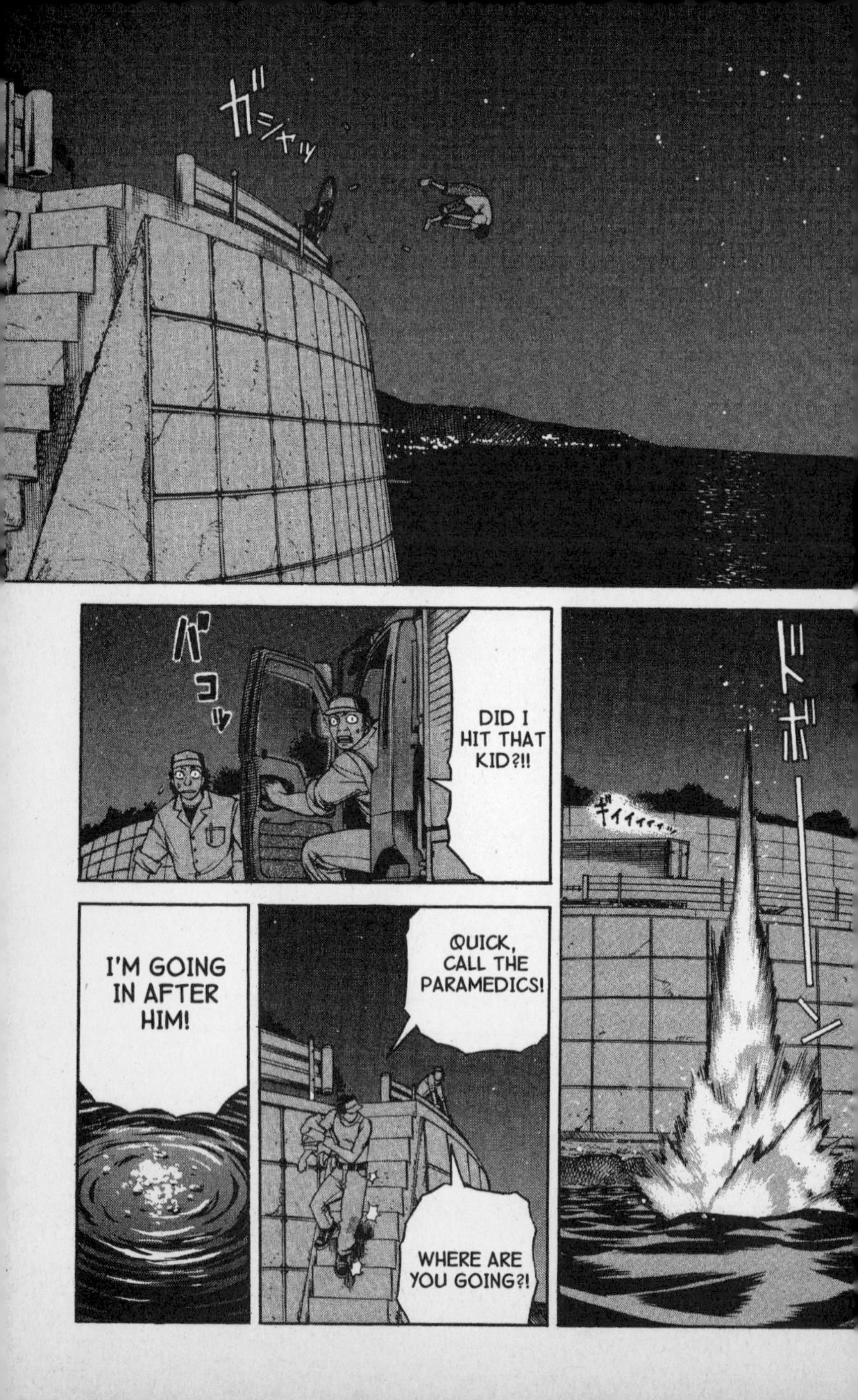
ガシャッ
ドボーーン
バコッ
DID I HIT THAT KID?!!
QUICK, CALL THE PARAMEDICS!
WHERE ARE YOU GOING?!
I'M GOING IN AFTER HIM!

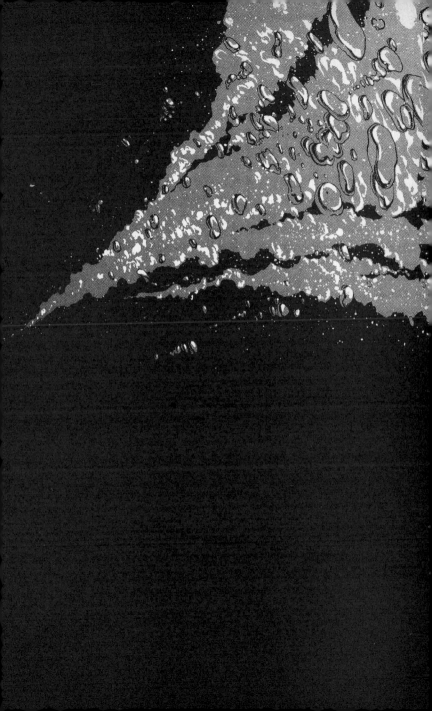

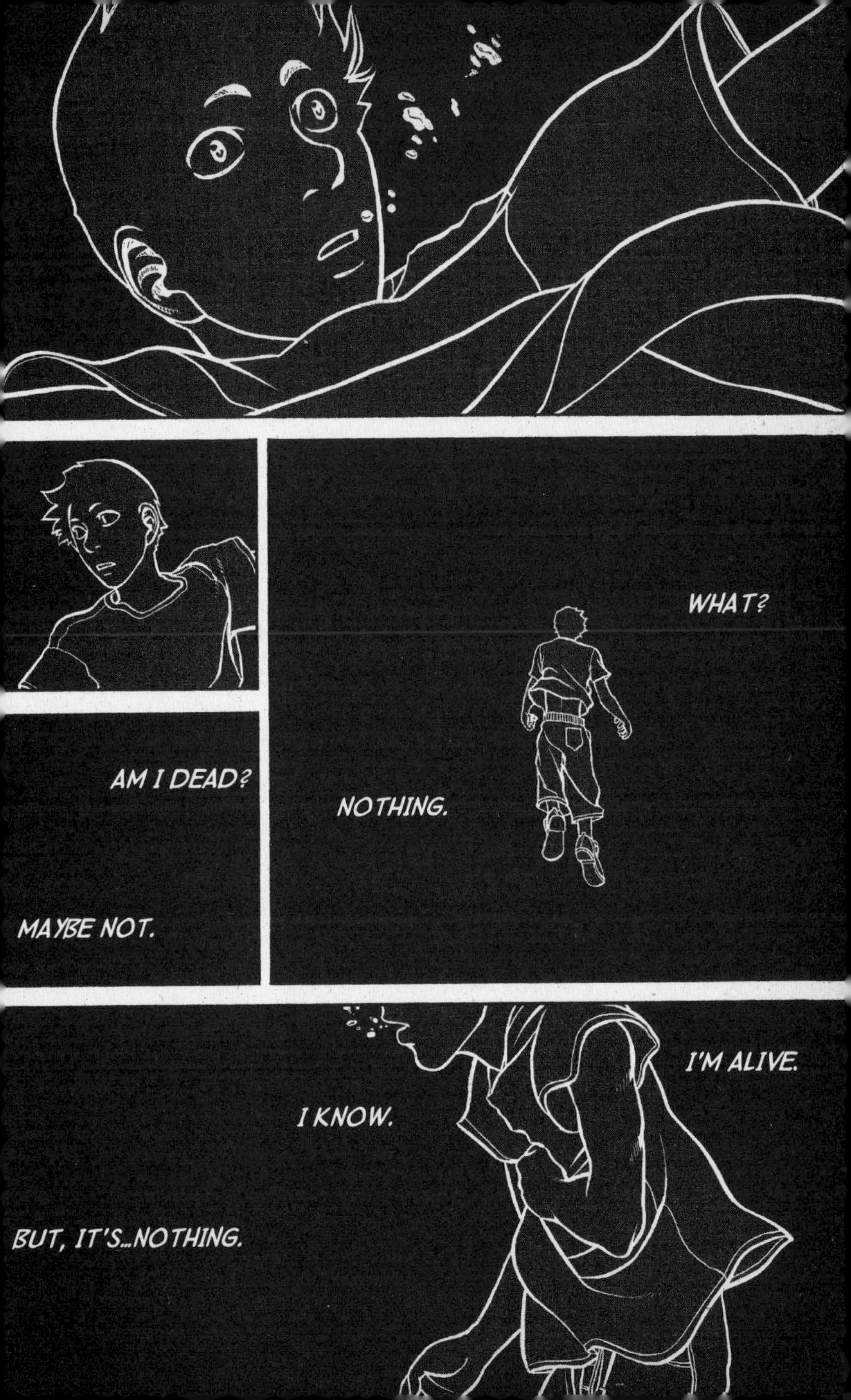
WHAT?
NOTHING.
AM I DEAD?
MAYBE NOT.
I'M ALIVE.
I KNOW.
BUT, IT'S...NOTHING.

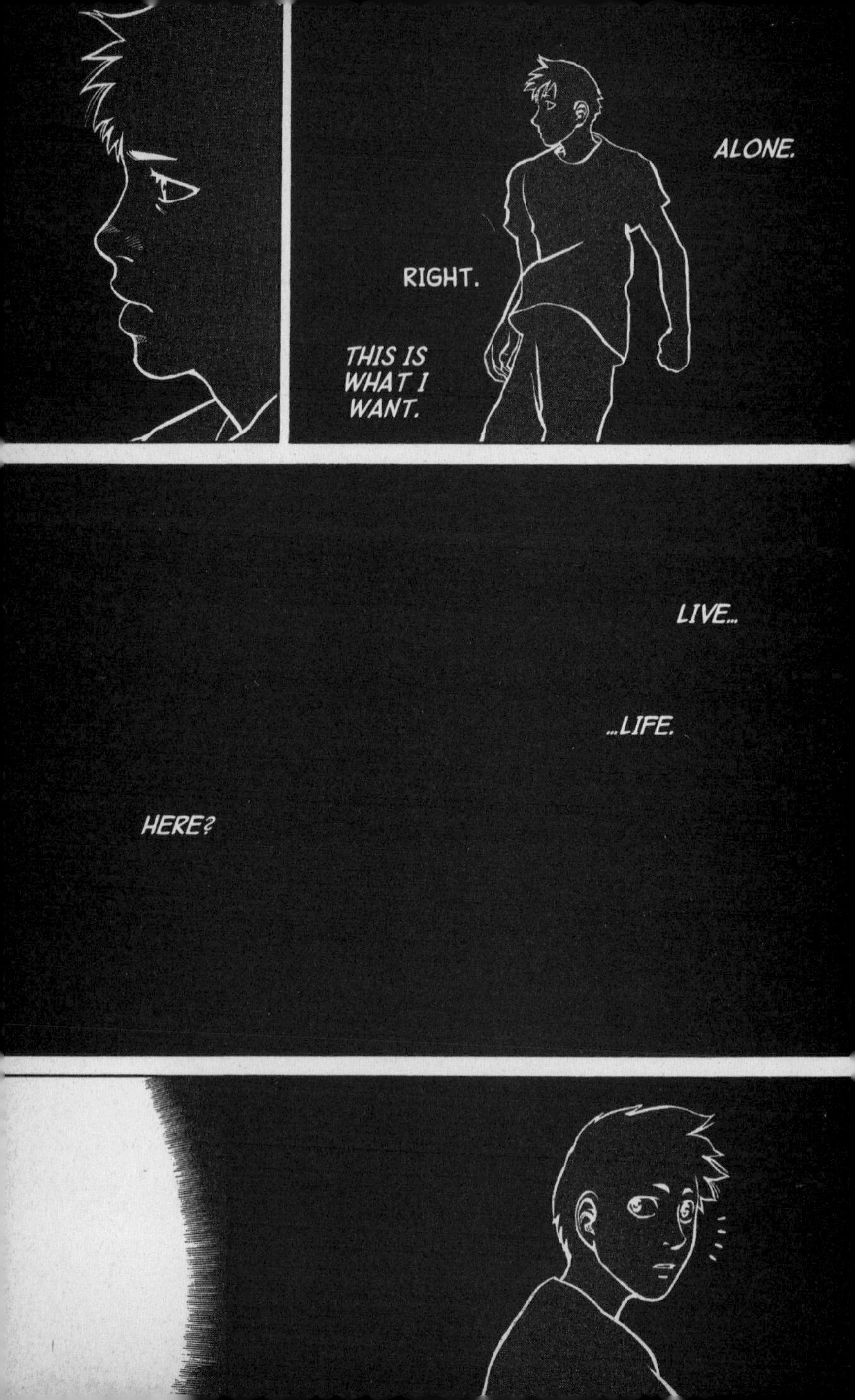
ALONE.
RIGHT.
THIS IS WHAT I WANT.
LIVE...
...LIFE.
HERE?

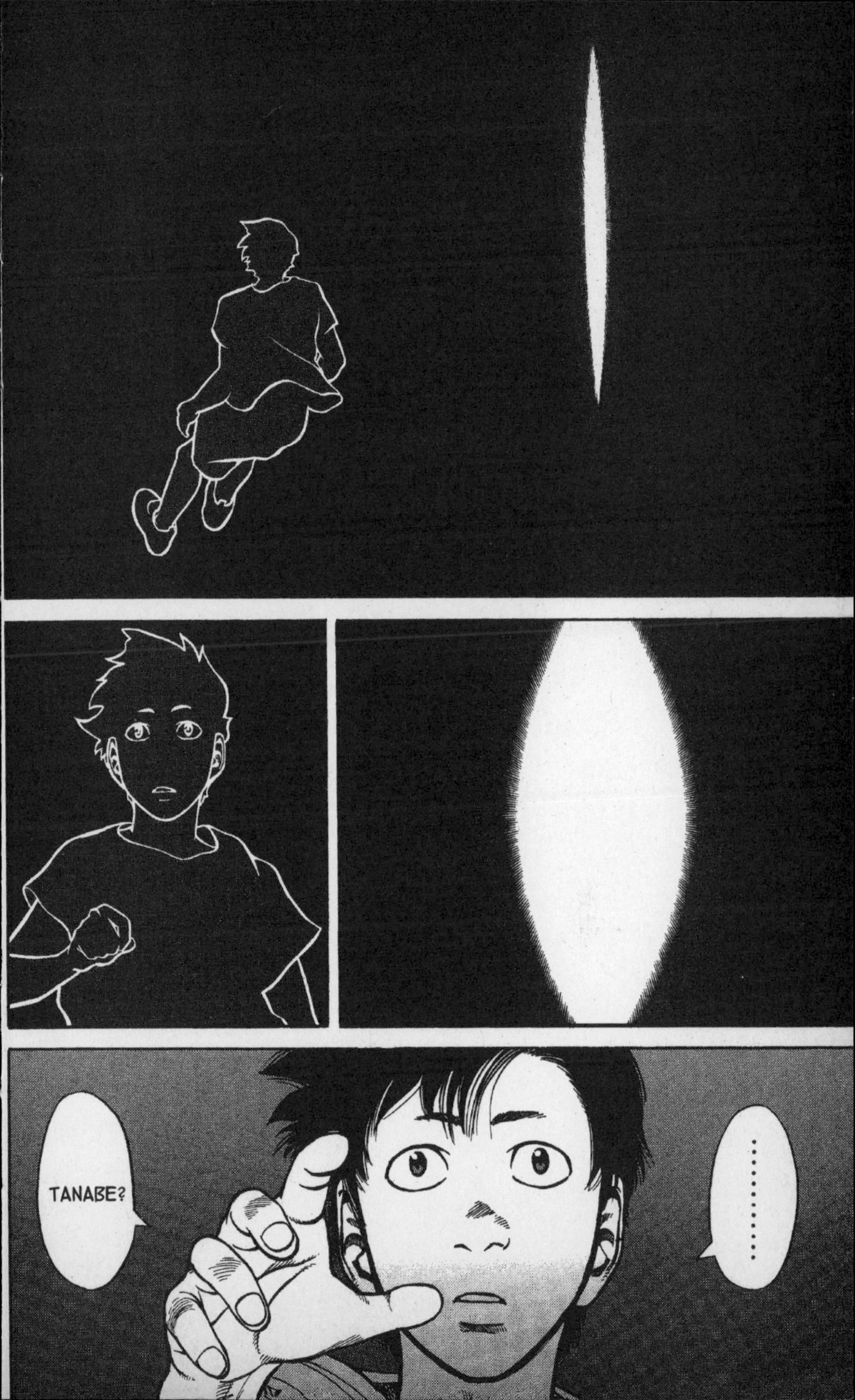
......
TANABE?

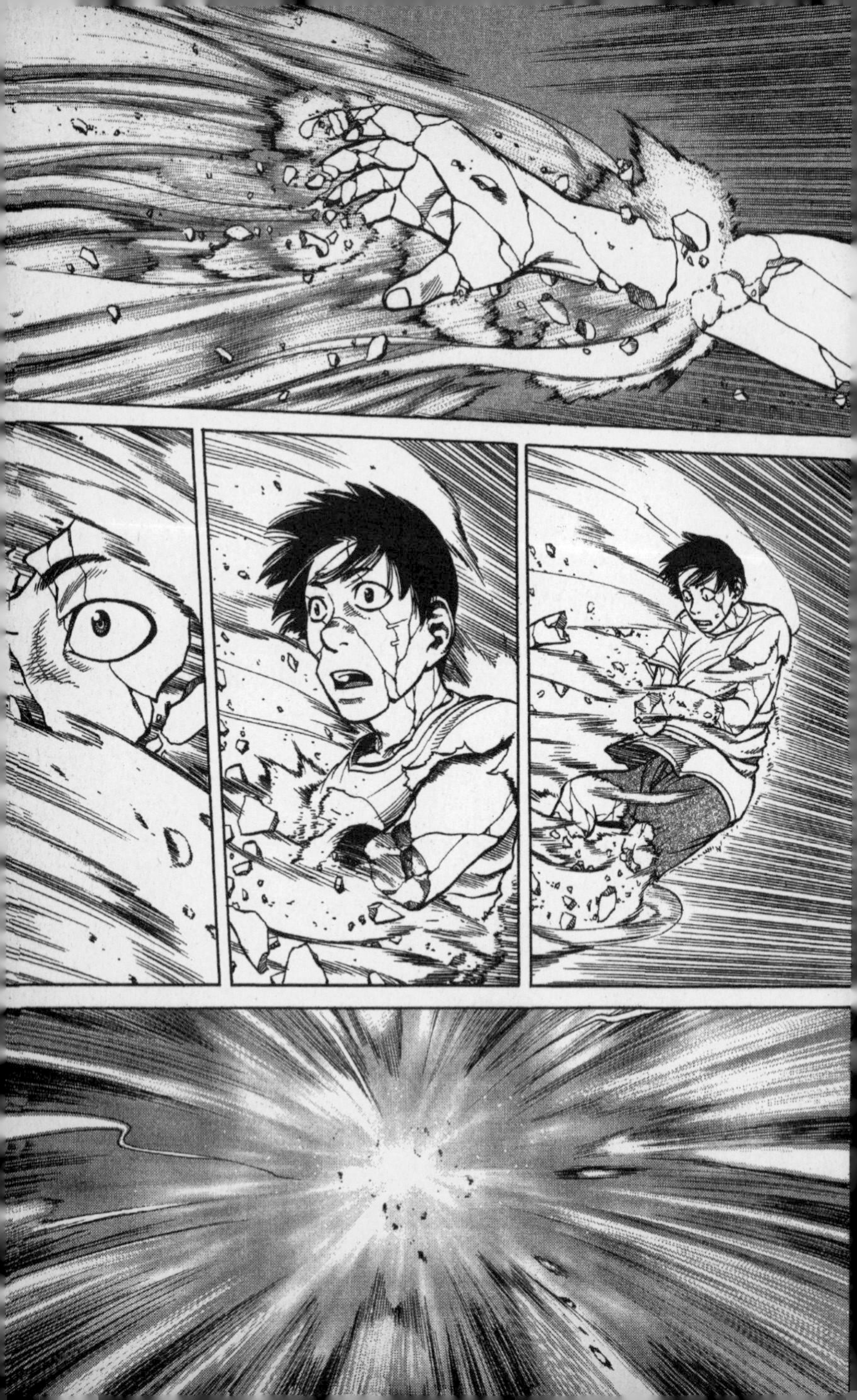

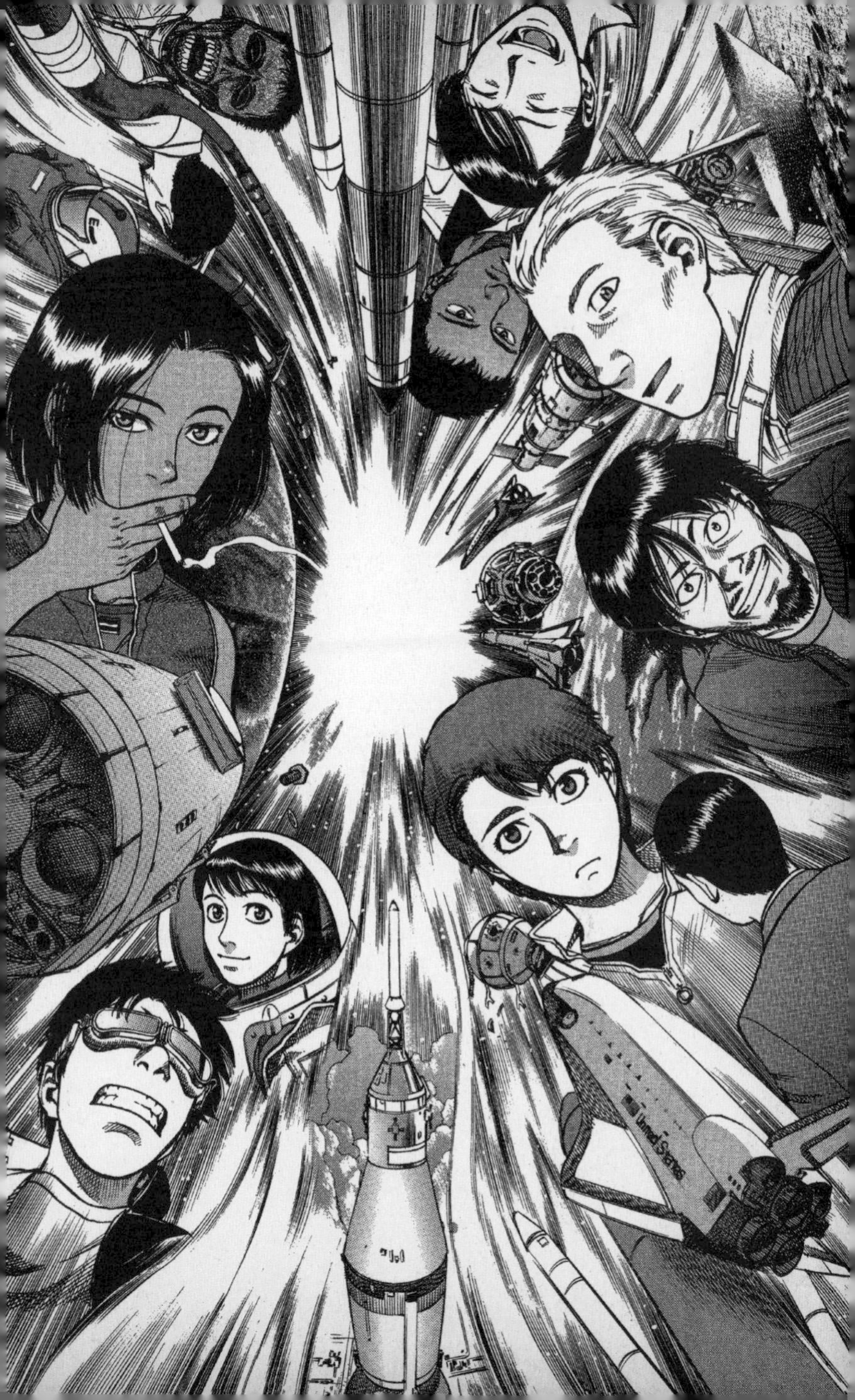
United States

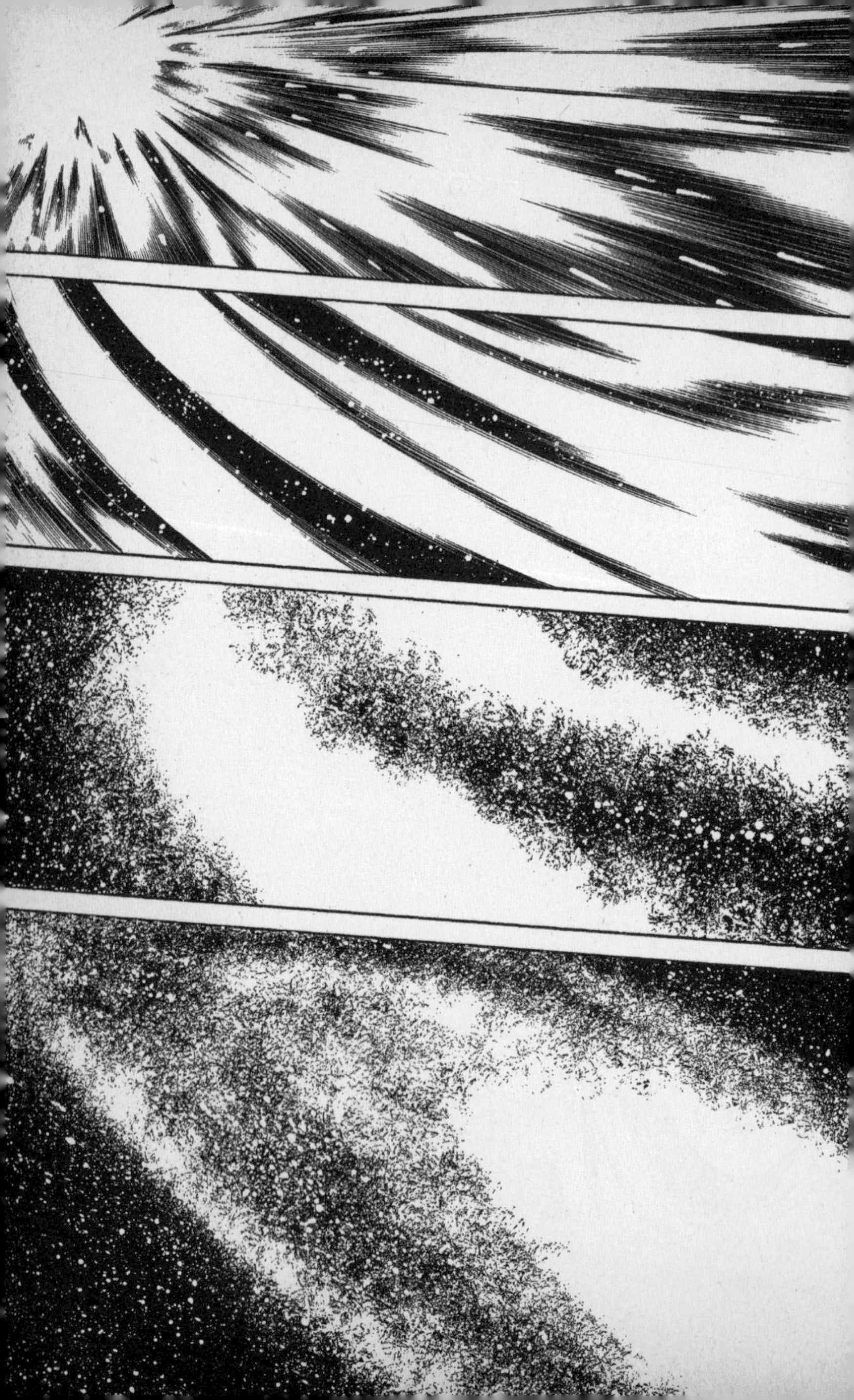

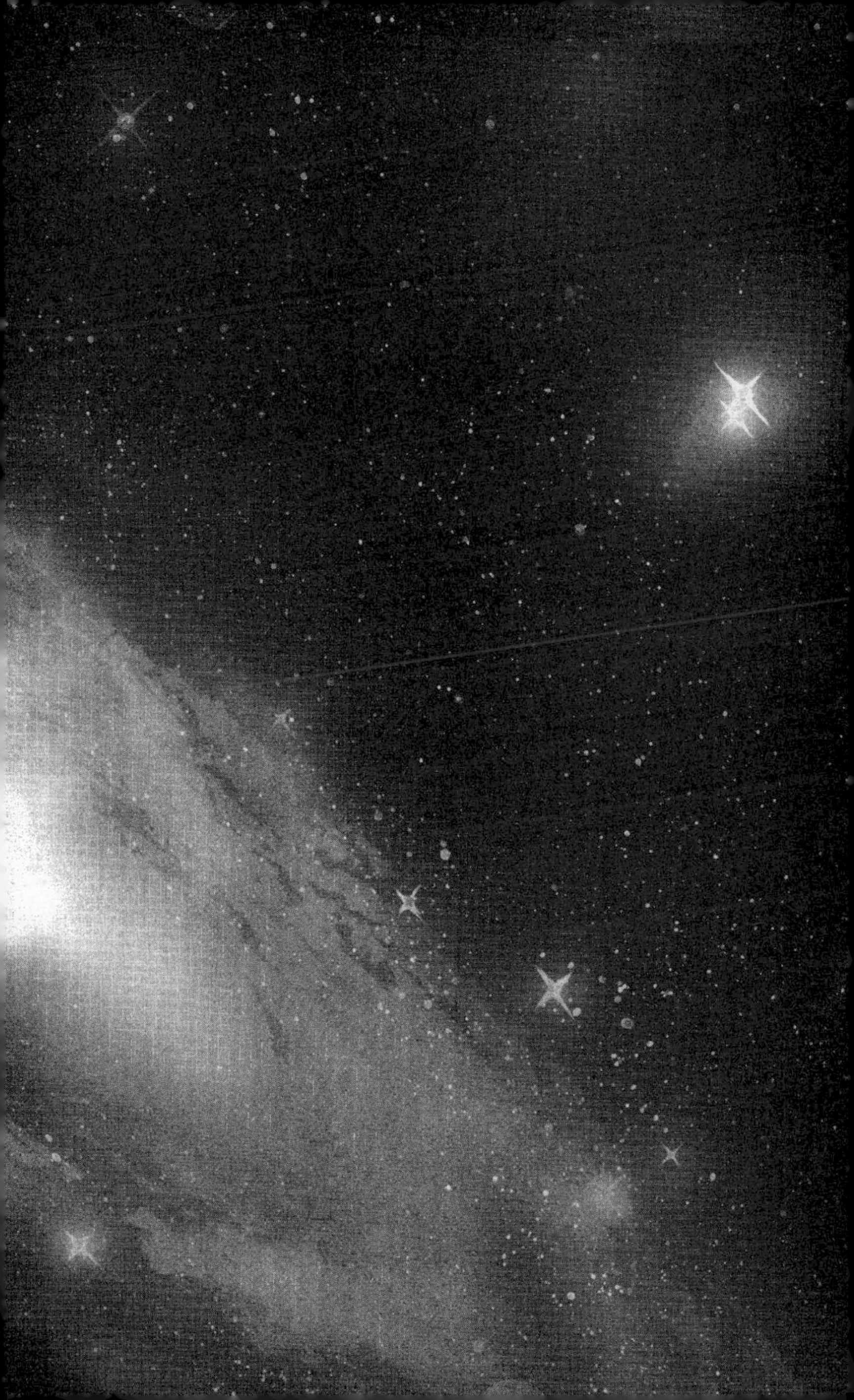

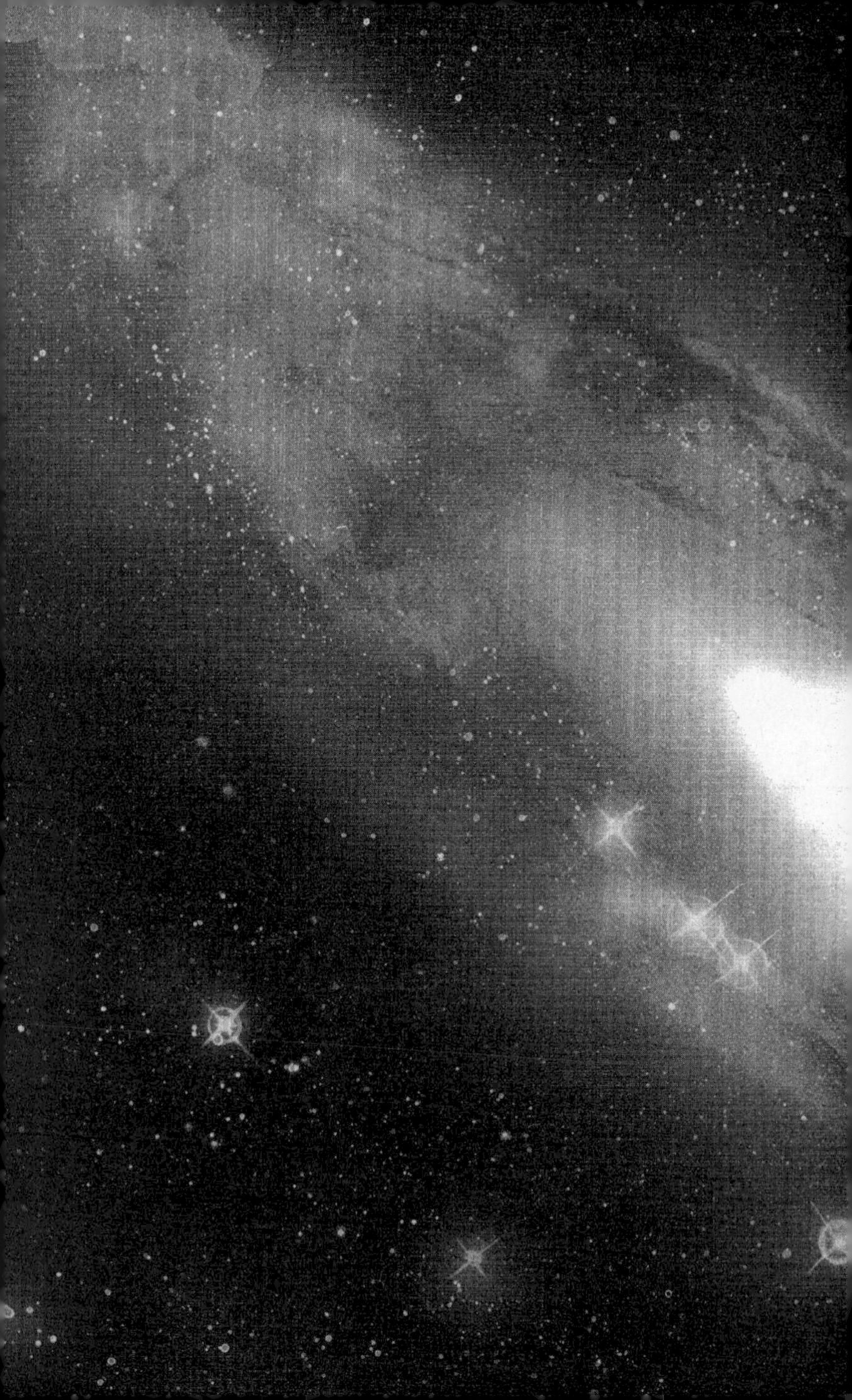

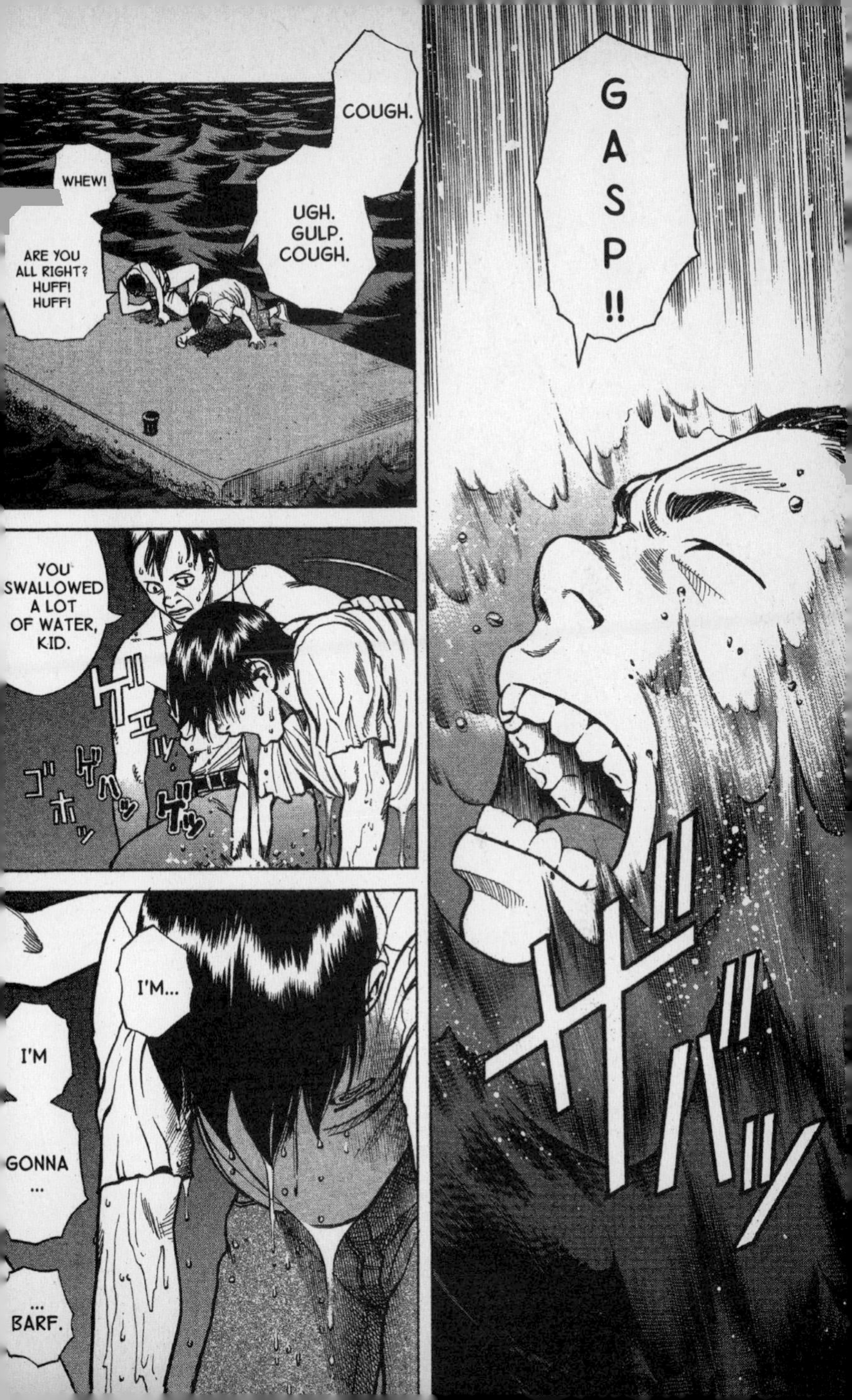
GASP!!
ザバッ
COUGH.
UGH. GULP. COUGH.
WHEW!
ARE YOU ALL RIGHT? HUFF! HUFF!
YOU SWALLOWED A LOT OF WATER, KID.
ゲェッ
ゲハッ
ゲッ
ゴホッ
I'M...
I'M
GONNA ...
... BARF.

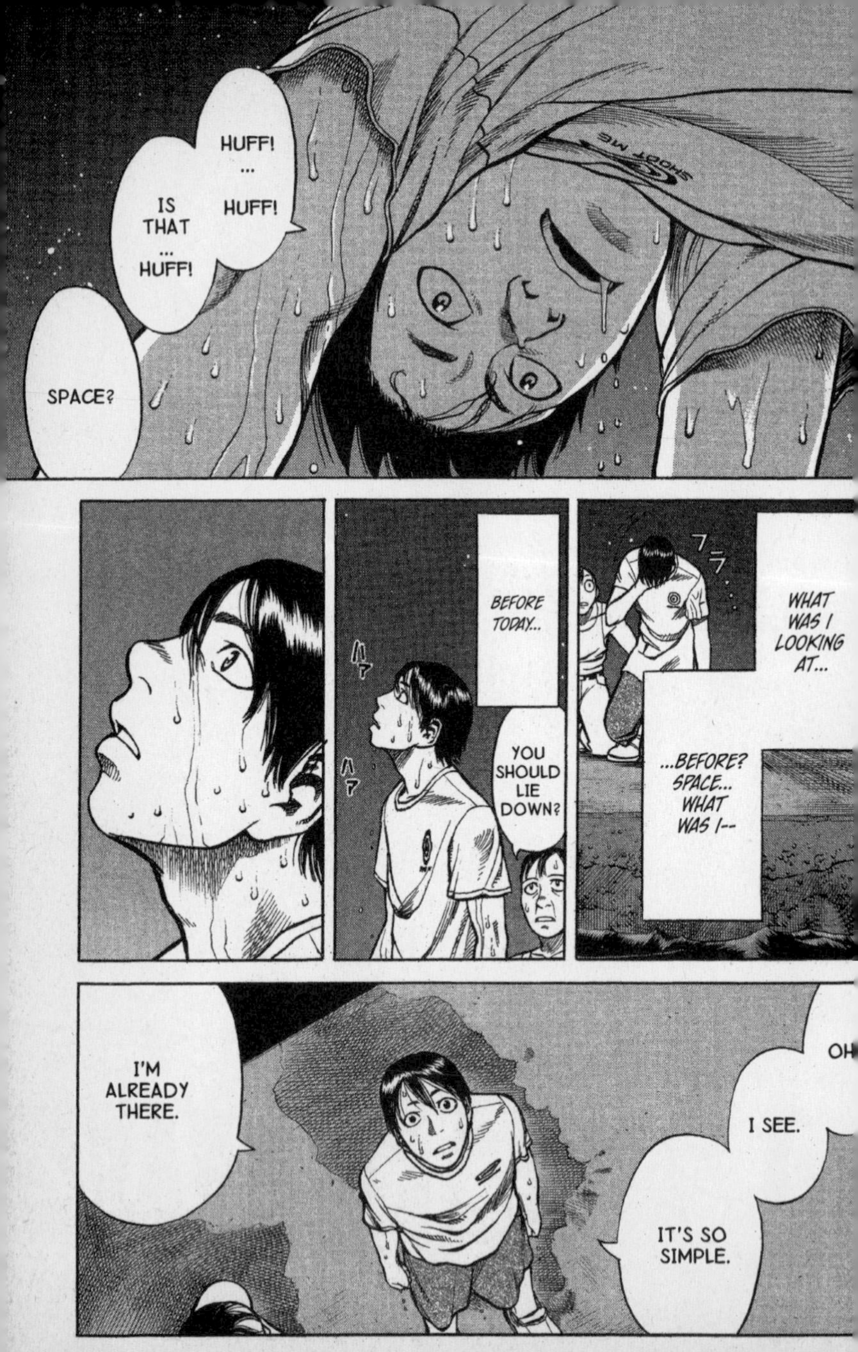
HUFF! ... HUFF!
IS THAT ... HUFF!
SPACE?
WHAT WAS I LOOKING AT...
...BEFORE? SPACE... WHAT WAS I--
フラ
BEFORE TODAY...
YOU SHOULD LIE DOWN?
ハァ
ハァ
OH
I SEE.
IT'S SO SIMPLE.
I'M ALREADY THERE.

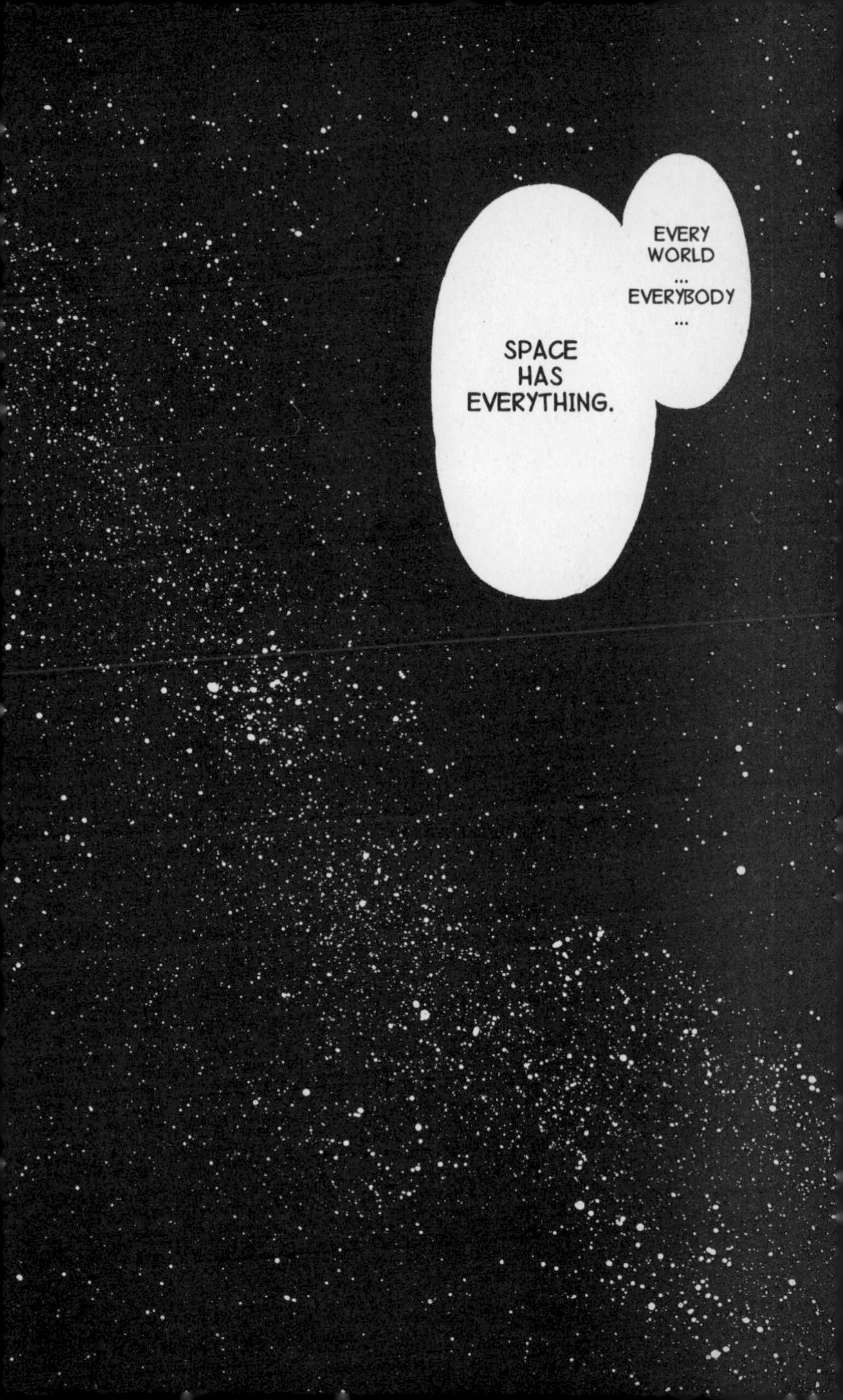
EVERY WORLD ... EVERYBODY ...
SPACE HAS EVERYTHING.

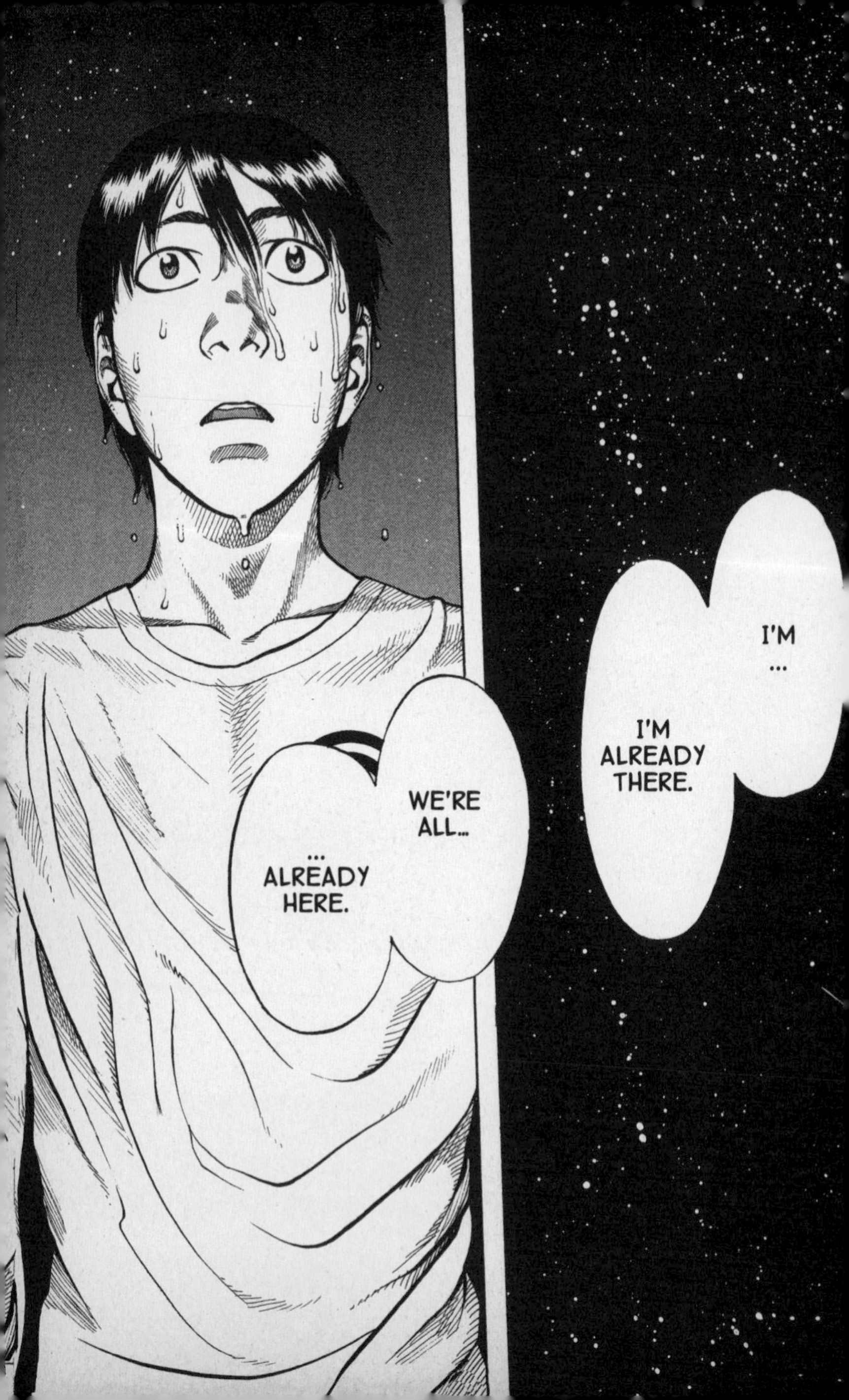
I'M ...
I'M ALREADY THERE.
WE'RE ALL...
... ALREADY HERE.

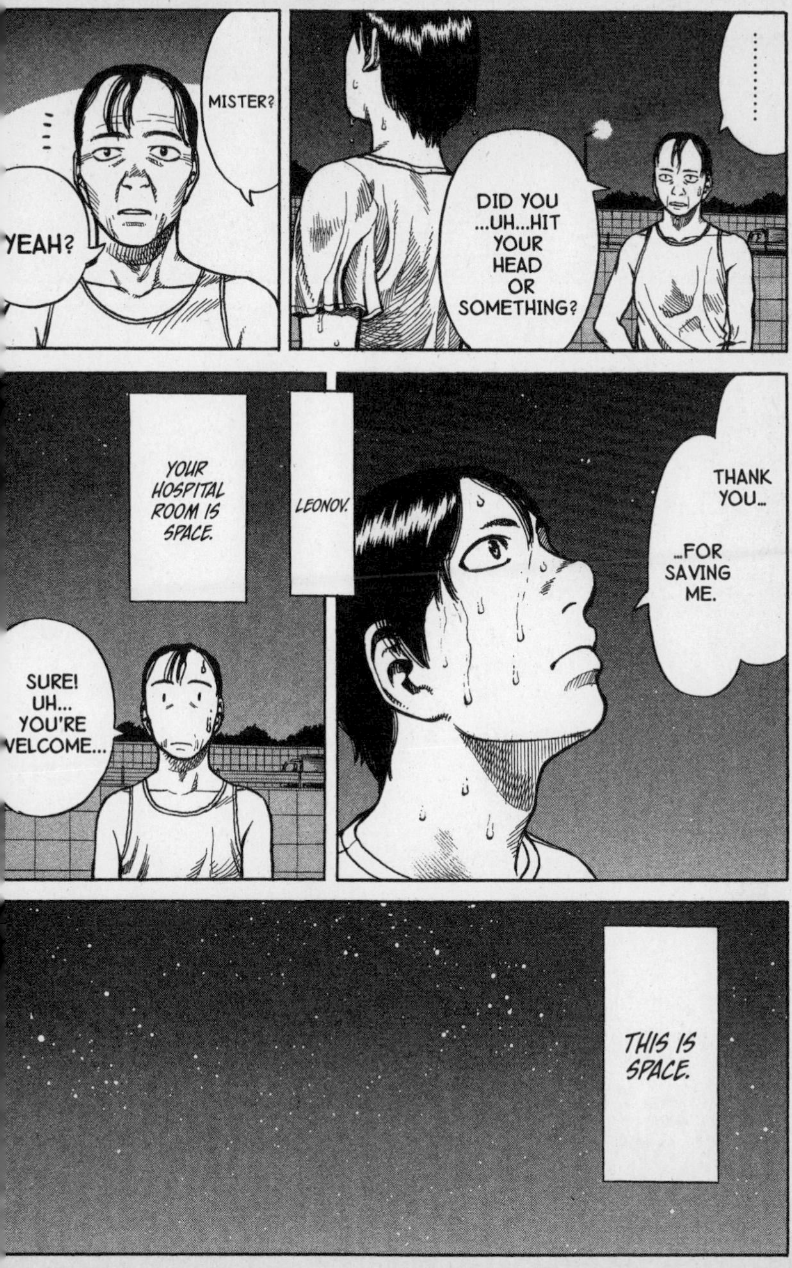
......
DID YOU ...UH...HIT YOUR HEAD OR SOMETHING?
MISTER?
...
YEAH?
THANK YOU...
...FOR SAVING ME.
LEONOV.
YOUR HOSPITAL ROOM IS SPACE.
SURE! UH... YOU'RE WELCOME...
THIS IS SPACE.

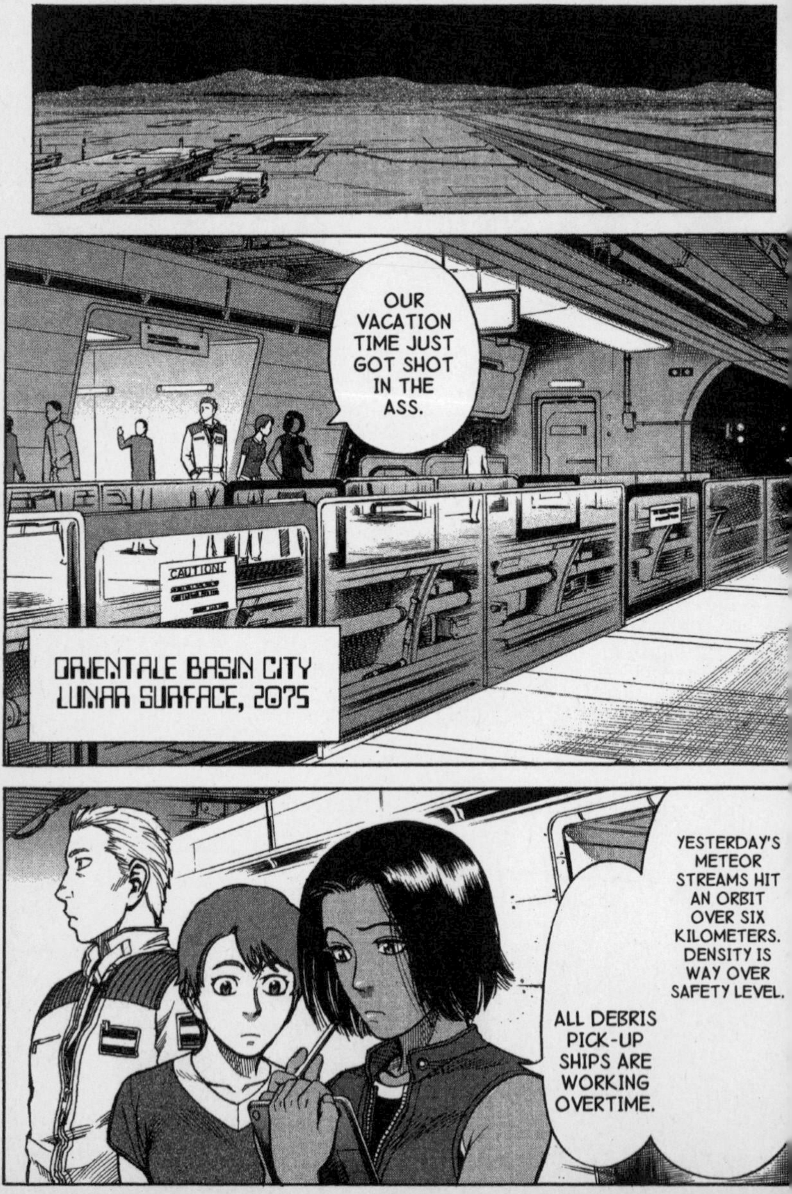
OUR VACATION TIME JUST GOT SHOT IN THE ASS.
CAUTION!
ORIENTALE BASIN CITY
LUNAR SURFACE, 2075
YESTERDAY'S METEOR STREAMS HIT AN ORBIT OVER SIX KILOMETERS. DENSITY IS WAY OVER SAFETY LEVEL.
ALL DEBRIS PICK-UP SHIPS ARE WORKING OVERTIME.

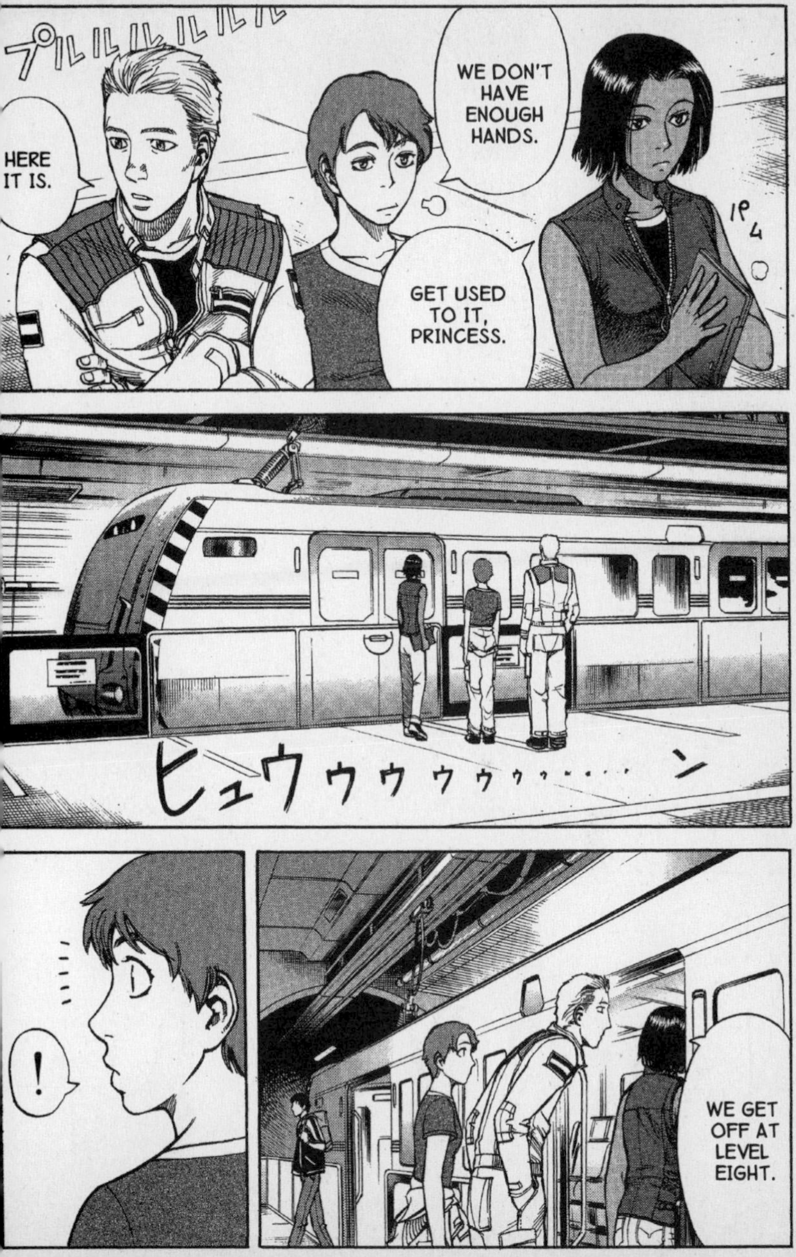
WE DON'T HAVE ENOUGH HANDS.
パム
GET USED TO IT, PRINCESS.
プルルルルル
HERE IT IS.
ヒュウウウウウウ・・・・ン
WE GET OFF AT LEVEL EIGHT.
!

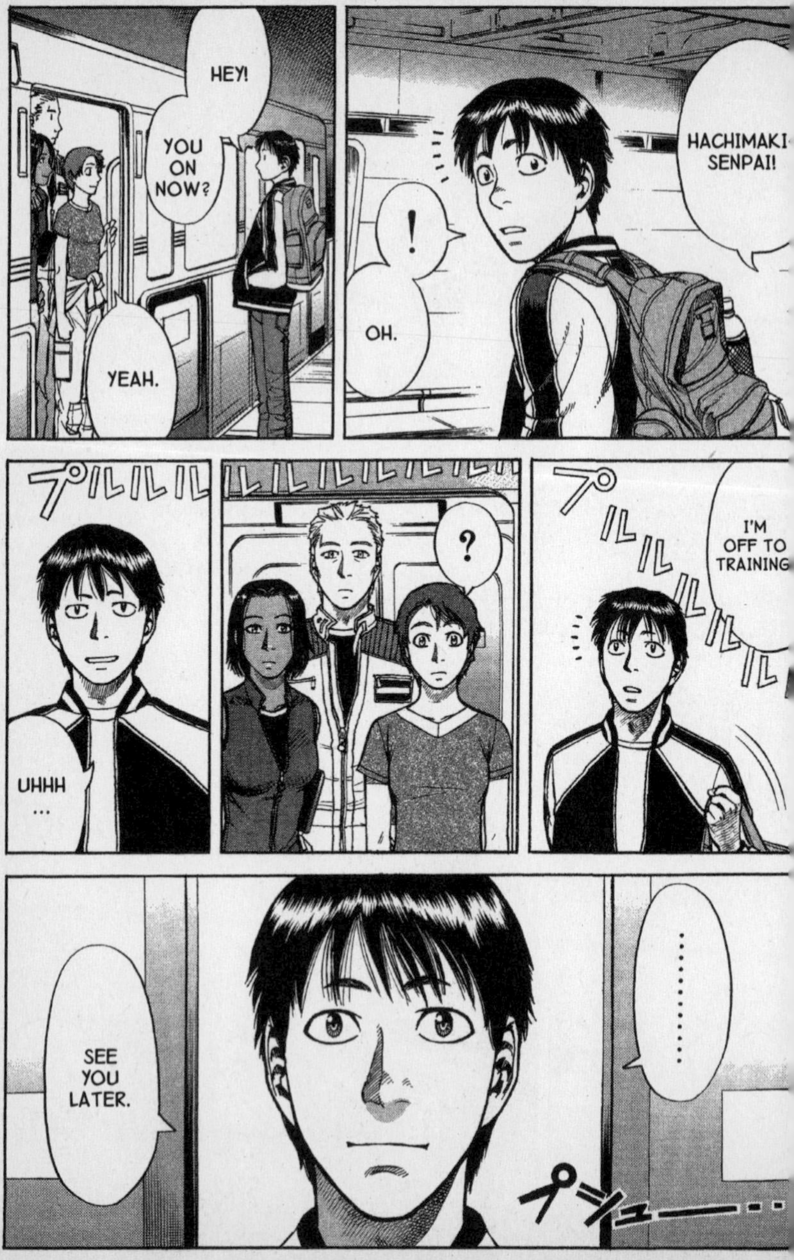
HACHIMAKI SENPAI!
!
OH.
HEY!
YOU ON NOW?
YEAH.
プルルルル
I'M OFF TO TRAINING
?
プルルルルルルルル
UHHH ...
......
プシュー・・
SEE YOU LATER.

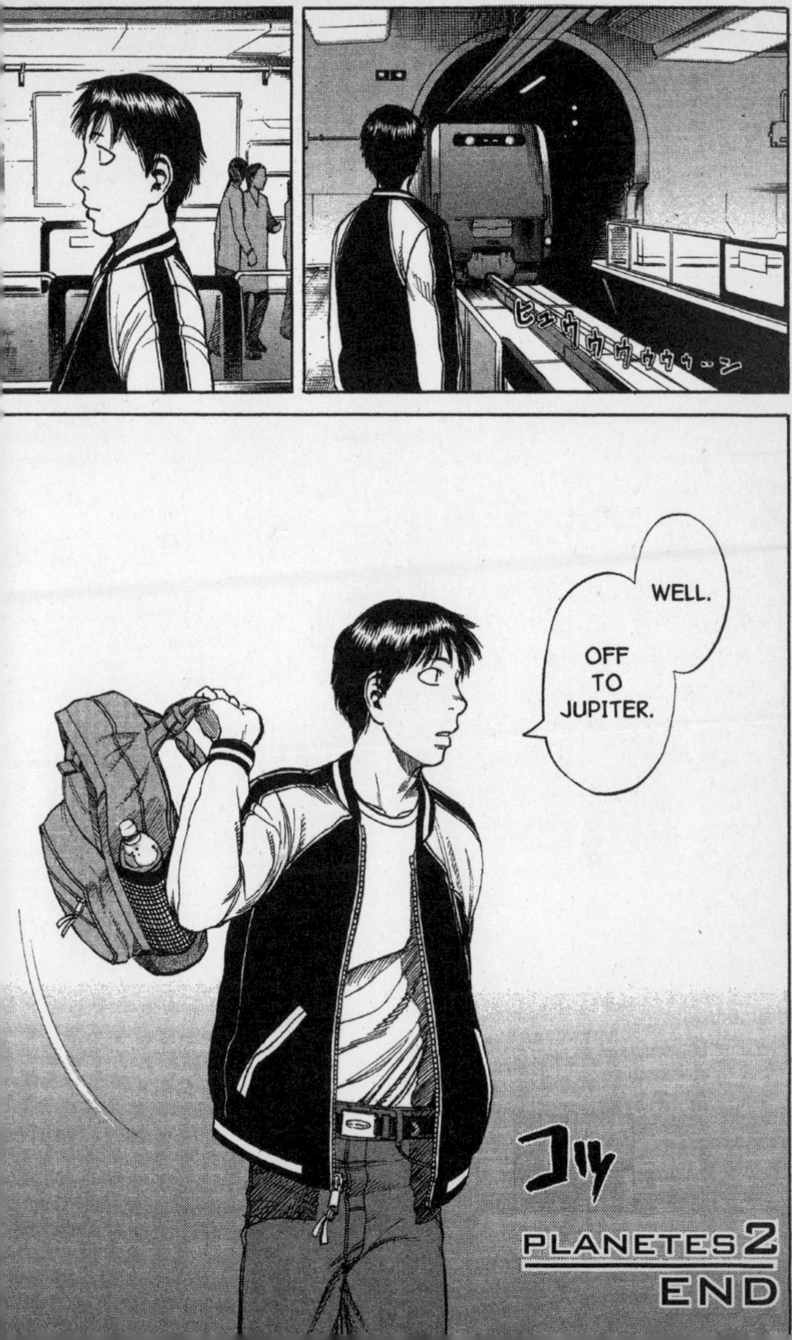
ヒュウウウウウゥ‥ン
WELL.
OFF TO JUPITER.
コッ
PLANETES 2
END

PLANETES

NEXT VOLUME...

After months of an excruciating selection process and the foiling of a terrorist plot to derail the pioneering undertaking, Hachimaki has been hired onto the first manned mission to Jupiter. However, his elation belies an emotional heaviness that he can't quite shake. It's been effecting his mood, his appetite, even his job performance. He seeks solace from his spiritual malaise in the company of young Tanabe, the very girl he felt exhaustingly irritating just a few short months ago. Will she have the answers he seeks? Or are both of them on a path of self-discovery?

Conceptualizing Space Travel

Kenji Miyazawa – Born in 1896, Kenji Miyazawa is one of Japan's most renowned authors. His poems, stories and novels reflect a strange time for Japanese culture as its deeply-rooted tradition began succumbing to the pressures of a modern, global society. In relation to the themes explored in Planetes, his writings capture the beauty of astronomical phenomena, not only on the purely aesthetic level, but also in understanding the science behind the motion and behavior of celestial objects. Just as Hachimaki finds himself driven by a passion for space travel but troubled by the solipsistic greed involved in conquering new frontiers, Miyazawa himself wanted to embrace the concept of mankind leaping into the stars, but would have been vexed by nations throughout the 20th century exploiting the new frontier to gain a strategic advantage over one another. His Buddhist philosophy informed dramatically his writing, as he searched tirelessly for the consanguinity betwixt all things. Though he is now a staple in Japanese literary history, he was only beginning to enjoy the success of his work when he was struck with an illness that claimed his life on September 23, 1933, at the untimely age of 37. One of his best-known stories, The Night of the Milky Way Train, features a pair of young boys on an imaginary trip through our galaxy, and it's a marvelous wonderland of science and spectacle.

Senior Lieutenant Yuri Alexeyevich Gagarin – On April 12, 1961, aboard the space capsule Vostok 1, this Russian cosmonaut became the first human to orbit the Earth. So momentous was this achievement that Lieutenant Gagarin not only became a nation hero for the Russian people, but the greatest space pioneer the world has yet known. A fervent student of mathematics and physics, one of his favorite readings growing up was the work of Russian rocket pioneer Konstantin Tsiolkovsky (see biography in Planetes Volume 1). In 1955, he took his first solo flight. And in 1957, on the very same day, at the tender age of 23, he graduated Orenburg and married his Vayla the woman that would be at his side through his illustrious career. In 1959, the young couple and their infant daughter moved to Star Town, a cosmonaut training facility just outside of Moscow. He was a brilliant man with a great sense of humor who enjoyed his work as much as he enjoyed relaxation, nature, friends, and, most importantly, family. After his historic extra-planetary flight, he embarked with his wife and children on a world tour as an ambassador of good will to a globe bowing under the mounting tensions of the Cold War. Though his dream was to return to space, Yuri Alexeyevich Gagarin was killed in 1968, test piloting a jet fighter for the Soviet Air Force.

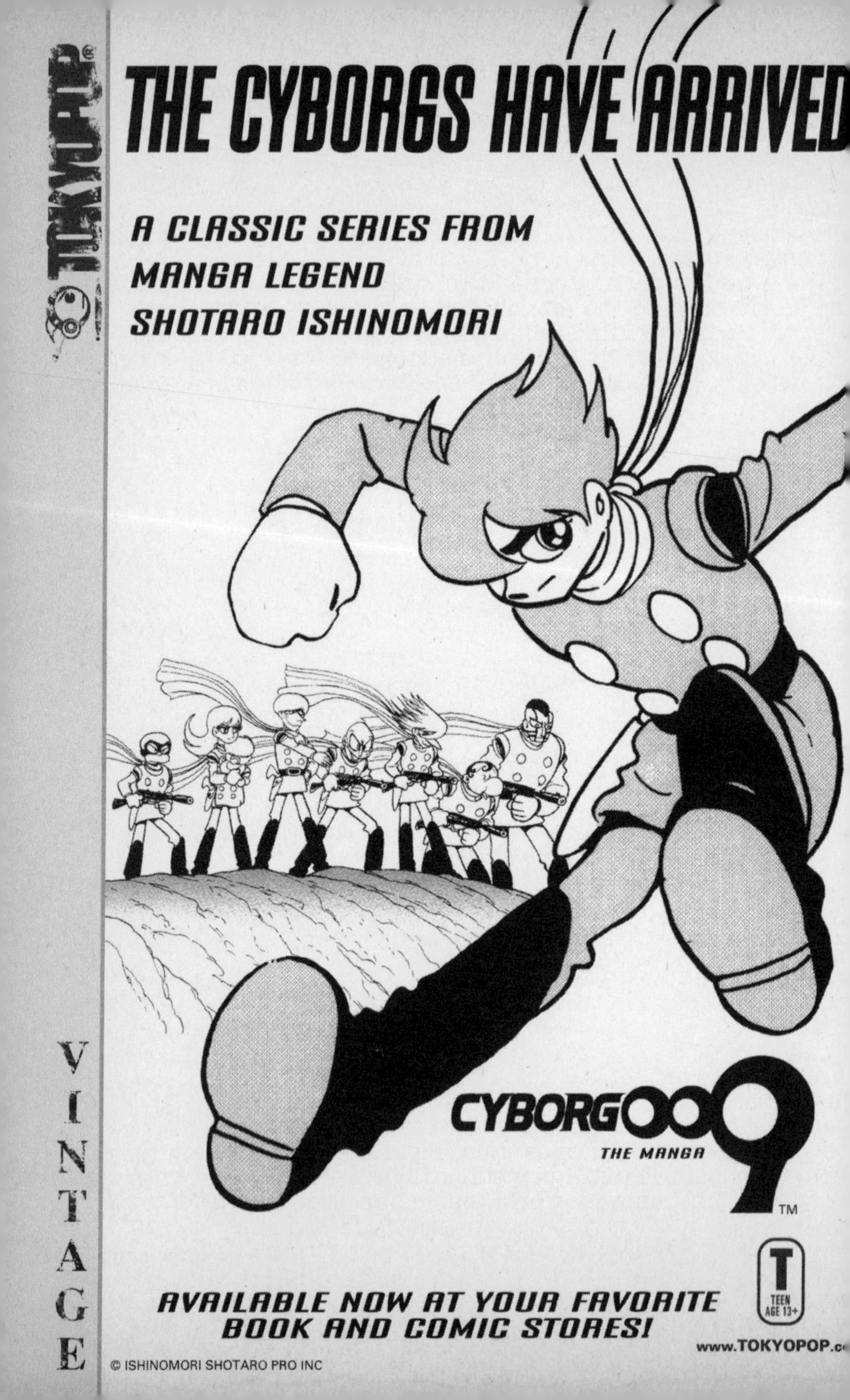
TOKYOPOP®
THE CYBORGS HAVE ARRIVED
A CLASSIC SERIES FROM
MANGA LEGEND
SHOTARO ISHINOMORI
CYBORG 009
THE MANGA
TM
T
TEEN
AGE 13+
AVAILABLE NOW AT YOUR FAVORITE
BOOK AND COMIC STORES!
www.TOKYOPOP.c
VINTAGE
© ISHINOMORI SHOTARO PRO INC

ALSO AVAILABLE FROM  TOKYOPOP®

REALITY CHECK
REBIRTH
REBOUND
REMOTE June 2004
RISING STARS OF MANGA December 2003
SABER MARIONETTE J
SAILOR MOON
SAINT TAIL
SAIYUKI
SAMURAI DEEPER KYO
SAMURAI GIRL REAL BOUT HIGH SCHOOL
SCRYED
SGT. FROG March 2004
SHAOLIN SISTERS
SHIRAHIME-SYO: SNOW GODDESS TALES December 2004
SHUTTERBOX
SNOW DROP January 2004
SOKORA REFUGEES May 2004
SORCEROR HUNTERS
SUIKODEN May 2004
SUKI February 2004
THE CANDIDATE FOR GODDESS April 2004
THE DEMON ORORON April 2004
THE LEGEND OF CHUN HYANG
THE SKULL MAN
THE VISION OF ESCAFLOWNE
TOKYO MEW MEW
TREASURE CHESS March 2004
UNDER THE GLASS MOON
VAMPIRE GAME
WILD ACT
WISH
WORLD OF HARTZ
X-DAY
ZODIAC P.I.

NOVELS

KARMA CLUB APRIL 2004
SAILOR MOON

ART BOOKS

CARDCAPTOR SAKURA
MAGIC KNIGHT RAYEARTH
PEACH GIRL ART BOOK April 2004

ANIME GUIDES

COWBOY BEBOP ANIME GUIDES
GUNDAM TECHNICAL MANUALS
SAILOR MOON SCOUT GUIDES

CINE-MANGA™

CARDCAPTORS
FAIRLY ODD PARENTS MARCH 2004
FINDING NEMO
G.I. JOE SPY TROOPS
JACKIE CHAN ADVENTURES
KIM POSSIBLE
LIZZIE MCGUIRE
POWER RANGERS: NINJA STORM
SPONGEBOB SQUAREPANTS
SPY KIDS
SPY KIDS 3-D March 2004
THE ADVENTURES OF JIMMY NEUTRON: BOY GENIUS
TRANSFORMERS: ARMADA
TRANSFORMERS: ENERGON May 2004

TOKYOPOP KIDS

STRAY SHEEP

For more information visit www.TOKYOPOP.com